eat

out in

pubs

The 2012 edition of our guide contains details of over 530 pubs. As ever, the crucial factor for selection in the guide is the quality of the food served, and though the style of cooking and the menus may vary from one pub to the next, our independent inspectors ensure that each and every pub listed reaches the required standards.
Cooking in British pubs continues to reach new heights, and there is an enormous amount of choice now available to diners. Some pubs proudly take the organic route with the support of small local suppliers, while others focus more on regional specialities and long-established local recipes. Some serve creative, contemporary cooking with more of an international flavour, but equally, there are plenty offering traditional British favourites too.
If you're having trouble choosing where to go, the descriptive texts give an insight into the individual character of each pub, highlighting what we found to be most memorable and charming, and the accompanying pictures reveal a little bit more of their personality.
Some of these pubs serve their food by the fireplace in the bar; others may have a more formal dining room, but whatever their style, they all have one thing in common: carefully prepared, flavoursome food made from fresh, quality ingredients.
Readers of the Michelin Eating out in Pubs guide write thousands of letters and emails to us every year, praising or criticising current entries or recommending new entries. Please keep these coming and help us to make the next edition even better.

MICHELIN
A better way forward

contents

SCOTLAND
North East
Northern Ireland
Yorkshire & The Humber
Isle of Man
IRELAND
North West
Republic of Ireland
East
ENGLAND
WALES
West Midlands
South
South West
Isle of Wight
Channel Islands

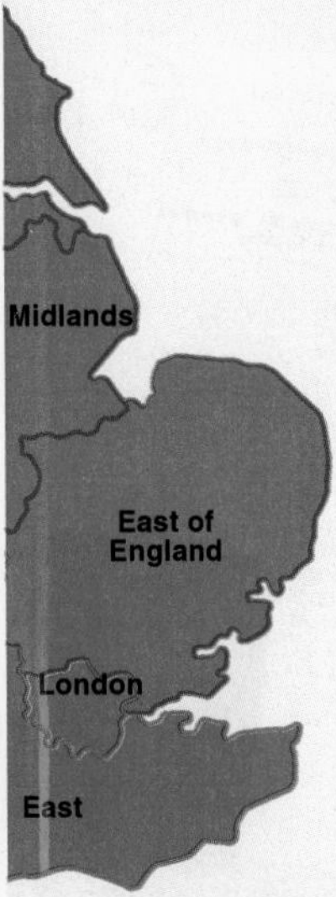

Midlands
East of England
London
East

How to use this Guide

How to find a pub

There are 3 ways to search for a pub in this guide:
- use the regional maps that precede each section of the guide
- use the alphabetical list of pubs at the end of the guide or
- use the alphabetical list of place names also at the end of the guide

Town / Village name

One of our favourite selections

Country or region and county names

Coloured pages border

- **England**
  - East Midlands
  - East of England
  - London
  - North East
  - North West
  - South East
  - South West
  - West Midlands
  - Yorkshire & The Humber
- **Scotland**
- **Wales**
- **Ireland**
  - Northern Ireland
  - Republic of Ireland

Hemingford Grey
England • East of England • Cambridgeshire
Cock
7
47 High St,
Hemingford Grey, PE28 9BJ
Tel.: (01480)463609
Website: www.thecockhemingford.co.uk.
Great Oakley Wagtail, Nethergate IPA, Brewsters Hophead and Oldershaw Newtons Drop
As you approach this 17C country pub you'll come across two doors: one marked 'Pub', leading to a split-level bar and the other marked 'Restaurant', leading to a spacious L-shaped dining room. Run by an experienced team, it has a homely feel, with warm fabrics, comfy seating and attractively papered walls throughout. In winter, the best spot is beside the fire and in summer, the most pleasant is by the French windows. Cooking rests firmly on the tried-and-tested side of things, with classic pub staples such as lamb shank and belly pork; good value set lunches; and a list of daily changing fish specials. A tempting sausage board also offers an appealing mix of several varieties of homemade sausage matched with mashed potato and sauces.
CLOSING TIMES
Open daily
booking essential
PRICES
Meals: a la carte £ 26/35
Typical Dishes
Rabbit & pork terrine
Pan-fried mackerel fillets with anchovy & olive tart
White chocolate & raspberry terrine
The village is 5 mi east of Huntingdon signposted off A 14.
Parking.
64

Name, address, telephone and website of the establishment

15

Entry number

Each pub or inn has its own entry number.

This number appears on the regional map at the start of each section to show the location of the establishment.

Pubs with bedrooms

For easy reference, those pubs that offer accommodation are highlighted.

in blue on the maps

Horningsea

England • East of England • Cambridgeshire

8 Crown and Punchbowl

High St,
Horningsea, CB25 9JG
Tel.: (01223)860643
Website: www.thecrownandpunchbowl.co.uk

No real ales offered

The clue that this is more of a dining than a drinking establishment lies in the fact that there's no real bar area. However, it still delivers on the pubby character, thanks to its beams, open fires and chunky wooden tables. The menu changes with the seasons but there are also daily specials and their popular 'sausage board'. There's a sophisticated element to the cooking – seared scallops are a permanent feature – and the kitchen can do traditional, such as the delicious blade of beef, as well as modern, with dishes like fish terrine with horseradish sorbet or the deconstructed millionaire's shortbread. There's a pleasant terrace and simple bedrooms available. Service has become a little less formal and is all the better for it.

CLOSING TIMES
Closed 26 December-1 January, dinner Sunday and bank holiday Monday

PRICES
Meals: a la carte £ 25/33
5 rooms: £ 75/95

Typical Dishes
Pan-fried asparagus with a poached egg
Pan-seared salmon with crushed new potatoes
Trio of desserts

Just off the A14, northeast of Cambridge. Parking.

65

Symbols

Meals served in the garden or on the terrace

A particularly interesting wine list

No dogs allowed

VISA Visa accepted

AE American Express accepted

Diners Club accepted

MasterCard accepted

Closing times Prices, rooms

Approximate range of prices for a three-course meal, plus information on booking and annual closures.

Some inns offering accommodation may close mid-afternoon and only allow guests to check in during evening hours. If in doubt, phone ahead.

Room prices range from the lowest-priced single to the most expensive double or twin.

Breakfast is usually included in the price.

Prices are given in £ sterling, except for the Republic of Ireland where €uro are quoted.

How to get there

Directions and driving distances from nearby towns, an indication of parking facilities and any other information that might help you get your bearings. Nearest Underground / train station indicated for London entries.

The blackboard

An example of a typical starter, main course and dessert, chosen by the chef.

Whilst there's no guarantee that these dishes will be available, they should provide you with an idea of the style of the cuisine.

The Pub of the year

The Pipe and Glass Inn

West End, South Dalton, Beverley
East Riding of Yorkshire

Tel: (01430) 810246

website : *www.pipeandglass.co.uk*

see page 484 for more details

Discovering a great new pub is a joyful thing and our team of full-time inspectors have once again travelled throughout Britain and Ireland in search of the best ones for this guide. Each year we also choose one to be crowned our 'Pub of the Year' – but what exactly merits this award? For us, it's a combination of factors, which include the warmth of the welcome and friendliness of the service, the character, the atmosphere and, of course, the food.

Its History

You could argue that The Pipe and Glass Inn has been providing succour to travellers since the 15th century, for it stands on the site of the original gatehouse to Dalton Park which would offer food and lodgings to those visiting the 'great house'. The present building replaced it in the 17th century, although there has been a certain amount of tinkering with it over the centuries. Today, the pub's bright façade gives few clues as to the jewel that is found within…

The Pub

The best things in life take time to mature. When James and Kate Mackenzie took over what was a shell of a pub in 2006, they were keen for it to evolve and mature organically, as time and money allowed. From the outset they showed their commitment to using local specialists by hiring a local carpenter to make the dining tables and they haven't stopped upgrading yet: the most recent development has been the addition of two very comfortable bedrooms, named 'Sage' and 'Thyme', and there are plans for more. The pub has a cosy bar and adjoining lounge, and a choice of three different dining areas, one of which comes with an impressively sized table that can seat up to 28.

Its Owners

Their steady approach has allowed James and Kate get to know their customers well and vice versa, which is probably one reason why the pub has such a warm feel. James, who does the cooking, grew up in Filey on the Yorkshire coast and arrived here with an impressive CV, having spent several years as Head Chef of The Star Inn at Harome. Kate, who also worked at The Star, oversees the service and has gathered around her a charming, young and enthusiastic team. They give the impression that nothing is too much trouble and never seem to lose their smiles, however busy, so it's hardly a surprise that this is a genuinely family friendly pub.

The Food

James's cooking has also matured over the years. It takes as its starting point the quality of the ingredients, which come from local suppliers and even occasionally from their own garden. Dishes have inherent heartiness – this is Yorkshire after all – but there's also an element of refinement to them and, at times, some subtle original touches but these are done without compromising on flavour. Moreover, James never forgets that, above all else, this is a pub, so for every wild sea trout tartar with fennel pollen, there's also a fish pie; for every loin of red deer with juniper cabbage, there are pork sausages with bubble and squeak.

Inspectors' favourites

All the pubs in this guide have been selected for the quality of their cooking. However, we feel that several of them deserve additional consideration as they boast at least one extra quality which makes them particularly special.

It may be the delightful setting, the charm and character of the pub, the general atmosphere, the pleasant service, the overall value for money or the exceptional cooking.
To distinguish these pubs, we point them out with our "Inspectors' favourites" Bibendum stamp.
We are sure you will enjoy these pubs as much as we have.

ENGLAND

EAST MIDLANDS

EAST OF ENGLAND

LONDON

NORTH EAST

NORTH WEST

Beer in the U.K. and Ireland

It's easy to think of beer as just bitter or lager. But that doesn't tell half the story. Between the two there's a whole range of styles and tastes, including pale ales, beers flavoured with spices, fruits and herbs, and wheat beers. It's all down to the skill of the brewer who'll juggle art, craft and a modicum of science to create the perfect pint.

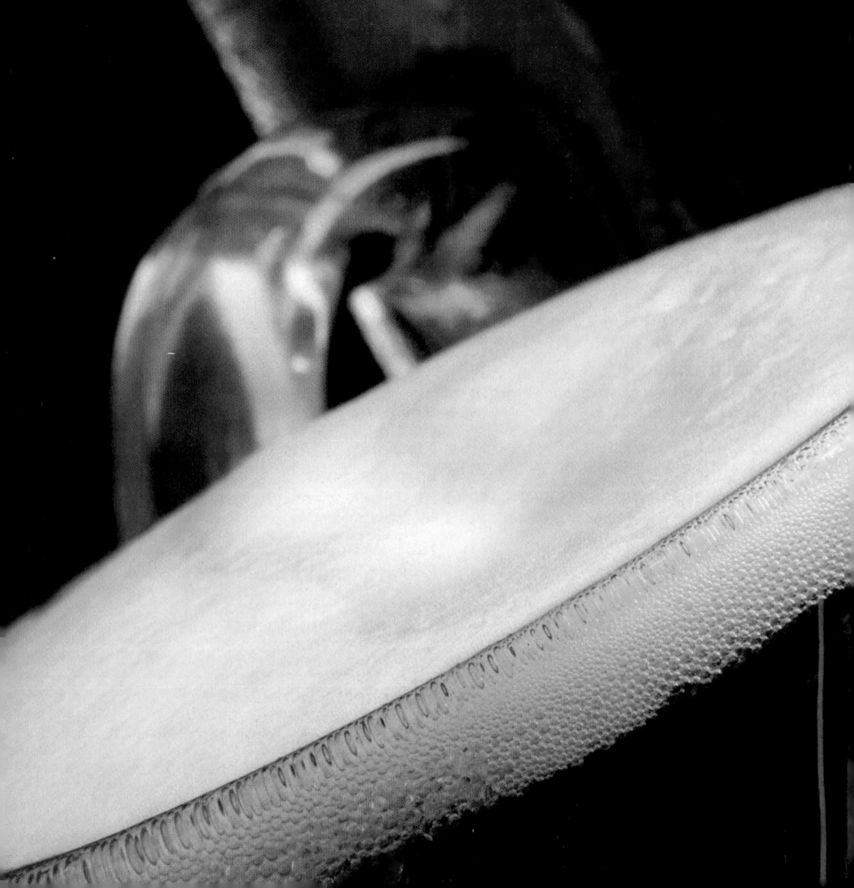

Grist and wort may sound like medieval hangover cures, but they're actually crucial to the brewing process. Malted barley is crushed into grist, a coarse powder which is mashed with hot water in a large vessel called a mash tun. Depending on what sort of recipe's required, the brewer will add different cereals at this stage, such as darker malt for stout. The malt's natural sugars dissolve and the result is wort: a sweet brown liquid, which is boiled with hops in large coppers. Then comes the most important process of all: fermentation, when the hopped wort is cooled and run into fermentation vessels. The final addition is yeast, which converts the natural sugars into alcohol, carbon dioxide and a host of subtle flavours.

Finally, a beer has to be conditioned before it leaves the brewery, and in the case of cask conditioned real ales, the beer goes directly into the cask, barrel or bottle. The yeast is still active in there, fermenting the beer for a second time, often in a pub cellar. All the time there's a delicate process going on as the beer is vulnerable to attack from micro-biological organisms. But as long as the publican cares about his beer, you should get a tasty, full-flavoured pint.

Beer's as natural a product as you can get. This is what's in your pint:

Barley
It's the main ingredient in beer and rich in starch. Malted before brewing to begin the release of sugars.

Hops
Contain resins and essential oils, and used at varying times to give beer its distinctive flavour. Early on they add bitterness, later on they provide a spicy or citrus zest.

Yeast
Converts the sugars from the barley into alcohol and carbon dioxide during fermentation. It produces compounds that affect the flavour of the beer.

Water
Burton and Tadcaster have excellent local water, and that's why they became great ale brewing centres. Meanwhile, the water of London and Dublin is just right for the production of stouts and porters.

Real quality

The modern taste for real ale took off over thirty years ago when it looked like the lager industry was in the process of killing off traditional "warm ale". There are several styles, but the most popular in England and Wales is bitter, which boasts a seemingly inexhaustible variety of appearance, scent and flavour. You can have your bitter gold or copper of colour, hoppy or malty of aroma, dry or sweet of flavour (sweet flavoured bitter? This is where the term "bitter" is at its loosest). Sometimes it has a creamy head; sometimes no head at all. Typically, go to a Yorkshire pub for the former, a London pub for the latter.

Mild developed its popularity in Wales and the north west of England in Victorian times. Often dark, it's a weaker alternative to bitter, with a sweetish taste based on its hop characteristics.

In Scotland, the near equivalent of bitter is heavy, and the most popular draught ales are known as 80 shilling (export) or 70 shilling (special). And, yes, they have a heavy quality to them, though 60 shilling ale – or Light – is akin to English mild.

Full-bodied and rich, stouts (and their rarer porter relatives) are almost a meal in themselves. They're famously black in colour with hints of chocolate and caramel, but it's the highly roasted yeast flavour that leaves the strong after taste.

YOU ALREADY KNOW THE MICHELIN GUIDE,
NOW FIND OUT ABOUT THE MICHELIN GROUP
MICHELIN
A better way forward

The Michelin Adventure

It all started with rubber balls! This was the product made by a small company based in Clermont-Ferrand that André and Edouard Michelin inherited, back in 1880. The brothers quickly saw the potential for a new means of transport and their first success was the invention of detachable pneumatic tyres for bicycles. However, the automobile was to provide the greatest scope for their creative talents.

Throughout the 20th century, Michelin never ceased developing and creating ever more reliable and high-performance tyres, not only for vehicles ranging from trucks to F1 but also for underground transit systems and aeroplanes.

From early on, Michelin provided its customers with tools and services to facilitate mobility and make travelling a more pleasurable and more frequent experience. As early as 1900, the Michelin Guide supplied motorists with a host of useful information related to vehicle maintenance, accommodation and restaurants, and was to become a benchmark for good food. At the same time, the Travel Information Bureau offered travellers personalised tips and itineraries.

The publication of the first collection of roadmaps, in 1910, was an instant hit! In 1926, the first regional guide to France was published, devoted to the principal sites of Brittany, and before long each region of France had its own Green Guide. The collection was later extended to more far-flung destinations, including New York in 1968 and Taiwan in 2011.

In the 21st century, with the growth of digital technology, the challenge for Michelin maps and guides is to continue to develop alongside the company's tyre activities. Now, as before,Michelin is committed to improving the mobility of travellers.

MICHELIN TODAY

WORLD NUMBER ONE TYRE MANUFACTURER

- 70 production sites in 18 countries
- 111,000 employees from all cultures and on every continent
- 6,000 people employed in research and development

Moving for a world

Moving forward means developing tyres with better road grip and shorter braking distances, whatever the state of the road.

CORRECT TYRE PRESSURE

RIGHT PRESSURE

- Safety
- Longevity
- Optimum fuel consumption

-0,5 bar

- Durability reduced by 20% (- 8,000 km)

-1 bar

- Risk of blowouts
- Increased fuel consumption
- Longer braking distances on wet surfaces

forward together
where mobility is safer

It also involves helping motorists take care of their safety and their tyres. To do so, Michelin organises "Fill Up With Air" campaigns all over the world to remind us that correct tyre pressure is vital.

WEAR

DETECTING TYRE WEAR

The legal minimum depth of tyre tread is 1.6mm.

Tyre manufacturers equip their tyres with tread wear indicators, which are small blocks of rubber moulded into the base of the main grooves at a depth of 1.6mm.

Tyres are the only point of contact between vehicle and road.

The photo below shows the actual contact zone.

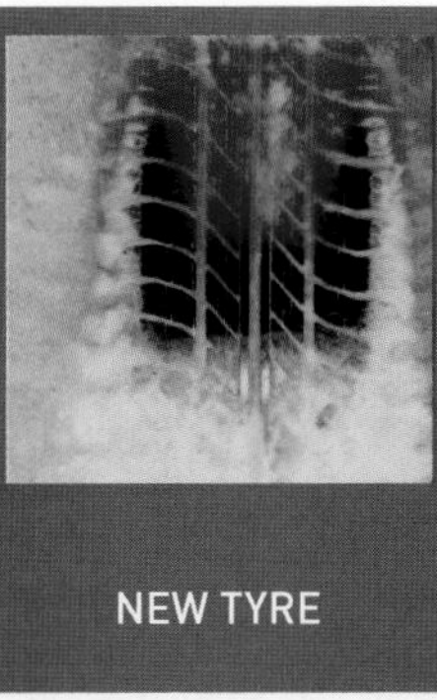

NEW TYRE

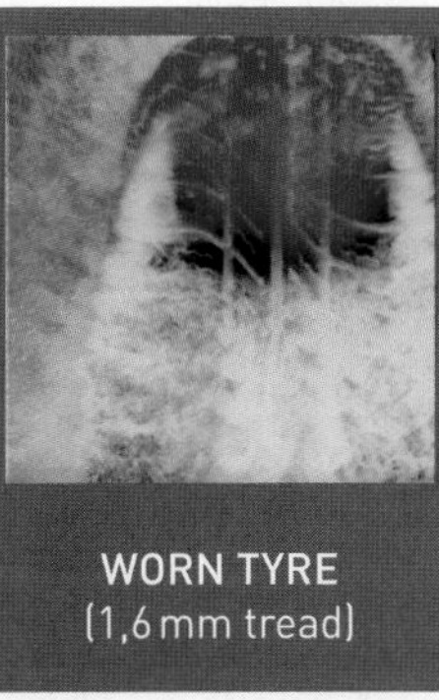

WORN TYRE
(1,6 mm tread)

If the tread depth is less than 1.6mm, tyres are considered to be worn and dangerous on wet surfaces.

Moving forward means sustainable mobility

INNOVATION AND THE ENVIRONMENT

By 2050, Michelin aims to cut the quantity of raw materials used in its tyre manufacturing process by half and to have developed renewable energy in its facilities. The design of MICHELIN tyres has already saved billions of litres of fuel and, by extension, billions of tonnes of CO2.

Similarly, Michelin prints its maps and guides on paper produced from sustainably managed forests and is diversifying its publishing media by offering digital solutions to make travelling easier, more fuel efficient and more enjoyable!

The group's whole-hearted commitment to eco-design on a daily basis is demonstrated by ISO 14001 certification.

Like you, Michelin is committed to preserving our planet.

Chat with Bibendum

Go to
www.michelin.com/corporate/fr
Find out more about Michelin's history
and the latest news.

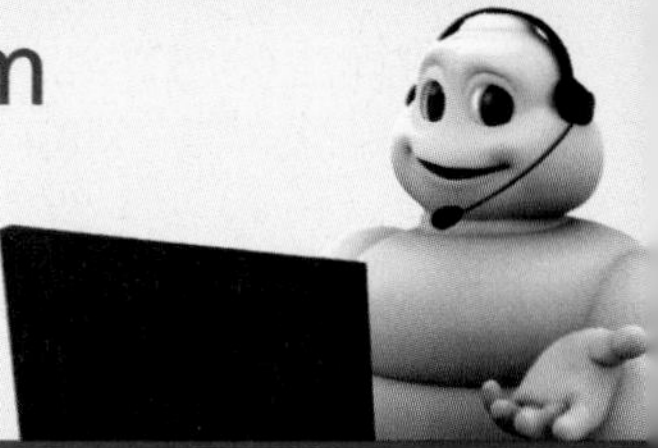

QUIZ

Michelin develops tyres for all types of vehicles. See if you can match the right tyre with the right vehicle…

Solution : A-6 / B-4 / C-2 / D-1 / E-3 / F-7 / G-5

A vision of England sweeps across a range of historic buildings, monuments and rolling landscapes. This image, taking in wild natural borders extending from the rugged splendour of Cornwall's cliffs to pounding Northumbrian shores, seeks parity with a newer picture of Albion: redefined cities and towns whose industrial past is being reshaped by a shiny, steel-and-glass, interactive reality. The country's geographical bones and bumps are a reassuring constant: the windswept moors of the south west and the craggy peaks of the Pennines, the summery orchards of the Kentish Weald, the "flat earth" constancy of East Anglian skies and the mirrored calm of Cumbria's lakes. The pubs of England have made good use of the land's natural bounty over the past decade; streamlined establishments have stripped out the soggy carpets and soggier menus and replaced them with crisp décor and fresh, inventive cooking. England's multi-ethnic culture has borne fruit in the kitchens of your local…

61
41

An area that combines the grace of a bygone age with the speed of the 21C. To the east (Chatsworth House, Haddon Hall and Burghley House) is where Pride and Prejudice came to life, while Silverstone to the south hosts the Grand Prix. Market towns are dotted all around: Spalding's cultivation of tulips rivals that of Holland, Oakham boasts its stunning Castle and Great Hall, and the legendary "Boston Stump" oversees the bustle of a 450 year-old market. The brooding beauty of the Peak District makes it the second most visited National Park in the world. Izaak Walton popularised the river Dove's trout-filled waters in "The Compleat Angler" and its surrounding hills are a rambler's dream, as are the wildlife habitats of the National Forest and the wind-swept acres of the pancake-flat fens. Above it all looms Lincoln Cathedral's ancient spire, while in the pubs, local ale – typically brewed in Bakewell, Dovedale or Rutland – slips down a treat alongside the ubiquitous Melton Mowbray pie.

Yorkshire & the Humber
North West
EAST
West Midlands
South East
MANCHESTER
SHEFFIELD
STOKE-ON-TRENT
NOTTINGHAM
LEICESTER
BIRMINGHAM
COVENTRY
Oldham
Huddersfield
Holmfirth
Barnsley
Thorne
Wigan
Leigh
Ashton-under-Lyne
Glossop
Stocksbridge
Peak District
Conisbrough
Doncaster
Altrincham
Hyde
Rotherham
Stockport
High Peak
Castleton
Bawtry
Maltby
Knutsford
Whaley Bridge
Chapel-en-le-Frith
National
Dronfield
Staveley
Worksop
East Retford
Northwich
Macclesfield
Buxton
Baslow
Chesterfield
Middlewich
Congleton
Bakewell
Chatsworth House
Park
Tuxford
Sandbach
Little Moreton Hall
Clay Cross
Hardwick Hall
Crewe
Kidsgrove
Leek
Matlock
Alfreton
Mansfield
Sutton-in-Ashfield
Newark-on-Trent
Newcastle-under-Lyme
Ashbourne
Ripley
Heanor
Southwell
Audlem
Belper
Hucknall
R. Trent
Market Drayton
Stone
Uttoxeter
Ilkeston
Derby
Bingham
Sudbury
Eccleshall
West Bridgford
Long Eaton
Stafford
Abbots Bromley
Burton-upon-Trent
Rempstone
Newport
Rugeley
Swadlincote
Shepshed
Loughborough
Cannock
Ashby de la Zouch
Melton
Gailey
Brownhills
Lichfield
Coalville
Walsall
Tamworth
Wolverhampton
Sutton Coldfield
Atherstone
Hinckley
Oadby
Uppingham
Dudley
Nuneaton
Market Harborough
Stourbridge
Bedworth
Lutterworth
Kidderminster
Halesowen
Solihull
Husbands Bosworth
Bewdley
Rugby
Stourport
Bromsgrove
Kenilworth
Rothwell
Wells
Redditch
Henley
Royal Leamington Spa
Wellingborough
Droitwich
Warwick
Worcester
Alcester
Southam
Daventry
Stratford-upon-Avon
Great Malvern
Evesham
Ettington
Pershore
Upton
Chipping Campden
Shipston-on-Stour
Towcester
Wolverton
Banbury
Broadway
Moreton
Tewkesbury
Winchcombe
Brackley
Milton Keynes
Stow-on-the-Wold
Chipping Norton
Buckingham
Bletchley
Gloucester
Cheltenham
OXFORD
WARWICK
WORCESTER
NORTHAM
LEICESTER
DERBY
STAFFORD
NOTTS

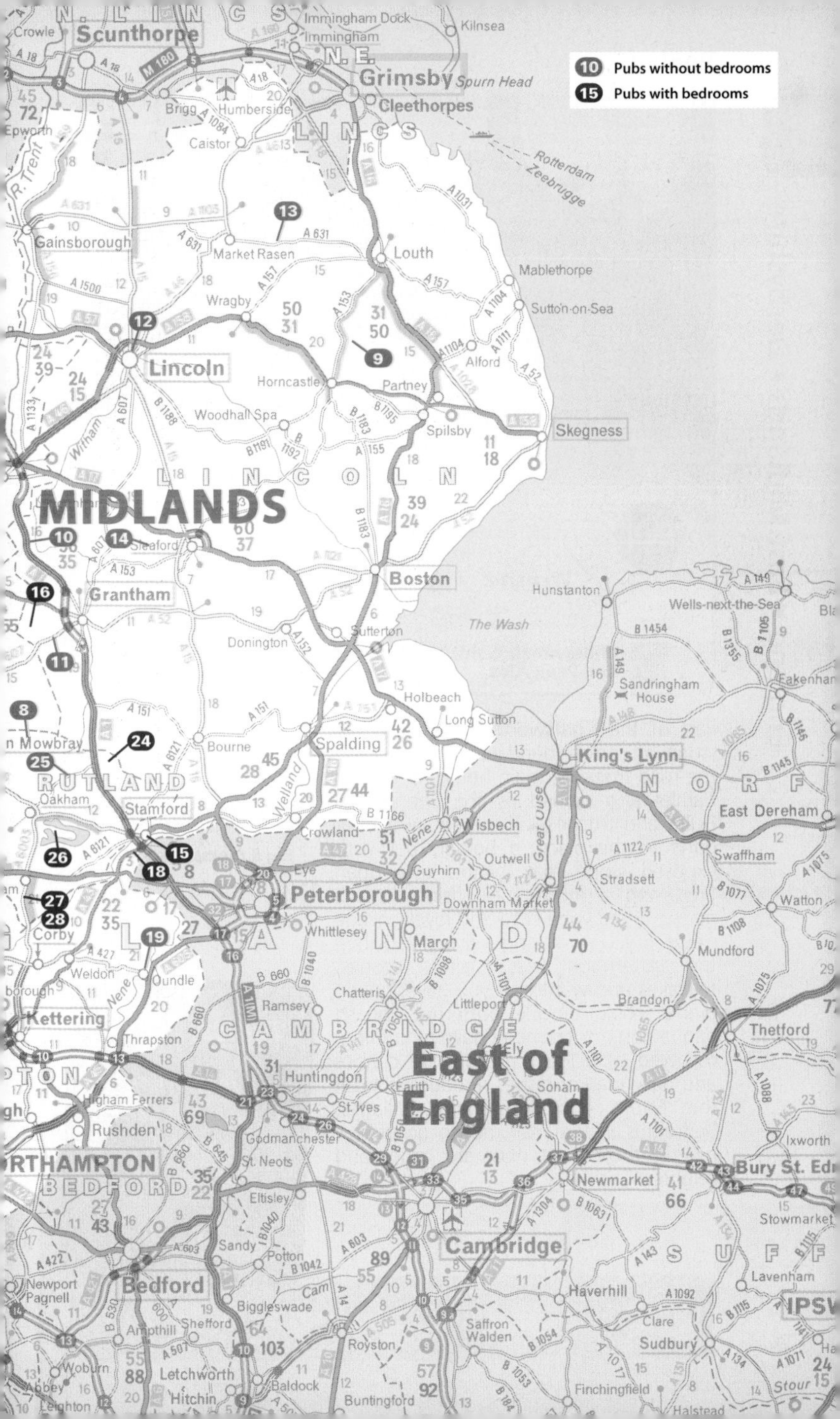

10 Pubs without bedrooms
15 Pubs with bedrooms
N. LINCS
N.E. LINCS
LINCS
LINCOLN
MIDLANDS
RUTLAND
East of England
NORF
CAMBRIDGE
NORTHAMPTON
BEDFORD
SUFF
Scunthorpe
Crowle
Immingham Dock
Immingham
Kilnsea
Grimsby
Spurn Head
Cleethorpes
Brigg
Humberside
Caistor
Epworth
R. Trent
Rotterdam
Zeebrugge
Gainsborough
Market Rasen
Louth
Mablethorpe
Sutton-on-Sea
Wragby
Alford
Lincoln
Horncastle
Partney
Woodhall Spa
Spilsby
Skegness
Witham
Sleaford
Grantham
Boston
Hunstanton
Wells-next-the-Sea
The Wash
Donington
Sutterton
Holbeach
Long Sutton
Sandringham House
Fakenham
Bourne
Spalding
King's Lynn
Mowbray
Oakham
Stamford
Welland
Crowland
Wisbech
Great Ouse
East Dereham
Nene
Outwell
Swaffham
Eye
Guyhirn
Stradsett
Peterborough
Downham Market
Watton
Corby
Whittlesey
March
Mundford
Weldon
Oundle
Chatteris
Ramsey
Littleport
Brandon
Kettering
Thrapston
Thetford
Ely
Huntingdon
Earith
Soham
Higham Ferrers
St. Ives
Rushden
Godmanchester
Ixworth
St. Neots
Bury St. Ed
Newmarket
Eltisley
Stowmarket
Sandy
Cambridge
Potton
Newport Pagnell
Bedford
Cam
Lavenham
Haverhill
Biggleswade
Clare
IPSW
Ampthill
Shefford
Saffron Walden
Royston
Sudbury
Woburn Abbey
Letchworth
Baldock
Finchingfield
Stour
Leighton
Hitchin
Buntingford
Halstead

Beeley

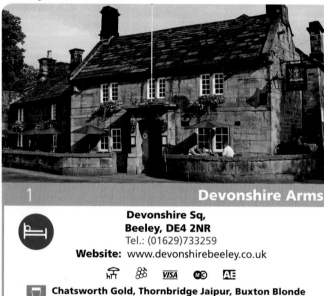

1 Devonshire Arms

Devonshire Sq,
Beeley, DE4 2NR
Tel.: (01629)733259
Website: www.devonshirebeeley.co.uk

VISA AE

Chatsworth Gold, Thornbridge Jaipur, Buxton Blonde and Peak Ales

Part of the Chatsworth Estate, this old stone inn can be found just minutes down the road from the main house, in a small hamlet also owned by the eponymous Duke and Duchess. There are two clear parts to the place: a homely bar with exposed stone, oak beams and open fires, and a modern extension with a glass-fronted wine cave and lovely village views. If you're making a flying visit then the 'Afternoon Feast' offers scones, teacakes and waffles; if you have longer, dinner could include butternut squash panna cotta or crumbed pavé of codling, followed by a list of Devonshire classics and daily market dishes. Produce is from the Estate and surrounding villages. Bedrooms in the main house boast low beams; those next door are larger and brighter.

Closing times
Open daily

Prices
Meals: a la carte £ 19/35

8 rooms: £ 114/217

Typical Dishes

Crab Scotch egg
Mr Hancock's bangers & mash
Bakewell tart

5 mi southeast of Bakewell by A 6 and B 6012. Parking.

2 Samuel Fox

Stretfield Rd,
Bradwell, S33 9JT
Tel.: (01433)621562
Website: www.samuelfox.co.uk

VISA

Black Sheep

This smart, stone-built pub stands out like a beacon in the Derbyshire village of Bradwell, its neutral colour schemes and rattan-style furniture giving it the fresh, light feel of an upmarket French bistro. It's run by a young couple and while he beavers away in the kitchen, she provides efficient, cheery service out the front. The set price lunch menu offers dishes such as corned beef hash with a fried egg, while the evening à la carte menu displays more ambitious dishes such as breast and leg of guinea fowl stuffed with wild mushrooms. Cooking is simple, reasonably priced and full of flavour, with game featuring strongly in winter and fish in summer. Four comfortable, modern bedrooms come with the added bonus of sherry and chocolates.

Closing times
Open daily

Prices
Meals: £ 15 (lunch)
and a la carte £ 19/29

4 rooms: £ 75/115

Typical Dishes

Home-smoked salmon
Braised shoulder of lamb
Gin & lime posset

12 mi northeast of Buxton by A 6 and B 6049. Parking.

3

Inn at Troway

Snowdon Ln,
Eckington, S21 5RU
Tel.: (01246)290751
Website: www.relaxeatanddrink.co.uk

VISA

Thornbridge ales - Jaipur and Wild Swan, Black Sheep and Old Speckled Hen

This early Victorian pub is set in a picturesque location and offers delightful views out over the rolling countryside; make the most of these by grabbing a seat either on the terrace or in the rear dining room. This is an area popular with walkers and the food is satisfyingly hearty; perfect for refuelling after a brisk morning hike. Among the earthy options available on the wide-ranging menu might be seven-hour braised brisket of beef, fisherman's pie or a good value mature steak; be sure to try the onion rings. For those who've given the walking a miss, lighter options listed on the blackboard include tapas-like plates like black pudding or local sausages. There's a fine selection of regional ales and staff bend over backwards to help.

Closing times
Open daily
booking advisable

Prices
Meals: £ 15 (lunch and early dinner) and a la carte £ 19/36

Typical Dishes

Chicken liver parfait
Thornbridge battered cod & chips
Sticky toffee pudding

7.5 mi southeast of Sheffield by A 61 and B 6056 (Eckington Rd). Parking.

4 **Chequers Inn**

Hope Valley,
S32 3ZJ
Tel.: (01433)630231
Website: www.chequers-froggatt.com

VISA AE

Peak Ales, Bakewell Best Bitter, Kelham Island Easy Rider, Bradfield Brewery Farmers Bitter

This 16C inn is built right into the stone boulders of Froggat Edge and even has a direct path from its garden up to the peak. As traditional inside as out, it's a comfortingly no-nonsense sort of place, boasting a cosy fire, gleaming brass, a large bar and a quieter, cosier room across the hall. The majority of diners are walkers, but the jolly team welcome one and all as if they were locals. Cooking is unfussy, wholesome and tasty, featuring traditional dishes that always include fish and chips, bangers and mash, and a pie. More imaginative specials appear on the blackboard alongside the starters and desserts – the latter of which usually includes a local Bakewell pudding. Weary travellers will find bedrooms comfy; the one to the rear is best.

Closing times
Closed 25 December

Prices
Meals: a la carte £ 24/30

5 rooms: £ 77/102

Typical Dishes

Seared scallops
Sage & Dijon mustard marinated pork
Bakewell pudding

Situated on the edge of the village. Parking.

Breedon on the Hill

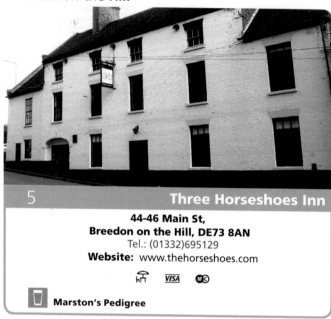

5 Three Horseshoes Inn

44-46 Main St,
Breedon on the Hill, DE73 8AN
Tel.: (01332)695129
Website: www.thehorseshoes.com

VISA

Marston's Pedigree

This large, whitewashed building may not look much like a pub but open the door and you can rest assured that you're in the right place. It's more dining pub than your typical village local but it's still characterful; full of books, artefacts and paintings. Numerous interlinking rooms allow you to create a different experience each time you come: choose maybe an antique table beside the exposed brick fireplace, an intimate corner in one of the smaller rooms, or in summer, a pleasant alfresco spot. A friendly, efficient team point out the blackboards that are scattered about the place, displaying classical, seasonal dishes which prove robust and flavoursome. If 3 courses is too much, don't worry – take something home from the shop for later.

Closing times
Closed 25-26 December, 1 January and Sunday dinner

Prices
Meals: a la carte £ 20/39

Typical Dishes

Chicken liver parfait
Derbyshire rib-eye steak with garlic butter
Chocolate whisky trifle

Signposted off A 42 between Castle Donington and Ashby de la Zouch. Parking.

6 **The Joiners**

Church Walk,
Bruntingthorpe, LE17 5QH
Tel.: (0116)2478258
Website: www.thejoinersarms.co.uk

VISA MC

Greene King IPA, Doombar

You can't help but feel that the locals had a part to play in the naming of this pub, which started life as the Joiners Arms and has since been renamed The Joiners. Set in a small rural village, this neat whitewashed building dates back to the 17C and boasts characterful wood floors and low beams. Run by an enthusiastic husband and wife team, it's more of a dining pub than a place for a casual drink; although the group of regulars crowded round the pine fitted bar would probably tell you otherwise. Menus display a mix of refined pub classics and more brasserie-style dishes, all cooked and presented in a straightforward yet effective manner. There's a good value set lunch and a wide selection of wines by the glass; Thursday is 'fish night'.

Closing times
Closed Sunday dinner and Monday
booking essential

Prices
Meals: £ 14 (lunch) and a la carte £ 26/30

Typical Dishes
Dressed Dorset crab
Scottish rib-eye steak
Liquorice panna cotta

Between Leicester and Husbands Bosworth off A 5199.

7

Red Lion Inn

2 Red Lion St,
Stathern, LE14 4HS
Tel.: (01949)860868
Website: www.theredlioninn.co.uk

Inspectors' favourites

VISA

Red Lion Ale, London Pride and Brewsters Marquis

Set in the village centre, this spacious whitewashed pub, with its rustic bar and characterful dining rooms, is very much part of the community. Whilst it maintains a healthy drinking trade, it's the food here that's the main attraction, with the seasonal produce growing in the kitchen garden helping to inform the menus and daily specials. The à la carte arrives with a map of the rest of their suppliers' locations on the back and it's reassuring that they don't stray far from the doorstep; you'll find sausages from the village butcher, game from the Belvoir estates and cheese from nearby dairies. Cooking is straightforward and unfussy, resulting in refined pub classics with the odd local or global twist. Service is friendly and attentive.

Closing times
Closed Sunday dinner
booking essential

Prices
Meals: £ 17 (lunch)
and a la carte £ 19/28

Typical Dishes
Twice-baked cheese soufflé, peas and walnut salad
Pan-fried calves liver, rösti potato, cabbage, bacon and mushrooms
Home-grown rhubarb Eton mess

8 mi north of Melton Mowbray by A 607. Parking.

8 **Berkeley Arms**

59 Main St,
Wymondham, LE14 2AG
Tel.: (01572)787587
Website: www.theberkeleyarms.co.uk

VISA MC

Marstons Pedigree, Greene King IPA and twice weekly changing guest ales

This attractive village pub dates back to the 16C and is currently under the control of an enthusiastic local couple, who have plenty of experience in the hospitality industry. As you enter a roaring fire greets you; turn left for the low-beamed bar with its tiled floor and pine tables or right for a slightly more formal dining room. The relaxed, personable service is overseen by charming owner Louise, while her husband, Neil, is hard at work behind the scenes, preparing an appealing seasonal menu of locally sourced produce. Dishes are gutsy and satisfying – there's a daily changing selection of bar snacks and a balanced à la carte of slightly more adventurous, modern offerings, such as braised pig cheek or sea bass with fennel and chorizo.

Closing times
Closed first 2 weeks January, 10 days summer, Sunday dinner and Monday lunch

Prices
Meals: £ 18 (lunch) and a la carte £ 21/32

Typical Dishes

Twice-baked cheese soufflé
Wild sea bass with fennel salad
Warm chocolate fondant

7 mi east of Melton Mowbray off B 676. In centre of village. Parking.

Belchford

9 **Blue Bell Inn**

1 Main Rd,
Belchford, LN9 6LQ
Tel.: (01507)533602

VISA

Black Sheep bitter and weekly changing local guest ales

Situated in a tiny village in the heart of the Lincolnshire Wolds, this whitewashed pub is a popular destination for those walking the Viking Way. You can't miss the big blue bell that hangs outside, however, when you delve deeper into it nobody really knows why it's there, since the pub was originally named after the bluebell flower. It's very much a traditional kind of place, boasting a cosy bar with exposed wooden beams, a typical black wood counter and old-style armchairs – as well as a linen-laid dining room – and despite being run by a young couple, still has an friendly, old-fashioned air. Dishes are listed on numerous blackboards above the fire in the bar and include sandwiches, old pub favourites and some more ambitious creations.

Closing times
Closed 2 weeks mid-January

Prices
Meals: a la carte £ 20/27

Typical Dishes

Crab & ginger salad
Twice-cooked pork belly
Sticky toffee pudding

4 mi north of Horncastle by A 153 and right hand turn east. Parking.

10 Wheatsheaf Inn

Main St,
Dry Doddington, NG23 5HU
Tel.: (01400)281458
Website: www.wheatsheaf-pub.co.uk

VISA

Timothy Taylor Landlord, Greene King Abbot Ale, Batemans XB and weekly guest ales

Set next to a characterful 17C church and overlooking a pretty village green, this smartly kept pub positively beckons you through the door. Once inside, you'll discover a cosy bar with a wood burning stove, settles scattered with cushions, and plenty of wood panelling, as well as a laid-back restaurant with upholstered chairs and painted stone walls; while to the rear, a small courtyard makes the perfect suntrap. The light bites lunch menu keeps things simple, offering unfussy dishes that keep the locals happy (such as beef, ale and mushroom pie), while the à la carte presents some more ambitious offerings like braised blade of beef – supplemented by daily blackboard specials in the evening. The local steaks and twice-baked chips are a hit.

Closing times
Closed Monday except bank holidays

Prices
Meals: £ 15 (lunch) and a la carte £ 23/28

Typical Dishes

Potted mackerel
Braised shoulder of lamb
Vanilla crème brûlée

11 mi northwest of Grantham by B 1174 and A 1. Parking.

11 **Gregory**

The Drift,
Harlaxton, NG32 1AD
Tel.: (01476)577076
Website: www.thegregory.co.uk

VISA MC

Deuchars, Theakston's and IPA

The Gregory has been serving the local community since the 19C, when workers from the eponymous family's estate made it their favourite haunt. When later relocated to its present spot, it was responsible for supplying the village with its coal. These days, the pub has a very modern feel, with a spacious dining room – for which you will need to book – and a smaller lounge. The menu offers a selection of pub classics, including plenty of steaks and homemade pies, alongside dishes such as risotto and fillet of sea bass. Sandwiches supplement at lunchtime, with old-fashioned puddings for afters. Thursday is steak night, whilst early evening Monday-Saturday means 'Super6ixes': six dishes, each available for the princely sum of six pounds.

Closing times
Closed dinner
25-26 December and
1 January

Prices
Meals: a la carte £ 21/33

Typical Dishes

Tempura king prawns
Monkfish Thai red curry
Lemon and lime panna cotta

2 mi southwest of Grantham by A 607. Parking.

12 **Wig & Mitre**

30-32 Steep Hill,
Lincoln, LN2 1LU
Tel.: (01522)535190
Website: www.wigandmitre.com

VISA MC AE D

Young's Golden Gold, Black Sheep, Batemans XB

Nestled among period shops on a steep hill, this well-established, part-14C pub is something of a Lincoln institution; standing midway between the castle (used as a court) – hence the 'Wig' – and the cathedral – hence the 'Mitre'. There's a cosy bar downstairs, and two period dining rooms and a light, airy beamed restaurant above. The menu changes quarterly, displaying largely classical dishes with the odd Mediterranean or Asian influence. There's a good value set selection weekdays and for those who enjoy a hearty homemade breakfast, they open at 9am. With wine books and maps dotted about the place, over 50 wines by the glass and a recommendation for every dish, it comes as no surprise to find that they own the next door wine shop too.

Closing times
Open daily

Prices
Meals: £ 16 and a la carte £ 21/30

Typical Dishes

Salmon fish fingers
Breast of chicken with Lincolnshire Poacher tart
Rhubarb & apple crumble

Close to the Cathedral. Lincoln Castle car parks adjacent.

13 Black Horse Inn

Magna Mile,
Ludford, LN8 6AJ
Tel.: (01507)313645
Website: www.blackhorseludford.co.uk

VISA

Tom Wood's, Fulstow, Skidbrooke Cyder and Great Newsome

Having moved from Lancashire to Lincolnshire to chase their dream of buying a pub and going it alone, Paul and Anna are in it for the long-haul. They may not have huge amounts of money but they do have passion and you have to admire their determination. The building itself might be a little worn but it has a warm, well-loved feel, with homely décor, simple furnishings and welcoming open fires. The horse racing prints are a reference to nearby Market Rasen, while the model planes are a tribute to the Lancaster Bomber veterans, who meet here for their reunions. The menu is concise, featuring good old-fashioned classics that always include some sort of steak. Plenty of pies and stews are on offer in winter, alongside ever-popular game dishes.

Closing times
Closed 2 weeks January, 25 December, Sunday dinner, Monday and bank holidays

Prices
Meals: £ 14 (lunch) and a la carte £ 20/28

Typical Dishes
Salt cod brandade
Confit lamb shoulder
Honey and pistachio baked apple

6 mi east of Market Rasen by A 631. Parking.

14 **Bustard Inn**

44 Main St,
South Rauceby, NG34 8QG
Tel.: (01529)488250
Website: www.thebustardinn.co.uk

VISA MC AE

Dixons Major, Batemans All Seasons, Sleaford Pale

From the outside it resembles a schoolhouse, but The Bustard Inn is hardly bookish. Its flag-floored bar is simple and uncluttered while its more spacious restaurant, with its cream-tiled floor and exposed brick, has a touch of the Mediterranean about it. Traditional pub favourites like sausage and mash and fish and chips are listed on the blackboard bar menu, while the restaurant's à la carte steps things up a gear with an array of modern-style dishes, ranging from pork and black pudding terrine or roast chump of lamb to glazed breast of Gressingham duck or pan-fried sea bream. Slay your thirst with a pint of specially brewed 'Cheeky Bustard' beer and enjoy reassuringly old-fashioned desserts like apple crumble or sticky toffee pudding.

Closing times
Closed 1 January, Sunday dinner and Monday

Prices
Meals: £ 19 (lunch) and a la carte £ 24/43

Typical Dishes

Purple sprouting broccoli with poached egg & hollandaise

Fillet of Lincolnshire beef

Iced rhubarb soufflé

4 mi west of Sleaford by A 17 and minor road south.
Parking.

15 **Bull & Swan**

St Martins,
Stamford, PE9 2LJ
Tel.: (01780)766412
Website: www.thebullandswan.co.uk

VISA AE

Adnams, Ufford Ales Ruperts Wardog, Oakham Ales J.H.B.

This stone-built pub started life as a medieval hall house, before being converted into a travellers inn during the late 1600s. It changed name several times until settling on the Bull & Swan in 1739, when it was taken over by Walter Robinson, a former coachman to the Earl of Exeter, and it remains the only public house south of the river. There's a characterful beamed bar with a lively atmosphere and a slightly more formal dining room. The wide-ranging menu offers something to suit all tastes, from sharing slates to classics such as Lincoln Red rib-eye steak or haslet with free range fried eggs and bacon; on Sundays try the roasting pot for four with all the trimmings. Stylish, individually designed bedrooms boast Egyptian cotton sheets.

Closing times
Open daily

Prices
Meals: a la carte £ 22/34
7 rooms: £ 90/110

Typical Dishes

Confit chicken & foie gras terrine
Roast chump of lamb
Poached rhubarb & strawberry Eton mess

0.5 mi south of the town centre on B 1081. Parking on London Rd.

16 **Chequers**

Main St,
Woolsthorpe by Belvoir, NG32 1LU
Tel.: (01476)870701
Website: www.chequersinn.net

VISA AE

Greene King IPA, Old Speckled Hen, Everards Tiger and regularly changing guest ales

If you like a side of history with your lunch then this quaint little village owned by the Belvoir Estate is the place to come. A pub has stood on this spot since 1692 – the first being run by the same family for 213 years – and it's just as much a community meeting place as ever. Locals nurse pints by the roaring fires, fixtures for the adjacent cricket pitch hang by the door and you can even sit beside the remains of the old village bread oven. Lunch is fairly simple, offering the likes of homemade burgers, pies and local sausages, while dinner adds things such as game or rib of beef for two; there's also a good value daily set menu and 7 dishes for £7 between 6 and 7pm. Crisply furnished, modern bedrooms are located in the old stables.

Closing times
Closed dinner
25-26 December and
1 January

Prices
Meals: £ 17 (weekdays)
and a la carte £ 21/33

4 rooms: £ 50/70

Typical Dishes

Pan-fried scallops
Duck breast with griottine cherry jus
Pineapple & chilli tarte Tatin

7.5 mi west of Grantham by A 607. Parking.

East Haddon

17 **Red Lion**

Main St,
East Haddon, NN6 8BU
Tel.: (01604)770223
Website: www.redlioneasthaddon.co.uk

VISA AE

Eagle IPA, Bombardier, Youngs London Cold

This thatched, honey-stone inn is located right in the heart of the attractive village of East Haddon and boasts a terrace to the front, along with pretty gardens to the rear. It was originally a farmhouse but has since been sympathetically extended, resulting in a pleasing mix of exposed beams and wood and slate floors, on which sit polished tables and comfy leather sofas. Food is taken seriously here, with the chef and one of the owners – both local boys – having spent time working at London's Rhodes 24. Menus offer upgraded pub classics, such as mutton cottage pie or venison and duck burger, and service is enthusiastic and attentive. Bedrooms are warm, welcoming and well-kept; one is in the old cottage next door, which dates back to 1798.

Closing times
Open daily

Prices
Meals: a la carte £ 20/26
5 rooms: £ 80/120

Typical Dishes

Grilled sardines
Slow-roasted pork belly
Chocolate doughnuts

8.5 mi northwest of Northampton off A428. Parking.

18 **Exeter Arms**

21 Stamford Rd,
Easton-on-the-Hill, PE9 3NS
Tel.: (01780)756321
Website: www.theexeterarms.net

VISA

Ufford White Hart, Wardog and seasonal guest ales

This 18C inn has been sympathetically yet stylishly restored by its owner, a local sheep farmer with a passion for good food. The interior has a unique charm and is adorned with copper pans, enamel signs, old hop sacks and bines, as well as an antique mangle and clothes horse. The bar is kept exclusively for the drinkers, who linger over pints from the owner's micro-brewery; while for dining there's a snug candlelit restaurant and a stylish conservatory with Lloyd Loom furnishings, that opens out onto the terrace. Menus offer the chef's signature dishes as well as tasty pizzas and 'home comforts', while in winter you'll find venison, partridge and pheasant from the local shoots. Stylish, well-appointed bedrooms boast smart modern bathrooms.

Closing times
Closed Sunday dinner

Prices
Meals: a la carte £ 23/38

6 rooms: £ 70/200

Typical Dishes

Tallington asparagus
Braised pork belly
Chocolate brownie

2.5 mi southwest of Stamford on A 43. Parking.

19 **Falcon Inn**

Fotheringhay,
PE8 5HZ
Tel.: (01832)226254
Website: www.thefalcon-inn.co.uk

VISA MC AE

Fuller's London Pride, Green King, IPA, Digfield Pools Nook, Ufford Ales, Nethergate Ales, Oakham Ales

In the pretty village of Fotheringhay – the birthplace of Richard III and the deathplace of Mary Queen of Scots – under the shadow of a large church, sits the attractive, ivy-clad Falcon Inn. It boasts a neat garden and a small paved terrace, a pleasant private dining annexe and a beamed bar with an unusual display of 15C bell clappers. You'll find the regulars playing darts and drinking real ales in the small tap bar, and the diners in the conservatory restaurant with its wicker chairs, formally laid tables and garden outlook. Good-sized menus include unusual combinations and some interesting modern takes on traditional dishes; you might find purple sprouting broccoli in your stilton soup or red pepper and dandelion dressing on your crab.

Closing times
Open daily

Prices
Meals: £ 16 (lunch)
and a la carte £ 23/32

Typical Dishes

Thai style crab salad
Rack of lamb
Chocolate nemesis

3.45 mi north of Oundle by A 427 off A 605. Parking.

Caunton Beck

Main St,
Caunton, NG23 6AB
Tel.: (01636)636793
Website: www.wigandmitre.com

VISA AE

Marston's Pedigree, Batemans GHA and Black Sheep

With tan coloured bricks and a wrought iron pergola this doesn't look much like your typical village pub; step inside, however, and locals supping cask ales will soon reassure you. When the weather's right, make for the large front terrace hung with colourful flower baskets. When it's not so good, head for the bar, with its scrubbed pine furniture and daily papers, or the traditional restaurant with its polished period tables and wheel-back chairs. Changing four times a year, the menu offers gutsy, manly cooking with the odd global influence. Daily specials include plenty of fish and there's a good value 3 course menu during the week. If breakfast is your thing, they open at 8am with the likes of smoked salmon, scrambled eggs and champagne.

Closing times
Open daily

Prices
Meals: £ 16 and a la carte £ 23/33

Typical Dishes

Portobello mushroom & sage risotto

Honey-glazed pork belly

Lemon & lime cheesecake

7 mi northwest of Newark by A 616, 6 mi past the sugar beet factory. Parking.

Colston Bassett

21 The Martins Arms

School Ln,
Colston Bassett, NG12 3FD
Tel.: (01949)81361
Website: www.themartinsarms.co.uk

VISA MC AE

Black Dog, Black Sheep, Greene King IPA, Timothy Taylor Landlord, Woodforde's Wherry, Old Speckled Hen

Blazing log fires cast a welcoming glow in the cosy bar of this creeper-clad pub; full of feminine touches like fresh flowers, comfy cushions, tea lights and gleaming copperware. Originally a farmhouse on the Martin family estate, it contains several articles salvaged from the original manor house, including the carved Jacobean fireplace and the old library shelves, now used to hold drinks in the bar. Said bar is the place for an impromptu lunch, while the period furnished dining rooms, adorned with hunting pictures, are more suited to a formal dinner – but be sure to book in advance. The menu has a strong masculine base with some Italian influences and the odd global flavour; portions are hearty and there's plenty of game in season.

Closing times
Closed dinner 25 December and Sunday

Prices
Meals: a la carte £ 27/33

Typical Dishes

Tempura scallops, cockles and pancetta salad

Fillet of cod with samphire

Rum baba with Chantilly cream

East of Cotgrave off A 46. Parking.

22 **Reindeer Inn**

Main St,
Hoveringham, NG14 7JR
Tel.: (01159)663629
Website: www.thereindeerinn.com

Inspectors' favourites

VISA MC

Black Sheep, Castle Rock Harvest Pale and Blue Monkey Original

Behind The Reindeer's modest exterior lies a characterful country inn, with low ceilings, wood beams and a snug bar replete with locals. It's a pleasant place to dine at any time of the year; in winter one appreciates the blazing log fire and the cosy, relaxed atmosphere, while in summer, the cricket pitch behind the pub becomes the focal point, with drinks delivered through a hatch when a game is in full swing. Reasonably priced menus offer an eclectic mix; alongside recognisable dishes like rib of beef and pan-fried calves liver, you will also find more unusual offerings like pork cheeks braised in cider or vegetable tagine. Regular themed evenings like fish and lobster night go down a storm – and they even provide a takeaway service.

Closing times
Closed 1 week May, 1 week October, Tuesday lunch, Sunday dinner and Monday

Prices
Meals: £ 10 (lunch) and a la carte £ 25/36

Typical Dishes
Smoked salmon with celeriac purée & poached egg
Lamb tagine and cous cous salad
Bread & butter pudding with apricot purée

5 mi south of Southwell by A 612. Parking.

23 **Full Moon**

Main St,
Morton, NG25 0UT
Tel.: (01636)830251
Website: www.themoonatmorton.co.uk

VISA MC

Greene King IPA, Blue Monkey Original, BG Sips, Oldershaws and Bombardier

Formerly three cottages and a shop, this modernised red-brick pub really is at the heart of village life: it organises a village scarecrow trail every Easter, holds civil wedding ceremonies and is particularly child friendly, with a wooden castle in the garden, a toy cupboard inside and a kids' menu that's bigger than most. Drinkers have their own space in the lounge, while dining takes place in the restaurant, which opens out onto the terrace and garden. Their motto is 'big flavours and no frills', so you'll find unfussy, boldly flavoured dishes featuring good quality ingredients, alongside a list of tasty blackboard specials; they also open early for breakfast, host monthly fish and vegetarian nights, and even provide a takeaway service.

Closing times
Closed Sunday dinner

Prices
Meals: a la carte £ 20/30

Typical Dishes

Crab cakes with salsa verde

Belly pork with bubble & squeak

Sticky toffee pudding

2.75 mi southeast of Southwell turning right off A 612 signposted Fiskerton. Parking.

24 The Olive Branch & Beech House

Main St,
Clipsham, LE15 7SH
Tel.: (01780)410355
Website: www.theolivebranchpub.com

VISA

Olive Ale, weekly changing guest ales.

You want the character and rusticity of a proper country inn but carefully crafted, highly accomplished food: enter The Olive Branch. It has the heart and soul of a real community pub – so you'll find farmers nursing pints beside the bar – but it also boasts a menu of well-prepared, classically based dishes and a friendly, informative serving team; not forgetting a truly charming garden and BBQ area. Cooking is flavoursome, robust and relies on fresh, local ingredients; and although descriptions may sound ordinary, the reality is anything but. Rather than chasing TV's bright lights, the chef gives cookery demonstrations in the old barn. Bedrooms provide a stylish contrast and include a host of extras. The homemade breakfasts are delightful.

Closing times
Open daily
booking essential

Prices
Meals: £ 21/28
and a la carte £ 25/41

6 rooms: £ 98/205

Typical Dishes

Salad of honey & mustard chicken
Whole baked sea bass
Sticky toffee pudding

9.5 mi northwest of Stamford by B 1081 off A 1. Parking.

Greetham

25 **Wheatsheaf Inn**

1 Stretton Rd,
Greetham, LE15 7NP
Tel.: (01572)812325
Website: www.wheatsheaf-greetham.co.uk

VISA

IPA, American Beauty and Newton's Drop

If you're on your way to Rutland Water, it's well worth diverting via this little village for a visit to the Wheatsheaf; mind the ducks as you pull in and be sure not to overshoot the parking space or you'll end up in the stream. The first thing you'll notice as you walk through the door is the aroma of freshly baked bread, which sits tantalisingly on the bar and is usually an onion foccacia on Sundays. The owners may have experience in London but they've wisely kept this as a family-friendly country pub complete with pool table and dartboard. Where they do use their experience is in the kitchen: robust, modern British cooking comes with hints of the Med, using cheaper cuts to keep prices down. Sunday lunch is a steal and desserts are a must.

Closing times
Closed first 2 weeks January, Monday except bank holidays and Sunday dinner

Prices
Meals: a la carte £ 19/30

Typical Dishes

Tiger prawns with garlic & lemon
Bavette steak & chips
Sticky ginger pudding

Just off the A1 on the B 668 to Cottesmore and Oakham. Parking.

26 **Finch's Arms**

Oakham Rd,
Hambleton, LE15 8TL
Tel.: (01572)756575
Website: www.finchsarms.co.uk

VISA AE

Timothy Taylor Landlord and Black Sheep

With its light sandstone walls and dark slate roof, this attractive 17C building is the very essence of a traditional country pub in outward appearance: inside, however, it offers a whole lot more. True, you'll find the regulars drinking real ales in a rustic bar among beams and flagstones but, the rest of the rooms take on a surprisingly Mediterranean feel, displaying round, stone topped tables and rattan chairs. Continue through yet further and to the rear of the pub you'll find its biggest draw: a large paved terrace, boasting beautiful views across Rutland Water. You can eat in any of the rooms – choosing from both classic and modern British dishes – but the terrace is definitely the place to be. Bedrooms are smart and stylish.

Closing times
Open daily

Prices
Meals: £ 16/20
and a la carte £ 21/27

10 rooms: £ 75/125

Typical Dishes

Seared fillet of beef with wasabi dressing

Cornish sea bass, basil mash & chorizo

Roasted pineapple with raspberry sorbet

3 mi east of Oakham by A 606. Parking.

Lyddington

27 Marquess of Exeter

52 Main St,
Lyddington, LE15 9LT
Tel.: (01572)822477
Website: www.marquessexeter.co.uk

VISA

Marston's Pedigree and Brakspear Bitter

This rather attractive 16C thatched pub is located in a pleasant village in the heart of the Rutland countryside. Locals gather in the cosy, flag-floored front bar, beside inglenook fireplaces and under characterful exposed beams; while, further on, there's a relaxed, rustic dining room with chunky scrubbed tables, old leather chairs and a range. The daily menu offers tasty, classical combinations that let good quality ingredients shine through – they even grow their own veg and keep chickens and pigs at the bottom of the garden. There's an appealing 'Lunch for Less' menu and specials written up on gilt mirrors, while the sharing plates – maybe rib of beef or shoulder of lamb – are firm favourites. Comfy bedrooms are found across the car park.

Closing times
Open daily

Prices
Meals: £ 15 (lunch)
and a la carte £ 26/31

17 rooms: £ 70/115

Typical Dishes

Chicken liver parfait
Grilled flat iron steak
Hot chocolate pudding

Just south of Uppingham, signposted off A 6003 in the middle of the village. Parking.

28 **Old White Hart**

51 Main St,
Lyddington, LE15 9LR
Tel.: (01572)821703
Website: www.oldwhitehart.co.uk

VISA

Grainstore Brewery Rutland bitter, Potbelly best and weekly changing guest ales

Set in the pleasant village of Lyddington, this 17C former coaching inn ticks all the right boxes. It boasts a neat garden, a smart canopy-covered terrace and several cosy open-fired rooms crammed full of old pictures and objets d'art. In keeping with the place, the monthly changing menu offers a selection of traditional pub dishes, cooked and served in a simple, unfussy manner. You might find roast loin of lamb, toad in the hole or pan-fried calves liver, followed by maybe lemon meringue pie or crumble of the day. If you fancy a bit of light competition, book yourself in for one of the petanque evenings, where you get plenty of game play before dinner. Bedrooms are modern and stylish – one has a spiral staircase leading to a private jacuzzi.

Closing times
Closed 25 December

Prices
Meals: £ 14 (lunch and early dinner) and a la carte £ 20/31

10 rooms: £ 60/95

Typical Dishes

Applewood smoked salmon with Norfolk crab

Homemade pork & sage sausages

Sticky toffee pudding

1.5 mi south of Uppingham off A 6003; by the village green. Parking.

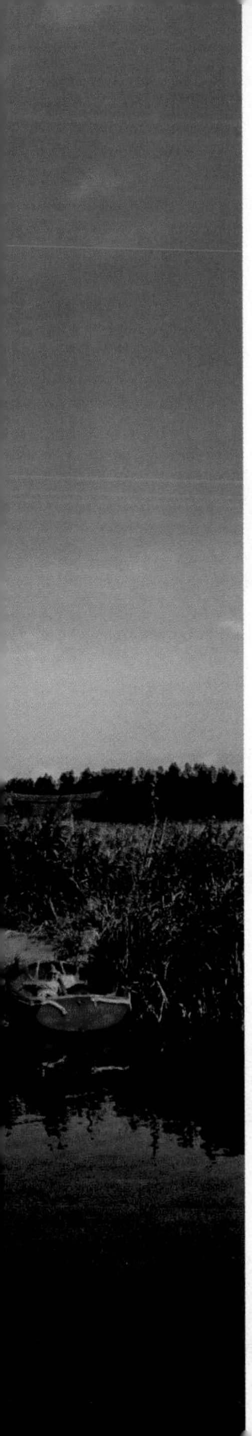

Wide lowland landscapes and huge skies, timber-framed houses, a frowning North Sea canvas: these are the abiding images of England's east. This region has its roots embedded in the earth and its taste buds whetted by local seafood. Some of the most renowned ales are brewed in Norfolk and Suffolk. East Anglia sees crumbling cliffs, superb mudflats and saltmarshes or enchanting medieval wool towns such as Lavenham. Areas of Outstanding Natural Beauty abound, in the Chilterns of Bedfordshire and Hertfordshire, and in Dedham Vale, life-long inspiration of Constable. Religious buildings are everywhere, from Ely Cathedral, "the Ship of the Fens", to the fine structure of Long Melford church. The ghosts of great men haunt Cambridge: Newton, Darwin, Pepys and Byron studied here, doubtless deep in thought as they tramped the wide-open spaces of Midsummer Common or Parker's Piece. Look out for Cromer crab, samphire, grilled herring, Suffolk pork casserole and the hearty Bedfordshire Clanger.

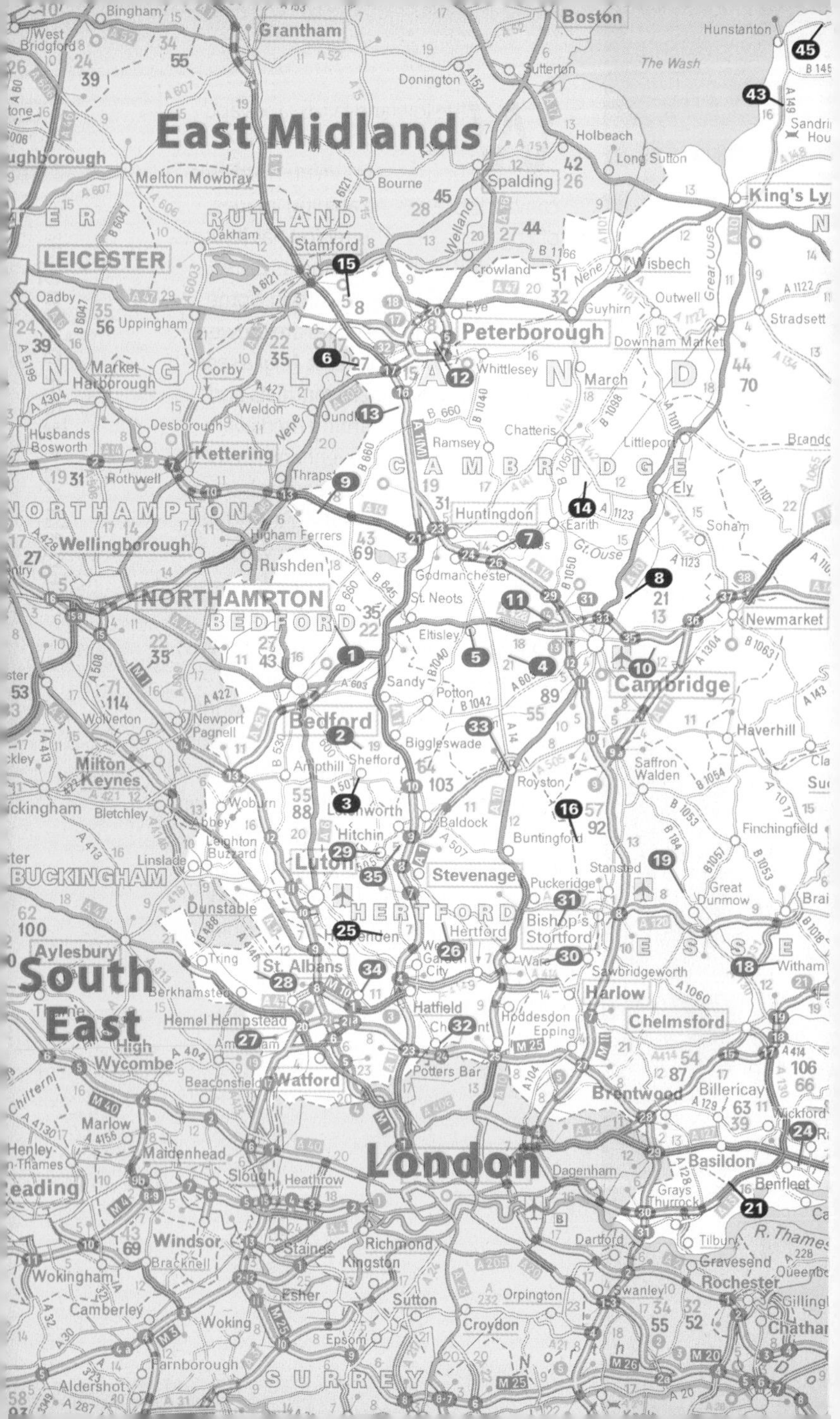
East Midlands
South East
London
Boston
Grantham
Bingham
West Bridgford
Hunstanton
The Wash
Donington
Sutterton
Holbeach
Long Sutton
Sandringham House
Loughborough
Melton Mowbray
Bourne
Spalding
King's Lynn
RUTLAND
Oakham
Stamford
Crowland
Wisbech
LEICESTER
Oadby
Uppingham
Eye
Guyhirn
Outwell
Stradsett
Peterborough
Downham Market
Whittlesey
Market Harborough
Corby
March
Weldon
Oundle
Husbands Bosworth
Desborough
Ramsey
Chatteris
Littleport
Brandon
Kettering
Rothwell
Thrapston
CAMBRIDGE
Ely
NORTHAMPTON
Huntingdon
Earith
Soham
Higham Ferrers
Wellingborough
St Ives
Gt. Ouse
Rushden
Godmanchester
Newmarket
St. Neots
BEDFORD
Eltisley
Cambridge
Sandy
Potton
Wolverton
Newport Pagnell
Bedford
Haverhill
Biggleswade
Milton Keynes
Ampthill
Shefford
Saffron Walden
Royston
Buckingham
Bletchley
Woburn Abbey
Letchworth
Baldock
Finchingfield
Leighton Buzzard
Hitchin
Buntingford
Linslade
Luton
Stevenage
Stansted
Great Dunmow
BUCKINGHAM
Puckeridge
Dunstable
HERTFORD
Bishop's Stortford
Hertford
Harpenden
Aylesbury
Tring
St. Albans
Welwyn Garden City
Ware
Sawbridgeworth
Witham
ESSEX
Berkhamsted
Hatfield
Harlow
Hemel Hempstead
Hoddesdon
Epping
Chelmsford
Thame
Amersham
High Wycombe
Watford
Potters Bar
Beaconsfield
Brentwood
Billericay
Wickford
Chiltern
Marlow
Henley-on-Thames
Maidenhead
Slough
Heathrow
Dagenham
Basildon
Benfleet
Reading
Grays Thurrock
Windsor
Staines
Richmond
Tilbury
R. Thames
Bracknell
Kingston
Dartford
Gravesend
Rochester
Wokingham
Esher
Sutton
Orpington
Swanley
Gillingham
Camberley
Woking
Croydon
Chatham
Epsom
Farnborough
Aldershot
SURREY
Welland
Nene
Great Ouse

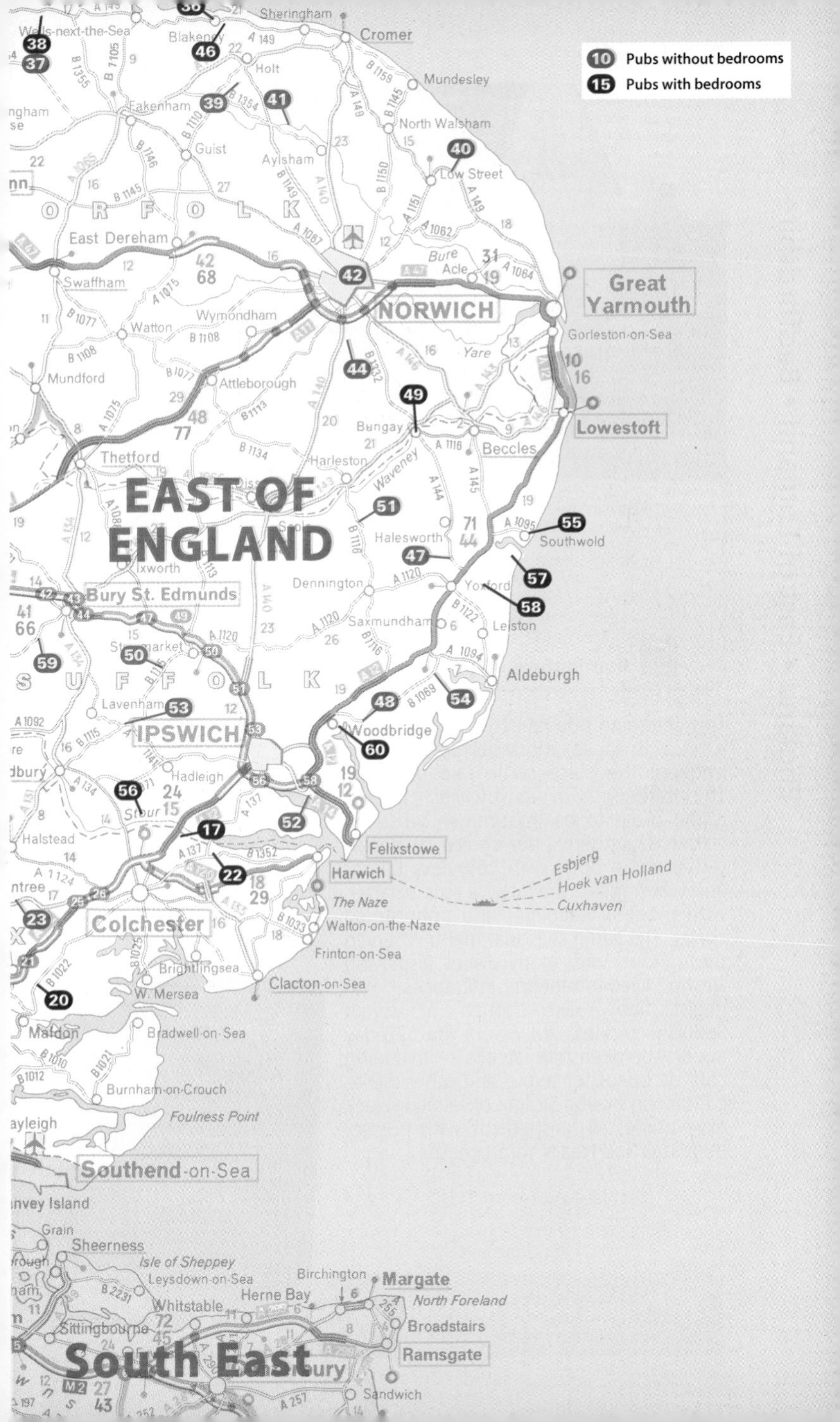
10 Pubs without bedrooms
15 Pubs with bedrooms
EAST OF ENGLAND
South East
NORFOLK
SUFFOLK
NORWICH
IPSWICH
Great Yarmouth
Lowestoft
Sheringham
Cromer
Wells-next-the-Sea
Blakeney
Holt
Mundesley
Fakenham
North Walsham
Guist
Aylsham
Low Street
East Dereham
Bure
Acle
Swaffham
Wymondham
Watton
Gorleston-on-Sea
Yare
Mundford
Attleborough
Bungay
Beccles
Thetford
Harleston
Waveney
Halesworth
Southwold
Ixworth
Dennington
Yoxford
Bury St. Edmunds
Saxmundham
Leiston
Stowmarket
Aldeburgh
Lavenham
Woodbridge
Hadleigh
Stour
Halstead
Felixstowe
Harwich
The Naze
Esbjerg
Hoek van Holland
Cuxhaven
Colchester
Walton-on-the-Naze
Frinton-on-Sea
Brightlingsea
W. Mersea
Clacton-on-Sea
Maldon
Bradwell-on-Sea
Burnham-on-Crouch
Foulness Point
Southend-on-Sea
Grain
Sheerness
Isle of Sheppey
Leysdown-on-Sea
Birchington
Margate
Herne Bay
North Foreland
Whitstable
Broadstairs
Sittingbourne
Ramsgate
Sandwich

1 Plough at Bolnhurst

Kimbolton Rd,
Bolnhurst, MK44 2EX
Tel.: (01234)376274
Website: www.bolnhurst.com

VISA

Buntingford, Adnam's and Grainstore ales

This charming pub has 15C origins and is a hit with locals and visitors alike, who frequent the place come rain or shine. The garden, with its trickling stream, is the place to be in summer, while on colder days there's the choice of bar or restaurant – both with cosy low beams and warm fires – the latter a little smarter, with modern wallpaper and upholstered chairs. The same seasonal menu is served throughout, with many dishes displaying strong Mediterranean influences. You might find roast chorizo or sweet Spanish pickles, followed by 28-day aged Aberdeenshire steaks – including côte de boeuf for two – and other dishes containing maybe Sicilian olive oil or black olive purée; all finished off with nursery puddings and Neal's Yard cheeses.

CLOSING TIMES
Closed 2 weeks January, Sunday dinner and Monday

PRICES
Meals: £ 19/25
and a la carte £ 27/37

Typical Dishes

Double baked goat's cheese soufflé

Confit of duck leg & roast sweet potatoes

Crème brûlée

On B 660 7 mi north of Bedford. Parking.

2 **Hare & Hounds**

The Village,
Old Warden, SG18 9HQ
Tel.: (01767)627225
Website: www.hareandhoundsoldwarden.co.uk

VISA

Youngs Bitter, Eagle IPA

With its ornate feature bargeboards and attractive manicured shrubs, this pub could easily appear on the front of any chocolate box. A charming building set in an idyllic village, it boasts four cosy rooms with brightly burning fires, bucket chairs and squashy banquettes, as well as a friendly team. If you're looking to eat, there's the choice of blackboard bar 'snacks' – although you could hardly call them so, as you might find fish and chips or pie of the day – or a monthly changing à la carte that offers robust, flavoursome dishes such as sea bass, pheasant or venison. Bread and pasta are made on the premises; meat is from local farms; fish is from sustainable stocks; and they have an allotment planted with various herbs, salad and berries.

CLOSING TIMES
Closed 26 December, 1 January, Sunday dinner and Monday except bank holidays

PRICES
Meals: a la carte £ 22/28

Typical Dishes

Chicken liver parfait
Veal burger with Montgomery cheddar
Mango & kiwi pavlova

3.5 mi west of Biggleswade by A 6001 off B 658. Parking here and at Village hall.

3 **Black Horse**

Ireland,
Shefford, SG17 5QL
Tel.: (01462)811398
Website: www.blackhorseireland.com

VISA AE

Fuller's London Pride, St Austell Tribute and Adnam's Best Bitter

Don't be deceived by the picture perfect chocolate box exterior; if you're looking for a quaint country inn you're in the wrong place. It may look traditional from the outside, but inside it's as stylish and modern as you can get. Contemporary light fittings are set amongst marble-style flooring and a granite-topped counter, and there's a walled courtyard complete with mirrors and fairy lights. The friendly staff serve an equally eclectic mix of generously portioned dishes. Lunch could include anything from suet crust pie to potted crab, while dinner might offer pork brawn followed by oxtail pudding or sweet potato tagine; finished off with good old-fashioned puddings. Accessed via a meandering garden path, bedrooms are comfy and delightfully cosy.

CLOSING TIMES
Closed 25-26 December, 1 January and Sunday dinner

PRICES
Meals: a la carte £ 23/38
2 rooms: £ 55

Typical Dishes
Salt & pepper squid
Vermouth-braised rabbit & pancetta
Coffee crème brûlée

1.5 mi northwest of Shefford by B 658 and Ireland rd. Parking.

4 **Willow Tree**

29 High St,
Bourn, CB23 2SQ
Tel.: (01954)719775
Website: www.thewillowtreebourn.com

VISA

Woodforde's Wherry, Black Sheep

It may be named after a majestic British tree, the likes of which you'll find blowing elegantly in the wind as you enter the car park, but this pub is far from your usual affair. The life-sized cow model in the garden is the first clue as to the quirky nature of the place, and is followed inside with the feeling of being inside a 'House and Homes' magazine, courtesy of chandeliers, gilt mirrors and the Louis XV style furniture dotted about the place. Menus offer everything from old pub classics to more ambitious dishes such as potted crab, baba ganoush, smoked fish lasagne or braised pheasant, with maybe lemon meringue pie or fig and almond tart to follow. They also have an appealing wine list, with most selections available by the glass.

CLOSING TIMES
Open daily

PRICES
Meals: a la carte £ 18/38

Typical Dishes

Cornish crab & smoked salmon millefeuille
Duck breast with saffron dauphinoise
Baileys crème brûlée

In the centre of the village. Parking.

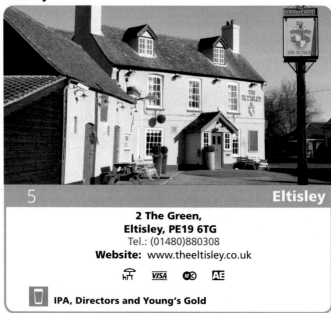

5 **Eltisley**

2 The Green,
Eltisley, PE19 6TG
Tel.: (01480)880308
Website: www.theeltisley.co.uk

VISA MC AE

IPA, Directors and Young's Gold

You might imagine that this chic, stylish gastro-pub is a strictly dining affair, but the contemporary bar is equally as welcoming to drinkers as diners; the latter, who can sit and watch their meal being prepared from the windows in the snug. For a more formal occasion head through to the restaurant, where grey walls meet wood and tile flooring, and bold designs are offset by swanky chandeliers. Large parties should ask for the 'Wurlitzer', a stylish high-backed semi-circular banquette, while for summer dining the terrace is ideal. Cooking is simple, unfussy and relies on quality local ingredients: meat is from nearby farms and vegetables, from their allotment. Everything from the bread and pasta to the desserts and ice cream is homemade.

CLOSING TIMES
Closed Monday in winter and Sunday dinner

PRICES
Meals: a la carte £ 22/37

Typical Dishes

Free range chicken & mushroom pressing

Rib-eye steak with beer-battered onion rings

Double chocolate brownie

Between St Neots and Cambridge, signposted off A 428. Parking.

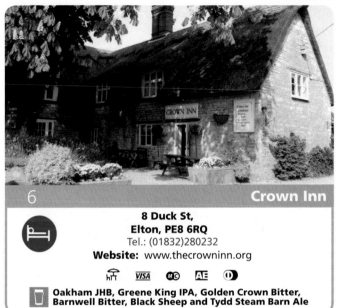

6 Crown Inn

8 Duck St,
Elton, PE8 6RQ
Tel.: (01832)280232
Website: www.thecrowninn.org

VISA MC AE

Oakham JHB, Greene King IPA, Golden Crown Bitter, Barnwell Bitter, Black Sheep and Tydd Steam Barn Ale

With its 17C honey-stone walls, charming thatched roof and lovely location in a delightful country parish, The Crown Inn really is a good old-fashioned pub. To start, sup a cask ale beside the characterful inglenook fireplace in the bar, then head through to the cosy dining room, large octagonal conservatory or out onto the spacious decked terrace. The same seasonally changing menu is served throughout, featuring old British favourites such as steak and ale pie or Lancashire hotpot, and often several dishes of a more Mediterranean persuasion. To finish, try the swan-shaped profiterole which swims on chocolate sauce. Individually designed bedrooms come in a mix of classic and modern styles; some have four-posters, sleigh beds or roll-top baths.

CLOSING TIMES
Closed Sunday dinner and Monday lunch

PRICES
Meals: a la carte £ 21/26
5 rooms: £ 65/95

Typical Dishes

Smoked haddock fishcake
Beef, ale & mushroom pie
Apple & blackberry crumble

Midway between Oundle and Peterborough signposted off A 605. Parking.

Hemingford Grey

7 **Cock**

47 High St,
Hemingford Grey, PE28 9BJ
Tel.: (01480)463609
Website: www.thecockhemingford.co.uk.

Inspectors' favourites

VISA MC AE

Great Oakley Wagtail, Nethergate IPA, Brewsters Hophead and Oldershaw Newtons Drop

As you approach this 17C country pub you'll come across two doors: one marked 'Pub', leading to a split-level bar and the other marked 'Restaurant', leading to a spacious L-shaped dining room. Run by an experienced team, it has a homely feel, with warm fabrics, comfy seating and attractively papered walls throughout. In winter, the best spot is beside the fire and in summer, the most pleasant is by the French windows. Cooking rests firmly on the tried-and-tested side of things, with classic pub staples such as lamb shank and belly pork; good value set lunches; and a list of daily changing fish specials. A tempting sausage board also offers an appealing mix of several varieties of homemade sausage matched with mashed potato and sauces.

CLOSING TIMES
Open daily
booking essential

PRICES
Meals: a la carte £ 26/35

Typical Dishes

Rabbit & pork terrine
Pan-fried mackerel fillets with anchovy & olive tart
White chocolate & raspberry terrine

The village is 5 mi east of Huntingdon signposted off A 14. Parking.

8 Crown and Punchbowl

High St,
Horningsea, CB25 9JG
Tel.: (01223)860643
Website: www.thecrownandpunchbowl.co.uk

VISA MC AE

No real ales offered

The clue that this is more of a dining than a drinking establishment lies in the fact that there's no real bar area. However, it still delivers on the pubby character, thanks to its beams, open fires and chunky wooden tables. The menu changes with the seasons but there are also daily specials and their popular 'sausage board'. There's a sophisticated element to the cooking – seared scallops are a permanent feature – and the kitchen can do traditional, such as the delicious blade of beef, as well as modern, with dishes like fish terrine with horseradish sorbet or the deconstructed millionaire's shortbread. There's a pleasant terrace and simple bedrooms available. Service has become a little less formal and is all the better for it.

CLOSING TIMES
Closed 26 December-1 January, dinner Sunday and bank holiday Monday

PRICES
Meals: a la carte £ 25/33
5 rooms: £ 75/95

Typical Dishes

Pan-fried asparagus with a poached egg
Pan-seared salmon with crushed new potatoes
Trio of desserts

Just off the A 14, northeast of Cambridge. Parking.

9 **Pheasant**

Village Loop Rd,
Keyston, PE28 0RE
Tel.: (01832)710241
Website: www.thepheasant-keyston.co.uk

VISA

Nethergate, Potbelly Brewery and Digfield

Since the former managers took over, this charming thatched pub has gone from strength to strength, despite becoming less 'village local' and more 'destination dining pub'. Set in a sleepy little hamlet and framed by colourful flowers, it offers the choice of classic or contemporary dining rooms. Flip over the daily changing menu and you'll find an explanation of what's in season, who supplied it and a glossary of terms. Flip it back and you'll find tasty homemade bread and hors d'oeuvres, followed by maybe a classic coq au vin or more international Thai black bream salad. One of the chefs spent time at London's St John restaurant, so you'll also find kidneys, ribs, tongues and hearts; the trimmings going into the popular pheasant burger.

CLOSING TIMES
Open daily
booking essential

PRICES
Meals: £ 22 (lunch)
and a la carte £ 28/40

Typical Dishes

Seared beef with wood sorrel, pennywort, pickled mushroom

Roasted saddle & tortelli of rabbit

Iced zabaglione parfait

Signposted off junction 15 of A 14. Parking.

10 Hole in the Wall

2 High St,
Little Wilbraham, CB21 5JY
Tel.: (01223)812282
Website: www.the-holeinthewall.com

Inspectors' favourites

VISA

Woodforde's Wherry, Buntingford's Sun Star and By George

It may be off the beaten track but that doesn't mean this pub has lost touch with the culinary world; far from it, in fact – and others could do well to follow in its footsteps. Many people look on this as an 'occasion' type of place but you're more than welcome to pop in just for a snack or a bowl of soup. The same menu is served throughout, offering traditional English cooking in flavoursome dishes, with local produce used wherever possible – and if you don't have time to visit the other 'hole in the wall', don't worry, the lunchtime à la carte provides particularly good value. The 15C part of the building boasts characterful low beamed ceilings, so mind your head or make for the more recently built, sympathetically designed extension.

CLOSING TIMES
Closed 2 weeks January, 2 weeks September-October, Sunday dinner and Monday except lunch on bank holidays

PRICES
Meals: a la carte £ 23/29

Typical Dishes

Pan-fried chicken livers on toast
Suffolk Barnsley chop
Cambridgeshire burnt cream

Just off the A 14 east of Cambridge, the Wilbrahams are signposted off A 1303. Parking.

Madingley

11 Three Horseshoes

High St,
Madingley, CB23 8AB
Tel.: (01954)210221
Website: www.threehorseshoesmadingley.com

VISA AE

Adnams, Timothy Taylor Landlord, Batemans and Everards Tiger

Set in a pretty village – famous for its stunning Hall – this pub, with its whitewashed walls and attractive thatched roof, fits right in. To the front, scrubbed wooden furniture is set beside a welcoming fireplace and small bar; to the rear, a more formal linen-laid conservatory with Lloyd Loom chairs looks out over the garden. The bar menu offers pork scratchings, olives and a concise three course selection, while the daily changing Italian à la carte – part written in Italian – features straightforward combinations and uncluttered, tasty dishes; maybe linguine di cozze or agnello arrosto. The bar has a great atmosphere, so if you're looking for a romantic table for two, make for the conservatory instead.

CLOSING TIMES
Open daily
booking advisable

PRICES
Meals: a la carte £ 22/38

Typical Dishes

Risotto primavera
Roast fillet of beef with snails, garlic & parsley
Chocolate ganache & toffee banana ice cream

West of Cambridge signposted off A 1303. Parking.

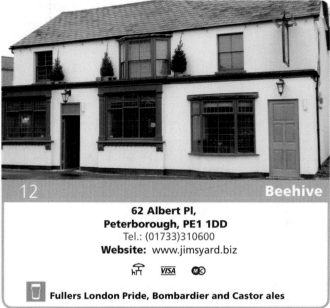

12 Beehive

62 Albert Pl,
Peterborough, PE1 1DD
Tel.: (01733)310600
Website: www.jimsyard.biz

Fullers London Pride, Bombardier and Castor ales

Just off the city centre ring road might not be your first choice of location for a pub but it's close at hand for the shoppers and has been stood here long enough that, despite having been closed for a while, the steady group of regulars are now returning. Owners James and Sharon have lived in the area all their lives and, remembering the pub in its heyday, jumped at the chance to get the place up and running again. It now has a smart, modern interior with stripped floorboards, a zinc-topped bar and a range of different seating. Lunch sees lighter offerings – the chicken liver pâté is a must – while dinner offers classics such as braised blade of beef or homemade pies; whatever you choose it will be well-presented, flavoursome and satisfying.

CLOSING TIMES
Closed 1 January and Sunday dinner

PRICES
Meals: a la carte £ 20/29

Typical Dishes

Chicken liver pâté
Merguez sausages with grain mustard mash
Panna cotta with pineapple carpaccio

In the centre of the city just off Bourges Boulevard. Pay and display parking across the road.

13 Village Bar (at Bell Inn)

Great North Rd,
Stilton, PE7 3RA
Tel.: (01733)241066
Website: www.thebellstilton.co.uk

Old Speckled Hen, Greene King IPA, Bishops Farewell Oakham Ales, Fools Nook Digfield Ales

It's hard to believe that this sleepy market town is just minutes off the A1, or that this 17C inn – famous as the birthplace of Stilton cheese – is set on what was once the most popular coaching route from York to London. Look closely however, and you can still see the distances to the major cities inscribed on what was the original archway from the road to the stables. Step inside and you have the choice of a characterful bar or more modern bistro setting. Classically based dishes are a step above your usual pub fare, so you might find wild boar and cranberry terrine, followed by grey mullet on tomato risotto or Label Anglaise chicken with parsnip potato pancakes. Cosy, traditionally styled bedrooms can be found in the adjoining inn.

CLOSING TIMES
Closed 25 December

PRICES
Meals: a la carte £ 20/30

Typical Dishes

Stilton pâté with pineapple chilli jam

Smoked haddock & spring vegetable risotto

Sticky toffee pudding

In the centre of the village. Parking.

14 **Anchor Inn**

Sutton Gault,
CB6 2BD
Tel.: (01353)778537
Website: www.anchor-inn-restaurant.co.uk

VISA MC AE

Weekly rotating guest ales including Hobsons Choice, Pegasus and Dionysus.

It may seem like a strange name for a pub that's nowhere near the coast – but it does have some watery connections. Built in 1650, this building was originally used to house the workers who created the Hundred Foot Wash in order to alleviate flooding in the fens. If you fancy a river view, head for the wood panelled rooms to the front of the bar, where you'll discover a pleasant outlook and a tempting menu, which might include smoked eel, pork loin in Parma ham, tea-infused duck or the house speciality of grilled dates wrapped in bacon. There are always some fish specials chalked on the board, while others occasionally use produce from the nearby Denham Estate. Neat, pine furnished bedrooms include two suites; one boasts river views.

CLOSING TIMES
Open daily

PRICES
Meals: £ 18 (weekday lunch) and a la carte £ 25/34

4 rooms: £ 89/155

Typical Dishes

Grilled dates wrapped in bacon

Pork tenderloin with cream cheese, nettles & bacon

Elderflower cheesecake

Off B 1381; from Sutton village follow signs to Sutton Gault; pub is beside the New Bedford River. Parking.

Ufford

15 White Hart

Main St,
Ufford, PE9 3BH
Tel.: (01780)740250
Website: www.whitehartufford.co.uk

VISA MC AE

Adnams, Ufford Ales - White Hart, Ruperts Wardog & Golden Drop

This delightful 17C inn stands at the centre of the charming village of Ufford. Outside, there's a super sun-trap of a terrace and garden, while inside there's a cosy bar housing an interesting collection of railway signs, farm implements and chamber pots, as well as a pleasant beamed restaurant with exposed stone walls and a lovely little conservatory. The menu offers a broad range of dishes, from simple sandwiches to starters of beetroot cured salmon or seared scallops with wild mushroom cream, followed by Thai-style fish casserole or creamy rabbit pie. Much of the meat comes from their farm and they also have a micro-brewery on-site. The sweet bedrooms are named after their beers – each has its own style and one boasts a four-poster.

CLOSING TIMES
Closed Sunday dinner

PRICES
Meals: a la carte £ 21/38
6 rooms: £ 70/110

Typical Dishes

Fishcake on smoked salmon & feta salad
Pan-fried fillet steak
Trio of crème brûlées

The village is signposted off B 660 northwest of Peterborough. Parking.

16 **Cricketers**

Clavering,
CB11 4QT
Tel.: (01799)550442
Website: www.thecricketers.co.uk

VISA AE

Adnams Broadside, Nethergates Jamies Tipple and Small Beer

Set in a charming village, this attractive whitewashed pub exudes plenty of old-world charm. Rustic brick walls and ancient wood beams are complemented by contemporary furnishings and stylish fittings, and there's a welcoming feel about the place. Cosy up beside the fire in the bar or head to the restaurant for a touch more formality. The same menu is served throughout and the cooking is precise, flavoursome and attractively presented; with the odd Italian touch thrown in. Good quality local produce is key, so you'll find plenty of regional meats, fresh fish and veg from the garden of the owners' son, Jamie Oliver. Bedrooms are split between the courtyard and pavilion: the former, simple and modern; the latter, more traditional.

CLOSING TIMES
Closed 25-26 December

PRICES
Meals: a la carte £ 24/34
14 rooms: £ 68/115

Typical Dishes

Bruschetta of home-smoked salmon & asparagus
Five spice Telmara Farm duck salad
Apricot custard tart with coconut ice cream

On the main road through the village close to the cricket pitch. Parking.

Dedham

17 **Sun Inn**

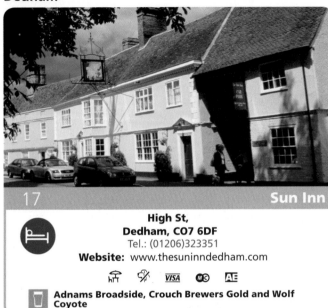

High St,
Dedham, CO7 6DF
Tel.: (01206)323351
Website: www.thesuninndedham.com

VISA

Adnams Broadside, Crouch Brewers Gold and Wolf Coyote

Set in an idyllic village in the heart of Constable Country, this brightly painted pub offers guests a slice of sun even when the skies are cloudy and grey. Log fires create a cosy feel, there's a superb burr elm bar counter, a two-tiered dining room and a pleasant garden and terrace. At lunchtime, the bar board tempts with a selection of doorstop sandwiches, terrines and tarts. The à la carte lists its simple, tasty dishes in Italian, followed by their English translation – if you don't mind sharing, try the antipasti; while options like lamb stew or pan-fried ox liver mean you can keep your meal all to yourself. Five contemporary bedrooms provide a restful night's slumber; Elsa, with its four-poster, is named after the resident ghost.

CLOSING TIMES
Closed 25-26 December

PRICES
Meals: £ 15 (weekdays) and a la carte £ 25/35

5 rooms: £ 65/160

Typical Dishes

Pea & broad bean bruschetta

Roasted turbot with asparagus & potato gnocchi

Saffron panna cotta with rhubarb marmalade

In the centre of the village. Parking.

18 Square & Compasses

Fuller Street,
CM3 2BB
Tel.: (01245)361477
Website: www.thesquareandcompasses.co.uk

VISA MC

Nethergate Stokers Ale, Crouch Vale Essex Boys, Dark Star Hophead and Over the Moon.

Hidden deep in the Essex countryside, down a labyrinth of lanes, you might just need that compass after all. A charming little pub with low beams, wood burning stoves and cosy character aplenty, this is a place that offers genuine hospitality from hands-on owners and a friendly team. It boasts a small locals bar with gravity fed casks and a dining room displaying numerous certificates and menus from the owners' pasts on its exposed brick walls. Unfussy menus offers the usual pub classics like home-cooked gammon or Stokers Ale pie, while the daily changing blackboards might list pies or terrines of locally shot game and pan-fried fish caught nearby. Unashamedly traditional homemade puddings feature the likes of spotted dick or rhubarb crumble.

CLOSING TIMES
Closed 1 January
booking essential

PRICES
Meals: a la carte £ 20/26

Typical Dishes

Chicken liver & port pâté
Grilled wing of skate with lemon, caper & parsley butter
Orange & passion fruit tart

Between Braintree and Chelmsford off the A 131. Parking.

Great Easton

19 **Green Man**

Mile End Green,
Great Easton, CM6 2DN
Tel.: (01371)852285
Website: www.thegreenmanrestaurant.com

VISA

Greene King IPA

This low slung, cottage style pub is as immaculate inside as it is out, with a smart, contemporary look. The original roof and wall beams have been retained, as has the large inglenook fireplace; there's a formal linen-clad restaurant, a neat garden and a sun-splashed terrace. Aside from the beer-batted cod with fat chips, dishes are more of a restaurant than a pub persuasion. One menu covers both lunch and dinner, supplemented by blackboard specials, which often include fish. You might come across tempura of salmon or pan-fried scallops, followed by lamb shank with honey-roast vegetables, duck breast with calvados and five spice or chicken stuffed with chestnut mousse and wrapped in bacon. Attentive, assured service completes the experience.

CLOSING TIMES
Closed two weeks January, Monday and Tuesday

PRICES
Meals: a la carte £ 25/38

Typical Dishes

Tempura prawns with wasabi mayonnaise

Sea bass with potato salad, smoked salmon & crayfish

Strawberry & champagne cheesecake

Signposted off the B 184 north of Great Dunmow. Parking.

20 The Bull

2 Maldon Rd,
Great Totham, CM9 8NH
Tel.: (01621)893385
Website: www.thebullatgreattotham.co.uk

Inspectors' favourites

VISA MC AE

London Pride, Bombardier and Adnams ales

Attractive roadside pub dating back to the 1500s and boasting a beautifully landscaped rear garden and distant views of West Mersea from the picnic tables at the front. Inside it's been modernised but still retains the pubby character you'd expect of a building its age. The beamed bar is split in two, with a snug that's frequented by the locals and a concise menu of pub favourites. At the back, is the more formal 'Willow Room', named after the large tree outside, which offers ambitious, elaborate, modern cooking crafted from local ingredients – maybe Maldon oysters or Epping Forest venison – alongside a few influences from the chef's native Scotland, such as haggis, neeps and tatties. Contemporary bedrooms are located in a nearby cottage.

CLOSING TIMES
Open daily

PRICES
Meals: £ 16 (lunch)
and a la carte £ 19/26

4 rooms: £ 59/85

Typical Dishes

Ham hock roulade with piccalilli.

Pan-seared pollock with surf clam broth.

Rhubarb crème brûlée.

Between Tiptree and Maldon on B 1022. Parking.

Horndon on the Hill

21 Bell

High Rd,
Horndon on the Hill, SS17 8LD
Tel.: (01375)642463
Website: www.bell-inn.co.uk

VISA MC AE

Greene King IPA, Crouch Vale Brewers Gold, Sharp's Doom Bar and Morland Original

If you're wondering about the hot cross buns, the story goes that past landlord Jack Turnell took over the pub on Good Friday, whereupon he nailed a bun to one of the beams; since then, a bun has been added every year – the cement version marking the wartime rationing. The Bell has been run by the same family for the last 50 years, although dates back nearly 12 times that. Drinkers will find themselves at home in the wood-panelled bar, while diners can choose from a beamed area or more formal restaurant. Cooking uses quality produce to create classically based dishes with a modern touch; maybe apple tart with a glass of malted milkshake. Bedrooms are styled after famous Victorian mistresses; those in Hill House display thoughtful extras.

CLOSING TIMES
Closed 25-26 December and bank holiday Mondays

PRICES
Meals: a la carte £ 22/37
15 rooms: £ 60/100

Typical Dishes

Mackerel fishcake with creamed horseradish
Herb-roasted lamb chump with crushed peas
Lemon & thyme crème brûlée

In the centre of the village. Parking.

22 Mistley Thorn

High St,
Mistley, CO11 1HE
Tel.: (01206)392821
Website: www.mistleythorn.com

VISA

Adnams, Sticklegs and various local guest ales

Set opposite the River Stour in the small coastal village of Mistley, this passionately run pub has become something of a local institution. Simplicity is the key here: the brightly coloured walls filled with local art create a stylish yet homely feel and the cooking is of a similarly comforting yet flavoursome vein. Tasty foccacia and fruity olive oil kick things off, followed by anything from burgers, fishcakes and steaks through to soufflés, terrines and shellfish – the tempting specials often featuring game or fish. If you look closely, there's the odd reference to owner Sherri's American/Italian childhood and her Mom's Cheesecake with homemade ice cream is now a permanent fixture. Spacious, wood-furnished bedrooms; some with river views.

CLOSING TIMES
Closed 25 December

PRICES
Meals: £ 15 (weekday lunch) and a la carte £ 19/33

8 rooms: £ 75/130

Typical Dishes
Beetroot, tomato & goat's cheese salad
Local fish stew with samphire & cockles
Dark chocolate cremoso, espresso parfait & salted almonds

In the centre of the village. Parking.

23 Compasses at Pattiswick

Compasses Rd,
Pattiswick, CM77 8BG
Tel.: (01376)561322
Website: www.thegreatpubcompany.co.uk

VISA MC

Adnams, Woodforde's Wherry and St Austell's Tribute

The Compasses started life as two estate workers' cottages. Now a smart pub, it boasts walls filled with wildlife photography and even a private room with its own terrace; but it's the cheery staff who really make the place. The best spot is in the barn-style restaurant, although spaces on the terrace are sought after too. Set weekday menus represent the best value but there's also the monthly changing à la carte and daily specials to consider; you might find pork pies or Welsh rarebit at lunchtime and braised lamb shank or seared tuna steak in the evening. Cooking is honest, simple and well done, with a huge amount of effort put into sourcing local ingredients. Venison is from the woods behind; pheasant and partridge, from local shoots.

CLOSING TIMES
Open daily

PRICES
Meals: a la carte £ 23/30

Typical Dishes

Sautéed wild mushrooms on toasted brioche

Herb-crusted lamb rack with champ

Glazed lemon tart with lime Chantilly

Between Braintree and Coggeshall signposted off A 120. Parking.

24 Woodmans Arms

Rayleigh Rd,
Thundersley, SS7 3TA
Tel.: (01268)775799
Website: www.thewoodmans.co.uk

VISA MC AE

Adnams Broadside, Courage Directors, Courage Best, Bombadier

Sometimes when a pub starts to serve good food, its drinkers – the locals – get somewhat sidelined; not so at The Woodmans Arms, where at least half the pub is dedicated to those supping pints and sipping wine, with large comfy sofas and bucket chairs to accommodate them. The neatly laid restaurant is decorated with old black and white photos; half screens cleverly separate the drinkers from the diners and a cheery young team see to the needs of all. The seasonal dishes are hearty and flavourful, and whilst traditional in the main – perhaps roast fillet of salmon or beer battered haddock – the menu might also include a Malaysian chicken salad or Cajan spiced whitebait. Lunchtime sees lighter choices such as baked potato or Welsh rarebit.

CLOSING TIMES
Open daily

PRICES
Meals: a la carte £ 25/35

Typical Dishes

Smoked chicken & ham hock terrine
Chump of lamb with parmentier sweet potatoes
Rhubarb & ginger crumble

Between Basildon and Southend-on-Sea off A 127. Parking.

25 **Brocket Arms**

Ayot St Lawrence,
AL6 9BT
Tel.: (01438)820250
Website: www.brocketarms.com

VISA

Sharp's Doom Bar, Nethergate Brocket Bitter and guest beers, Adnams and Woodford Wherry

Opposite George Bernard Shaw's old house, behind the uneven walls and leaded windows of this small 14C inn, you'll find a cosy, characterful bar with flag floors, dark wood beams and exposed brick; not forgetting a huge inglenook fireplace that you can sit inside and a monk's hole hidden up the chimney. The good value bar menu is designed with ramblers in mind and there are regular summer BBQs, however the chef's talent is best displayed through his 'menu du jour' – served mainly in the traditional, wood-furnished restaurant – which offers a good range of original, flavoursome combinations; maybe smoked ham scrumpet with piccalilli, followed by slow-braised ox cheeks in stout. Bedrooms are simple and comfortable, some are set in the courtyard.

CLOSING TIMES
Closed Sunday dinner

PRICES
Meals: £ 25 and a la carte £ 23/28

6 rooms: £ 95/125

Typical Dishes

Scotch egg with curry sauce

Roasted fillet of pork with duck egg & red wine sauce

Orange blossom crème brûlée

2.75 mi west of Welwyn signposted off B 656. Parking.

26 Tilbury

Watton Rd,
Datchworth, SG3 6TB
Tel.: (01438)815550
Website: www.thetilbury.co.uk

VISA MC AE

Brakspear Oxford Gold, Brakspear Best

Chef Paul Bloxham now seems to spend more time behind the stoves at The Tilbury than on TV, save for the odd appearance on Market Kitchen – and for the pub, that can only be a good thing. Owners Paul and Paul know where it's at when it comes to local, seasonal produce and the cover of the menu will reassure any sceptic, listing the ingredients that will feature each month, alongside their provenance and other ethical considerations they take into account when sourcing produce. The menu ranges from wild mushrooms on toast to Herdwick mutton chops, followed perhaps by Bramley apple crumble. On a summer's day head for the smartly dressed tables on the terrace; otherwise, just sit back among the artwork or beside the roaring fire and enjoy.

CLOSING TIMES
Closed Sunday dinner

PRICES
Meals: £ 18 (lunch)
and a la carte £ 25/33

Typical Dishes
Squid & coriander risotto, pork belly & scallop
Guinea fowl, chicory, onions & pickled mushrooms
Plate of lemon desserts

4 mi southeast of Stevenage signposted off A 602. Parking.

Flaunden

27 Bricklayers Arms

Hogpits Bottom,
Flaunden, HP3 0PH
Tel.: (01442)833322
Website: www.bricklayersarms.com

VISA MC AE

Doombar, London Pride, Rebellion IPA, and Trings beer of the month

This pub is tucked away by itself on the outer reaches of a small hamlet, so you'll need a good navigator when trying to find it. Part-built in 1722, it was originally two cottages, before becoming a butcher's, a blacksmith's and later, an alehouse. Inside it's rather smart, with polished tables and fresh flowers everywhere; the areas to the side of the bar being more formally laid than those in front. This isn't the place for a quick snack (a glance at the menu will show there are none), but somewhere serving good old-fashioned, French-inspired dishes. Sunday lunch is a real family affair and if you've only time for a fleeting visit, have a hearty pudding on the terrace. The wine list is a labour of love, featuring boutique Australian wines.

CLOSING TIMES
Closed 25 December

PRICES
Meals: a la carte £ 26/39

Typical Dishes
Home-smoked fish plate
Fillet of Herefordshire beef with green peppercorn sauce
Crêpe filled with Cointreau mascarpone & citrus fruit

5 mi northeast of Amersham signposted off the A404. Parking.

28 **Alford Arms**

Frithsden,
HP1 3DD
Tel.: (01442)864480
Website: www.alfordarmsfrithsden.co.uk

VISA AE

Marlow Rebellion, IPA, Tring Sidepocket and Sharp's Doom Bar

Set among the network of paths that run across the Chilterns, this attractive Victorian pub is a popular destination for hikers – and when you're trying to squeeze your car into a tight space on the narrow country lane, arriving by foot may suddenly seem the better option. A pleasant garden overlooks the peaceful village green – where you might spot the odd Morris dancer or two – and the warm bar welcomes four-legged friends as equally as their owners. The traditional menu has a strong British stamp and follows the seasons closely, so you're likely to find salads and fish in summer and comforting meat or game dishes in winter; these might include belly pork with sticky parsnips, lamb and rabbit shepherd's pie or a tempting blackboard special.

CLOSING TIMES
Closed 25-26 December

PRICES
Meals: a la carte £ 22/28

Typical Dishes

Local rabbit & hazelnut terrine

Whole roast sea bream with pearl barley

Marsala roast peach & gingerbread trifle

4.5 mi northwest of Hemel Hempstead signposted off A 4146. Parking.

29 Radcliffe Arms

31 Walsworth Rd,
Hitchin, SG4 9ST
Tel.: (01462)456111
Website: www.radcliffearms.com

VISA AE

Buntingford, Tring, Red Squirrel and Grain, Milton

Named after a renowned local family, the Radcliffe Arms enjoys its position as a true neighbourhood pub. It might have been modernised but this is still a friendly, relaxed place for the town's drinkers to gather, supping on gravity fed real ales or debating which of the 13 varieties of gin or 28 wines by the glass are best. The central bar is surrounded by a mix of wooden tables and chairs, and there's a small conservatory to the rear. Tasty cooking includes a few pub classics but it's more about well-presented, restaurant-style dishes here; you might find beetroot risotto, daube of beef or the locals' favourite, tiger prawns with chilli sauce. If you fancy it, you can even visit both before and after work, as they open at 8am for breakfast.

CLOSING TIMES
Open daily

PRICES
Meals: a la carte £ 27/42

Typical Dishes

Goat's cheese panzerottis & beetroot carpaccio

Slow cooked blade of beef

Tarte Tatin

A short walk from the high street in the direction of the station. Parking.

30 Fox and Hounds

2 High St,
Hunsdon, SG12 8NH
Tel.: (01279)843999
Website: www.foxandhounds-hunsdon.co.uk

VISA MC AE

Adnams Bitter, Adnams Broadside, Red Squirrel and Saffron Blonde ales

London to Hertfordshire isn't the biggest of moves but swapping the hustle and bustle of crowded streets for the peace and quiet of the countryside is a move that childhood sweethearts James and Bianca – now husband and wife – believe is well worth making. If the weather's good, sit in the garden or on the terrace; if not, find a spot in the pleasant bar or dining room. Menus are concise, offering tasty, unfussy dishes that display a clear understanding of flavours. There are a few pub classics alongside more restaurant-style dishes such as salt and pepper squid or scallops with herb butter, and there's a popular seafood bar outside in the summer too. All of the pastas are homemade, they smoke their own fish and desserts are not to be missed.

CLOSING TIMES
Closed 26 December, Sunday dinner and Monday

PRICES
Meals: £ 17 (weekdays) and a la carte £ 26/35

Typical Dishes

Palourde clams with chorizo

Calves liver persillade with potato cake

Apple tart with salted caramel ice cream

Between Hertford and Harlow signposted off A 414, in the village centre. Parking.

Much Hadham

31 Hoops Inn

Perry Green,
Much Hadham, SG10 6EF
Tel.: (01279)843568
Website: www.hoops-inn.co.uk

VISA

Adnams, Meantime and local seasonal ales

This smart whitewashed pub is located in a pretty hamlet, opposite what was once the home of sculptor Henry Moore, and is the perfect place to eat when visiting his studios. It's not large but it is brimming with character, thanks to low beamed ceilings and a wood burning stove, along with a few more modern touches. It's now owned by the Henry Moore Foundation, so you'll find his designs printed in the textiles and exclusive access from the garden to the grounds of his estate. When it comes to the cooking, it's fresh, tasty and vibrant. At lunch, choose between light bites and pub favourites; in the evening, from the likes of a tasting plate of starters, hanger steak and pork T-bone. Puddings change daily and are presented on small blackboards.

CLOSING TIMES
Closed Sunday dinner and Monday

PRICES
Meals: a la carte £ 18/27

Typical Dishes

Treacle cured salmon

Hanger steak, roasted shallots & horseradish butter

Warm apple Bakewell tart

2.75 mi southeast of the village; follow sign to Henry Moore Foundation.

32 **Sun at Northaw**

1 Judges Hill,
Northaw, EN6 4NL
Tel.: (01707)655507
Website: www.thesunatnorthaw.co.uk

Adnams Explorer, Squirrel Conservation and Saffron Brewery's Saffron Blonde

This restored, part-16C pub sits by the village green. Deceptively spacious, it's contemporary in style, with a traditional edge. Cooking is original, so expect a wide range of dishes like crispy pigs' ears, spiced lamb pie, red gurnard or maybe even sea urchin. There's a strong regional slant here too: ingredients are sourced from the East of England, there are local ales and ciders behind the bar – as well as some English bottles on the wine list – and the toilet walls are even papered with Ordnance Survey maps of the area. Look out for wooden crates of veg scattered about the place and expect to see a chef coming to grab an onion or two. Service is friendly and the pub's affectionate spaniel, Smudge, may well wander over to welcome you too.

CLOSING TIMES
Closed Sunday dinner and Monday

PRICES
Meals: £ 18 (weekday lunch) and a la carte £ 27/37

Typical Dishes

Lamb scrumpet with caper salad

Whole Norfolk plaice with surf clams, peas & samphire

Chocolate terrine with strawberries

Beside village green on main road through the village. Parking.

33 Cabinet at Reed

High St,
Reed, SG8 8AH
Tel.: (01763)848366
Website: www.thecabinetatreed.co.uk

VISA

Woodforde's Wherry, Fullers London Pride, and Timothy Taylor

Set foot in Reed and you'll be transported back to days of old, when houses were surrounded by moats and the pub was the hub of the village. The houses are now ringed by large grass verges but all roads still lead to The Cabinet. Behind its white clapperboard exterior this pub hides a delightful brick-floored snug, a cosy open-fired bar and a small, simply laid restaurant. There's an air of informality about the place which is echoed in the menus, so you'll find a list of dishes that the owners would like to eat themselves. Cooking is flavoursome but dishes aren't always what they seem, as traditional recipes are given a more modern twist. The set lunches provide particularly good value and the warming casseroles and pies are a hit in winter.

CLOSING TIMES
Closed 25 December, 1 January and Monday lunch

PRICES
Meals: £ 16/26
and a la carte £ 23/35

Typical Dishes

Baked duck egg & smoked salmon
Sea bass with tomatoes & olives
Chocolate pot and Bourbon biscuit

3 mi south of Royston signposted off A 10. Parking.

34 **Blue Anchor**

145 Fishpool St,
St Albans, AL3 4RY
Tel.: (01727)855038
Website: www.theblueanchorstalbans.co.uk

VISA

McMullens IPA, Country bitter and Rusty Anchor

The Blue Anchor is a relative newcomer to the Hertfordshire pub scene; although owner Paul Bloxham – TV chef and owner of sister pub, The Tilbury – is no stranger to the trade. The pub is nicely set, close to the historic city centre, opposite Verulamium Park, and boasts a pleasant pub-meets-bistro style. The front bar is the most atmospheric of the rooms but on a sunny day head for the lovely garden, which runs right down to the River Ver. Paul has a passion for seeking out the best local producers and letting the seasons inform his cooking, so you'll find top notch ingredients and plenty of homemade and home-smoked products. Dishes are rustic and robust, and even the simplest offerings are taken seriously. Service is chirpy and swift.

CLOSING TIMES
Closed Sunday dinner

PRICES
Meals: £ 17 (lunch)
and a la carte £ 22/30

Typical Dishes

Plate of homemade charcuterie

John Dory with almonds & borlotti beans

Tonka bean crème brûlée

Off the High St past the cathedral. Parking.

35 **Fox**

Willian,
SG6 2AE
Tel.: (01462)480233
Website: www.foxatwillian.co.uk

VISA

Brancaster Best, The Wreck, Malthouse Bitter, Woodeforde's Wherry, Adnams Bitter and Fuller's London Pride

Set right in the heart of the village, this bright, airy pub is extremely popular. At lunchtime, drinkers and diners vie for tables in the bar, while in the evenings the local drinkers pull rank and those wanting a meal head for the dining room. Light wood floors and matching furniture feature throughout and the keener eye will notice a host of subtle references to Norfolk – home to the owner's other two pubs. Crisps and olives are provided while you study the menu and tasty homemade chocolates finish things off. There's plenty of seafood on offer here, with the likes of haddock rarebit, black bream or herb-crusted cod and always a good choice of game in season. For those who just can't decide, 'The Fox Slate' provides the perfect solution.

CLOSING TIMES
Closed Sunday dinner

PRICES
Meals: a la carte £ 21/33

Typical Dishes

Brancaster Staithe oysters
Pan-roasted fillet of sea bass
Basil infused panna cotta

3 mi northeast of Hitchin by A 505 and side road. Parking.

36 **White Horse**

4 High St,
Blakeney, NR25 7AL
Tel.: (01263)740574
Website: www.blakeneywhitehorse.co.uk

VISA AE

Adnams Broadside, Adnams Bitter, Woodfordes Wherry, Yetmans

Maybe you've spent the afternoon wandering the beautiful north Norfolk coastline, spotting the various species of bird that flock along the marshes, or on a boat trip out to Blakeney Point to see the seals basking on the sandbanks. The invigorating sea air will no doubt have stoked your appetite, so head for something hearty to eat at this brick and flint former coaching inn. The same à la carte menu is served in all areas and changes according to what's freshly available and in season. Dishes might include grilled lemon sole or pot roast suckling pig, with puddings like hot chocolate fondant or crème brûlée. Bedrooms have modern facilities and come in various shapes and sizes; some decorated in the bright blues and yellows of the seaside.

CLOSING TIMES
Closed 25 December
booking advisable

PRICES
Meals: a la carte £ 20/34
9 rooms: £ 50/140

Typical Dishes

Roast pigeon breast with foie gras risotto
Roast mackerel salad
Mandarin panna cotta

Just off the quay. Parking.

37 Jolly Sailors

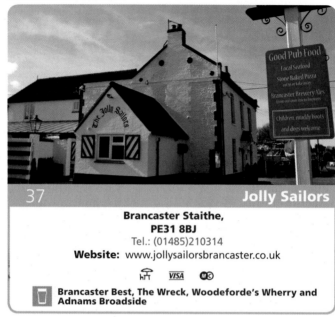

Brancaster Staithe,
PE31 8BJ
Tel.: (01485)210314
Website: www.jollysailorsbrancaster.co.uk

VISA

Brancaster Best, The Wreck, Woodeforde's Wherry and Adnams Broadside

Already the owner of two successful pubs, Clifford Nye decided to add a more casual younger sister to his collection. Dating back over 250 years, The Jolly Sailors is a refreshing break from the norm – retaining much of its original rustic character despite having been spruced up. The open fire provides a focal point and the 'Children, Dogs and Well Behaved Parents' sign reminds you that all are welcome. The menu may be simple but it works well: there's a selection of baguettes, ploughman's and light bites, as well as freshly made pizzas – with a create your own option – and a selection of main dishes that could include curry or liver and bacon. There's also a pie and fish of the day, and usually some local oysters from the beds out front.

CLOSING TIMES
Open daily

PRICES
Meals: a la carte £ 17/23

Typical Dishes

Brancaster mussels
Steak & ale pie
Warm triple chocolate brownie

Just off the quay. Parking.

38

White Horse

Brancaster Staithe,
PE31 8BY
Tel.: (01485)210262
Website: www.whitehorsebrancaster.co.uk

VISA MC

Woodforde's Wherry, Adnam's Best Bitter, Brancaster Best, The Wreck, Malthouse bitter and Oyster Catcher

With glorious views over the Brancaster Marshes and Scolt Head Island, a seat on this pub's sunny back terrace or in the spacious rear conservatory is a must. If the tables here are all taken, then the landscaped front terrace may not have the views, but it's got the parasols, the heaters and the lights to make up for it. Foodwise, the oft-changing menus provide ample choice, with seafood being a highlight, you might find local Cromer crab, Brancaster oysters or fish from the boats at the end of the car park. The pub's popularity means that service can sometimes suffer under the strain but with the coastal views to provide a distraction you might not even notice. Bedrooms are comfy; those in the rear extension each have their own terrace.

CLOSING TIMES
Open daily
booking essential

PRICES
Meals: a la carte £ 22/28
15 rooms: £ 77/134

Typical Dishes

Brancaster oysters
Grilled local smoked haddock with asparagus
Lemon tart

On A 149 Hunstanton to Wells rd. Parking.

Hunworth

39 **Hunny Bell**

The Green,
Hunworth, NR24 2AA
Tel.: (01263)712300
Website: www.hunnybell.co.uk

VISA MC AE

Woodfords Wherry, Adnams, Eldgoods, Oakham, Wolf and Abbott ales

Following a sympathetic renovation and extension, this 18C whitewashed pub with its smart country interior looks the bee's knees. Exposed brickwork, stone flooring and restored wooden beams are offset by bold modern feature walls, and there's an appealing conservatory and smart wood-furnished patio overlooking the green. The owners' experience really shines through, resulting in a keenly priced, seasonal menu that's modern-European meets traditional pub. For main course you might discover local pork sausages or sage-roast chicken breast, while at either end of the meal the chef proudly presents homemade breads and sorbets. The baby of the Animal Inns family, it is as sound as a bell and 'Hunny' is sure to be the buzz word for miles around.

CLOSING TIMES
Open daily

PRICES
Meals: a la carte £ 25/34

Typical Dishes

Dressed Cromer crab, feta cheese & pink grapefruit salad
Chump of lamb
Baked egg custard tart

On the green. Parking.

40 **Ingham Swan**

Sea Palling Rd,
Ingham, NR12 9AB
Tel.: (01692)581099
Website: www.theinghamswan.co.uk

VISA

Woodforde's Brewery ales including Wherry, Mardlers, Admiral's Reserve

This attractive thatched pub, dating from the 14C and sitting in the shadow of a fine 11C church, lies in a small hamlet known for its delightful cricket field – all in all, a charming scene of English pastoral splendour. The cosy beamed interior is equally characterful and while this is clearly more of a dining pub, drinkers are still welcome. The one area which does break with tradition is the cooking, which is far from straightforward but clearly skilled; dishes are made up of many ingredients, albeit in classic combinations, and presentation adopts a contemporary style; even the fillet of beef is elevated to something a lot more interesting. Wine dinners and cookery classes are popular events. Bedrooms are too modest for us to recommend.

CLOSING TIMES
Closed 25-26 December
booking essential at dinner

PRICES
Meals: £ 19/28
and a la carte £ 22/41

Typical Dishes

Hot roast foie gras
Pan-fried wild sea bass
Vanilla crème brûlée

In the centre of the village. Parking.

Itteringham

41 Walpole Arms

The Common,
Itteringham, NR11 7AR
Tel.: (01263)587258
Website: www.thewalpolearms.co.uk

Inspectors' favourites

VISA

Adnams Bitter and Broadside, Woodforde's Wherry and one guest ale

This red-brick inn has all the old-fashioned charm of one who has been providing hospitality since the 18C. The Mediterranean-influenced menus are modified daily, as dictated by suppliers and seasons, with tasty, well-prepared dishes such as baby octopus in red wine and tomato sauce or escabeche of red mullet to start, followed by fillet of salmon with saffron mash, Morston mussels or sauté of veal with potato gratin. The formal restaurant, with its low ceilings and clothed tables, makes a becoming backdrop for a dinner date; the gardens and terrace are great come summer, while the rustic, beamed bar is definitely the most characterful seat in the house. If you're after something simpler to eat, the pub classics will oblige.

CLOSING TIMES
Closed 25 December and Sunday dinner

PRICES
Meals: a la carte £ 20/31

Typical Dishes

Salt & pepper squid salad

Hake fillet, creamed peas, leeks & bacon

Buttermilk pudding with summer berries

In the centre of the village. Parking.

42 Mad Moose Arms

2 Warwick St,
Norwich, NR2 3LD
Tel.: (01603)627687
Website: www.madmoose.co.uk

VISA MC AE

Oakham, Woodfords, London Pride and Wolf

The Mad Moose Arms is very much a neighbourhood haunt and you're likely to find the locals in their droves as you step through the doorway. It's a 'proper' pub, with cosy burgundy walls, plenty of tables and a busy, buzzy atmosphere; even more so during match times, when you'll find excited groups clustered around the TVs. Large blackboards list an enticing array of dishes that range from light bites to substantial pub favourites – but if you're after something a little more formal, head upstairs. Here you'll find period chairs set around smartly laid tables, bold silvery wallpaper, gilt chandeliers and an interesting menu of more ambitious, classically based dishes. Presentation is modern; amuse bouches and pre-desserts also feature.

CLOSING TIMES
Closed 25 December

PRICES
Meals: a la carte £ 21/30

Typical Dishes

Warm smoked mackerel with pickled red cabbage & herb oil

Seared hake with chive butter sauce

Chocolate terrine with fresh orange sorbet

Off Unthank Road. Local on-street parking.

Snettisham

43 **Rose and Crown**

Old Church Rd,
Snettisham, PE31 7LX
Tel.: (01485)541382
Website: www.roseandcrownsnettisham.co.uk

VISA

Adnams, Woodforde's Wherry and one regularly changing guest ale

Its warren of rooms and passageways, uneven floors and low beamed ceilings place the Rose and Crown squarely into the quintessentially English bracket of inns; the larger dining rooms, the paved terrace and the children's play area in the garden add some 21C zing to the pub's 14C roots. Cooking is gutsy by nature and makes good use of local produce, with neatly presented dishes such as peppered tuna carpaccio or pan-roast salmon on offer alongside trusty classics like sausage and mash or steak and chips. Service is efficient, they are well used to being busy and a good crowd of locals from the village can often be found enjoying a tipple or two at the bar. Bedrooms are quite a contrast to the rustic pub: light, airy and modern in style.

CLOSING TIMES
Open daily

PRICES
Meals: a la carte £ 21/29
16 rooms: £ 70/110

Typical Dishes

Goat's cheese with walnut & red onion tartlet

Steak burger & French fries

Apricot bread & butter pudding

In the middle of the village. Parking.

44

Wildebeest Arms

82-86 Norwich Rd,
Stoke Holy Cross, NR14 8QJ
Tel.: (01508)492497
Website: www.thewildebeest.co.uk

Inspectors' favourites

VISA MC AE

Selection of Adnams ales

With its wicker fence and chairs, tribal tree trunk tables and wild animal artefacts, this pub offers a taste of the African savannah in the unlikely setting of Norfolk. Despite the pub's exotic undertones, the food is more European in flavour, with seasonal main courses such as seared pigeon breast, rump of English lamb, and butternut squash, leek and parmesan risotto and desserts like vanilla panna cotta. Cooking is distinctly modern in style, with neatly presented dishes in well judged portions. The set lunch and dinner menus represent very good value for money and service comes from friendly, well organised staff who handle busy periods with aplomb. Should it begin to approach balmy African temperatures, head for the pleasant terrace.

CLOSING TIMES
Closed 25 December
booking essential

PRICES
Meals: £ 17/22
and a la carte £ 25/35

Typical Dishes
Local asparagus with poached egg & white onion purée
Fillet of sea bream with chorizo & red pepper sauce
Dark chocolate fondant

Just off the A 140 5.5 mi south of Norwich. Parking.

Thornham

45 **Orange Tree**

High St,
Thornham, PE36 6LY
Tel.: (01485)512213
Website: www.theorangetreethornham.co.uk

VISA

Woodforde's Wherry, Adnams Southwold Bitter, Crouch Vale Brewers Gold

You're guaranteed a warm welcome from the chatty staff at this popular 17C inn, as is your pooch, who can sit with you in the relaxed, open-fired bar while gnawing on a 'Scooby Snack'. If you fancy a more intimate affair, leave your four-legged friend at home and head for the contemporary restaurant, where wine racks temptingly adorn the walls. A vast array of menus offers everything from bar classics to restaurant-style dishes, via a list of vegetarian choices and daily specials. Flavours are vibrant and well-defined, many with an international feel, and they often arrive on boards or slates; you might find Brancaster crab spaghetti, chicken Tikka Jalfrezi or garlic butter roast calves liver. Compact modern bedrooms complete the picture.

CLOSING TIMES
Open daily

PRICES
Meals: a la carte £ 25/35
6 rooms: £ 65/110

Typical Dishes

Warm fish platter
Pan-fried fillet of wild halibut
Norfolk apple & rhubarb crackle crumble

4.5 mi northeast of Hunstanton on A 149. Parking.

46 Wiveton Bell

Blakeney Rd,
Wiveton, NR25 7TL
Tel.: (01263)740101
Website: www.wivetonbell.com

VISA MC AE

Woodforde's Wherry, Once Bittern and Yetmans Red

Situated in a beautiful area surrounded by salt marshes and nature reserves, The Wiveton Bell makes the ideal stop off point for walkers following the coastal path. The neatly kept garden provides a fantastic location for stargazing at night and hosts an attractive flower display by day; while inside the pub there's a comfy, modern bar leading to an airy conservatory – which is brightened yet further by a convivial atmosphere and the cheery team. Traditional menus offer salads, light meals and largely British-based dishes, alongside a few more international influences; you might find Thai fish cakes, Briston pork belly or fisherman's pie. Charming bedrooms come complete with a continental tuckbox, so keep your PJs on and have breakfast in bed.

CLOSING TIMES
Closed 25 December
booking essential

PRICES
Meals: a la carte £ 21/29
4 rooms: £ 90/140

Typical Dishes

Pigeon, ham hock & chicken terrine
Cley smokehouse poached haddock
Chocolate torte

Signposted off the A 149 just south of Blakeney. Parking.

Bramfield

47 **Queen's Head**

The Street,
Bramfield, IP19 9HT
Tel.: (01986)784214
Website: www.queensheadbramfield.co.uk

VISA MC AE

Adnams Bitter and Broadside

Run by a dedicated husband and wife team, this characterful, cream-washed pub has been in the family for more than 11 years. Set in the heart of a small country village beside an attractive thatched church, it boasts two rooms; the largest, with its high beamed ceiling and scrubbed tables opening out onto a flower-filled garden. The central bar has lots to catch the eye, with shelves crammed full of books and a selection of homemade preserves, chutneys and cakes for sale. There's a blackboard snack menu and a daily changing, classically based à la carte, which is formed around the latest local, seasonal and organic produce – much from the local soil association farm just up the road. You'll often find local bands playing on a Friday night.

CLOSING TIMES
Closed 25 December

PRICES
Meals: a la carte £ 21/30

Typical Dishes
Organic dates wrapped in Bramfield bacon
Roasted free range pork belly with beetroot salsa
Pavlova with Suffolk cream

In the centre of the village. Parking.

48 **British Larder**

Orford Rd,
Bromeswell, IP12 2PU
Tel.: (01394)460310
Website: www.britishlardersuffolk.co.uk

VISA

Adnams Bitter, Woodforde's Wherry, Adnams Broadside

Once down-at-heel, this 17C pub has been modernised in its look and transformed into a beacon for Suffolk produce, courtesy of its owners who have a passion for all things local. They even encourage their customers to donate produce to the pub – a blackboard behind the bar will list what 'glut is required' and any produce brought in is weighed and an agreed price is credited against the customer's next meal. The kitchen handles these ingredients deftly and will sometimes use modern techniques such as water-baths. Deli sharing boards feature at lunch, while dinner is more structured. The pub itself is smart and contemporary but still has an appealingly rustic edge. The enthusiastic owners also hold regular wine events and cookery classes.

CLOSING TIMES
Closed Sunday dinner and Monday in winter except December

PRICES
Meals: a la carte £ 28/40

Typical Dishes

Chicken & ham terrine with pickled beetroot

Lamb rump, shoulder croquette & crushed minted potatoes

Strawberry arctic roll

2.5 mi northeast of Woodbridge on the A 1152. Parking.

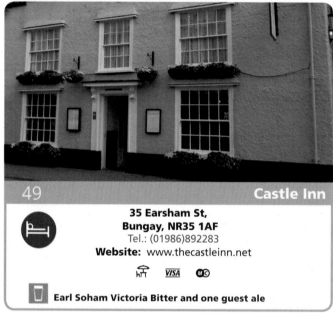

49 **Castle Inn**

35 Earsham St,
Bungay, NR35 1AF
Tel.: (01986)892283
Website: www.thecastleinn.net

VISA

Earl Soham Victoria Bitter and one guest ale

This sky-blue pub's open-plan interior includes dining areas and an intimate rear bar – the perfect spot for a postprandial coffee or for a flick through the foodie magazines. Cooking is country based; fresh, simple and seasonal, and while lunchtime might see sausage and mash or fisherman's pie on offer alongside sandwiches, the evening menu might include pan-seared pigeon breast or duck leg confit. The Innkeeper's platter is a perennial favourite and showcases local produce, including a great pickle made by the Rocking Grannies – keep an eye out for the cake stands too, with their homemade cakes and cookies. Themed evenings include pie and wine night and film and food night, complete with popcorn. Bedrooms are homely, warm and comfortable.

CLOSING TIMES
Closed 25 December

PRICES
Meals: £ 19 (lunch)
and a la carte £ 20/30

4 rooms: £ 70

Typical Dishes

English asparagus with deep-fried poached egg

Bungay pigeon in Parma ham

Vanilla & ginger baked apple

In the centre of town. Parking.

50 Buxhall Crown

Mill Rd,
Buxhall, IP14 3DW
Tel.: (01449)736521
Website: www.thebuxhallcrown.co.uk

St Austell's Tribute, Thwaites Wainwright, Greene King IPA and St Edmund

This part-16C country pub is set off the beaten track, with a bright, yellow-painted dining room which looks out to Buxhall Windmill. Head down into the cosy, low beamed bar for beer straight from the barrel – while you're here take a look over the blackboard menu of seasonal dishes. These tend towards the classics so expect choices like rack of English lamb or steak and chips alongside pub favourites such as sausage and mash; at the weekends, when it's busier, they step things up a gear, adding a few more modern touches. There's a great value, weekly changing 2 course set menu, a decent selection of Suffolk cheeses and classic desserts like lemon tart; release your inner child with some fun puds featuring space dust and penny chews.

CLOSING TIMES
Closed 25 December and Sunday dinner

PRICES
Meals: £ 16 (lunch) and a la carte £ 19/31

Typical Dishes

Duck taco stack

Smoked haddock fishcake & Welsh rarebit

Chocolate pavlova with raspberry compote

3.5 mi west of Stowmarket. Signposted off the B 1115. Parking.

Fressingfield

51 Fox & Goose Inn

Church Rd,
Fressingfield, IP21 5PB
Tel.: (01379)586247
Website: www.foxandgoose.net

VISA

Adnams Best Bitter and Southwold ales

Attractive 16C pub stood opposite the village green, built by – and still owned by – the 14C church next door. Inside it delivers all you would expect of a pub its age: wooden beams, tiled floors and open fireplaces, while for those who enjoy a more alfresco experience, there's a pleasant terrace overlooking the duck pond on the green. Choose an East Anglian ale from the casks behind the bar to sup alongside a good old classic pub dish or opt for a more restaurant-style offering from the good value weekly lunch menu. If you fancy an altogether more sophisticated experience however, head upstairs to the comfy lounge and linen-clad dining room, where dishes are modern with touches of originality and you'll find many more ingredients on the plate.

CLOSING TIMES
Closed 1 week early January, 25-30 December and Monday
booking advisable

PRICES
Meals: £ 18 (lunch) and a la carte £ 29/36

Typical Dishes

King scallops with cauliflower purée & sherry caramel
Fillet of beef with thyme jus
Plum tarte Tatin with lemongrass ice cream

By the village green. Parking.

52 **Ship Inn**

Church Ln,
Levington, IP10 0LQ
Tel.: (01473)659573
Website: www.theshipinnlevington.co.uk

VISA

Adnams, Southwold Bitter, Broadside and Explorer

There may well be a new captain at the helm but it's steady as she goes for The Ship Inn. Reputedly built from ships' timbers, and crammed with nautical memorabilia, the small rooms of this characterful 14C pub soon fill up with customers but, as they don't take bookings, it's wise to arrive early. Start with dishes like stilton and leek tart or seared scallops, followed by pan-fried lemon sole or salmon and tiger prawn brochette. With its emphasis on local seafood, the menu changes daily, but there's always plenty of non-fish dishes too, from belly of Blythburgh pork to char-grilled rib-eye steak. On a warm day, the picnic tables are a great place from which to watch the distant boats; if it gets too draughty, try the rear terrace instead.

CLOSING TIMES
Open daily
bookings not accepted

PRICES
Meals: a la carte £ 22/31

Typical Dishes

Sweet chilli & garlic tiger prawns

Liver & bacon with Madeira jus

Coffee panna cotta, espresso syrup & dark chocolate mousse.

Midway between Ipswich and Felixstowe signposted off A 14. Parking.

Monks Eleigh

53 **Swan**

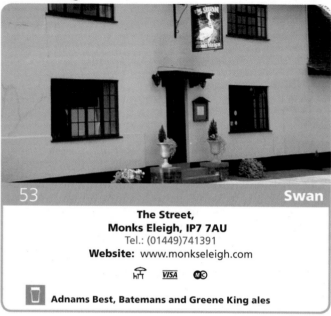

The Street,
Monks Eleigh, IP7 7AU
Tel.: (01449)741391
Website: www.monkseleigh.com

VISA

Adnams Best, Batemans and Greene King ales

The Swan's owners may originally hail from the north, but they have fully embraced their adopted home of East Anglia, and the wealth of produce the area offers provides ample inspiration for the frequently changing, seasonal menu of generous, flavourful dishes. Depending on the ingredients fresh in, these might include smoked haddock fish pie with creamy mash or lamb tagine with apricots, almonds and couscous, and – thanks to Nigel's background – often include a smattering of Italian influences. Everything is made on-site; from the bread and terrines to the classic British puddings and ice creams. The thatched pub's beamed interior is fresh and bright, and the bubbly Carol serves locals and newcomers alike with warmth and efficiency.

CLOSING TIMES
Closed 2 weeks July, 25-26 December, Sunday dinner and Monday

PRICES
Meals: £ 18 and a la carte £ 21/35

Typical Dishes
Suffolk asparagus with parmesan & balsamic
Sirloin steak with blue cheese & compote of onions
Perry jelly with vanilla ice cream

3.5 mi southeast of Lavenham on A 1141. Parking.

54 **Crown Inn**

Bridge Rd,
Snape, IP17 1SL
Tel.: (01728)688324
Website: www.snape-crown.co.uk

VISA MC AE

Adnams; Bitter and Broadside

With its low ceilings, open fires and mismatched wooden chairs, this characterful 400 year old building on the outskirts of the village really is a true country pub. It's not just local ingredients that you'll find on the menu but produce that's recently been picked from the owner's garden or plucked off his trees – and the eggs, milk and meats are equally as fresh, as they keep pigs, calves, goats, turkey, quail and rescued battery hens out the back. As you would expect, cooking is seasonal and simply done, with light bites on offer at lunch and more substantial dishes such as confit duck or rib-eye steak at dinner. The blackboard specials always include a market fish of the day and to finish, there's a selection of tasty nursery puddings.

CLOSING TIMES
Open daily

PRICES
Meals: a la carte £ 19/29

Typical Dishes

Home-reared pork terrine with medlar jelly
Orford wild bass with asparagus risotto
Iced rhubarb parfait

On B 1069, just north of Snape Maltings. Parking.

55 Crown

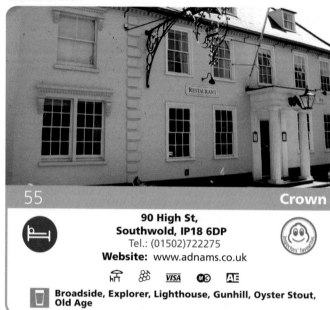

90 High St,
Southwold, IP18 6DP
Tel.: (01502)722275
Website: www.adnams.co.uk

VISA MC AE

Broadside, Explorer, Lighthouse, Gunhill, Oyster Stout, Old Age

This 17C former coaching inn sits on the high street of a charming town, near to the brewery and only a hop, skip and a jump away from the sea. Its traditionally styled bar and dining room are often buzzing with diners and the small, oak-panelled, nautically themed locals bar is a great place for a leisurely pint or two of Adnams of an afternoon. The same modern, seasonal menu is served throughout: choose from dishes such as pan-fried sea bass, Cromer crab cakes, sausage and mash or cottage pie, with perhaps a sticky toffee pudding or some homemade ice cream for dessert. Arrive early to avoid disappointment, however, as they don't take bookings. Individually styled bedrooms have a contemporary feel; those towards the rear are the quietest.

CLOSING TIMES
Open daily

PRICES
Meals: a la carte £ 22/37
14 rooms: £ 100/195

Typical Dishes

Trio of local wild rabbit
Wild Lowestoft sea bass
Chocolate mousse

In the town centre. Parking.

56 **Crown**

Stoke-by-Nayland,
CO6 4SE
Tel.: (01206)262001
Website: www.crowninn.net

VISA AE

Adnams BB, Brewers Gold, Woodford's Wherry

Set overlooking the Box and Stour river valleys, in a hillside village in the Dedham Vale, this substantial 16C pub is a lovely place to visit, with its large lawned gardens and a smart wood-furnished patio. Step inside and you'll find various little rooms and semi open-plan snugs, where wood and flag flooring gives way to boldly coloured walls. If you're into wine, there are over 30 by the glass; while a large glass-fronted room displays a selection of top quality bottles. Menus change every three weeks and feature the latest seasonal produce sourced from nearby farms and estates, supplemented by a daily catch and seafood specials. Spacious bedrooms take on either contemporary or country cottage styles; some have French windows and a terrace.

CLOSING TIMES
Closed 25-26 December

PRICES
Meals: a la carte £ 23/38
11 rooms: £ 80/200

Typical Dishes

Crispy lamb's sweetbreads

Gressingham duck breast with aubergine purée

White chocolate & pistachio mousse

In the centre of the village. Parking.

57 **Anchor**

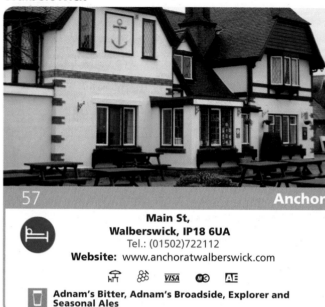

Main St,
Walberswick, IP18 6UA
Tel.: (01502)722112
Website: www.anchoratwalberswick.com

VISA AE

Adnam's Bitter, Adnam's Broadside, Explorer and Seasonal Ales

Unusually for a pub, The Anchor is housed in an Arts and Crafts building. It's a welcoming, relaxing place, run by an enthusiastic, friendly team; there's a pleasant terrace and a path leading directly from the garden to the beach. But enough about the pub – for it's all about the food, wine and beer here. Owners Sophie and Mark are passionate about sourcing local, seasonal produce – with some ingredients even coming from their own allotment. Dishes are prepared with real care and global flavours punctuate the menu, so alongside British classics like fish and chips, you'll find Asian dressings, Indian spicing, tapas platters and risottos. Simple chalet bedrooms; breakfast like a king on choices such as smoked haddock and jugged kippers.

CLOSING TIMES
Open daily

PRICES
Meals: a la carte £ 23/33
8 rooms: £ 95/150

Typical Dishes

West Mersea oysters
Scallops with artichoke purée
Hot chocolate pudding

In the centre of the village. Parking.

58 Westleton Crown

The Street,
Westleton, IP17 3AD
Tel.: (01728)648777
Website: www.westletoncrown.co.uk

VISA MC AE

Adnams and one local guest ale

This good-looking red-brick 17C former coaching inn, set in a pretty little village, delivers what you'd expect and a little bit more. The bar welcomes you with its beams and open fires but venture a little further in and you'll find an attractive and surprisingly modern conservatory, as well as an appealing terrace and garden. Mercifully, the same seasonally pertinent menu is offered throughout, so you can eat your suet pudding or the more sophisticated breast of guinea fowl with confit spring roll anywhere you choose. Those staying overnight not only have their own pleasant sitting room but will find that the bedrooms, which are named after birds, come in a crisp, uncluttered style and have particularly luxurious bathrooms.

CLOSING TIMES
Open daily

PRICES
Meals: a la carte £ 28/38
34 rooms: £ 80/120

Typical Dishes

Oven roasted Suffolk quail

Roast neck of Suffolk lamb with fennel risotto

The Crown's own Arctic roll

In the centre of the village. Parking.

59 **The White Horse**

Rede Rd,
Whepstead, IP29 4SS
Tel.: (01284)735760
Website: www.whitehorsewhepstead.co.uk

VISA MC

Adnams Bitter, Broadside and Explorer

The attractive copper-topped bar is the hub of this cheerfully run 17C village pub, not long refurbished. There are three further areas to choose from: to the left is a beamed and characterful room which fills up quickly; to the right the brighter Gallery, so named as its shows local artists' work; and, thirdly, a back room for larger parties which leads out to the large garden. But everyone likes to assemble in the bar to look at the large menu with each dish displayed on a separate blackboard. The kitchen's strength lies in the more conventional dishes like liver and bacon, grilled kippers and the pub's own homemade sausages. It's owned by a couple who established their reputation at The Beehive in nearby Horringer.

CLOSING TIMES
Closed 1 week in January, 25-26 December and Sunday dinner

PRICES
Meals: a la carte £ 12/20

Typical Dishes

Creamy fish soup
Pan-fried loin of venison with bubble & squeak
Vanilla and rhubarb compote with vanilla ice cream

Well signposted off the A 143, 4.5 mi south of Bury St Edmunds. Parking.

60 **Crown**

Thoroughfare,
Woodbridge, IP12 1AD
Tel.: (01394)384242
Website: www.thecrownatwoodbridge.co.uk

VISA MC AE

Any two of Adnams Bitter, Adnams Broadside, London Time keg ales

With its farmers' markets and a main street full of restaurants and cafés, the delightful riverside town of Woodbridge is up there with the best of them when it comes to foodie credentials; and all the more so since the arrival of The Crown. After a top-to-toe, 21C makeover, this colourfully painted pub retains little evidence of its 17C roots; a glass-roofed, granite-floored bar sits at its centre, with four smart dining areas set around it. Bedrooms are stylish, with good facilities and service is polite and friendly, coping well when busy. The extensive menu offers everything from salads and starters like cockle and samphire fritters through to main dishes like meatballs, fish pie or duck. Look out for the skiff and the sporks.

CLOSING TIMES
Open daily

PRICES
Meals: £ 20 and a la carte £ 24/32
10 rooms: £ 110/180

Typical Dishes

Seared king scallops with pancetta & rocket

Roast loin & braised leg of rabbit

Iced strawberry parfait

At town centre crossroads. Parking.

Twenty-first century London may truly be called the definitive world city. Time zones radiate from Greenwich, and global finances zap round the Square Mile, while a vast smorgasbord of restaurants is the equal of anywhere on the planet. A stunning diversity of population now calls the capital its home, mixing and matching its time between the urban sprawl and enviable acres of green open space. From Roman settlement to banking centre to capital of a 19C empire, London's pulse has rarely missed a beat. Along the way, expansion has gobbled up surrounding villages, a piecemeal cocktail with its ingredients stirred to create the likes of Kensington and Chelsea, Highgate and Hampstead, Twickenham and Richmond. Apart from the great range of restaurants, London boasts over three and a half thousand pubs, many of which now see accomplished, creative cooking as an integral part of their existence and appeal. And you can find them sprinkled right the way across from zones one to five…

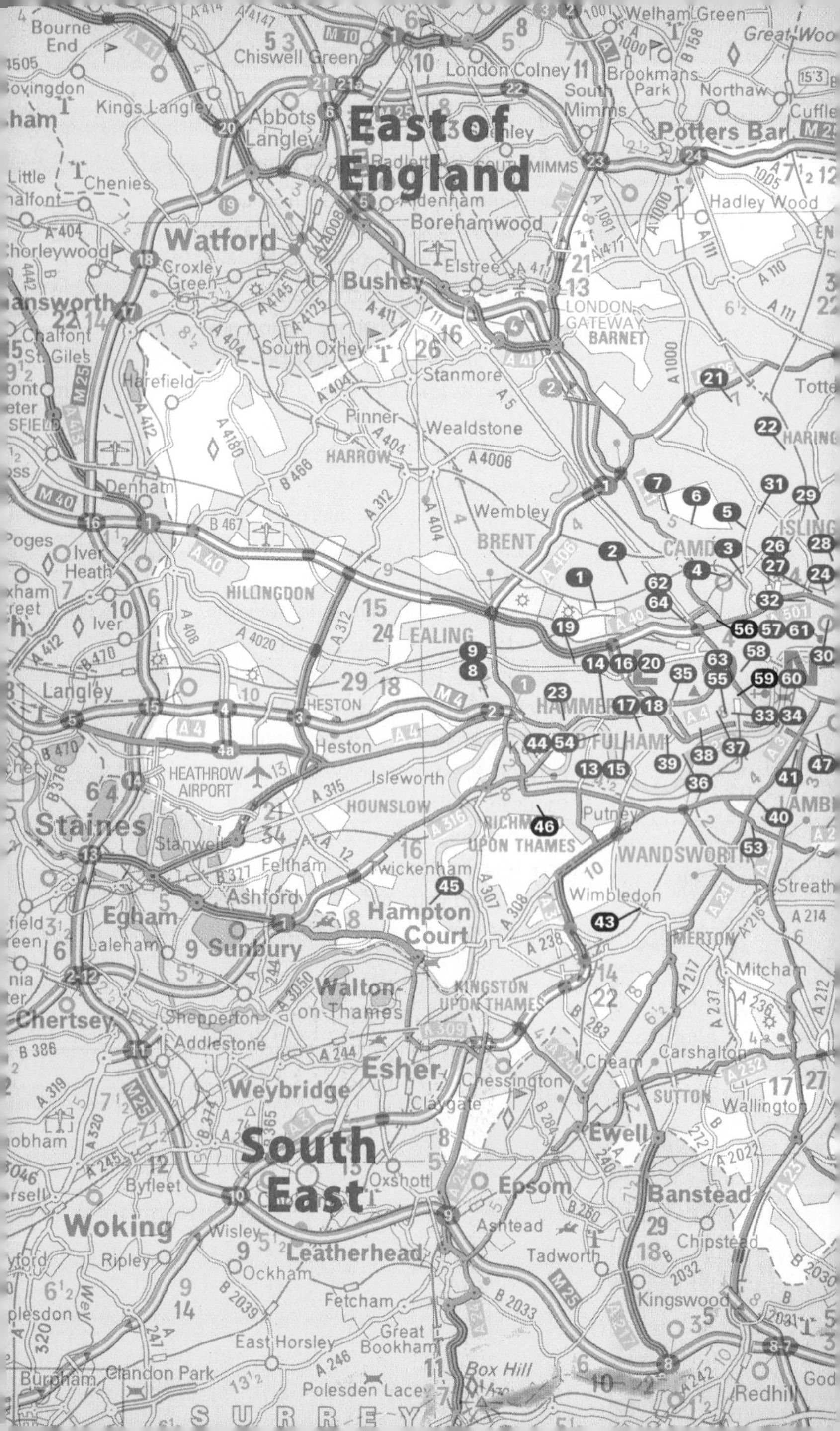

East of England
South East
Bourne End
Chiswell Green
London Colney
Welham Green
Brookmans Park
Northaw
Bovingdon
Kings Langley
Abbots Langley
South Mimms
Potters Bar
Little Chalfont
Chenies
Aldenham
Borehamwood
Hadley Wood
Chorleywood
Watford
Croxley Green
Elstree
Bushey
London Gateway
Barnet
Chalfont St Giles
South Oxhey
Stanmore
Harefield
Pinner
Wealdstone
Harrow
Denham
Wembley
Brent
Iver Heath
Iver
Hillingdon
Ealing
Langley
Heston
Heathrow Airport
Isleworth
Hounslow
Staines
Stanwell
Feltham
Twickenham
Richmond upon Thames
Putney
Wandsworth
Wimbledon
Egham
Ashford
Hampton Court
Sunbury
Merton
Mitcham
Streatham
Laleham
Walton-on-Thames
Kingston upon Thames
Chertsey
Shepperton
Addlestone
Esher
Cheam
Carshalton
Chessington
Sutton
Wallington
Weybridge
Claygate
Ewell
Byfleet
Oxshott
Epsom
Banstead
Woking
Wisley
Leatherhead
Ashtead
Tadworth
Chipstead
Ripley
Ockham
Kingswood
Fetcham
Great Bookham
East Horsley
Clandon Park
Box Hill
Polesden Lacey
Redhill
Surrey

East of England
South East
LONDON
12 Pubs without bedrooms
43 Pubs with bedrooms
Fyfield
High Ongar
Epping
N. Weald Bassett
Chipping Ongar
Cheshunt
Waltham Abbey
Epping Forest
Loughton
Abridge
Kelvedon Hatch
Ingatestone
Pilgrims Hatch
Brentwood
Ingrave
Stapleford Abbotts
Chigwell
Basildon
WALTHAM FOREST
REDBRIDGE
Romford
HAVERING
Hornchurch
Upminster
Langdon
HACKNEY
Ilford
BARKING AND DAGENHAM
Bulphan
TOWER HAMLETS
NEWHAM
South Ockendon
Orsett
Beckton
Aveley
THURROCK
Grays Thurrock
Chadwell St Mary
Tilbury
Blackwall Tunnel
Woolwich
GREENWICH
Dartford Crossing
Erith
BEXLEY
Northfleet
Dartford
Swanscombe
LEWISHAM
Sydenham
Sidcup
Wilmington
Darenth
Istead Rise
Swanley
Longfield
Hartley
Farningham
Meopham
BROMLEY
West Wickham
CROYDON
Orpington
Eynsford
Ash
West Kingsdown
New Addington
Sanderstead
Biggin Hill
Otford
Warlingham
North Downs
Woldingham
Ightham
W. Malling
Borough Green
Caterham
Sundridge
Sevenoaks
Knole
Mereworth
Westerham
Oxted
Mote
Shipbourne

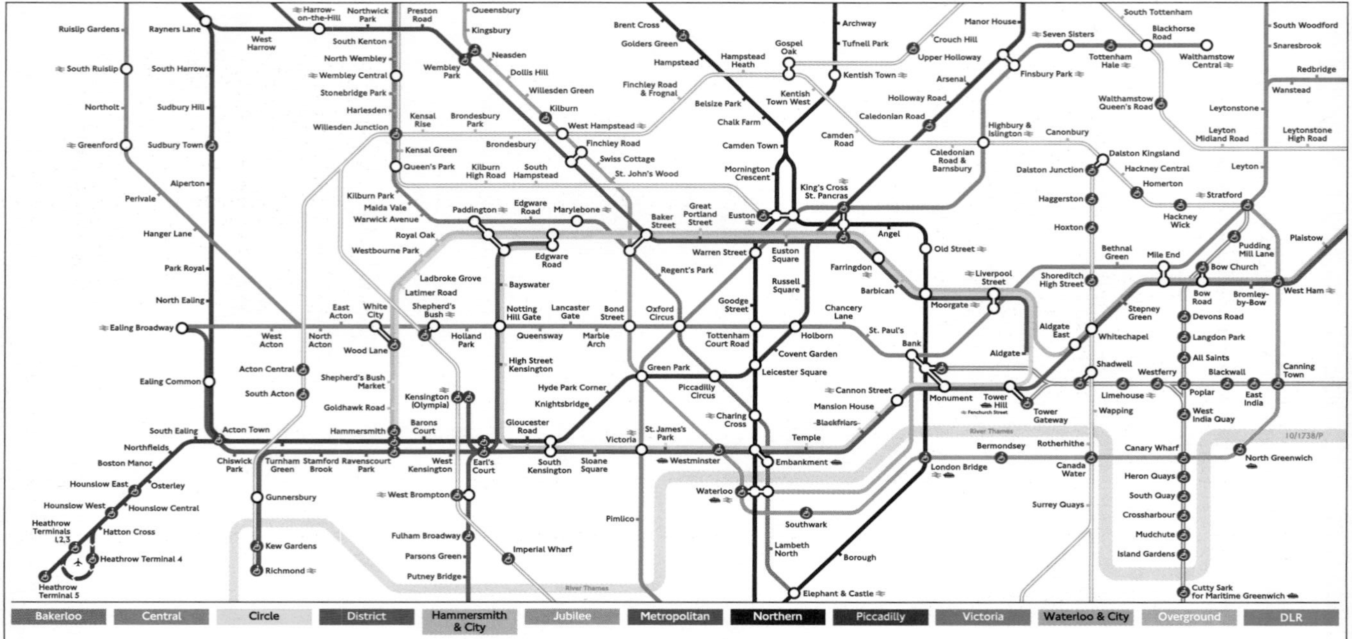

MAYOR OF LONDON

Website
tfl.gov.uk

24 hour travel information
0843 222 1234*

*You pay no more than 5p per minute if calling from a BT landline. There may be a connection charge. Charges from mobiles or other landline providers may vary.

Transport for London

UNDERGROUND

Reg. user No. 11/1981/P

Version C 02.2010

Improvement works may affect your journey, please check before you travel

Correct at time of going to print

1 Paradise by way of Kensal Green

19 Kilburn Ln,
Kensal Green, W10 4AE
Tel.: (020)89690098
Website: www.theparadise.co.uk

VISA MC

Charles Wells's Bombardier

Their slogan is 'they love to party at Paradise' and, frankly, who can blame them? This is so much more than just a pub, it's a veritable fun palace – upstairs plays host to everything from comedy nights to film clubs and you can even 'host your own roast' with friends in a private room. If you're coming in to eat then grab a squashy sofa in the Reading Room off the bar and share some of the terrific snacks; or sit in the dining room where the cooking is showy but satisfyingly robust. Whether it's potted meats, terrines, chateaubriand or poached turbot, it's clear that this is a very capable kitchen. The atmosphere throughout is great and helped along in no small way by a clued-up team who know their food.

CLOSING TIMES
Open daily
dinner only and lunch Saturday and Sunday

PRICES
Meals: a la carte £ 21/36

Typical Dishes

Scallops with sweetcorn & pancetta

Rib-eye steak with triple cooked chips

Sticky toffee pudding

⊖ *Kensal Green.*

2 Salusbury

50-52 Salusbury Rd,
Queen's Park, NW6 6NN
Tel.: (020)73283286
Website: www.thesalusbury.co.uk

VISA MC AE D

Adnam's Broadside and Bitter

The Salusbury was never one to worry unduly about its looks: its appeal lay simply in the quality of its cooking. Now a refit has smartened it up somewhat but the imperturbable atmosphere is unchanged and the service is as youthful and sprightly as ever. The pub comes divided in two, with a bar on one side and a dining room in sage green, with a subtle Edwardian feel, on the other. The kitchen has a pronounced Italian accent and the menu is divided according to cooking method so that under the 'roast' section you might find whole sea bream in a salt crust and under 'fried', crispy squid with lemon; dishes are as big in flavour as they are in size. Much of their produce is also available to buy in their shop next door.

CLOSING TIMES
Closed 25-26 December and Monday lunch

PRICES
Meals: a la carte £ 20/30

Typical Dishes

Octopus salad with chickpeas & tomato

Pappardelle with duck ragu

Chocolate fondant

⊖ Queen's Park.

3 **Bull and Last**

168 Highgate Rd,
Dartmouth Park, NW5 1QS
Tel.: (020)72673641
Website: www.thebullandlast.co.uk

VISA MC

Sharp's Doom Bar, Mad Goose, Sambrooks Wandle and Black Sheep

The Bull and Last understands absolutely what makes a good foodie pub and top of that list would be a menu that reflects the time of year and the weather outside: come on a snowy December night – when you'll be greeted by the aroma of cloves and mulled wine – and you can dine on pumpkin soup, mutton broth and apple strudel. The menu changes with every service and even the nibbles, such as lamb fritters and sweet anchovies, reveal the cleverness of the kitchen. The chefs also know their way around an animal: the charcuterie boards of terrines, parfaits and rillettes are well worth ordering. This Victorian pub, spread over two floors with a slightly quieter upstairs, has plenty of charm and character and is always busy so booking is vital.

CLOSING TIMES
Closed 24- 25 December
booking essential

PRICES
Meals: a la carte £ 27/33

Typical Dishes
Stuffed lamb's heart with celeriac remoulade
Lamb with spiced aubergine, chickpeas & coriander
Churros with yoghurt sorbet

⊖ Tufnell Park. Free parking in the neighbourhood.

4 **Engineer**

65 Gloucester Ave,
Primrose Hill, NW1 8JH
Tel.: (020)77220950
Website: www.the-engineer.com

VISA

Charles Wells Bombardier and St Peters

Although speculation remains as to the identity of the original engineer, what is certain is that this is a great local, which is at the heart of the local community. It's divided equally between bar and dining room, with a terrific garden terrace to boot; and it's always busy, with occasional live music on Sundays adding to the fun. The reverse of the menu name checks the suppliers – always a reassuring act – and there are usually a couple of vegetarian options along with a separate menu of the day's specials. The steak and fabulous baker fries are a constant and cooking is wholesome and generally gutsy. The wine list is printed within old cartoon annuals; wines are decently priced and divided up according to their character.

CLOSING TIMES
Closed 1 week Christmas

PRICES
Meals: a la carte £ 26/44

Typical Dishes
Asparagus with poached egg & hollandaise
Honey-glazed lamb with figs, pine nuts & spring onions
Steamed marmalade pudding

⊖ *Chalk Farm. On-street parking meters.*

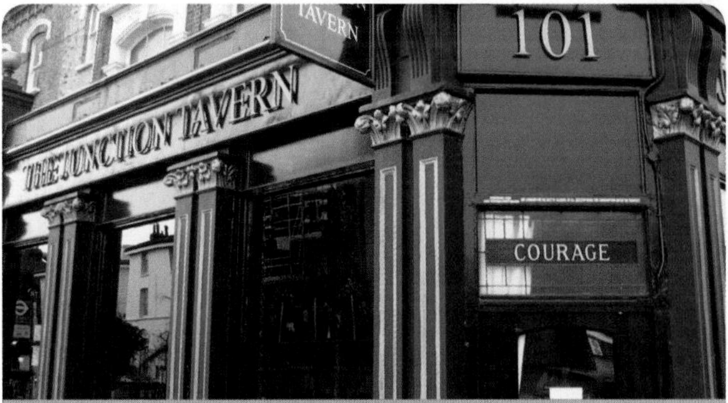

5 Junction Tavern

101 Fortess Rd,
Tufnell Park, NW5 1AG
Tel.: (020)74859400
Website: www.junctiontavern.co.uk

VISA

Sambrook's Wandle and 10-15 guest beers per week from independent regional brewers

Over the years, Tufnell Park has appealed to young urban professionals because, along with its pretty Victorian terraces, it has a belligerent edge to add a little credibility. The Junction Tavern fits in well. The menu changes daily and portion size has been slightly reduced to give more balance to the menu as a whole; the cooking remains unfussy and relies on good flavours. There's plenty of choice, from light summer dishes such as grilled sardines and seared tuna to the more robust rib-eye and pork belly. Staff are a chatty bunch who know their beers – they offer weekly changing guest ales and hold a popular beer festival; the 'pie and a pint' choice remains a favourite. Commendably, they also offer tap water without being prompted.

CLOSING TIMES
Closed 24-26 December and 1 January

PRICES
Meals: a la carte £ 23/31

Typical Dishes

Smoked mackerel rillette

Sea bass with roast fennel & chorizo

Pear & almond tart with Jersey cream

⊖ Tufnell Park. Pay & display parking in nearby streets.

6 Magdala

2A South Hill Park,
Hampstead, NW3 2SB
Tel.: (020)74352503
Website: www.the-magdala.com

VISA

Greene King IPA, Fuller's London Pride and twice weekly changing guest ales

The Magdala is divided into three: on the right-hand side is the locals bar – you can eat here but not many do as it's a little dark and you'll feel like an impostor. Just go left, grab a seat anywhere and you'll be served. The third part of the operation is the upstairs, used as an extension at weekends or for hosting the monthly comedy club or fortnightly quiz. There's nothing on the menu to frighten the horses: there are burgers, sausages, paella and charcuterie plates or meze to share. However, the cooking is undertaken with greater care than you expect and you end up feeling as though you're in a country pub miles from the city. The owner certainly found a novel solution to the problem of keeping her chef – Reader, she married him.

CLOSING TIMES
Open daily

PRICES
Meals: a la carte £ 22/30

Typical Dishes

Chicken liver pâté
Pork belly, celeriac mash & Savoy cabbage
Double chocolate brownie

⊖ Belsize Park. Pay & display parking outside the pub; heath car park 5 min walk.

7 **Wells**

30 Well Walk,
Hampstead, NW3 1BX
Tel.: (020)77943785
Website: www.thewellshampstead.co.uk

VISA MC AE

Everards Tiger and Black Sheep

The Wells is named after Chalybeate Well which, in 1698, was given to the poor of Hampstead – it's about 30 yards away, next to that BMW. Equidistant between Heath and High Street, this handsome pub is split in two: downstairs is the busier, more relaxed part of the operation, while upstairs you'll find a formally dressed dining room. Apart from a couple of extra grilled dishes downstairs, the two areas share a menu, which is cleverly balanced to satisfy all appetites from spirited dog walker to leisurely shopper. Salads or seared scallops can be followed by sea bass, assorted pasta or duck confit; puds are good and they do a decent crumble. Add a commendable range of ales and wines and you have a pub for all seasons.

CLOSING TIMES
Open daily

PRICES
Meals: a la carte £ 28/38

Typical Dishes

Tomato, watermelon, feta & pumpkin seed salad

Plaice with caper, lemon & parsley butter

Apple & rhubarb crumble

⊖ Hampstead. Parking in Well Road.

8 **Bollo**

13-15 Bollo Ln,
Acton Green, W4 5LR
Tel.: (020)89946037
Website: www.thebollohouse.co.uk

VISA MC AE

Greene King IPA and Olde Trip, Abbot Ale

The Bollo is a large, handsome Victorian pub whose glass cupola and oak panelling give it some substance and personality in this age of the generic pub makeover. Tables and sofas are scattered around in a relaxed, sit-where-you-want way and the menu changes as ingredients come and go. The kitchen appeals to its core voters by always including a sufficient number of pub classics like the Bollo Burger, the haddock or fishcakes. But there is also a discernible southern Mediterranean influence to the menu, with regular appearances from the likes of chorizo, tzatziki, bruschetta and hummus. This is a pub where there's always either a promotion or an activity, whether that's the '50% off a main course' Monday or the Wednesday quiz nights.

CLOSING TIMES
Open daily

PRICES
Meals: a la carte £ 20/31

Typical Dishes

Scallops with black pudding & minted pea purée

Rabbit with cider, wholegrain mustard mash & Savoy cabbage

Citrus cheesecake

⊖ Chiswick Park. Parking meters.

9 Duke of Sussex

75 South Par,
Acton Green, W4 5LF
Tel.: (020)87428801
Website: www.realpubs.co.uk

VISA MC

Skinners Betty Stogs and ales from Camden Brewery and Fullers

Perhaps it's part of the plan but the Duke of Sussex seems like a typical London pub, even from the front bar, but step through into the dining room and you'll be in what was once a variety theatre from the time when this was a classic gin palace, complete with proscenium arch, glass ceiling and chandeliers. If that wasn't unusual enough, you could then find yourself eating cured meats or fabada, as the menu has a strong Spanish influence. Traditionalists can still get their steak pies and treacle tart but it's worth being more adventurous and trying the sardines, the paella and the crema Catalana. This is a fun, enthusiastically run and bustling pub and the kitchen's enthusiasm is palpable. On Mondays it's BYO; Sunday is quiz night.

CLOSING TIMES
Closed dinner 25 December and Monday lunch

PRICES
Meals: a la carte £ 23/28

Typical Dishes

Razor clams with chorizo

Pork chop escalivada with salsa picante

Santiago tart

Chiswick Park. Parking on adjacent street.

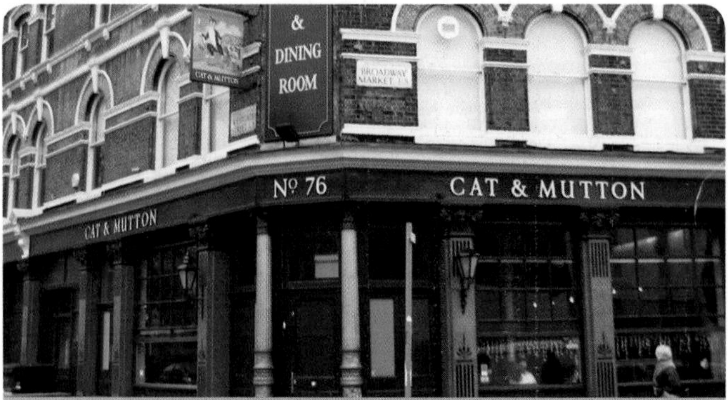

10 Cat & Mutton

76 Broadway Mkt,
Hackney, E8 4QJ
Tel.: (020)72545599
Website: www.catandmutton.co.uk

VISA MC

Old Speckled Hen, Adnams Broadside, Bombardier

The Cat & Mutton has been a fixture here since the 1700s, when it was a drovers' inn quenching the thirst of farm workers bringing their livestock down from East Anglia. The streets round here might still frighten out-of-towners and the pub may now look a little frayed around the edges but step inside, look past the rough and ready character, and the young staff will make you feel reassuringly welcome. The open kitchen adds a little theatre to proceedings and the relatively concise menu changes often. The cooking is straightforward but is also undertaken with more care than you expect. Their beef is organic and in the evening steaks stand out amongst the more elaborate dishes. It's upstairs for quiz nights and art classes.

CLOSING TIMES
Closed 25-26 December and Sunday dinner

PRICES
Meals: £ 15 (dinner) and a la carte £ 24/34

Typical Dishes
Scallops with white bean purée & smoked black pudding
Roast pheasant, champ & black cabbage
Vanilla rice pudding brûlée

⊖ Bethnal Green.

11 Prince Arthur

95 Forest Rd,
Hackney, E8 3BH
Tel.: (020)72499996
Website: www.theprincearthurlondonfields.com

VISA MC AE

Adnams Bitter and monthly changing guest ales

Those who judge by first impressions will probably walk on by as this slightly scruffy corner pub would struggle to entice anyone on looks alone. To be honest, the inside isn't much keener on the eye, apart from the stuffed animals and the postcard collection, but then this isn't about appearances, more about good food and convivial company. Sit anywhere in the U-shaped room and the amiable staff will be quick to come over. The menu reads appealingly: smoked salmon, terrines, fish and chips, sausage and mash – but the cooking is done with unexpected care and more than a little skill; fish from Billingsgate is handled particularly deftly. Just thinking about the deep-fried jam or cherry sandwich for dessert will be enough to seal an artery.

CLOSING TIMES
Closed 25-26 December
dinner only and lunch Saturday-Sunday

PRICES
Meals: a la carte £ 26/41

Typical Dishes

Poached duck egg, spinach & onion tart

Roast rump of lamb with sweetbreads & minted peas

Pineapple tarte Tatin

⊖ Bethnal Green.

12 Princess of Shoreditch

76-78 Paul St,
Shoreditch, EC2A 4NE
Tel.: (020)77299270
Website: www.theprincessofshoreditch.com

VISA MC AE

Meantime Pale Ale, Sambrooks Wandle, Tring Side Pocket for a Toad

The old girl may change hands now and then but she remains as popular as ever. The ground floor is your proper pub; drinkers are the mainstay but they get an appealing and appropriate menu where platters of sausage, charcuterie and cheese are the highlights, along with pies of the cottage or pork variety. For more mellow surroundings follow the fairy lights up to a warm, candlelit room. Here, the menu displays greater ambition. The cooking is more European in its influence and, despite the occasional affected presentation, it's clear the kitchen has confidence and ability. Flavours are good, techniques are sound and parfaits are a real highlight. The pub prides itself on the friendliness of its staff and upstairs is no different.

CLOSING TIMES
Closed 24-26 December

PRICES
Meals: £ 18 (lunch)
and a la carte £ 25/32

Typical Dishes

Ham hock with spring bean & pea salad
Sea bass with orange & tomato gazpacho
Sticky toffee pudding

⊖ Old Street. On-street parking meters.

13 Anglesea Arms

35 Wingate Rd,
Hammersmith, W6 0UR
Tel.: (020)87491291
Website: www.anglesea-arms.com

VISA MC

Otter Bitter, Otter Ale, Adnams Light House, Sharp's Doom Bar

The Anglesea Arms proves that you can update a pub while still respecting its heritage. Its windows are etched with the inviting words 'Pies and Hams' and 'Stout and Oysters' and above the door is 'Mon Mam Cymru', Mother of Wales, as the Isle of Anglesey is known. The wood-floored, wood-panelled bar has a cluttered, lived-in feel and gets very crowded, so if you're in for eating head for the brighter rear dining room, with its part-glass ceiling and exposed kitchen. The blackboard menu might change between services and can be a little unbalanced with lots of starters, fewer mains and a limited number of puddings but the cooking is robust and has a strong British bias, with the likes of pig's head terrine, smoked eel and game featuring.

CLOSING TIMES
Closed 25-27 December

PRICES
Meals: a la carte £ 20/52

Typical Dishes

Lamb's fry with mousserons & mustard

Grey mullet with samphire & roast tomatoes

Boiled orange cake with orange curd

⊖ Ravenscourt Park.

14 **Crabtree**

4 Rainville Rd,
Hammersmith, W6 9HA
Tel.: (020)73853929
Website: www.thecrabtreeW6.co.uk

VISA

Triple fff Moondance, Nethergate Three Point Nine, Cottage Golden Arrow and Adnams Extra

On a sunny day few things in life beat being by the river in a London pub and The Crabtree certainly makes the most of its location. Its beer garden, with its barbeque-style menu, can hold up to 200, while the dining room boasts its own terrace overlooking the river – and if you haven't yet booked for lunch on Boat Race day then you're probably already too late. A variety of ploys are used to fill the equally large interior of this Victorian beauty, from BYO Mondays to quiz nights on Tuesdays. For lunch the selection varies from ciabatta sarnies to shepherd's pie; the evening menu is more adventurous. The kitchen does things properly – parfaits and terrines are highlights and fish is perfectly timed – but vegetarians are also looked after.

CLOSING TIMES
Open daily

PRICES
Meals: a la carte £ 24/34

Typical Dishes

Pressed ham hock terrine with piccalilli
Pan-fried skate wing with lemon and caper butter
Sticky toffee pudding

⊖ Barons Court.

15 Dartmouth Castle

26 Glenthorne Rd,
Hammersmith, W6 0LS
Tel.: (020)87483614
Website: www.thedartmouthcastle.co.uk

VISA AE

Sharps Doom Bar, Cornish Coaster, Otter Bitter, Black Sheep and Timothy Taylor Landlord

The view one way is of offices, the other, smart Victorian terraced houses, so this pub has to satisfy a wide variety of customers and their differing needs – and it does so with aplomb. Plenty just come in for a drink but you can eat on either of the two floors, although the ground floor has the better atmosphere and opens out onto a small terrace; just order at the bar and leave them your credit card. The Mediterranean exerts quite an influence on the large menu, whose prices are more than fair. Pasta appears to come in two sizes – big or even bigger – and the antipasti dish for two is great for sharing over a bottle of wine. Sandwiches use ciabatta, and desserts like tiramisu or panna cotta finish things off nicely.

CLOSING TIMES
Closed 24 December-2 January and Saturday lunch

PRICES
Meals: a la carte £ 18/31

Typical Dishes

Smoked salmon salad with horseradish & baby beets

Confit duck leg with crushed potatoes

Coconut rice pudding

⊖ Hammersmith.

16 **Harwood Arms**

Walham Grove,
Fulham, SW6 1QP
Tel.: (020)73861847
Website: www.harwoodarms.com

Inspectors' favourites

VISA MC AE

Sambrooks Junction, Bath Gem

Its reputation may have spread like wildfire but what many visitors find most reassuring is how unaffected the Harwood Arms has remained. The reason for its success is largely down to the shared passion of the three owners and it came as no surprise that the change in the kitchen in 2011 resulted in no drop in the standard of the food. The cooking remains very seasonal and properly British; faggots, nettle soup, beef cheeks and Hampshire lamb all make regular appearances. There is obvious skill in the cooking but none of the dishes ever seem out of place in this relaxed environment – it's cooking that's all about carefully matched ingredients and great flavours, and not about technique and ego. The bar snacks are pretty good too.

CLOSING TIMES
Closed 26-29 August, 25-28 December, 1 January and Monday lunch
booking essential

PRICES
Meals: a la carte £ 30/34

Typical Dishes
Rabbit, prune & bacon faggots
Glazed Aylesbury duck leg & Douglas fir sausage
Chilled rice pudding with Grasmere gingerbread

⊖ *Fulham Broadway.*

17 Havelock Tavern

57 Masbro Rd,
Brook Grn, Hammersmith, W14 0LS
Tel.: (020)76035374
Website: www.havelocktavern.com

VISA MC AE

Sambrooks Wandle, Adnams Regatta, Purity Pure UBU, Sharps Doom Bar

Head straight for the bar where smiley, somewhat dishevelled looking staff will organise a drink, open a tab and add your name to the list of those waiting for a table, which are allocated on a first-come-first-served basis. This actually appears to add to the atmosphere as everyone is forced to rub shoulders in the bar first, where you'll find bowls of pistachios and olives while you wait. The blackboard menu changes with each service and cooking is on the stout side so you're better off sharing a nibble like chipolatas and mustard or pickled quail egg, before choosing a pie or steak; only if your appetite is really healthy will you have room for crumble and custard. The busier the place gets, the better the service.

CLOSING TIMES
Closed 25-26 December

PRICES
Meals: a la carte £ 21/30

Typical Dishes

Grilled mackerel with beetroot & smoked bacon

Chicken & mint tagine

Toasted banana bread with toffee sauce

⊖ Kensington Olympia. On-street pay & display parking.

18 My dining room

18 Farm Ln,
Fulham, SW6 1PP
Tel.: (020)73813331
Website: www.mydiningroom.net

VISA MC AE

Greene King IPA

'My dining room' is the archetypal gastropub of our day: yes, there's a bar with an open fire and a smattering of locals, but the bar's modern, the fire is gas and the locals are in suits. Head through 'The Lounge' and you'll get to a smart dining room, all silver and velvet, with John Garrett photos on the walls. Again, the menu is not that of your typical boozer: the kitchen displays a classical education and throws in a few French influences with their tartiflettes and cassoulets; there are even modern touches like foie gras with apple crumble. Add an impressive selection of wine by the glass and it's perhaps no surprise to learn that the owner is actually French. Al Murray's Pub Landlord wouldn't know where to look.

CLOSING TIMES
Open daily

PRICES
Meals: £ 14/20
and a la carte £ 21/37

Typical Dishes

Tartiflette
Slow-cooked garlic roast chicken
Tarte Tatin with cider sorbet

⊖ Fulham Broadway. On-street parking meters free after 8.30pm.

19 Princess Victoria

217 Uxbridge Rd,
Shepherd's Bush, W12 9DH
Tel.: (020)87495886
Website: www.princessvictoria.co.uk

VISA MC AE

Timothy Taylor Landlord, Sambrooks Wandle and Hook Norton Old Hooky

London has a wealth of fine Victorian gin palaces but few are as grand as The Princess Victoria. From the friezes to the etched glass, the portraits to the parquet floor, the last restoration created a terrific pub. Mind you, that's not all that impresses: there's a superb, wide-ranging wine list, with carafes and glasses providing flexibility; enticing bar snacks ranging from quail eggs to salt cod croquettes; a great menu that could include roasted skate wing or homemade pork and herb sausages; and, most importantly, cooking that's executed with no little skill. Those with proclivities for all things porcine will find much to savour – charcuterie is a passion here and the board may well include pig's cheeks and rillettes.

CLOSING TIMES
Closed 24-28 December

PRICES
Meals: £ 13 (lunch)
and a la carte £ 21/34

Typical Dishes
Crispy lamb sweetbreads with tuna sauce
Roast breast, confit leg & sausage of Madgetts Farm duck
Rhubarb, strawberry & pecan crumble

⊖ *Shepherd's Bush.*

20 **Sands End**

135-137 Stephendale Rd,
Fulham, SW6 2PR
Tel.: (020)77317823
Website: www.thesandsend.co.uk

VISA MC AE

Black Sheep, St Austell's Tribute

Sands End is probably not the best known part of London, or indeed Fulham, but no doubt its residents prefer it that way so they can keep their eponymous pub to themselves. It's a cosy, warm and welcoming one, with a central bar offering some nifty homemade snacks, but try resisting because the main menu – which changes every few days – is pretty appealing itself. There's a distinct British bias which amounts to more than merely name-checking the birthplace of the ingredients. Winter dishes like braised lamb neck or roast partridge with Savoy cabbage are particularly pleasing and West Mersea oysters a good way of starting things off. There's a well-chosen and equally equitably priced wine list that sticks mostly to the Old World.

CLOSING TIMES
Closed 25-26 December
booking advisable

PRICES
Meals: a la carte £ 32/42

Typical Dishes

House-cured beef with onions & confit baby carrots

Pan-fried sea bream with fennel, radish, mint & ricotta

Spiced apple & berry crumble

⊖ *Fulham Broadway.*

21 Clissold Arms

105 Fortis Green,
Fortis Green, N2 9HR
Tel.: (020)84444224
Website: www.clissoldarms.co.uk

VISA MC AE

Timothy Taylor Landlord, Fuller's London Pride, Harveys Sussex

Such is the growing reputation of The Clissold Arms that it may soon be better known for the quality of its cooking than its more long-standing claim to fame – that of having played host to The Kinks' first gig. Come at lunch and the menu and atmosphere make you feel you're in a proper pub, where you can expect classics like fishcakes or steak sandwiches. At dinner it all looks more like a restaurant, with loftier prices and slightly more ambitious, but still carefully prepared, dishes. The place is a lot bigger than you expect and, while staff could do with a little more guidance, it's often busy with locals grateful to have somewhere other than chain restaurants in their neighbourhood. The decked terrace has recently been extended.

CLOSING TIMES
Open daily

PRICES
Meals: a la carte £ 18/30

Typical Dishes
Stuffed figs with Monte Enebro cheese & honey dressing
Salmon & haddock fishcakes, pea purée & poached egg
Lemon lavender crème brûlée

⊖ East Finchley. Parking.

22 Queens Pub and Dining Room

26 Broadway Par,
Crouch End, N8 9DE
Tel.: (020)83402031
Website: www.thequeenscrouchend.co.uk

VISA AE

Adnams Gunhill and three weekly changing guest ales

From the original mahogany panelling to the beautiful stained glass windows and ornate ceiling, this pub offers a striking example of Victoriana. Originally built as a hotel, its dining room is particularly attractive and is separated from the bar by a glass door; those looking for a little more intimacy should ask for a table on the raised section. The open kitchen recognises that the locals want classic pub food in this environment and doesn't disappoint. The blackboard acknowledges the pub's main suppliers and the menu evolves seasonally, with traditional British comfort food being the main attraction. Along with the specials, look out for their autumn 'Sausage and Ale' festival – what can compete with Toad in the Hole and a pint?

CLOSING TIMES
Open daily

PRICES
Meals: a la carte £ 24/29

Typical Dishes

Chilli squid & chorizo salad

Corn-fed chicken with broad bean risotto

Hot chocolate fondant

On-street parking meters.

23 Devonshire Arms

126 Devonshire Rd,
Chiswick, W4 2JJ
Tel.: (020)87422302
Website: www.devonshirearmspub.com

VISA

Harveys Sussex, Sambrooks Wandle, Woodfordes Wherry, Old Hookey, 6X, Otter

Those behind the Drapers Arms in Islington are now at the helm of this roomy, characterful neighbourhood pub and they've given it a makeover true to its Edwardian roots. The front room is the cosier spot and is dominated by the central bar which allows plenty of space for drinkers. The menu changes twice daily and dishes are vibrant and appealing, courtesy of the French and Mediterranean influences. Starters vary from a half pint of prawns to a pigeon breast salad, grilled bavette or Cornish mackerel with broad bean relish. There's a thoughtfully compiled wine list of around 70 bins with a good selection by the glass and carafe. The relaxed yet friendly service provided by the young team add further to the pleasant local atmosphere.

CLOSING TIMES
Open daily
booking advisable

PRICES
Meals: a la carte £ 20/25

Typical Dishes

Duck foie gras & pigeon terrine
Braised breast of lamb
Dark chocolate brownie

⊖ Turnham Green. On-street parking meters in the adjacent streets.

24 **Barnsbury**

209-211 Liverpool Rd,
Islington, N1 1LX
Tel.: (020)76075519
Website: www.thebarnsbury.co.uk

VISA MC AE

Selection of weekly changing guest ales

The young owner may have a background in some of London's more fashionable dining establishments, but he's turned The Barnsbury back into a proper local pub as he felt it had become too much like a restaurant. That being said, the food is still done well and the menu is appealing, with tarts, salads, potted shrimps and mussels jostling for attention alongside Toulouse sausages, risottos and steaks served with the ubiquitous triple-cooked chips; the homemade puds are especially good. Lunch trade is not big in these parts so the midday menu is more limited. Chandeliers fashioned from wine glasses are dotted around the place and add character; but do sit in the more atmospheric front bar rather than the dining area at the back.

CLOSING TIMES
Closed 24-26 December
dinner only and lunch Friday-Sunday

PRICES
Meals: a la carte £ 20/35

Typical Dishes

Charcuterie board
Rump of lamb with parsley mash
Hot chocolate fondant with strawberry ice cream

⊖ Highbury & Islington. On-street parking meters.

25

Drapers Arms

44 Barnsbury St,
Islington, N1 1ER
Tel.: (020)76190348
Website: www.thedrapersarms.com

VISA

Truemans Runner, Harvey's Sussex, Sambrooks' Wandle and Thornbridge Jaipur.

Unless meeting the in-laws, your best bet is to stay on the ground floor of this handsome Georgian pub, as the more demure surroundings of the upstairs dining room, with its powder blue walls and flickering candlelight, are slightly at odds with the muscular nature of the cooking. This is the sort of food that prompts the rolling up of sleeves and the generous pouring of wine. Snail and chorizo soup, game terrine, Barnsley chop and onglet: flavours here pack a veritable punch and the kitchen recognises a decent ingredient when it sees one. The owners never forget that this is a pub and so prices are kept at sensible levels. Even the wine list plays its part by offering most of its largely French and Spanish selection for under £30.

CLOSING TIMES
Open daily
booking advisable at dinner

PRICES
Meals: a la carte £ 24/32

Typical Dishes

Grilled razor clams
Barnsley chop with anchovy dressing
Buttermilk pudding with rhubarb

⊖ *Highbury & Islington.*

26 Fellow

24 York Way,
King's Cross, N1 9AA
Tel.: (020)78334395
Website: www.thefellow.co.uk

VISA MC AE

Hopback Summer Lightning, Sharps Doom Bar, HSB and Youngs

It was just a matter of time before a few decent pubs opened around the rapidly developing area of King's Cross. The Fellow is one of the busiest, attracting a youthful and local clientele; it also manages to give the impression it's been here for years. Eating happens on the dark and atmospheric ground floor, with drinkers heading upstairs to the even more boisterous cocktail bar. The menu is quite a sophisticated little number but the kitchen is up to the task. Start with ham hock terrine or potted crab, followed by roast rump of lamb or grilled haddock with champ. Desserts such as apple tart display a lightness of touch. The serving team are a bright, capable bunch. There is an outdoor terrace but you'll be surrounded by smokers.

CLOSING TIMES
Closed 25 December and Sunday dinner

PRICES
Meals: a la carte £ 26/33

Typical Dishes

Ox heart with tomatoes & mustard cress

Grey mullet with fennel & pearl onions

Tarte Tatin with cream

⊖ King's Cross St Pancras. 2 min walk from Tube and mainline station.

27 Green

29 Clerkenwell Gn,
Finsbury, EC1R 0DU
Tel.: (020)74908010
Website: www.thegreenec1.co.uk

VISA MC

Adnam's Broadside, Timothy Taylor Landlord and Bath Ales Gem

29 Clerkenwell Green dates from 1580 and had become a tavern by 1720. It's therefore fitting that, after decades being used firstly as offices and then as a restaurant, The Green is now back to being known as a pub. Appetising and imaginative bar snacks like hog shank on toast are to be had in the ground floor bar, but the intimate upstairs is where the real eating goes on. Here you'll find an appealing menu of fresh, seasonal ingredients which might include Devon crab, Cornish mackerel, Wiltshire trout or Suffolk pork. The traditional fish pie is a favourite of many and the puds on the blackboard continue the British theme. Lunches get pretty busy with those wearing suits but dinner is more relaxed and the clientele in less of a hurry.

CLOSING TIMES
Closed 25-30 December

PRICES
Meals: a la carte £ 24/34

Typical Dishes

Roquefort & apple salad

Roast bavette with béarnaise sauce

Treacle tart with banana custard

⊖ Farringdon.

28 House

63-69 Canonbury Rd,
Canonbury, N1 2DG
Tel.: (020)77047410
Website: www.thehouse.islington.com

VISA AE

Adnams Ales

The front terrace is certainly an appealing feature in summer but, thanks to its warm atmosphere and candlelit tables, The House is just as welcoming on a winter's night. The regulars relaxing around the bar exude a general sense of localness and on the whole they prefer the sort of food that goes well with a pint; it's others who come looking for something a little special on the menu. The kitchen is intelligent enough to appreciate these two different markets in equal measure, so puts just as much effort into a shepherd's pie or a burger as it does with the sea bass or partridge. Weekends are busy, especially the breakfasts, but check first as The House often holds wedding receptions for those who've got hitched at Islington Town Hall.

CLOSING TIMES
Closed Monday except bank holidays

PRICES
Meals: a la carte £ 20/30

Typical Dishes

Seared scallops & risotto

Oven-baked canon of lamb

'Islington mess' meringue

⊖ *Highbury & Islington.*

29 **Northgate**

113 Southgate Rd,
Islington, N1 3JS
Tel.: (020)73597392

VISA

Deuchar's IPA, Fuller's London Pride and Black Sheep.

The Northgate is decked out in the usual gastropub aesthetic of mismatched furniture and local artists' work for sale on the walls; at the back you'll find tables laid up for dining and an open kitchen. You'll also find an extraction fan that's so strong you can feel its tug. Staff are pretty laid back, at times almost to the point of somnolence; go with a similarly relaxed frame of mind to avoid irritation. Where the pub scores is in the food: there's a strong Mediterranean influence on the vast blackboard. You'll find merguez and chorizo sausages, assorted pastas, a bit of Greek and some French – all in generously sized portions with the emphasis on flavour. Finish with something a little closer to home like treacle tart.

CLOSING TIMES
Closed 1 January
dinner only and lunch Saturday-Sunday

PRICES
Meals: a la carte £ 20/29

Typical Dishes

Goat's cheese & vegetable tart

Pot-roast chicken with fettucine

Flourless chocolate cake

⊖ Dalston Kingsland (rail). Free on-street parking after 6.30pm.

30 **Peasant**

240 St John St,
Finsbury, EC1V 4PH
Tel.: (020)73367726
Website: www.thepeasant.co.uk

VISA MC AE

Crouch Vale Brewers Gold, Trumans Runner and Brodies Special

Come along too early in the evening and you'll find the bar four deep with city boys having a quick pint on the way home. However, things do quieten down later and, when they do, you'll notice what a characterful spot this is. Most of the eating gets done upstairs in the dining room with its dimmed chandeliers, open fire and circus-themed posters. The cooking has been simplified and returned to a core of British dishes accompanied by the occasional Mediterranean note. The result is that it is far more satisfying and the well-judged dishes – whether braised rib of beef with horseradish mash or roast pollock with shrimps – all largely deliver on flavour. You will need a side dish or two with your main course, which can push up the final bill.

CLOSING TIMES
Closed 25 December-1 January and bank holidays except Good Friday
booking essential

PRICES
Meals: a la carte £ 23/30

Typical Dishes

Pork & prune terrine
Sea bass with asparagus & beetroot
Strawberries with meringue

⊖ Farringdon. On-street parking meters nearby; also free parking at weekends after 1.30pm.

31 St John's Tavern

91 Junction Rd,
Archway, N19 5QU
Tel.: (020)72721587
Website: www.stjohnstavern.com

VISA AE

Sharp's Cornish Coaster, Timothy Taylor Landlord, Redemption Urban Dusk and other changing guest ales

Too many diners arrived expecting Clerkenwell's St John restaurant – hence the addition of 'tavern' to the name of this pub, which has long been a beacon of hope on drab old Junction Road. The dark colours and fireplace in the dining room may make it look like somewhere for a winter's night but staff keep things light and perky throughout the year. The menu changes daily and the open kitchen puts some thought into the vegetarian choices, be they the courgette and cheddar tart or the squash and halloumi parcels; but they also know how to fire up the heat when cooking a pork chop or rib-eye. The wine list is sensibly priced, with enough carafes to make up for the 125ml glasses, although Black Sheep bitter is a popular alternative.

CLOSING TIMES
Closed 25-26 December and 1 January
dinner only and lunch Friday-Sunday
booking advisable at dinner

PRICES
Meals: a la carte £ 24/33

Typical Dishes

Jellied pig's head
Hake steak with saffron potato & chorizo stew
Honeycomb pavlova

⊖ Archway. Pay & display parking bays; free after 6.30pm.

32 **Well**

180 St John St,
Finsbury, EC1V 4JY
Tel.: (020)72519363
Website: www.downthewell.com

VISA MC AE

No real ales offered

The Well is perhaps more of a locals pub than many others found around these parts. It's all quite small inside but, thanks to some huge sliding glass windows, has a surprisingly light and airy feel, and the wooden floorboards and exposed brick walls add to the atmosphere of a committed metropolitan pub. Monthly changing menus offer modern dishes ranging from potted shrimps to foie gras and chicken liver parfait or sea trout and samphire, as well as classic English puddings like Eton Mess and some particularly good cheeses. The downstairs bar with its seductive lighting and fish tank is only available for private hire; check out the picture of a parched desert and a well which follows the curve of the wall on your way down.

CLOSING TIMES
Closed 25-26 December

PRICES
Meals: a la carte £ 23/33

Typical Dishes

Braised ox cheek, grilled tongue & pickled onions

Rose veal escalope with fried duck egg

Chocolate tart with Guinness ice cream

⊖ *Farringdon. On-street parking meters.*

33 Admiral Codrington

17 Mossop St,
Chelsea, SW3 2LY
Tel.: (020)75810005
Website: www.theadmiralcodrington.com

Inspectors' favourites

VISA MC AE

Caledonia 80 Shillings and Summer Ale

The Admiral Codrington is a smart, dependable affair as befits an establishment named after a hero of the Battles of Trafalgar and Navarino. What was once the HQ of the Sloane Ranger movement is now known for the quality of its food, although it still attracts a pretty smart crowd. The main bar and terrace are quite subdued during the day but get busy in the evening when all the eating is done in the neat, comfortable restaurant with its sliding glass roof. The menu can't quite decide whether this is a pub or a restaurant and so covers all bases from chilli salt squid to roast beef; coq au vin to fish and chips and includes some baguettes at lunch. Service can sometimes lack a little personality but the young team do get the job done.

CLOSING TIMES
Closed 25-26 December

PRICES
Meals: a la carte £ 23/43

Typical Dishes

Chilli salt squid with coriander

The Admiral's cod with a herb crust

Sticky toffee pudding

⊖ *South Kensington. Parking in the adjacent streets.*

34 Builders Arms

13 Britten St,
Chelsea, SW3 3TY
Tel.: (020)73499040
Website: www.geronimo-inns.co.uk

VISA MC AE

Charles Wells Bombardier, Sharp's Doom Bar and Adnams Best

The Builders Arms is very much like a packed village local – the only difference being that, in this instance, the village is Chelsea and the villagers are all young and prosperous. The inside delivers on the promise of the smart exterior but don't expect it to be quiet as drinkers are welcomed just as much as diners. In fact, bookings are only taken for larger parties but just tell the staff that you're here to eat and they'll sort you out. The cooking reveals the effort that has gone into the sourcing of some decent ingredients; the rib of beef for two is a perennial favourite. Dishes are robust and satisfying and are not without some flair in presentation. Wine is also taken seriously and their list has been thoughtfully put together.

CLOSING TIMES
Open daily

PRICES
Meals: a la carte £ 22/34

Typical Dishes

Prawn & avocado tian
Navarin of lamb with glazed new potatoes
Lemon & sultana cheesecake

⊖ South Kensington.

35 **Cadogan Arms**

298 King's Rd,
Chelsea, SW3 5UG
Tel.: (020)73526500
Website: www.thecadoganarmschelsea.com

VISA MC AE

Fuller's London Pride, Adnams Bitter and monthly changing guest ales

The Martin brothers seem to have the King's Road covered, with The Botanist dominating the Sloane Square end and The Cadogan Arms doing its thing at the other. The tiled entrance step reads 'luncheon, bar and billiards' which sounds appealingly like a lost afternoon, and it is clear that this is still a proper, blokey pub. The upstairs billiard tables are available by the hour and, while you eat, you'll feel the beady eyes of the various stuffed and mounted animals on the walls staring at you. The cooking is appropriately gutsy; juicy Aberdeen Angus rib-eye, golden-fried haddock, Dexter Beef and Welsh lamb are all staples of the menu. Starters and desserts are a little showier – perhaps something for the ladies? Staff catch the mood just so.

CLOSING TIMES
Closed 25-26 December
booking advisable at dinner

PRICES
Meals: a la carte £ 24/33

Typical Dishes

Wild nettle & watercress soup

Cornish lemon sole, samphire, shrimps & capers

Rhubarb crumble & custard

⊖ *South Kensington.*

36 Chelsea Ram

32 Burnaby St,
Chelsea, SW10 0PL
Tel.: (020)73514008

VISA MC

Youngs Bitter and Wells Bombardier

It's easy to see why the Chelsea Ram is such a successful neighbourhood pub: it's somewhat secreted position means there are few casual passers-by to upset the peace, the locals appreciate the relaxed and warm feel of the place and the pub provides them with just the sort of food they want. That means proper pub grub, with highlights being things on toast, like chicken livers or mushrooms, and the constant presence of favourites like The Ram burger or haddock and leek fishcake; prices are fair and portions large. They do take bookings but somewhat reluctantly, as they always want to keep a table or two for that spontaneous visit. The Chelsea Ram's winning formula is that it's comfortable just being what it is – a friendly, reliable local.

CLOSING TIMES
Closed Sunday dinner

PRICES
Meals: a la carte £ 22/26

Typical Dishes

Grilled fig salad with goat's cheese & toasted hazelnuts

Pork belly with crushed potato & mushy peas

Tiramisu

⊖ Fulham Broadway. On-street parking meters and single yellow lines.

37 Lots Road Pub & Dining Room

114 Lots Rd,
Chelsea, SW10 0RJ
Tel.: (020)73526645
Website: www.lotsroadpub.com

VISA MC AE

Sharp's Doom Bar and one regularly changing guest ale

Lots Road Pub and its customers are clearly happy with one another as it has introduced a customer loyalty scheme, whereby anyone making their fifth visit is rewarded with a discount. Lunch is geared more towards those just grabbing a quick bite but dinner sees a choice that could include oysters, mussels or a savoury tart; the Perthshire côte de boeuf is the house speciality. There are also pies and casseroles, in appropriate pub-like sizes, and even salads for those after something light. Service remains bright and cheery, even on those frantic Thursday nights when the pub offers 'Thursday Treats' with wine tasting and nibbles. The only disappointment is the somewhat ordinary bread for which they make a not insubstantial charge.

CLOSING TIMES
Open daily

PRICES
Meals: a la carte £ 20/30

Typical Dishes

Tomato & rocket soup
Cumberland sausage, mash, crispy onions & gravy
Sticky toffee pudding

⊖ Fulham Broadway.

38 **Phoenix**

23 Smith St,
Chelsea, SW3 4EE
Tel.: (020)77309182
Website: www.geronimo-inns.co.uk/thepheonix

VISA MC AE

Harvey's Sussex Best, Sharp's Doombar and Cornish Coaster

The same menu is served throughout and, while the bar has plenty of seating and a civilised feel, head to the warm and comfortable dining room at the back if you want a more structured meal or you're impressing a date. Blackboard specials supplement the menu which keeps things traditional: fish on a Friday, a pasta of the day and the likes of fishcakes or sausage and mash with red onion jam. For lunch, you'll find some favourites for late-risers, like eggs Benedict and, in winter, expect the heartening sight of crumbles or plum pudding. Wines are organised by their character, with nearly 30 varieties offered by the glass. The side dishes can bump up the final bill but The Phoenix remains a friendly and conscientiously run Chelsea local.

CLOSING TIMES
Closed 25 December

PRICES
Meals: a la carte £ 21/34

Typical Dishes

Smoked salmon, pickled courgette & sour cream

Fishcake with spinach & poached egg

Rhubarb strudel

⊖ Sloane Square. On-street parking meters.

39 Pig's Ear

35 Old Church St,
Chelsea, SW3 5BS
Tel.: (020)73522908
Website: www.thepigsear.com

VISA MC AE

Sam Brook's Wandle Junction and Uley Pigs Ear

This Chelsea pub may not look much like a foodie spot from the outside, or indeed from the inside, but it does have a refreshing honesty to it. Lunch is in the rough-and-ready ground floor bar, decorated with everything from 'Tintin' pictures to covers of 'Sounds' newspaper. There's a decent choice of 5-6 main courses and a wine list on a blackboard. With its wood panelling and dressed tables, the upstairs dining room provides quite a contrast, but the atmosphere is still far from starchy. Here the menu displays a little more ambition but cooking remains similarly earthy and the wine list has plenty of bottles under £30. The kitchen knows its way around an animal: slow-cooked dishes such as pork cheeks are done particularly well.

CLOSING TIMES
Open daily

PRICES
Meals: a la carte £ 15/25

Typical Dishes
Roast bone marrow with shallots & capers
Poached chicken breast with girolles, summer vegetables & shaved truffle
White chocolate parfait

⊖ *Sloane Square. 25min on foot.*

40 Bobbin

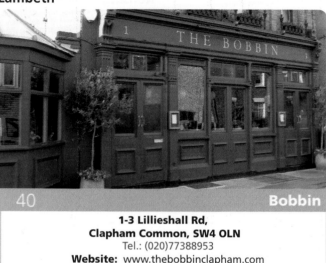

1-3 Lillieshall Rd,
Clapham Common, SW4 0LN
Tel.: (020)77388953
Website: www.thebobbinclapham.com

VISA MC AE

Harvey's Sussex Bitter and Sambrook's Wandle Ale

You'll find the Bobbin in a quiet residential street which, combined with its warm service, cosy bar and the Wednesday Quiz night, makes it feel like a proper local. You can eat in the bar or in the conservatory, from a menu which changes every six weeks and offers a choice of five starters and five mains. The charcuterie boards are great for sharing but vegetarians are also looked after, with the likes of leek, nettle and artichoke cannelloni. The kitchen sticks to using what's in season and, refreshingly, they don't feel they have to name-check every supplier to prove it. This pub may never set the world on fire yet that's part of its charm: they seem to have got everything right and are just, well, bobbin' along nicely.

CLOSING TIMES
Open daily

PRICES
Meals: a la carte £ 19/27

Typical Dishes

Charcuterie board
Roast chicken with grilled polenta & green beans
Chocolate sponge

⊖ Clapham Common. Free on-street parking after 6.30 pm.

41 **Canton Arms**

177 South Lambeth Rd,
Stockwell, SW8 1XP
Tel.: (020)75828710
Website: www.cantonarms.com

inspectors' favourites

VISA

Betty Stogs, Black Sheep, Summer Lightning and Timothy Taylor Golden Best

Its appreciative audience prove that the demand for fresh, honest, seasonal food is not just limited to smart squares in Chelsea or Islington. The oval-shaped bar dominates the room, with the front half busy with drinkers and the back laid up for diners, although it's all very relaxed and you can eat where you want. The kitchen's experience in places like the Anchor & Hope and Great Queen Street is obvious on their menu which features rustic, earthy British food, of the sort that suits this environment so well. Lunch could be a kipper or tripe and chips; even a reinvented toasted sandwich. Dinner sees a short, no-nonsense menu offering perhaps braised venison or grilled haddock, with daily specials like steak and kidney pie for two.

CLOSING TIMES
Closed Christmas-New Year, Monday lunch, Sunday dinner and bank holidays

PRICES
Meals: a la carte £ 19/27

Typical Dishes

Salt cod brandade, toast & olives

Confit duck leg, Arroncina beans & romesco sauce

Chocolate pot

⊖ Stockwell. Free parking in the evening.

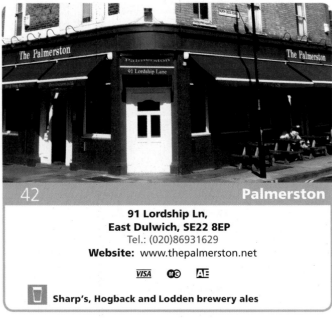

42 **Palmerston**

91 Lordship Ln,
East Dulwich, SE22 8EP
Tel.: (020)86931629
Website: www.thepalmerston.net

VISA MC AE

Sharp's, Hogback and Lodden brewery ales

It's not just for the locals – those passing through for a visit to the Horniman Museum or Dulwich Picture Gallery must also be pleased to have somewhere so welcoming in which to extend their stay in SE22. You can sit anywhere, although there is a section at the back with wood panelling and a mosaic floor which they call 'the dining room'. The menus tend to evolve on a monthly basis, with influences ranging from the Med to Asia. The bread is good, which usually augurs well and, refreshingly, the dishes come with just the ingredients described on the menu. Add a well-priced weekday menu and a host of engaging young staff and it's little wonder the pub attracts such a wide range of ages, which in turn creates a pleasant atmosphere.

CLOSING TIMES
Open daily

PRICES
Meals: £ 16 (lunch)
and a la carte £ 25/32

Typical Dishes

Grilled asparagus with poached egg, balsamic & parmesan

Bollito misto with salsa rossa

Lemon meringue pie

⊖ East Dulwich (rail). Free on-street parking in the evening.

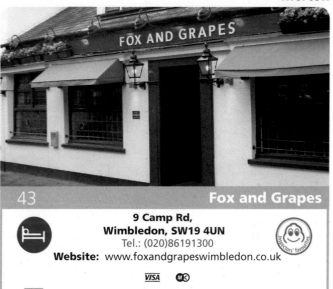

43

Fox and Grapes

9 Camp Rd,
Wimbledon, SW19 4UN
Tel.: (020)86191300
Website: www.foxandgrapeswimbledon.co.uk

Inspectors' favourites

VISA MC

Sharp's Doom Bar, Black Sheep and Fuller's London Pride

Claude Bosi first made his mark in Ludlow where, along with his Hibiscus restaurant, he also had a pub. When he moved to London the plan was to open a pub again once his restaurant was established and this he duly did in 2011. Cedric, his brother, runs the show and one look at the menu confirms their credentials as honorary Brits: this is proper pub food. Their prawn cocktail is hugely popular, as is the Cumberland sausage with mash, the ale battered hake and Angus sirloin. Scotch egg is made with wild boar, and junket makes an appearance, which makes you forgive their sneaking in the odd Gallic touch like snails and some of the over-formality. Thankfully, the pub's bigger than it looks as it's very popular. It also has three cosy bedrooms.

CLOSING TIMES
Closed 25 December
booking advisable

PRICES
Meals: £ 20 (lunch)
and a la carte £ 26/38
3 rooms: £ 125

Typical Dishes

Pork & bramley apple pie

Brown ale battered hake & chips

Hazelnut tart & clotted cream ice cream

⊖ Wimbledon. Located on the edge of Wimbledon Common. On-street parking.

44 **Brown Dog**

28 Cross St,
Barnes, SW13 0AP
Tel.: (020)83922200
Website: www.thebrowndog.co.uk

VISA AE

Westerham Brewery Grasshopper, Twickenham Original, Wandle Sam Brown Brewery

Thankfully, changes of ownership don't appear to mean much here – perhaps you really can't teach an old dog new tricks – because The Brown Dog remains a terrific neighbourhood pub and the locals clearly love it just the way it is. Mind you, this pretty Victorian pub is so well hidden in the maze of residential streets that it's a wonder any new customers ever find it anyway. The look fuses the traditional with the modern and service is bubbly and enthusiastic. Jugs of iced water arrive without prompting and the cleverly concise menu changes regularly. A lightly spiced crab salad or pint of prawns could be followed by a succulent rump of lamb, while puddings not only display a terrific lightness of touch but are also very commendably priced.

CLOSING TIMES
Closed 25-26 December

PRICES
Meals: a la carte £ 20/30

Typical Dishes

Grilled cuttlefish & chorizo salad

Sea bream fillet with crushed Jersey Royal potatoes

Lemon & strawberry posset

⊖ *Barnes Bridge (Rail).*

45 King's Head

123 High St,
Teddington, TW11 8HG
Tel.: (020)31662900
Website: www.whitebrasserie.com

VISA MC

Fuller's London Pride, Sharp's Doom Bar, Twickenham Spring Ale

Britain has its pubs and France its brasseries; The King's Head does its bit for the entente cordiale by combining both. Raymond Blanc's team has given this Victorian pub a tidy makeover and, although there might not be much character left, they have created a suitably warm environment. The brasserie at the back is run by a pleasant, enthusiastic team and the menus offer all comers plenty of choice. Classic brasserie dishes such as Toulouse sausages and beef stroganoff come with a satisfyingly rustic edge, while the dual-nationality element is maintained through the inclusion of a ploughman's board alongside the charcuterie. Steaks on the charcoal grill are popular and families are lured in by the decent kiddies menu.

CLOSING TIMES
Open daily

PRICES
Meals: £ 14/16
and a la carte £ 19/26

Typical Dishes

Smoked Cornish mackerel with horseradish cream

Cod with samphire & roast tomato sauce

Rhubarb & custard with honeycomb

⊖ Teddington (Rail). On-street parking.

46 **Victoria**

10 West Temple Sheen,
East Sheen, SW14 7RT
Tel.: (020)88764238
Website: www.thevictoria.net

VISA

Fuller's London Pride, Harveys, Butcombe

Many pubs claim to be genuine locals – The Victoria is the real deal: it sponsors local clubs and the chef is patron of the local food festival; he also holds cookery workshops at the school next door. This is a beautifully decorated pub, with a restored bar with a wood burning stove and plenty of nooks and crannies; a few steps down and you're in the more formal conservatory overlooking the terrace. The cooking is modern British with the odd international note. Warm homemade bread could be followed by Scotch egg with roast beetroot, cod with a white bean stew and, to finish, blood oranges with rhubarb sorbet. Produce is local where possible: veg is from Surrey and honey from Richmond. Service is engaging and there are simple bedrooms available.

CLOSING TIMES
Open daily

PRICES
Meals: a la carte £ 28/30
7 rooms: £ 115/125

Typical Dishes

Tartar of red snapper
Hake wrapped in Serrano ham
Apple tarte Tatin

⊖ Mortlake (Rail). Just off Upper Richmond Rd. West (A205) by Coval St and Temple Sheen.

47

Anchor & Hope

36 The Cut,
Southwark, SE1 8LP
Tel.: (020)79289898

VISA MC

Youngs Ordinary, Charles Wells Bombardier and weekly changing guest ales

The Anchor & Hope is still running at full steam and its popularity shows no sign of abating. It's not hard to see why: combine a menu that changes with each service and is a paragon of seasonality, with cooking that is gutsy, bold and wholesome, and you end up with immeasurably rewarding dishes like suckling kid chops with wild garlic, succulent roast pigeon with lentils or buttermilk pudding with poached rhubarb. The place has a contagiously congenial feel and the staff all pull in the same direction; you may spot a waiter trimming veg or a chef delivering dishes. The no-reservation policy remains, so either get here early or be prepared to wait – although you can now book for Sunday lunch, when everyone sits down at 2pm for a veritable feast.

CLOSING TIMES
Closed Christmas-New Year, Sunday dinner, Monday lunch and bank holidays

PRICES
Meals: a la carte £ 23/32

Typical Dishes

Duck hearts on toast
Rib of beef with chips & béarnaise
Muscat caramel custard

⊖ Southwark. On-street parking meters.

48 **Garrison**

99-101 Bermondsey St,
Bermondsey, SE1 3XB
Tel.: (020)70899355
Website: www.thegarrison.co.uk

VISA MC AE

Adnams Bitter and St Peter's Organic Ale

'Sweet' is not an adjective that could apply to many of London's pubs but it does seem to fit The Garrison. The service has a certain natural charm and the place has a warm, relaxed vibe, while its mismatched style and somewhat vintage look work well. Open from 8am for smoothies and breakfast, it gets busier as the day goes on – and don't bother coming for dinner if you haven't booked. Booth numbers 4 and 5, opposite the open kitchen, are the most popular while number 2 at the back is the cosiest. The menu has a distinct Mediterranean flavour; salads dominate the starters and steaks and braised meats sit alongside pasta and fresh fish options. Puddings are more your classic pub variety. The owners' other place, Village East, is just down the street.

CLOSING TIMES
Closed 25-27 December
booking essential at dinner

PRICES
Meals: a la carte £ 23/30

Typical Dishes

Razor clams, roast tomato & garlic sauce
Smoked haddock with poached egg & chive beurre blanc
Sticky toffee pudding

⊖ *London Bridge.*

49 Gun

27 Coldharbour,
Canary Wharf, E14 9NS
Tel.: (020)75155222
Website: www.thegundocklands.com

VISA MC AE

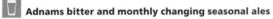

Adnams bitter and monthly changing seasonal ales

The 18C Gun may have had a 21C makeover but that doesn't mean it has forgotten its roots: its association with Admiral Lord Nelson, links to smugglers and ties to the river are all celebrated in its oil paintings and displays of assorted weaponry. The dining room and the style of service are both fairly smart and ceremonial, yet The Gun is a pub where this level of formality seems appropriate. Dockers have now been replaced by bankers, the majority of whom rarely venture beyond the 35-day aged steak. This is a shame as the menu cleverly combines relatively ambitious dishes such as game or John Dory with more traditional local specialities like eel and oysters. Even the dessert menu offers a mix, from soufflés to stewed plums.

CLOSING TIMES
Closed 25-26 December

PRICES
Meals: £ 18 (lunch)
and a la carte £ 28/49

Typical Dishes
Pork belly, snails, garlic & peppered chicory
Roast duck breast, confit leg & shepherd's pie
Apple charlotte with vanilla custard

⊖ Blackwall (DLR). Marsh Wall car park; on-street parking meters.

50 Morgan Arms

43 Morgan St,
Bow, E3 5AA
Tel.: (020)89806389
Website: www.capitalpubcompany.com/The-Morgan-Arms

VISA MC AE

Sharp's Doom Bar, Atlantic, Adnam's Best Bitter and Timothy Taylor Landlord

This former boozer's clever makeover respects its heritage while simultaneously bringing it up to date. The bar's always busy while the dining area is more subdued. You'll find the kitchen keeps its influences mostly within Europe but also understands just what sort of food works well in a pub. The daily changing menu usually features pasta in some form and staples like whitebait - which come devilled in this instance - assorted tarts and the perennial favourite, fishcakes accompanied by a poached egg. What's more, prices are kept at realistic levels which make this pub appealing to those who live nearby and who like a little spontaneity in their lives. Look out for the occasional themed evening and charity auction.

CLOSING TIMES
Closed 25 December

PRICES
Meals: a la carte £ 24/34

Typical Dishes

Pork & chicken terrine
Red mullet & squid with spicy chickpeas & minted yoghurt
Passion fruit crème brûlée

⊖ Bow Road. Parking meters in Tredegar Square until 6.30pm; after 6.30pm parking outside.

51 Narrow

44 Narrow St,
Limehouse, E14 8DP
Tel.: (020)75927950
Website: www.gordonramsay.com

VISA AE

Greene King St Edmunds, Adnam's Broadside and monthly changing guest ales

Despite receiving some negative publicity a while back, when it was revealed that certain dishes in Gordon Ramsay's pubs are prepared in a central kitchen, The Narrow does not seem to be any less frenetic. This 'logistical cooking', as they describe it, is used for dishes requiring a lengthy cooking process, such as the slow-roasted pork belly or beef braised in Guinness. However it gets there, the food on the plate is tasty, seasonal and laudably British, be it devilled kidneys, Morecambe Bay brown shrimps, a chicken pie or a sherry trifle. What is also certain is that no other London pub has better views, as one would expect from a converted dockmaster's house; just be sure to request a table in the very appealing conservatory.

CLOSING TIMES
Open daily
booking essential

PRICES
Meals: £ 22 (lunch)
and a la carte £ 24/36

Typical Dishes

Crayfish cocktail
Breast of chicken, gem lettuce, peas & cider sauce
Bread & butter pudding

⊖ Limehouse (DLR). Parking.

52 Owl & Pussycat

34 Redchurch St,
Spitalfields, E2 7DP
Tel.: (020)34870088
Website: www.owlandpussycatshoreditch.com

VISA MC AE

Brakspear Bitter, Ringwood Best, Ringwood 49er and Marston's IPA

As they did with The Fellow in King's Cross, the owners like to open pubs at the embryonic stage of a neighbourhood's gentrification. This was a run down East End boozer called The Crown which now has a raggedly modish look, with ironic touches of Victoriana to match the Edward Lear name. The ground floor is for drinkers and snackers; dining is done upstairs, where a concise but constantly changing and appealingly stout British menu is offered in the evening. Pork terrines, a crayfish cocktail or even oysters and Guinness may be followed by a Barnsley chop or a proper pie. Their puds, like lavender rice pudding and rhubarb crumble, are the kind that should be compulsory in all pubs. Bread and filtered water are provided gratis.

CLOSING TIMES
Closed 25-26 December, 1 January and bank holidays

PRICES
Meals: a la carte £ 25/43

Typical Dishes
Deep-fried skate cheeks with creamed leek & bacon
Rib-eye steak with Bordelaise sauce & dripping chips
Apple tart with butterscotch sauce

⊖ Shoreditch. On-street parking meters.

53 **Avalon**

16 Balham Hill,
Balham, SW12 9EB
Tel.: (020)86758613
Website: www.theavalonlondon.com

VISA MC AE

Timothy Taylor Landlord, Sharp's Doom Bar and Tribute

So Avalon really does exist…and it comes in the shape of a huge, atmospheric pub topped with an illuminated sign that makes it hard to miss on Balham Hill. Sir Edward Coley Burne-Jones prints add a suitably mythical edge to the aesthetic of the long bar and here you can order the sort of snacks that go well with a pint. Head through to the tiled and characterful rear dining room for their seasonal menu which is of the sort to appeal to a broad constituency. You'll find everything from a pie of the day and steaks to dishes of a more Mediterranean persuasion like whole grilled bream with caponata or gnocchi with porcini mushrooms. Once the team warm up, service is pleasant and the large summer terrace at the back is a great feature.

CLOSING TIMES
Closed 25-26 December and 1 January
booking advisable

PRICES
Meals: a la carte £ 25/30

Typical Dishes
Rabbit & ham terrine with pickled baby carrots
Mackerel with beetroot tortelloni & horseradish cream
Green tea crème brûlée

⊖ Clapham South.

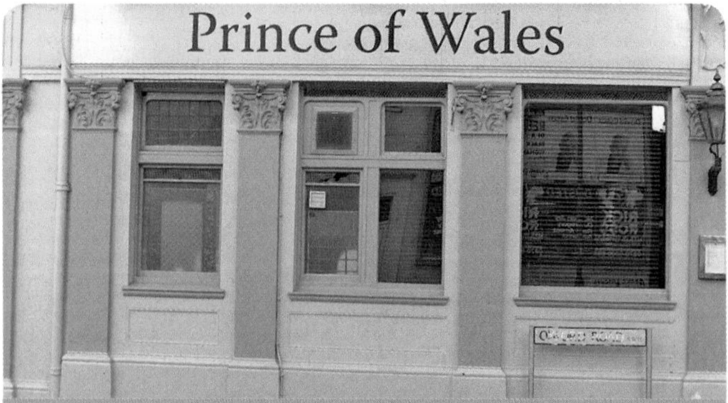

54 Prince of Wales

138 Upper Richmond Rd,
Putney, SW15 2SP
Tel.: (020)87881552
Website: www.princeofwalesputney.co.uk

VISA MC AE Diners

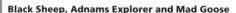

Black Sheep, Adnams Explorer and Mad Goose

You'll feel the warmth as soon as you enter. The bar, whose walls are lined with tankards, is usually packed with a mix of drinkers and diners, perhaps enjoying homemade Scotch eggs or fish with triple-cooked chips; you'll feel as though you just want to join in the fun. There is a quieter space behind the bar but if you want something completely different then go down a few steps and you'll find a grand and lavishly kitted out baronial-style dining room. The daily changing menu is full of seasonality and diversity. Oysters, Asian salads or charcuterie can be followed by beef Bourguignon or some terrific game, and there's usually a great selection of ice creams to finish. Sunday lunch is a family affair, with spit-roast chicken a speciality.

CLOSING TIMES
Closed 23 December-1 January and Monday lunch except bank holidays

PRICES
Meals: a la carte £ 27/43

Typical Dishes

Wild rabbit & pork terrine

Stone bass with fried oysters & rock samphire

Buttermilk pudding with poached peaches

⊖ *East Putney.*

55 **Ebury**

11 Pimlico Rd,
Victoria, SW1W 8NA
Tel.: (020)77306784
Website: www.theebury.co.uk

VISA MC

Fuller's London Pride

Grab a passing waiter to get yourself seated otherwise they'll assume you've just come for a drink at the bar and will ignore you. Once you've got your feet under one of the low-slung tables, however, you'll find everything moves up a gear. This is a rather smart affair and provides an object lesson in how to draw in punters. That means a varied menu, from burger to black bream, assorted salads that show some thought, three vegetarian dishes and main courses that display a degree of originality. Add to that a conscientious kitchen, a wine list that offers plenty by the glass and carafe, and weekend brunch that goes on until 4pm and it's little wonder the place is always so busy. The waiters come with French accents and self-confidence.

CLOSING TIMES
Open daily

PRICES
Meals: a la carte £ 30/39

Typical Dishes

Beetroot & goat's cheese salad

Loin of pork, mango, fennel & capers

Verbena jelly with pineapple carpaccio

⊖ *Sloane Square. Pay & display in the street.*

56 Grazing Goat

6 New Quebec St,
Marylebone, W1H 7RQ
Tel.: (020)77247243
Website: www.thegrazinggoat.co.uk

VISA MC AE

Deuchars and Doom Bar

The Portman Estate, owners of some serious real estate in these parts and keen to raise the profile of its investment, encouraged an experienced pub operator more at home in Chelsea and Belgravia to venture a little further north and take over the old Bricklayers Arms. Renamed in homage to a past Lady Portman (who grazed goats in a field where the pub now stands as she was allergic to cows' milk), it is now a smart city facsimile of a country pub. It's first-come-first-served in the bar but you can book in the upstairs dining room. Pub classics are the order of the day, such as pies or Castle of Mey steaks, and Suffolk chicken is cooked on the rotisserie. The eight bedrooms are nicely furnished, with their bathrooms resembling Nordic saunas.

CLOSING TIMES
Open daily
booking essential at dinner

PRICES
Meals: a la carte £ 30/45
8 rooms: £ 195/225

Typical Dishes

Chilli salt squid with lime dressing

28 day dry-aged Castle of Mey rib-eye steak

Caramel and banana cheesecake

⊖ Marble Arch.

57 **Larrik**

32 Crawford Pl,
Marylebone, W1H 5NN
Tel.: (020)77230066
Website: www.thelarrik.com

VISA MC AE D

Timothy Taylor, Sharp's Doom Bar, Black Sheep and Hook Norton

Its airy feel and capable service mean that The Larrik has always been popular with larger groups and now, thanks to the obvious ambition of the owner, it's attracting plenty more customers for the quality of its food; so it's no surprise to find the place packed by 1pm on a daily basis. Try to sit at the front where it's brighter and more fun. Freshly made and substantial salads, a luxurious chicken liver parfait, plump salmon and haddock fishcakes with hollandaise and rewardingly rich desserts like chocolate brownies confirm a kitchen that's well grounded in the basics and aware of what people want from a pub. Add regularly changing real ales and you have a pub that's set to be part of the local landscape for some time to come.

CLOSING TIMES
Closed 25 December

PRICES
Meals: £ 13 (dinner) and a la carte £ 25/37

Typical Dishes
Chicken liver parfait
Fishcake with poached egg, hollandaise sauce & pea purée
Chocolate brownie

⊖ *Edgware Road. On-street parking meters.*

58 Only Running Footman

5 Charles St,
Mayfair, W1J 5DF
Tel.: (020)74992988
Website: www.therunningfootmanmayfair.com

VISA MC AE

Wells Bombardier and Youngs

Apparently the owners added 'only' to the title when they found out that theirs was the only pub in the land called 'The Running Footman'. Spread over several levels, it offers cookery demonstrations and private dinners along with its two floors of dining. Downstairs is where the action usually is, with its menu offering pub classics from steak sandwiches to fishcakes, but you can't book here and it's always packed. Upstairs is where you'll find a surprisingly formal dining room and here they do take reservations. Its menu is far more ambitious and European in its influence but the best dishes are still the simpler ones, with desserts a strength. You can't help feeling that you would be having a lot more fun below stairs, though.

CLOSING TIMES
Open daily

PRICES
Meals: a la carte £ 21/37

Typical Dishes

Beetroot, walnut & goat's curd salad
Beer-battered haddock, chips & mushy peas
Chocolate mocha tart with strawberries

⊖ Green Park.

59 **Orange**

37 Pimlico Rd,
Victoria, SW1W 8NE
Tel.: (020)78819844
Website: www.theorange.co.uk

VISA MC AE

The Famous Belgium, Harvey's and Adnams Bitters

The Belgravia-Victoria-Pimlico quarter is clearly working for the team behind The Thomas Cubitt and Pantechnicon Rooms because their latest pub, The Orange, is within shouting distance of their other two and appears to be equally busy. There are a couple of differences: this pub has bedrooms, nicely decorated and named after the local streets, and the food is a little more down-to-earth and family-friendly. Pizza in the bar from their wood-fired oven is always a popular choice; there's Film Night on Mondays and, unusually, the first floor restaurant is noisier than the bar. The building's stucco-fronted façade may be quite grand but the colonial feel inside and the particularly friendly service create a pleasantly laid-back atmosphere.

CLOSING TIMES
Open daily

PRICES
Meals: a la carte £ 24/41
4 rooms: £ 185/205

Typical Dishes

Spiced calamari with chilli & lime dressing

Roast rump of Devon lamb, parmesan potato & aubergine

Dark chocolate & orange tart

Sloane Square.

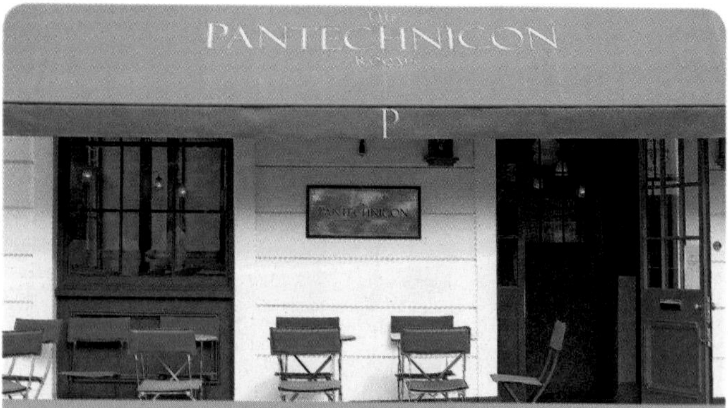

60 **Pantechnicon**

10 Motcomb St,
Belgravia, SW1X 8LA
Tel.: (020)77306074
Website: www.thepantechnicon.com

VISA MC AE

Adnams Bitter

The name 'Pantechnicon' either refers to a large removal wagon or the antique repository which once sat on Motcomb Street until it was destroyed by fire in the 1870s. It's no clearer inside, as you'll find both sepia photos of assorted removal vehicles as well as a painting depicting the fire. But one thing is certain: this is the antithesis of a spit 'n' sawdust pub. The ground floor is first-come-first-served and is always lively but upstairs is an altogether more gracious affair, designed for those who like a little formality with their pheasant. The cooking is traditional but with a twist. Oysters are a perennial; there's a decent salad selection and they set their stall by the traceability of their mature Scottish steaks.

CLOSING TIMES
Closed 25 December-1 January

PRICES
Meals: a la carte £ 32/46

Typical Dishes
Devon crab with avocado, grapefruit & crisp bread
Braised pork belly with black pudding croquette
Cocoa bean brûlée with cinnamon doughnuts

⊖ Knightsbridge .

61 **Portman**

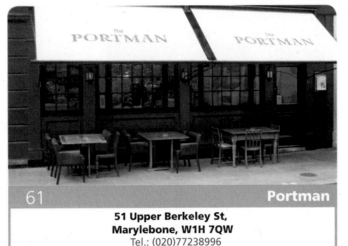

51 Upper Berkeley St,
Marylebone, W1H 7QW
Tel.: (020)77238996
Website: www.theportmanmarylebone.com

VISA MC AE

London Pride, Rebellion, Trumans, Caledonian, Theakstons

When it went by the name of The Masons Arms this pub was widely known for its gruesome history. It was here that the condemned, on their way to Tyburn Tree gallows, would take their last drink, which purportedly led to the phrase "one for the road". Reincarnated as The Portman, the pub these days boasts a less disreputable clientele who are more attracted by the quality of the cooking. Food is served all day and you can choose to eat in the busy ground floor bar or in the unexpectedly formal upstairs dining room, all thick-pile carpet and starched tablecloths. Fortunately, the style of food remains thoroughly down-to-earth and satisfying and is accompanied by a well-organised wine list and an interesting selection of cocktails.

CLOSING TIMES
Open daily

PRICES
Meals: a la carte £ 22/31

Typical Dishes

Chicken liver parfait
Fillet of sea trout, Jersey Royals & asparagus with lemon
Passion fruit cheesecake

⊖ *Marble Arch.*

62 Prince Alfred & Formosa Dining Room

5A Formosa St,
Bayswater and Maida Vale, W9 1EE
Tel.: (020)72863287
Website: www.theprincealfred.com

VISA MC AE

Youngs Bitter and Charles Wells' Bombardier

Original plate glass, panels and snugs make The Prince Alfred a wonderful example of a classic Victorian pub. Unfortunately, the eating is done in the Formosa Dining Room extension on the side but at least it's a lively room with capable cooking. There's a rustic theme running through the menu, with a strong British accent, so traditionalists will enjoy the fish pie, potted trout, steak and ale pie and calves liver but there are also risottos, parfaits and terrines for those whose tastes are more continental. The open kitchen is not averse to sprucing up some classics, for example your burger arrives adorned with foie gras and truffles. Prices are realistic, even with a charge made for bread, and the friendly team cope well under pressure.

CLOSING TIMES
Open daily

PRICES
Meals: £ 16 (lunch)
and a la carte £ 25/39

Typical Dishes

Crispy goat's cheese with balsamic strawberries

Slow-roast lamb with stuffed roast peppers

Yoghurt panna cotta

⊖ Warwick Avenue. Parking by Warwick Avenue station (2min on foot).

63 Thomas Cubitt

44 Elizabeth St,
Victoria, SW1W 9PA
Tel.: (020)77306060
Website: www.thethomascubitt.co.uk

Inspectors' favourites

VISA MC AE

Adnams' Southwold BItter and IPA

The Thomas Cubitt is a pub of two halves: on the ground floor it's perennially busy and you can't book which means that if you haven't arrived by 7pm then you're too late to get a table. However, you can reserve a table upstairs, in a dining room that's a model of civility and tranquillity. Here, service comes courtesy of a young team where the girls are chatty and the men unafraid of corduroy. Downstairs you get fish and chips; here you get pan-fried fillet of brill with oyster beignet and truffled chips. The cooking is certainly skilled, quite elaborate in its construction and prettily presented. So, take your pick: upstairs can get a little pricey but is ideal for entertaining the in-laws; if out with friends then crowd in downstairs.

CLOSING TIMES
Closed Christmas and New Year
booking essential

PRICES
Meals: a la carte £ 29/49

Typical Dishes

Chilli salt squid with citrus pepper sauce
Organic beef burger
Rhubarb Bakewell tart

⊖ Sloane Square. Parking meters in Elizabeth Street.

64 **Waterway**

54 Formosa St,
Bayswater and Maida Vale, W9 2JU
Tel.: (020)72663557
Website: www.thewaterway.co.uk

VISA AE

Sharp's Doom Bar and Cornish Knocker

A canalside setting offering refreshment to passing narrowboaters; a large terrace besieged by drinkers; and live music on a Thursday night – it sounds like a pub and even has the necessary warmth and bustle, but inside it's all surprisingly smart. There's a bar occupying one side and a restaurant the other, with no sign anywhere of any spit or sawdust. The menu and cooking are both comparable to the most urbane of urban gastropub: the muscular flavours of black pudding with chorizo and hen's egg are in contrast to its delicate presentation, while fillet of bream with prawn mash reveals the kitchen's lighter touch. Things tail off somewhat with desserts but prices are realistic. Service is youthful, bubbly and capable.

CLOSING TIMES
Open daily

PRICES
Meals: a la carte £ 26/36

Typical Dishes

Char-grilled squid with goat's cheese fritters

8oz Hereford rib-eye steak with char-grilled vegetable skewers

Strawberry Eton mess

⊖ Warwick Avenue.

This region cradles some of England's wildest and most dramatic scenery typified by Northumberland National Park, a landscape of rolling purple moorlands and roaring rivers bursting with salmon and trout. Kielder Forest's mighty wilderness has been called "the country's most tranquil spot" while Bill Bryson has waxed lyrical upon the glories of Durham Cathedral. Those who love the wind in their hair are equally effusive about the eleven-mile footpath that accompanies the pounding waves of Durham's Heritage Coast; further north are the long, dune-backed beaches of Northumberland. Rambling across the region is Hadrian's Wall, 73 miles of iconic Roman history, while a modern slant on architectural celebrity is proffered by the Millennium Bridge, BALTIC Centre and Angel of the North. The famously bracing air whets hearty appetites for local Cheviot lamb, Coquetdale cheese or Holy Island oysters. And what could be more redolent of the North East than a breakfast of Craster kippers?

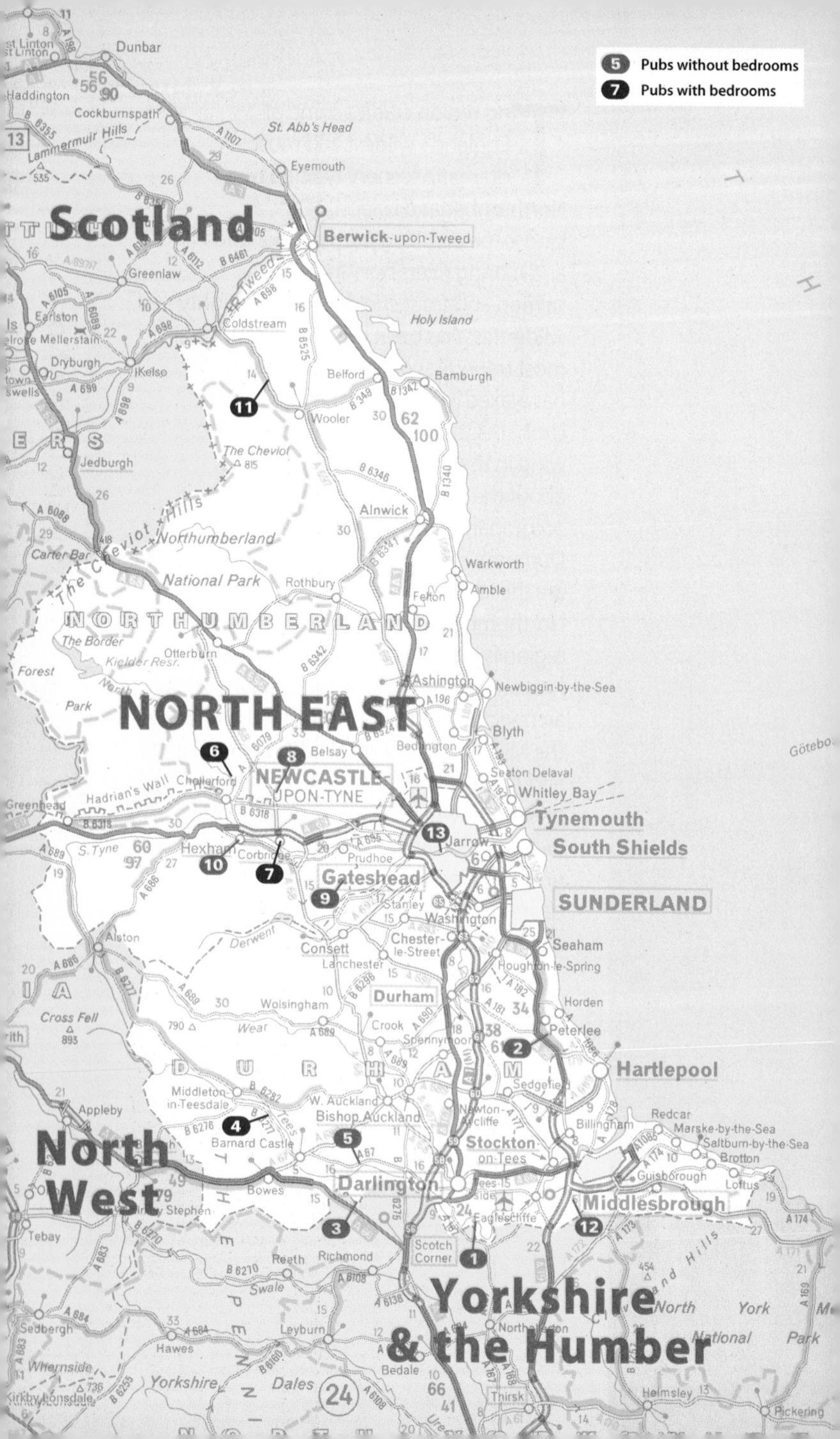
5 Pubs without bedrooms
7 Pubs with bedrooms
Scotland
NORTH EAST
North West
Yorkshire & the Humber
NORTHUMBERLAND
DURHAM
Dunbar
Haddington
Cockburnspath
Lammermuir Hills
St. Abb's Head
Eyemouth
Berwick-upon-Tweed
Greenlaw
Earlston
Mellerstain
Coldstream
Dryburgh
Kelso
Holy Island
Belford
Bamburgh
Wooler
Jedburgh
The Cheviot
Alnwick
Carter Bar
Cheviot Hills
Northumberland National Park
Rothbury
Warkworth
Amble
Felton
The Border
Otterburn
Kielder Resr.
Forest Park
Ashington
Newbiggin-by-the-Sea
Blyth
Belsay
Bedlington
Seaton Delaval
Whitley Bay
Chollerford
NEWCASTLE-UPON-TYNE
Hadrian's Wall
Greenhead
Tynemouth
South Shields
Hexham
Corbridge
Prudhoe
Jarrow
Gateshead
SUNDERLAND
Stanley
Washington
Alston
Consett
Chester-le-Street
Seaham
Lanchester
Houghton-le-Spring
Durham
Horden
Cross Fell
Wolsingham
Crook
Peterlee
Spennymoor
Hartlepool
Sedgefield
Middleton-in-Teesdale
W. Auckland
Bishop Auckland
Newton Aycliffe
Redcar
Marske-by-the-Sea
Appleby
Billingham
Saltburn-by-the-Sea
Barnard Castle
Stockton-on-Tees
Brotton
Guisborough
Loftus
Bowes
Darlington
Middlesbrough
Kirkby Stephen
Eaglescliffe
Tebay
Scotch Corner
Reeth
Richmond
Swale
North York Moors National Park
Sedbergh
Hawes
Leyburn
Northallerton
Whernside
Yorkshire Dales
Bedale
Kirkby Lonsdale
Thirsk
Helmsley
Pickering

1 **Bay Horse**

45 The Green,
Hurworth on Tees, DL2 2AA
Tel.: (01325)720663
Website: www.thebayhorsehurworth.com

Inspectors' favourites

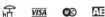

VISA MC AE

Cumberland, Bitter & Twisted and regularly changing guest ale

Set on a long grassy street in an attractive village, this early 18C creamwashed pub is framed by colourful planters and hanging baskets, and boasts a pleasant rear terrace and garden. Drinkers and diners mingle amongst antique chairs, low stools and leather banquettes in the open-fired bar area and the relaxed, informal atmosphere continues through into the dining room. For special occasions the private first floor room definitely adds some style, with its 20 foot Victorian table and adjoining lounge. Menus offer something for everyone, featuring classics such as moules marinierè, daube of beef or omelette Arnold Bennett, as well as familiar pub favourites. Dishes range in their presentation from simple and rustic to modern and intricate.

CLOSING TIMES
Closed Sunday dinner

PRICES
Meals: £ 17 (lunch)
and a la carte £ 25/33

Typical Dishes

Mussels, roasted red peppers, chorizo & potatoes
Pressed belly pork & Toulouse sausage
Caramelised rice pudding

5.5 mi south of Darlington; signed off A 167; in the middle of the village. Parking.

2 **Castle Eden Inn**

Stockton Rd,
Castle Eden, TS27 4SD
Tel.: (01429)835137
Website: www.castleedeninn.com

VISA MC AE

Timothy Taylor Landlord, Black Sheep, Copper Dragon Golden Pippin, Nel's Best and Consett's Red Dust

You'll find this substantial former coaching inn on what was once the main road into London. If there's space, grab a table in the front garden, if not, head inside, where you'll discover a large, stylish bar and formal, linen-laid dining room brightened with large vases of lilies. Menus offer a bewildering array of choice. The traditional bar menu is served all day and offers the likes of ham, egg and chips and shepherd's pie, while the main à la carte features more substantial dishes such as ham hock and pease pudding or cannon of local lamb. There's also a monthly changing set menu that follows the seasons and daily specials such as local Lindisfarne oysters or net caught langoustines. Suppliers are name-checked on the back of the menu.

CLOSING TIMES
Open daily

PRICES
Meals: a la carte £ 22/31

Typical Dishes

Potted ham hock, pease pudding & stottie cake

Cannon of lamb with braised shank faggot & mint jelly

Treacle tart

7 mi northwest of Hartlepool by A 179, A 19 and on B 1281, at edge of village. Parking.

3 **Oak Tree Inn**

Hutton Magna,
DL11 7HH
Tel.: (01833)627371

VISA MC AE

Black Sheep, Charles Wells Bombardier, Timothy Taylor Landlord

They say good things come in small packages and that's definitely the case with this charming whitewashed pub. Found on the main street of a small hamlet, it consists of a single room with a proper old-fashioned counter, six wooden tables flanked by green settles and a bench table for the locals. Claire – who both serves the drinks and delivers the food – provides a warm welcome at the bar, while behind the scenes in the kitchen, Alastair single-handedly holds the fort. The menu takes on a fairly formal format, offering generous portions of hearty, flavoursome cooking with a rustic French feel: you might find confit belly pork, onion and thyme tart or best end of lamb. More wide-ranging flavours such as cumin and chilli often appear too.

CLOSING TIMES
Closed 24-27 December, 31 December, 1 January and Monday
dinner only
booking essential

PRICES
Meals: a la carte £ 27/34

Typical Dishes

Venison & black pudding shepherd's pie
Monkfish wrapped in pancetta with carrot, ginger & little gem
Lemon, mascarpone & pistachio semi-freddo

7 mi southeast of Barnard Castle off A 66. Parking.

4 **Rose and Crown**

Romaldkirk,
DL12 9EB
Tel.: (01833)650213
Website: www.rose-and-crown.co.uk

Inspectors' favourites

VISA

Theakston Best Bitter, Black Sheep Bitter and Allendale Best Bitter

Set next to a Saxon church in the middle of three village greens – looking out over a water pump and some stocks – is this quintessential 18C English village inn. There's a wonderfully atmospheric front bar displaying plenty of brass, a warmly decorated brasserie and, tucked away to the rear, a cosy lounge boasting an impressive grandfather clock. Between the bar and brasserie menus there's a good range of dishes, with a core of classics and some more substantial offerings at dinner. While in the evening, residents tend to favour the traditional linen-laid dining room with its china-filled dresser and seasonally changing four course menu. Split between the inn and the courtyard, bedrooms boast designer décor, flat-screen TVs and Bose radios.

CLOSING TIMES
Closed 24-26 December

PRICES
Meals: a la carte £ 22/33
12 rooms: £ 95/185

Typical Dishes

Cotherstone cheese soufflé

Pan-fried wood pigeon, onion marmalade & juniper sauce

Sticky walnut tart

3.5 mi southeast of Middleton-in-Teesdale on B 6277; on the village green, next to the church. Parking.

5 **Bridgewater Arms**

Winston,
DL2 3RN
Tel.: (01325)730302
Website: www.thebridgewaterarms.com

VISA AE

Timothy Taylor Landlord and Greene King IPA

It may seem an odd name for a pub located within a former school but it makes sense when you learn that it once stood beside the old bridge, next to the water. Inside, it's light and spacious, with a 2 foot copperplate alphabet edging the ceiling, a programme from the 1957 Jack and the Beanstalk production above the bar – you might even find some of the cast members sitting underneath it – and a more formal dining room behind. The daily changing menu has a strong seafood base, offering the likes of Manx Queenies, sweet herrings and salt and chilli squid, followed by maybe roast lobster salad or Dover sole – but they offer first-rate steaks and racks of lamb too. The charming owner splits his time between the kitchen and the front of house.

CLOSING TIMES
Closed 25-26 December, Sunday and Monday

PRICES
Meals: a la carte £ 22/36

Typical Dishes
Grilled half-shell Queenie scallops
Monkfish with a curried prawn risotto
Turkish delight ice cream

5 mi east of Barnard Castle by A 67, on B 6274. Parking.

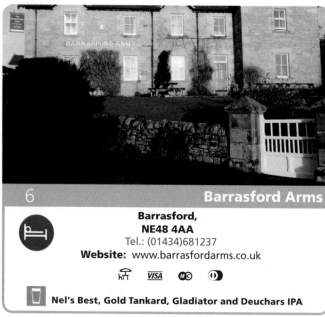

6 **Barrasford Arms**

Barrasford,
NE48 4AA
Tel.: (01434)681237
Website: www.barrasfordarms.co.uk

VISA

Nel's Best, Gold Tankard, Gladiator and Deuchars IPA

In the heart of the Northumbrian countryside, close to Kielder Water and Hadrian's Wall, sits this family-run 19C stone inn, providing an ideal base for exploring the North Tyne Valley. Retaining its traditional character, the pub provides the perfect home from home. The cosy fire is a huge draw, as are the regular vegetable, darts and quoits competitions, but the star attraction is the food. Menus differ between lunch and dinner; the former being a touch less formal. Local rib-eye is a permanent feature, as is the twice-baked cheese soufflé, and many come for the local game, which is handled deftly. The owner works closely with his suppliers to ensure that the ingredients remain tip-top. Comfortable bedrooms are sensibly priced.

CLOSING TIMES
Closed January, Christmas, Monday Feb-March, Sunday dinner and Monday lunch

PRICES
Meals: £ 16 (weekday lunch) and a la carte £ 22/30

7 rooms: £ 50/85

Typical Dishes

Twice-baked Cheddar cheese soufflé

Rib-eye steak & chips

Sticky pistachio meringue

7 mi north of Hexham signed off A 6079. Parking.

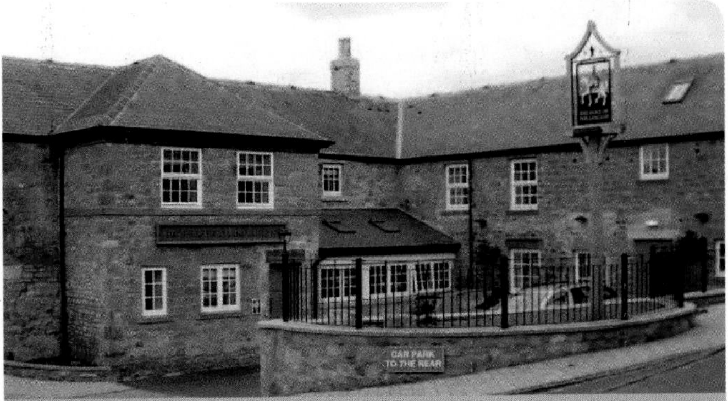

7 Duke of Wellington

Newton,
Corbridge, NE43 7UL
Tel.: (01661)844446
Website: www.thedukeofwellingtoninn.co.uk

VISA MC

Timothy Taylor Landlord, Tyneside Blonde and regularly changing guest ales

Dating from the early 1600s, this is reputedly the oldest licensed premises in the county and, despite being tucked away down a twisty single track, it's clear that a good few people know about it. The first thing you'll notice as you approach is the great valley view and when the sun's shining, a spot on the terrace is definitely the place to be. Inside it has a smart, modern country style, with a large, open-fired bar displaying stone walls and a more formal dining room with its tables already laid. Breakfast includes local eggs Benedict; lunch features pub classics; while dinner offers more interesting dishes such as rabbit and tarragon terrine or saddle of roe deer. Stylish, luxurious bedrooms come with character, courtesy of exposed beams.

CLOSING TIMES
Open daily
booking advisable

PRICES
Meals: a la carte £ 22/32
7 rooms: £ 90/135

Typical Dishes

Smoked salmon with hot potato salad
Grilled plaice with samphire, cockles, clams and braised celery
Chocolate cake with vanilla ice cream

3 mi east of Corbridge by A 6350 and A 69 in the centre of the village. Parking.

Great Whittington

8 Queens Head Inn

Great Whittington,
NE19 2HP
Tel.: (01434)672267
Website: www.the-queens-head-inn.co.uk

VISA

Wylam Brewery Gold Tankard, High House Farm Brewery Maften Magic

A wonderful mural above the fire in the bar depicts the Queens Head Inn as it once was; in fact, this cosy room was at one time all that existed of what is considered by some to be the oldest inn in Northumberland. Its 400 year old thick brick walls have now been breached and the rear extension houses a dining room filled with bookshelves, old farming implements and general bric à brac. The lunchtime menu offers anything from filled stotties to duck spring rolls, while the evening menu might mean homemade game terrine, twice-baked soufflé, lamb's liver and bacon or honey-roast Barbary duck; with lamb and Galloway beef supplied by the farm next door. Service is as friendly as it comes, and a couple of courses shouldn't break the bank.

CLOSING TIMES
Closed Sunday dinner, Monday and Tuesday

PRICES
Meals: a la carte £ 17/33

Typical Dishes
Ham hock terrine
Chicken stuffed with goat's cheese & Parma ham
Key lime pie

6 mi north of Corbridge by A 68 off B 6318. Parking.

9 **Feathers Inn**

Hedley on the Hill,
NE43 7SW
Tel.: (01661)843607
Website: www.thefeathers.net

VISA

Mordue Workie Ticket, Wylam Northern Kite, Consett Red Dust and Hexhamshire Devil's Elbow

All three rooms in this characterful village centre pub have their bookshelves crammed with cookbooks and their walls filled with photos of those who supply their produce, both of which suggest that this is a place which takes its food seriously. The kitchen certainly does things properly, whether that's making its own black pudding or preparing the popular game dishes. The food is generous in both flavour and size and seasonality plays a large part – the menu changes on a daily basis and it's worth exploring the selection of local cheeses. The pub has a warm and welcoming feel, thanks to its large central fireplace and stove and feels genuinely part of the local community. It also offers really nice views of the surrounding countryside.

CLOSING TIMES
Open daily

PRICES
Meals: a la carte £ 20/29

Typical Dishes

Pea, mint & asparagus terrine

Slow-cooked shoulder of local roe deer

Burnt Northumbrian cream

6 mi north of Consett by A 694, B 6309 and minor road.
Parking.

10 Rat Inn

Anick,
Hexham, NE46 4LN
Tel.: (01434)602814
Website: www.theratinn.com

VISA AE

Wylam Brewery Gold, Allendale Curlew's High House, Hexhamshire Devils Water and Mordues Workie Ticket

A) Rat catchers once used this as a meeting place, B) It was once home to a large rat, C) The local snitch lived here during the Jacobite rebellion. Unfortunately nobody knows the answer as to how this 18C drovers' inn got its name, so just sit back and enjoy the pleasant Tyne valley views and tasty, wholesome cooking. Situated in a small hillside hamlet, it's the perfect place to escape the rat race of the city, with its multi-levelled garden boasting arbours and picnic sets, and a traditional interior displaying wooden beams and an open range. The daily blackboard menu is concise but covers a good range of dishes, from pub classics such as cottage pie to more ambitious rack of lamb for two. Produce is fresh, good quality and locally sourced.

CLOSING TIMES
Closed Sunday dinner and Monday except bank holidays lunch

PRICES
Meals: a la carte £ 21/31

Typical Dishes

Free range duck eggs en cocotte
Roast Northumbrian rib of beef for two
Ginger sponge

1.5 mi north of Hexham off A 69. Parking.

11

Red Lion Inn

Main Rd,
Milfield, NE71 6JD
Tel.: (01668)216224
Website: www.redlioninn-milfield.co.uk

VISA

Wylam ales, Black Sheep and regularly changing local guest ale

This classical stone pub started life in the mid-1700s as a drovers' inn before becoming a stopping point for the mail stagecoach between 1785 and 1835. It really is the heart of the village, so if you'd rather not catch up with the latest sporting events, head for the open-fired dining room instead of the bar. The menu has a traditional feel and offers plenty of choice, showcasing produce from both England and across the border. Dishes range from prawn cocktail to scallops with black pudding, the Shetland mussels are not to be missed and the hearty homemade burger has become a cult dish. Specials are chalked up the board and if you manage to make it to pudding you'll be rewarded with a tasty nursery selection. Bedrooms are simple and homely.

CLOSING TIMES
Open daily
booking advisable

PRICES
Meals: a la carte £ 18/25
2 rooms: £ 25/50

Typical Dishes
Wild mushroom bruschetta with poached egg
Rump steak, chunky chips, onion rings & tomato
Homemade meringues with rhubarb

7 mi southeast of Coldstream by A 697. In the village centre.
Parking

Maltby

12 Chadwicks Inn

High Ln,
Maltby, TS8 0B9
Tel.: (01642)590300
Website: www.chadwicksinnmaltby.co.uk

VISA MC

Copper Dragon Brewery

Originally named The Pathfinder, this pub dates back over 200 years and was where the Spitfire pilots used to stop for a noggin before flying out on their missions. It's now run by local celebrity Gary Gill, who, when he's not at the pub, can be found commentating on regional BBC football matches. In warmer weather find a spot in the garden or on the sheltered patio area; in winter, head for the large, open-fired bar or either of the two dining rooms with their smartly laid, polished tables. Choose between sandwiches or a daily changing set menu at lunchtime, and from a selection of tapas dishes like Girolle salad or truffled venison in the afternoons. The main à la carte features ambitious, intricate dishes and service is fittingly formal.

CLOSING TIMES
Closed 25 December, 1 January and Monday
booking advisable

PRICES
Meals: £ 16 (lunch) and a la carte £ 26/40

Typical Dishes
King scallops & Thai spiced white crab beignet
Rump of lamb & braised lamb breast with sweet potato purée
Strawberry jelly & Chantilly cream

3 mi south of Middlesborough by A 19 and A 1045. Parking at rear.

13 Broad Chare

25 Broad Chare,
Newcastle upon Tyne, NE1 3DQ
Tel.: (0191)2112144
Website: www.thebroadchare.co.uk

VISA MC

Wylam Gold Tankard and Rocket Best Bitter, Honkers Goose Island, Trashy Blonde and Black Sheep

Owned by Terry Laybourne and set next to its sister operation Caffé Vivo, Broad Chare really hit the ground running. It's located in the heart of the city, close to the theatre and law courts and, with its 'Proper Beer, Proper Food' motto, has become a hit with the locals. The snug ground floor with its low level stool seating offers a choice of over 42 ales and a bar snack menu featuring the likes of Scotch eggs, cauliflower with curried mayonnaise and deep-fried pig's ears – affectionately named 'Geordie Tapas'. Dining also takes place upstairs, where you'll find everything from a tasty 'on toast' selection to hearty daily specials such as steak and kidney pudding, followed by tasty nursery desserts, including steamed sponge with custard.

CLOSING TIMES
Closed 25 December and Sunday dinner
booking advisable

PRICES
Meals: a la carte £ 19/34

Typical Dishes
Hand-raised pork pie
Steak & kidney pudding
Steamed syrup sponge with custard

In the city centre. Parking nearby.

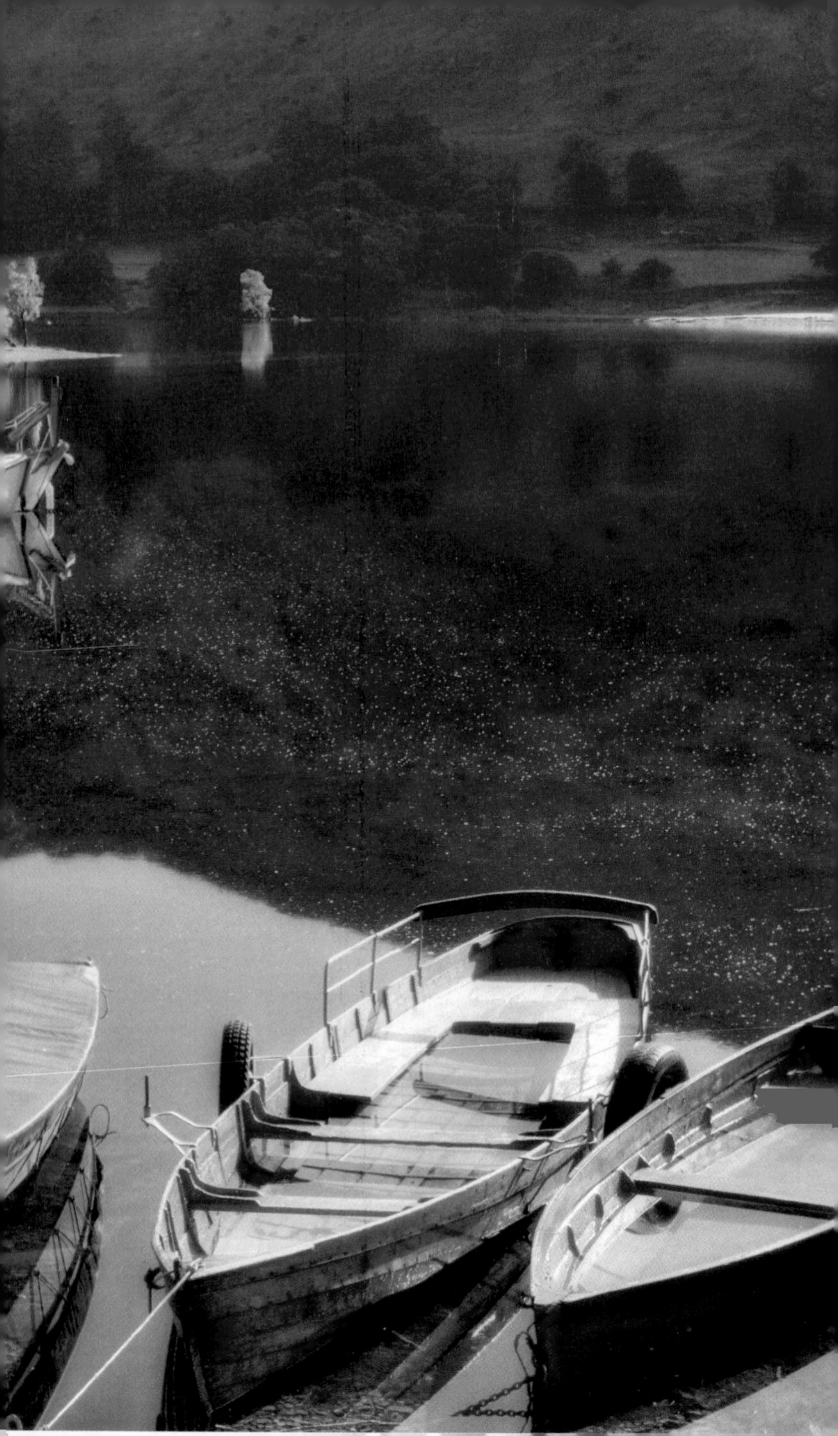

Energised by Liverpool's swagger as 2008's European City of Culture, the north west feels like a region reborn. Dovetailed by the confident sophistication of a reinvigorated Manchester, the country's oldest industrial heartland boasts an impressive cultural profile. And yet arty urban centres are a million miles away from the rural grandeur of the region: trails and paths criss-cross the area all the way from the Solway Firth to Cheshire. Cumbria is a walker's paradise: from Hadrian's Wall to the glories of the Lake District, and along the vast shoreline of Morecambe Bay with its rich gathering of waders and wildfowl, there's a vivid contrast in scenery. The architectural landscape of the region covers the ages, too. Lancaster Castle reverberates to the footsteps of ancient soldiers, while Chester's walled city of medieval buildings is a true gem. Blackpool is now Europe's biggest seaside resort while the flavour of the north west is hotpot, black pudding and Morecambe Bay shrimps.

5 Pubs without bedrooms
9 Pubs with bedrooms
Scotland
NORTH
North East
Yorkshire & the Humber
Dumfries
Carlisle
Workington
Whitehaven
Barrow-in-Furness
Morecambe
Lancaster
Penrith
Keswick
Kendal
Ambleside
Windermere
Cumbria
Lake District
Cumbrian Mountains
Solway Firth
Wigtown Bay
Luce Bay
Mull of Galloway
Burrow Head
St. Bees Head
Point of Ayre
ISLE OF MAN
Douglas
Ramsey
Peel
Ballaugh
Snaefell
Port Erin
Port St. Mary
Castletown
Ronaldsway
Stranraer
Glenluce
Drummore
Port William
Wigtown
Whithorn
Isle of Whithorn
Gatehouse of Fleet
Castle Douglas
Kirkcudbright
Ringford
Dalbeattie
New Abbey
Auchencairn
New Galloway
Lockerbie
Langholm
Canonbie
Longtown
Gretna
Annan
Bowness-on-Solway
Brampton
Greenhead
Hadrian's Wall
Hexham
Corbridge
Chollerford
NEWCASTLE UPON TYNE
Alston
Silloth
Abbey Town
Wigton
Thursby
Aspatria
Bothel
Maryport
Cockermouth
Skiddaw
Derwent water
Buttermere
Frizington
Egremont
Gosforth
Scafell Pikes
Grasmere
Coniston
Bowness
Patterdale
Ullswater
Broughton-in-Furness
Greenodd
Ulverston
Dalton
Millom
Grange-Over-Sands
Carnforth
Appleby
Cross Fell
Brough
Kirkby Stephen
Orton
Tebay
Sedbergh
Whernside
Kirkby Lonsdale
Ingleton
Barnard Castle
Middleton-in-Teesdale
Bowes
Wolsingham
Reeth
Hawes
Leyburn
Threshfield
Settle
Yorkshire Dales
Forest Park

IRISH SEA
BLACKPOOL
Fleetwood
Cleveleys
Lytham St. Anne's
Southport
Ainsdale
Formby
LIVERPOOL
Liverpool Bay
Bootle
Wallasey
Hoylake
Birkenhead
Bebington
LANCASHIRE
Preston
Blackburn
Clitheroe
Gisburn
Padiham
Burnley
Nelson
Colne
Keighley
Skipton
BRADFORD
Halifax
Accrington
Rawtenstall
Todmorden
Brighouse
Rochdale
Leyland
Darwen
WEST
Bury
Bolton
Ormskirk
Skelmersdale
Wigan
Leigh
St. Helens
Warrington
Widnes
Runcorn
Altrincham
Oldham
MANCHESTER
Ashton-under-Lyne
Hyde
Stockport
Knutsford
Wilmslow
Whaley Bridge
Buxton
Macclesfield
Congleton
Northwich
Frodsham
Winsford
Middlewich
Sandbach
Crewe
Nantwich
Tarporley
Chester
Ellesmere Port
CHESHIRE
Kidsgrove
Little Moreton Hall
Leek
Newcastle-under-Lyme
STOKE-ON-TRENT
Audlem
Uttoxeter
East Midlands
West Midlands
Whitchurch
Wem
Hodnet
Wrexham
Wrecsam
Ruabon
Ellesmere
Oswestry
Llangollen
Corwen
Bala
Berwyn
Wales
Mold
Yr Wyddgrug
Flint
Fflint
Queensferry
Holywell
Mostyn
Prestatyn
Rhyl
Denbigh
Dinbych
St. Asaph
Abergele
Colwyn Bay / Bae Colwyn
Llandudno
Great Ormes Head
Conwy
Penmaenmawr
Llanfairfechan
Llanrwst
Betws-y-Coed
Capel Curig
Carnedd Llewelyn
Bethesda
Bangor
Beaumaris
Menai Bridge
Llangefni
ANGLESEY
Amlwch
Llanerchymedd
Holyhead / Caergybi
Holy Island
Rhosneigr
Isle of Anglesey
Newborough
Caernarfon
Caernarfon Bay
Llanberis
Snowdon
Snowdonia
Beddgelert
Blaenau Ffestiniog
Ffestiniog
Penrhyndeudraeth
Porthmadog
Criccieth
Pwllheli
Abersoch
Aberdaron
Nefyn
Lleyn Peninsula
Harlech
GWYNEDD
Cerrigydrudion
Penmachno
National
and
Belfast
Dublin
Larne
Long Preston
Ilkley
Bingley
Huddersfield
Holmfirth
Peak District
Bakewell

1 **The Wizard**

Macclesfield Rd,
Alderley Edge, SK10 4UB
Tel.: (01625)584000
Website: www.ainscoughs.co.uk

VISA MC AE

Thwaites Original and Storm Brewery guest ales

With its flag floors, wood beams and open fires, this 200 year old pub is full of character and charm. Being dog friendly, it attracts its fair share of walkers, and its mix of drinkers and diners – and the resulting vibrant atmosphere – make it feel like a proper pub. Small tapas-style plates like grilled halloumi or devilled chipolatas give drinkers something to nibble on. There are lunchtime sandwiches and pub favourites like pies, burgers and beef dripping chips, as well as more substantial dishes like lamb hotpot or roast pork belly, with the occasional Mediterranean influence. Cooking makes good use of seasonal, local produce and is flavourful, straightforward and very good value. Service is polite and attentive, if rather too formal.

CLOSING TIMES
Closed 25 December

PRICES
Meals: a la carte £ 25/38

Typical Dishes

Caesar salad, fresh anchovies, bacon & parmesan

Rump of lamb Niçoise

Rum & raisin crème brûlée

1.25 mi southeast of Alderley Edge on B 5087.

2 **Yew Tree Inn**

Long Ln,
Spurstow, Bunbury, CW6 9RD
Tel.: (01829)260274
Website: www.theyewtreebunbury.com

VISA

Stonehouse Station Bitter and four guest ales

This handsome part red brick, part black and white timbered pub is the younger sister of the Bull at Shocklach and upon opening, was welcomed by the locals with outstretched arms. Once inside, you'll find it isn't as big as you first thought – but there's room enough for one and all, whether that's locals with pints gathered to organise the latest village events or diners attending one of the regular themed evenings. Find a seat in the central bar or one of smaller rooms boasting wood and quarry tile flooring, mahogany panels and open fires. Extensive menus offer local and homemade produce, with dishes ranging from fish pie to braised ox cheeks; while the black pudding salad, chips in dripping and Cheshire Brie for two are must tries.

CLOSING TIMES
Open daily

PRICES
Meals: a la carte £ 23/28

Typical Dishes

Ballottine of rabbit with prune purée

Crisp belly pork, black pudding hash & creamed cabbage

Manchester tart

7.5 mi northwest of Nantwich by A 51, A 534 and A 49. Parking.

3

Fox and Barrel

Foxbank,
Cotebrook, CW6 9DZ
Tel.: (01829)760529
Website: www.foxandbarrel.co.uk

VISA

Deuchars IPA, Moorhouse Best, and Tinners

With wood-panelled walls filled with framed pictures and shelves lined with books, you could be mistaken for thinking you're in a Brunning and Price pub, but then that's probably because the owners have both worked for the group in the past. The front bar with its wood burning stove is very much the drinkers' domain, while the smart terrace and large garden, complete with vintage tractor, attract one and all. Menus change virtually daily and offer plenty of originality and interest; you might find twice-baked cheese soufflé followed by loin of venison with spiced red cabbage, alongside old favourites like fish and chips. Dishes are generously proportioned, neatly presented and sensibly priced – and there's a good list of wines by the glass too.

CLOSING TIMES
Closed dinner 25-26 December and 1 January

PRICES
Meals: a la carte £ 23/30

Typical Dishes
Oxtail risotto
Pan-fried cod loin
Eton mess

On A 49 northeast of Tarporley. Parking.

4

Pheasant Inn

Higher Burwardsley,
CH3 9PF
Tel.: (01829)770434
Website: www.thepheasantinn.co.uk

VISA MC AE

Weetwood Best, Weetwood Eastgate, Weetwood Cheshire Cat and Spitting Feathers Farmhouse Ale

Set on a large sandstone outcrop in the middle of the Cheshire plains, this characterful stone pub boasts great views over the surrounding area. Popular with walkers following the Sandstone Trail, it boasts reclaimed beams, stone columns and gas fires. One room is fairly pubby with a leather-furnished snug; the other, similar in style but with more formal seating. The huge windows are a real feature – and tables by them are extremely sought-after – but the best place to sit is on the terrace itself. Extensive daily menus offer refined pub favourites, as well as some Mediterranean-influenced dishes, and sandwiches are available throughout the afternoon. Spacious, beamed bedrooms in the main building; more modern rooms with views in the barn.

CLOSING TIMES
Open daily

PRICES
Meals: a la carte £ 17/30
12 rooms: £ 75/150

Typical Dishes

Prawn & crayfish salad
Lemon, thyme & apple stuffed belly pork with ratatouille
Plum Bakewell tart

2.5 mi southeast of Tattenhall. Parking.

5 Duke of Portland

Penny's Ln,
Lach Dennis, CW9 8SY
Tel.: (01606)46264
Website: www.dukeofportland.com

VISA MC AE D

Jennings Cock a Hoop, Marston's Pedigree, Brakspear's Oxford Gold and Ringwood Best Bitter

This cream-washed inn sits on the main road through the village, welcoming drinkers and diners alike. The former tend to gather in the high-ceilinged main bar or the relaxing, leather-furnished lounge. The latter have two choices: a raised area close to the bar and – the more popular option – a smart, contemporary side room which houses a mounted stag's head, shot in 1931 by the Duke of Portland. The lengthy à la carte menu offers dishes that won't scare the horses; the daily specials provide a little more interest. Good quality, organic ingredients are sourced from local farmers and artisan suppliers, who are proudly name-checked on the menu. A paved rear terrace offers an appealing alfresco option should the weather choose to acquiesce.

CLOSING TIMES
Open daily

PRICES
Meals: £ 17 and a la carte £ 19/30

Typical Dishes

Chilli beef fillet & garlic mash
Middle-Eastern spiced sea bass fillet
Warm chocolate brownie

3.5 mi west of Northwich by B 5082. Parking.

6 **Bells of Peover**

The Cobbles,
Lower Peover, WA16 9PZ
Tel.: (01565)722269

VISA MC AE

Robinsons Brewery Dizzy Blonde and XB

So, why does this refurbished 16C former coaching inn have the Stars and Stripes flying over it? Because, apparently, Generals Eisenhower and Patton were stationed nearby and were regulars. And the Bells? No, not from the church tower but the name of a family who once owned it. These days the pub offers a range of options: from scrumpy and snacks to a full culinary extravaganza. In the bar and the two ground floor dining rooms you'll find a large, appealing menu of classic pub dishes, done well. Up three steps and you enter into 'fine dining' territory, where the ingredients are of a more luxurious (and pricey) nature. Service can be a little over formal, particularly downstairs, but should relax a little over time.

CLOSING TIMES
Open daily

PRICES
Meals: a la carte £ 21/42

Typical Dishes

Potted langoustines & shrimps

Chump of lamb with mint sauce

Strawberry & Pimm's trifle

Off the B 5081 which runs through the village. Parking.

7

Church Green

Higher Ln,
Lymm, WA13 0AP
Tel.: (01925)752068
Website: www.thechurchgreen.co.uk

VISA MC AE

Old Speckled Hen and Deuchars IPA

Standing on the green next to St Mary's Church, the original inn burnt down and was later replaced by this double gable-fronted Victorian pub beside Lymm Dam. The experienced chef-owner, Aiden Byrne (who appeared on BBC2's the Great British Menu) is supported by a pleasant, well-structured team, and takes pride in the pub's kitchen garden, which supplies everything from beetroot to soft fruits. The open-plan bar and restaurant are decorated in modern browns and creams and there's a pleasant conservatory and attractive decked terrace to the rear. Throughout the afternoon, the lounge-bar offers simple, pub-style dishes but things step up a gear in the evening with more ambitious offerings such as pork with scallops or beetroot poached salmon.

CLOSING TIMES
Open daily
booking essential

PRICES
Meals: £ 40 and a la carte £ 24/40

Typical Dishes

Foie gras with hazelnut risotto
Wing rib of beef
Caramel parfait, milk and honey

7 mi west of Altrincham by A 56. Parking.

8 Swettenham Arms

Swettenham,
CW12 2LF
Tel.: (01477)571284
Website: www.swettenhamarms.co.uk

VISA MC AE

Tatton Brewery, Landlord, Bollington Best, Sharp's Doom Bar, Pride of Pendle, Black Sheep

If you rely on your sat nav you may well end up in the middle of the local ford, but this pub's well worth the search once you find it. Formerly a nunnery, it's been in the capable hands of the Cunninghams for many years now; although there's still the occasional ghostly sighting of a nun. Its beaten copper bar, welcoming open fireplaces and shiny horse brasses mean that tradition reigns, which is a surefire hit with both drinkers and diners. The seasonally changing menu provides plenty of choice, from sharing platters and satisfying pub classics to carefully prepared, well-presented restaurant-style dishes, such as Boudin sausage or rack of local lamb with basil mousse. Find time to stroll around the lavender meadow or RHS arboretum.

CLOSING TIMES
Open daily

PRICES
Meals: a la carte £ 17/40

Typical Dishes

Black pudding, Scotch egg, watercress salad
Poached fillet of wild sea trout with a lemon sabayon sauce
Peach Melba

Between Holmes Chapel and Congleton, signposted off the A 54. Parking.

9 **Drunken Duck Inn**

Barngates,
Ambleside, LA22 0NG
Tel.: (01539)436347
Website: www.drunkenduckinn.co.uk

VISA

Barngates Brewery: Chesters Strong & Ugly, Tag Lag, Cracker, Mothbag, Westmorland Gold and Red Bull Terrier

Situated in the heart of the beautiful Lakeland countryside, this attractive inn takes its name from an old legend about a landlady, some ducks and a leaky beer barrel. The popular fire-lit bar is the cosiest place to sit, among hop bines, pictures of the hunt and old brewery advertisements; but there are also two more formal dining rooms. The same menu is served throughout, offering simple lunches and much more elaborate dinners, with prices to match; cooking is generous and service, attentive. Ales come from the on-site micro-brewery and are made with water from their own tarn. Boutique, country house bedrooms – some with patios – boast extremely comfy beds and country views. Afternoon tea can be taken in the lounge or residents' garden.

CLOSING TIMES
Closed 25 December
booking essential

PRICES
Meals: a la carte £ 22/46
17 rooms: £ 117/295

Typical Dishes

Duck cottage pie
Beef fillet, shallot purée, creamed potatoes
Chocolate parfait

3 mi southwest of Ambleside by A 593 and B 5286 on Tarn Hows road. By the crossroads at the top of Duck Hill. Parking.

10 Hare & Hounds

Bowland Bridge,
LA11 6NN
Tel.: (015395)68333
Website: www.hareandhoundsbowlandbridge.co.uk

VISA

Guest ales from Cumbrian breweries

This charming 17C Lakeland pub is situated in the delightful village of Bowland Bridge, where Arthur Ransome wrote the book 'Swallows and Amazons'. There's a large terrace with chunky wooden tables to the front, leading through into a rustic, open-fired inner with stone walls, black and white village photos and exposed beams draped with hop bines. Menus offer typical, hearty, pub-style dishes – such as homemade pies or Lakeland hotpot with black pudding and home-pickled cabbage – and much of the produce is locally sourced. There's also a fine selection of ales to choose from, including 'Hair of the Dog', which is specially brewed for them by a nearby brewery. Bedrooms are well-equipped and elegant with smart bathrooms; some have roll-top baths.

CLOSING TIMES
Open daily

PRICES
Meals: a la carte £ 22/27
3 rooms: £ 80

Typical Dishes

Cumberland sausage & black pudding terrine
Beef & ale pie
Passion fruit crème brûlée

In the village centre. Parking.

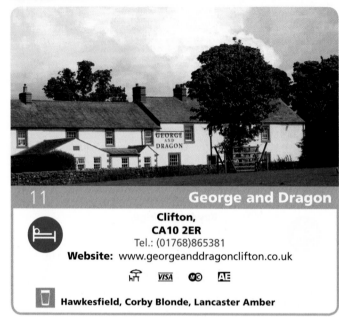

11 George and Dragon

Clifton,
CA10 2ER
Tel.: (01768)865381
Website: www.georgeanddragonclifton.co.uk

VISA MC AE

Hawkesfield, Corby Blonde, Lancaster Amber

Enter The George and Dragon and you'll soon realise you've come somewhere a bit special. It's owned by prominent Cumbrian landowners, the Lowther family, and the food is as fresh as it gets, with organic meats including lamb and Shorthorn beef from their estate's farms, seasonal game from the surrounding woods and moors, and vegetables from the kitchen gardens. Dishes might include fish pie, chicken livers on toast or grilled local black pudding, and cooking is simple and effective. Although fully refurbished, the 18C coaching inn has lost none of its traditional character, helped along nicely by flagstones, fires, hop bines, rugs and sofas; plus photos which tell tales of the Lowther Estate from days long past. Smart, modern bedrooms.

CLOSING TIMES
closed 26 December

PRICES
Meals: a la carte £ 22/39
10 rooms: £ 75

Typical Dishes

Twice-baked cheese soufflé
Venison liver, wild garlic mashed potato & onion gravy
Crème brûlée

On A6 in centre of village. Parking.

12 **Punch Bowl Inn**

Crosthwaite,
LA8 8HR
Tel.: (01539)568237
Website: www.the-punchbowl.co.uk

VISA

Barngates Bewery - Westmorland Gold, Tag Lag, Cumberland Brewery - Corby Blonde

Nestled among the hills in the heart of the picturesque Lyth Valley, this attractive 17C inn enjoys a truly delightful setting. The views are glorious, but the pub itself is charming too, boasting cosy open fires, exposed wooden beams and trailing hop bines. Dining takes place in the rustic bar and more formal restaurant; lunch features some interesting takes on classical dishes, such as venison sausage and mash or macaroni cheese with truffles – but the kitchen's ambition is most evident at dinner, where dishes display a degree of complexity that you wouldn't usually find in a pub. Individually styled bedrooms boast quality linen and smart bathrooms with roll-top baths and fluffy towels; 'Noble' features twin tubs and 'Danson', the best views.

CLOSING TIMES
Open daily

PRICES
Meals: a la carte £ 21/39
9 rooms: £ 120/305

Typical Dishes

Glazed Lancashire cheese soufflé
Roasted duck breast in honey
Bread & butter pudding

5.25 mi west of Kendal by All Hallows Lane; next to the church. Parking.

Kirkby Lonsdale

13 Sun Inn

6 Market St,
Kirkby Lonsdale, LA6 2AU
Tel.: (015242)71965
Website: www.sun-inn.info

VISA MC

Timothy Taylor Landlord, Hawkshead Best Bitter, Thwaites Wainwrights and Kirkby Lonsdale Monumental Blond

'Sourced locally' means exactly that at the 17C Sun Inn: meat regularly comes from the butcher down the road; cheese comes from the famous Churchmouse cheese shop next door and if lamb is on the menu, you can be pretty certain it recently frolicked in a nearby field. Everything you would look for in a pub is here; from the rustically refurbished restaurant with its seasonal menu of appealingly presented, generously proportioned dishes, to the busy locals bar with its scrubbed wooden floors, comfy seats and open fire; from the splendid selection of real ales and the cleverly formulated wine list to the hands-on owners and their competent staff. Immaculately kept bedrooms have a modern feel, with great lighting and good quality linen.

CLOSING TIMES
Closed Monday lunch

PRICES
Meals: £ 20 (lunch)
and a la carte £ 29/34

11 rooms: £ 72/154

Typical Dishes

Ham hock terrine
Welsh sea bass with clam chowder sauce
Dark chocolate fondant

5.5 mi southeast of Junction 36 on M6. Long stay car park in Booth Rd.

14 **Black Swan**

Kirkby Stephen,
CA17 4NG
Tel.: (01539)623204
Website: www.blackswanhotel.com

VISA

Black Sheep Ale & Bitter, John Smiths & guest ales

This part-Victorian, family-run inn really is at the centre of the local community – it's not just the only pub, but also the only shop in this pleasant village; and it's so remotely set that the staff are trained as the first response team for local 999 calls too. The pub itself boasts a bar, two dining rooms and a linen-laid restaurant, while over the road, a huge garden stretches down to Scandal Beck – providing the location for their annual music festival. The same menu is served throughout and features filling pub classics, with more restaurant-style specials appearing in the evening. Staff remain polite and friendly, even at the busiest times. Cosy bedrooms are largely antique-furnished; one is more modern and boasts a four-poster.

CLOSING TIMES
Closed 25 December

PRICES
Meals: a la carte £ 18/29
15 rooms: £ 60/125

Typical Dishes

Terrine of smoked trout, mackerel & salmon

Pan-fried lamb's liver with smoked bacon

Vanilla & white chocolate panna cotta

5 mi southwest of Brough by A 685. Parking.

Lupton

15 Plough

Cow Brow,
Lupton, LA6 1PJ
Tel.: (015395)67700
Website: www.theploughatlupton.co.uk

VISA MC AE

Kirkby Lonsdale Monumental, Jennings Cumberland Ale, Coniston Bluebird Bitter

Younger sister to the Punch Bowl at Crosthwaite, the Plough is set on the main road that links the Lake District to North Yorkshire and, like its sister pub, is starting to gain a reputation in the local area. There's a cosy, homely feel to the place, which is made up of two neutrally hued rooms filled with an assortment of quality antique tables and comfy sofas set around a wood burning stove. The cheery, knowledgeable team serve up a pleasing mix of pub and restaurant-style dishes: you'll find a selection of grills, alongside a list of tasty small plates – such as Queenie scallops or Serrano ham – that can be mixed and matched as you please with an enticing array of side dishes. Smart, individually styled bedrooms complete the picture.

CLOSING TIMES
Open daily

PRICES
Meals: a la carte £ 18/29
5 rooms: £ 100/195

Typical Dishes

Courgette fritters, honey & Lancashire cheese
Spiced lamb shank
Mixed berry and rhubarb crumble

4.75 mi northwest of Kirkby Lonsdale on A 65.

16 **Highwayman**

Nether Burrow,
LA6 2RJ
Tel.: (01524)273338
Website: www.highwaymaninn.co.uk

VISA MC AE

Thwaites Original, Lancaster Bomber and Wainwright

It's rumoured that this sizeable 18C coaching inn with its lovely terrace was once the midnight haunt of the local highwaymen. Set on the border of three counties – Cumbria, Lancashire and Yorkshire – it makes the most of its setting, with produce so local that a meal almost constitutes a geography lesson. The extensive menu notes the provenance of every ingredient, while on the back page a large map locates and names suppliers. Cooking is hearty and rustic with a comforting feel; you might find Thornby Moor Dairy cheese on toast with Sillfield Farm sweet-cured bacon, followed by heather-reared Lonk lamb Lancashire hotpot and then jam roly poly. Order from the efficient team at the open-fired, stone-floored bar or at any of the pay points.

CLOSING TIMES
Closed 25 December

PRICES
Meals: a la carte £ 19/38

Typical Dishes

Twice-baked chestnut mushroom soufflé
Herdwick mutton shepherd's pie
Elderflower syllabub & jelly

2 mi south of Kirkby Lonsdale by A 65 and A 683. Parking.

Sizergh

17 Strickland Arms

Sizergh,
LA8 8DZ
Tel.: (01539)561010
Website: www.thestricklandarms.com

VISA

Lancaster Bomber, Wainwrights, Langdale Tup, Coniston Bluebird, Hawkshead Bitter, Loweswater Gold

Originally the coach house for next door Sizergh Castle, this sizeable building dates back over 250 years and attracts a diverse range of clientele, from local workers, to visitors from the nearby caravan park and even the Strickland family from the aforementioned castle. There's a characterful, shabby-chic feel to the place and always a few tables reserved by the bar for the locals, who like to sit over a real ale or two. Menus feature classical pub dishes, with daily specials chalked on the board; maybe goat's cheese tart, potted shrimps or steak and ale pie – and all in generous portions. Thursdays are fish nights, Sundays often feature live music and there's a popular beer festival in August with a hog roast, folk music and entertainers.

CLOSING TIMES
Closed 25 December

PRICES
Meals: a la carte £ 20/28

Typical Dishes

Potted Morecambe Bay shrimps

Sweet-cured pork loin steak with local black pudding

Sticky toffee pudding

3 mi southwest of Kendal by A 391. Parking.

18 Queen's Head

Troutbeck,
LA23 1PW
Tel.: (01539)432174
Website: www.queensheadtroutbeck.co.uk

VISA AE

Ginger Tom, XB, Unicorn, Dizzy Blonde, Double Hop, Cumbrian Way

This passionately run pub is found in the most delightful setting and makes a great stop off point if you're heading for the Kirkstone Pass. It's amazingly characterful inside, consisting of a beamed bar with an unusual 'four-poster' counter (lined with a huge selection of whiskies), and several interlinking rooms which boast a vast array of memorabilia. Seating varies from heavy wooden settles to high-backed leather chairs but the best spot has to be the terrace with its fantastic hill views. The extensive menu changes six times a year and ranges from nibbles and their fun signature dish, a chip butty with homemade tomato sauce, through to cottage pie and fillet steak. Smart bedrooms boast strong comforts. Rooms 10 and 11 have the best views.

CLOSING TIMES
Open daily

PRICES
Meals: £ 20 and a la carte £ 24/42
15 rooms: £ 75

Typical Dishes

Foie gras & chicken liver parfait
Confit of duck leg
Lemon posset with Chardonnay jelly

4 mi north of Windermere by A 592. Parking.

19 **Brown Horse Inn**

Winster,
LA23 3NR
Tel.: (01539)443443
Website: www.thebrownhorseinn.co.uk

VISA

Winster Valley Brewery's Best Bitter, Old School, Hurdler, Lytham Lowther

This simple coaching inn has always been popular with the locals; but even more so since the creation of its on-site brewery. It has a shabby-chic style, with flagged floors, antique dressers and a real mix of furniture. In one corner, a miniature model of the bar (made by one of the regulars) and a London Underground map of local pubs provide talking points; while the split-level terrace is a real draw. Seasonal menus feature produce from the fields out back and game comes from shoots they organise themselves. Dishes are designed with hungry walkers in mind; the blackboard specials are a little more adventurous and often include home-reared pork. Bedrooms are a mix of classical and boutique styles; the latter have French windows and terraces.

CLOSING TIMES
Open daily

PRICES
Meals: a la carte £ 22/33
9 rooms: £ 50/100

Typical Dishes

Trio of smoked fish
Breast of duck, duck toast, blood orange caramel
Strawberry crème brûlée

4 mi south of Windermere by A 5074. Parking.

20 **Derby Arms**

Witherslack,
LA11 6RH
Tel.: (015395)52207
Website: www.thederbyarms.co.uk

VISA

Wainwright, Bomber, Hawkshead, Jolly Boys Indurance, Celebration

This substantial 19C coaching inn is named after the owners of the nearby Halecat Estate, who have been the Earls of Derby since 1485. Located on the main road from Kendal to Ulverston, it was rescued after several years standing empty, and is now a characterful shabby-chic style of place, with rug-covered floors, open fires and hop-hung beams. A bowl of water welcomes your four-legged friends, there's a small community shop filled with local produce to the rear and theme nights are common. Cooking is rustic yet refined, offering the likes of pâté or black pudding followed by steak pie or sausage and mash; with treacle tart or sticky toffee pudding to follow. Classical bedrooms display antique furniture; some boast views or roll-top baths.

CLOSING TIMES
Open daily

PRICES
Meals: £ 10 (lunch and early dinner)/16 and a la carte £ 22/32

6 rooms: £ 50/85

Typical Dishes
Homemade duck & chicken liver pâté
Fillet of Fleetwood haddock with Jolly Boys batter
Raspberry & mascarpone cheesecake

In centre of hamlet off the main A 590 Grange over Sands to Kendal road. Parking

21

Victoria

29 Stamford St,
Altrincham, WA14 1EX
Tel.: (0161)6131855

VISA MC AE

Old Speckled Hen and Young's Waggle Dance

The Victoria is a very traditional looking pub, set in a quiet part of the town centre, with flower pots on the windowsills and a few pavement tables. Its appealing interior comes as a pleasant surprise; a single room with a wooden bar at its centre and half the tables left for drinkers; the other half laid up for diners. Lunchtime sees sandwiches, light bites and a few dishes from the evening à la carte, which are classically based but with a modern twist; maybe smoked duck crumpet, steak and kidney pudding or jugged wild rabbit. The emphasis is on locally sourced ingredients, so expect beef from Ashlea Farm, Pendrill's cheese and Dunham Massey Farm ice cream. There's a good value early evening set menu and friendly service from a young team.

CLOSING TIMES
Closed 1 January, 26 December and Sunday dinner

PRICES
Meals: a la carte £ 24/33

Typical Dishes

Pigeon pasty with pearl barley stew

Jugged wild rabbit with PX sherry & prunes

Honeycomb & mead sundae

Pay & display parking outside; free at night.

22 **White Hart Inn**

51 Stockport Rd,
Lydgate, Oldham, OL4 4JJ
Tel.: (01457)872566
Website: www.thewhitehart.co.uk

VISA MC AE

Timothy Taylor's Best and Landlord, J.W. Lees and weekly changing local guest ales

Set overlooking Saddleworth Moor, this stone-built inn has undergone various sympathetic extensions over the years; which are now home to a private dining room, a formal restaurant, a function room and 12 antique-furnished bedrooms. The bar boasts a dark wood counter, exposed beams and open fires, while photos of the owner's travels to various mountains in the Highlands, Rockies, China and Tibet hang on the walls; ironically, he once got thrown out of this pub for underage drinking before eventually buying it himself. Menus are fairly lengthy, displaying modern, brasserie-style dishes and a few classics – you might find chicken liver parfait, goat's cheese salad, pot-roast chicken or local sausages and mash – and all at very reasonable prices.

CLOSING TIMES
Closed 26 December

PRICES
Meals: £ 20 (Sunday lunch) and a la carte £ 26/35

12 rooms: £ 95

Typical Dishes

Tandoori king prawns with cumin-roasted belly pork

Pot-roast lamb rump with cauliflower purée

Chocolate delice with salted caramel

3 mi east of Oldham by A 669 on A 6050. Parking.

Arkholme

23 Redwell Inn

Arkholme,
LA6 1BQ
Tel.: (015242)21240
Website: www.redwellinnarkholme.co.uk

VISA

Regularly changing guest ales from Bowland, Hawkshead and Lancaster breweries

This attractive 16C stone inn takes its name from the well that stands to the rear of the pub, whose bricks turned red due to minerals leached from the water. It's one of those places that's a real family affair, with the son behind the scenes in the kitchen and mum and dad looking after the guests. The rustic bar boasts a few sofas, scrubbed tables and a wood burning stove, as well as a large display of homemade breads for sale, while the restaurant in the old coach house is a little more formal. The same menu is served throughout and offers something for everyone, from potted shrimps to Grandma Singletons Lancashire cheese pasty or a classic fish pie. There's also a nibbles section, serving the likes of homemade Scotch eggs with HP sauce.

CLOSING TIMES
Open daily
booking advisable

PRICES
Meals: £ 16 (lunch)
and a la carte £ 16/39

Typical Dishes

Shrimp & home-smoked mussel risotto
Fell-bred rump of lamb with blackened aubergine
Duck egg tart

6 mi southwest of Kirkby Londale on B 6254. Parking.

24 **Red Pump Inn**

Clitheroe Rd,
Bashall Eaves, BB7 3DA
Tel.: (01254)826227
Website: www.theredpumpinn.co.uk

VISA

Moorhouse's, Timothy Taylor Landlord, Hawskhead Brewery and Tirril

Dine in this pub's traditional restaurant or in the rustic bar. The fire-lit snug is a charming place to idle away an hour or two, while the valley sunsets make the terrace a fantastic place for a drink. Local produce features highly on the seasonal menus, with dishes like super-slow-roasted Pendle belly pork or hot-smoked Dunsop trout paté. With local shoots in and around the Forest of Bowland, game is the speciality, so you'll also see dishes like venison ravioli and pan-fried breast of pheasant. Dessert might mean steamed lemon sponge pudding or a selection of regional cheeses; beers include local and guest ales, with Black Sheep on draught. Sleep in one of the spacious, modern bedrooms; wake up to views of Pendle Hill or Longridge Fell.

CLOSING TIMES
Closed 2 weeks January and Monday except bank holidays

PRICES
Meals: £ 15 (weekdays) and a la carte £ 18/28
3 rooms: £ 75/115

Typical Dishes

Pan-seared pigeon, apple & black pudding
Rabbit leg confit with haggis fritters
Blackcurrant sponge & compote

3 mi northwest of Clitheroe by B 6243 and minor road northwest. Parking.

25 Clog & Billycock

Billinge End Rd,
Pleasington, Blackburn, BB2 6QB
Tel.: (01254)201163
Website: www.theclogandbillycock.com

VISA MC AE

Thwaites Original, Wainwrights, Lancaster Bomber and Bloomin ale

This popular sandstone pub was originally called the Bay Horse, before being renamed after a fashion trend often sported by the former landlord – who liked to wear the quirky combination of clog shoes and a billycock hat. The addition of a large extension means the pub is now modern and open-plan. The neutrally hued walls are filled with photos of their local suppliers and the extensive menus offer a strong Lancastrian slant; you might find Morecambe Bay shrimps, Port of Lancaster smoked fish or Ribble Valley beef, alongside tasty sharing platters. Most produce comes from within 20 miles and suppliers are plotted on a map on the back of the menu. Cooking is rustic and generous; prices are realistic; and the service is friendly and organised.

CLOSING TIMES
Closed 25 December

PRICES
Meals: a la carte £ 20/33

Typical Dishes

Potted Goosnargh duck
Line-caught haddock & chips
Bramley apple crumble

2 mi west of Blackburn, signed off A 677. Parking.

26 Bay Horse Inn

Bay Horse Ln,
Forton, LA2 0HR
Tel.: (01524)791204
Website: www.bayhorseinn.com

VISA MC

Lancaster Blonde, Moorhouse's Pendle Witch, Wainwright and Black Sheep

Flanked by the A6 and M6, and just a stone's throw away from the main Euston to Glasgow railway line, it's hard to believe how peaceful it is here. Burgundy walls, low beamed ceilings, a stone fireplace and characterful corner bar provide a cosy, welcoming atmosphere, while the rear dining room overlooks an attractive summer terrace and a pleasant wooded garden. The young owner is passionate about sourcing the freshest seasonal produce and you'll always find local offerings such as Andrew Ireland's black pudding, Port of Lancaster smoked salmon and Cumbrian lamb on the menu, with dishes ranging from good old pub classics right through to more modern, sophisticated fare. Beautifully appointed bedrooms are housed nearby in 'The Old Corn Store'.

CLOSING TIMES
Closed Sunday dinner and Monday except bank holidays

PRICES
Meals: £ 22 (lunch) and a la carte £ 22/36

2 rooms: £ 75/89

Typical Dishes

Hot smoked salmon with crab & avocado purée

Chump of lamb with creamed pearl barley

Chocolate pot

1.25 mi north by A 6 on Quernmore Rd. Parking.

27

Duke of York Inn

Brow Top,
Grindleton, BB7 4QR
Tel.: (01200)441266
Website: www.dukeofyorkgrindleton.com

VISA MC AE

Thwaites Original and Black Sheep Best Bitter

This ivy-clad pub sits on the main road running through this pleasant hamlet, in the heart of the Trough of Bowland. If its character you're after, dine in the rustic bar with its flag floors and wood burning stove. The more modern alternative is the smart, airy dining room, adorned with wine bottles and a large mirror. There are sandwiches at lunchtime and a great value set lunch and early evening menu; the seasonal à la carte offers plenty of regional choices and a decent selection of fish, often including lobster. Dishes might include steak and Grindleton ale pudding or roast loin and rack of Pendleton lamb; produce is commendably local, with herbs from the chef-owner's garden. Regular events include monthly wine nights and a pudding club.

CLOSING TIMES
Closed 25 December, Monday except bank holidays and Tuesday following bank holidays

PRICES
Meals: £ 14 and a la carte £ 24/39

Typical Dishes

Pork belly & black pudding with apple salad

Fillet of halibut & asparagus

Yorkshire rhubarb

3 mi northeast of Clitheroe signed off A 671. Parking.

28 Borough

3 Dalton Sq,
Lancaster, LA1 1PP
Tel.: (01524)64170
Website: www.theboroughlancaster.co.uk

VISA MC

Hawkshead Best Bitter, Charles Wells Bombardier, Lancaster Brewery and Kirkby Lonsdale ales

Set on the same cobbled square as the town hall, this pub has previously spent time as the mayor's house, a working men's club and a coffee importer's business. At the front is the characterful bar, its walls covered in old pictures of the city; the rear area is for dining and beyond that, there's an enclosed terrace. Extensive menus offer hearty, filling pub dishes like steak, hotpot or pie and peas; the DIY deli boards are a popular choice and, since local artisan producers are well used, you can expect shrimps from Morecambe Bay and fish from Fleetwood. Beer is given due respect, with local bitters, German lager and some unusual bottled ales. Regular comedy nights and a weekly poker class happen in the grand first floor former lounge.

CLOSING TIMES
Closed 25 December

PRICES
Meals: a la carte £ 19/32

Typical Dishes

Morecambe Bay potted shrimps

Steamed steak & ale pudding

Apple & berry crumble

In Dalton Square adjacent to the Town Hall on the one-way system. Parking in Dalton Square.

Little Eccleston

29 **Cartford Inn**

Cartford Ln,
Little Eccleston, PR3 0YP
Tel.: (01995)670166
Website: www.thecartfordinn.co.uk

VISA

Regularly changing selection from Bowland, Moorhouses and Hawkeshead Breweries

A gentle and ongoing makeover is transforming this 17C coaching inn into an attractive dining venue which blends original features with contemporary styling. Gallic touches alert you to the nationality of the owner, who provides friendly, efficient service with his young, local team. Get cosy next to the open fire on a cold winter's evening; come summer, dine alfresco overlooking the River Wyre and the Trough of Bowland. Menus offer something to suit your every mood; from sandwiches and wood platters of local produce to popular pub favourites like oxtail suet pudding, fish pie, lamb hotpot or steak and chips. Bedrooms are a cut above your typical pub: individually styled, with modern facilities, feature walls and antique French furniture.

CLOSING TIMES
Closed 25 December and Monday lunch

PRICES
Meals: a la carte £ 18/28
15 rooms: £ 65/190

Typical Dishes
Smoked Lancashire cheese, red onion & courgette tartlet
Oxtail and beef in real ale suet pudding
Cartmel village shop sticky toffee pudding

7 mi east of Blackpool by A 585 and A 586. Parking.

30 Three Fishes

Mitton Rd,
Mitton, BB7 9PQ
Tel.: (01254)826888
Website: www.thethreefishes.com

VISA MC AE

Lancaster Bomber, Wainwrights. Hen Harrier and Pride of Pendle, Moorhouses

From Morecambe Bay shrimps to Ribble Valley beef and Goosnargh chicken to Fleetwood fish, the menu here reads like a paean to Lancastrian produce. Regional specialities abound and local suppliers are celebrated as food heroes in the striking photos which adorn the pub's walls. The seasonally changing menus are extensive, meaning no matter how many times you come back, you can always try something new, and this a truly family-friendly pub, with children's menus which pay much more than lip service to your little ones. Sunday lunch is popular, when a roast is also available – but this modern country inn is deservedly busy all week long, packed with people keen to try tasty, satisfying dishes made with the best the North West has to offer.

CLOSING TIMES
Closed 25 December

PRICES
Meals: a la carte £ 21/33

Typical Dishes

BBQ corn-fed chicken wings with ginger
Battered scampi, crispy squid & chips
Lemon meringue pie

2.5 mi northwest of Whalley on B 6246. Parking.

31 **Inn at Whitewell**

Forest of Bowland,
Whitewell, BB7 3AT
Tel.: (01200)448222
Website: www.innatwhitewell.com

VISA

Copper Dragon, Blond Witch, Timothy Taylors

This 14C creeper-clad inn sits high on the banks of the River Hodder, in prime shooting and fishing country, in the heart of the Trough of Bowland. Antique furniture and a panoramic view of the valley make the spacious bar the most atmospheric place to sit. Other similarly styled rooms boast the character but not the view; for a more formal meal, head for a linen-laid table in the raised-level, valley-facing restaurant. Classic menus offer wholesome, regionally inspired dishes like Lancashire hotpot or fillet of local beef. Spacious bedrooms are split between the inn and nearby coach house. Some are traditional in style with four-posters and antique baths; others are more contemporary. A well-stocked vintners also sells cookbooks and guides.

CLOSING TIMES
Open daily

PRICES
Meals: a la carte £ 16/43
23 rooms: £ 88/200

Typical Dishes

Terrine of Goosnargh duckling
Confit shoulder of Lonk lamb
Chocolate brownie

6 mi northwest of Clitheroe by B 6243. Parking.

32 **Freemasons**

8 Vicarage Fold,
Wiswell, BB7 9DF
Tel.: (01254)822218
Website: www.freemasonswiswell.co.uk

Bowland Brewery, Three B's, Prospect

Charming, welcoming, warm and chatty are all adjectives which apply to the staff here, so it's no wonder that they're busy. Of course service counts for little if the food's not right; but, again, here the Freemasons comes up trumps. Chef Steven Smith likes to create modern versions of traditional pub dishes; think good old chicken Kiev reborn as organic chicken breast and Kiev with potato purée, wild mushrooms and thyme; or trifle: not as your mother made it, but with Pedro Ximenez jelly, baked quince and warm Madeleines. Flag floors, low beams and open fires feature downstairs, while the first floor boasts an elegant, antique-furnished dining area with a country house feel, as well as a comfortable lounge and two semi-private dining rooms.

CLOSING TIMES
Closed Monday except bank holidays

PRICES
Meals: £ 17 (weekdays) and a la carte £ 28/46

Typical Dishes

Tandoori-roast monkfish with pig's trotter nuggets

Goosnargh chicken with asparagus

Custard tart with rhubarb arctic roll

Signposted off A 671 east of Whalley. Some parking in the village.

Wrightington Bar

33 Mulberry Tree

9 Wood Ln,
Wrightington Bar, WN6 9SE
Tel.: (01257)451400
Website: www.themulberrytree.info

VISA MC

Black Sheep ales

Such are the choices available at this spacious 19C pub, you may find yourself frozen in the grip of indecision. Firstly, where to sit: at one of the linen-clad tables in the formal dining area or in the more laid-back bar area? Next comes the tricky bit: what to eat. The menu is virtually the same in both parts of the pub, but with more than twenty starters and even more main courses to choose from you might need more than the customary five minutes to decide. There's something for everyone, from Sichuan chicken livers, oysters and fishcakes, to steaks, suet pudding and mushroom risotto, with plenty of pubby classics like fish and chips and sausage and mash. Dishes come in generous portions and at prices that won't break the bank.

CLOSING TIMES
Open daily

PRICES
Meals: a la carte £ 27/40

Typical Dishes

Twice-baked goat's cheese soufflé

Whole roasted sea bass & stir-fried Asian vegetables

Hot chocolate pudding

3.5 mi northwest of Standish by A 5209 on B 5250. Parking.

The south east abounds in handsome historic houses once lived in by the likes of Disraeli and the Rothschilds, and it's no surprise that during the Plague it was to leafy Chalfont St Giles that John Milton fled. It is characterised by rolling hills such as the Chilterns with their ancient beechwoods, and the lilting North and South Downs, which cut a rural swathe across busy commuter belts. The film and television worlds sit easily here: Hambleden and Turville, in the Chilterns, are as used to the sound of the autocue as to the crunch of ramblers' boots. Meanwhile, James Bond's Aston Martin glistens in Beaulieu's Motor Museum, in the heart of the New Forest. Spinnaker Tower rivals HMS Victory for dominance of the Portsmouth skyline, while in Winchester, the Great Hall, home for 600 years to the Arthurian round table, nods acquaintance with the eleventh century Cathedral. Good food and drink is integral to the region, from Whitstable oysters and Dover sole to established vineyards.

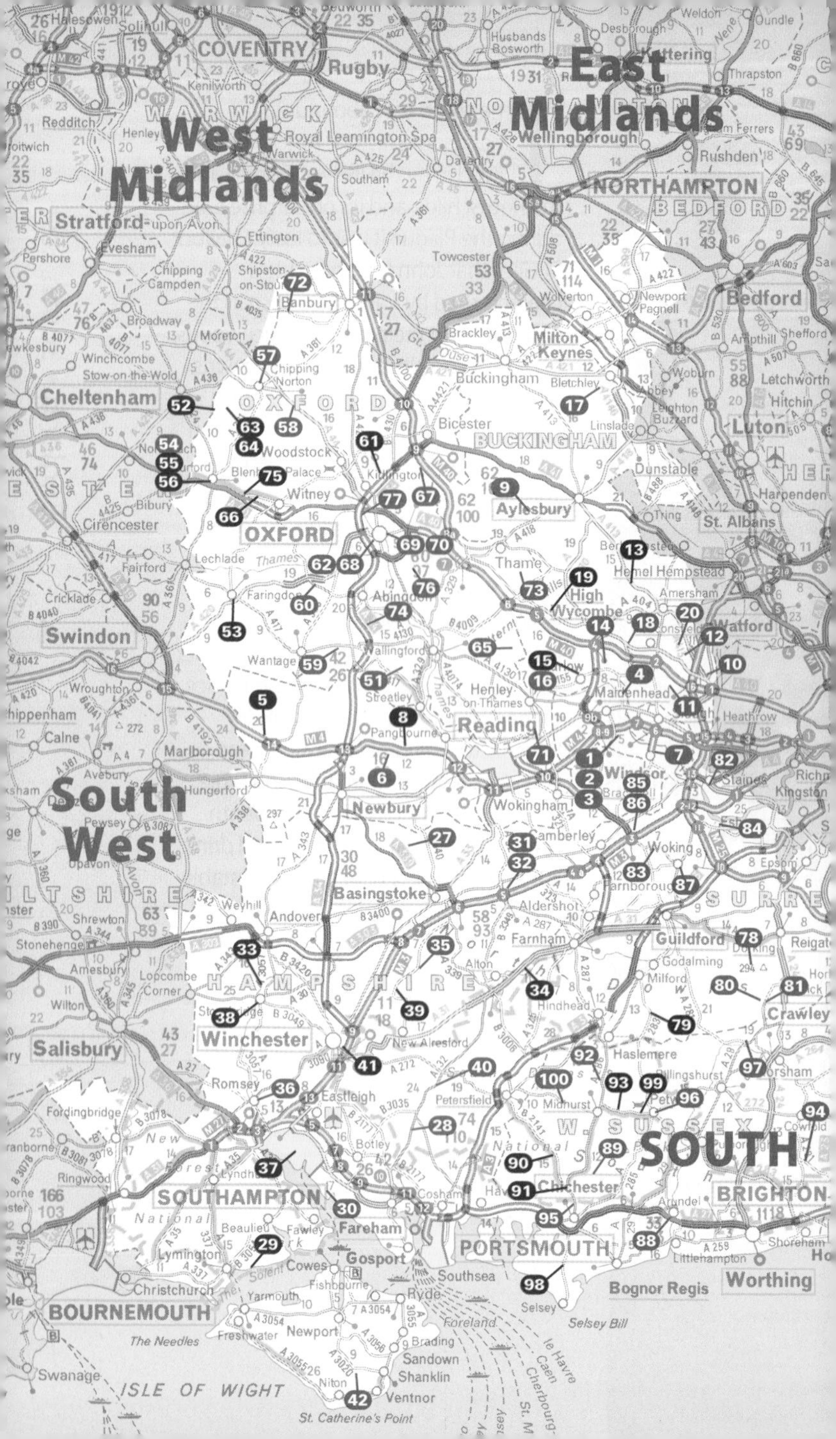

West Midlands
East Midlands
South West
SOUTH
COVENTRY
Rugby
Royal Leamington Spa
Warwick
Stratford-upon-Avon
Evesham
Cheltenham
Cirencester
Swindon
Banbury
Chipping Norton
Woodstock
Witney
OXFORD
Abingdon
Wallingford
Bicester
Aylesbury
Thame
High Wycombe
Maidenhead
Reading
Newbury
Henley-on-Thames
Wokingham
Windsor
Camberley
Basingstoke
Andover
Winchester
Salisbury
Southampton
SOUTHAMPTON
Eastleigh
Romsey
Fareham
Gosport
PORTSMOUTH
Chichester
Bognor Regis
Worthing
BRIGHTON
Crawley
Guildford
Woking
Farnham
Aldershot
Haslemere
Petersfield
Midhurst
BOURNEMOUTH
Christchurch
Lymington
Cowes
Newport
Ryde
Sandown
Shanklin
Ventnor
ISLE OF WIGHT
NORTHAMPTON
Wellingborough
Kettering
Milton Keynes
Bedford
Luton
Watford
St. Albans
Hemel Hempstead
Amersham
Marlborough
Hungerford
Devizes
Amesbury
Stonehenge
Towcester
Brackley
Buckingham
Bletchley
Leighton Buzzard
Dunstable
Daventry
Southsea
Selsey Bill
St. Catherine's Point
The Needles
Swanage

6 Pubs without bedrooms
8 Pubs with bedrooms
East of England
London
EAST
CAMBRIDGE
ESSEX
KENT
E. SUSSEX
Thetford
Brandon
Bungay
Littleport
Chatteris
Ramsey
Ely
Huntingdon
Earith
St. Ives
Soham
Scole
Halesworth
Godmanchester
St. Neots
Newmarket
Bury St. Edmunds
Ixworth
Dennington
Yoxford
Saxmundham
Eltisley
Stowmarket
Potton
Biggleswade
Lavenham
Haverhill
Clare
IPSWICH
Woodbridge
Royston
Saffron Walden
Sudbury
Hadleigh
Baldock
Buntingford
Finchingfield
Stour
Halstead
Felixstowe
Stevenage
Puckeridge
Stansted
Great Dunmow
Braintree
Harwich
The Naze
Hertford
Bishop's Stortford
Colchester
Walton-on-the-Naze
Welwyn Garden City
Ware
Sawbridgeworth
Witham
Frinton-on-Sea
Brightlingsea
Clacton-on-Sea
Harlow
W. Mersea
Hatfield
Hoddesdon
Chelmsford
Cheshunt
Epping
Maldon
Bradwell-on-Sea
Potters Bar
Brentwood
Billericay
Burnham-on-Crouch
Wickford
Foulness Point
Rayleigh
Basildon
Benfleet
Southend-on-Sea
Grays Thurrock
Canvey Island
Dartford
Tilbury
R. Thames
Grain
Sheerness
Gravesend
Queenborough
Isle of Sheppey
Rochester
Leysdown-on-Sea
Birchington
Margate
Orpington
Gillingham
Herne Bay
North Foreland
Croydon
Chatham
Whitstable
Broadstairs
Sittingbourne
Faversham
Ramsgate
Canterbury
Knole
Sandwich
Redhill
Sevenoaks
Maidstone
Deal
Tonbridge
Southborough
Ashford
South Foreland
East Grinstead
Royal Tunbridge Wells
Biddenden
Terminal
Dover
Crowborough
Tenterden
Cuckfield
Hawkhurst
Hythe
Folkestone
Haywards Heath
Heathfield
Uckfield
New Romney
Tunnel-so
Chann
Rye
Lydd
Hailsham
Battle
Cap Blanc
Winchelsea
Dungeness
Wissar
Lewes
Cap Gris Nez
Polegate
Bexhill
Hastings
Newhaven
Seaford
Eastbourne
Wimereux
Beachy Head
Boulogne
PAS DE CALAIS
le Portel
Dieppe
Hardelot-Plage

Bray

1 Crown

High St,
Bray, SL6 2AH
Tel.: (01628)621936
Website: www.thecrownatbray.co.uk

VISA MC AE D

Greene King IPA, Brains, Old Speckled Hen, Wadworth 6X, Spitfire, Deuchars IPA

Not content with owning just one pub in the village of Bray, Heston Blumenthal has added a second to his portfolio. This charmingly restored 16C building began life as two cottages and an old bike shop – hence the confusion with the doors as you approach; tip, head for the middle one. Drinkers mingle with diners beside roaring fires in the bar, sat amongst sturdy dark oak columns and below low beams; while next door there's a lighter, cottagey style dining room. Heston may be firmly involved in the compilation of the menu but that doesn't mean his young chef is kept from stamping his mark on the dishes. Cooking is robust, flavoursome and British in essence, ranging from ploughman's, through sausage and mash, to lemon sole with potted shrimps.

CLOSING TIMES
Open daily

PRICES
Meals: a la carte £ 21/35

Typical Dishes

Potted duck, grilled bread & cornichons
Angus burger & fries
Strawberry Eton mess

1 mi south of Maidenhead by A 308. Parking.

2 **Hinds Head**

High St,
Bray, SL6 2AB
Tel.: (01628)626151
Website: www.hindsheadhotel.co.uk

Inspectors' favourites

VISA MC AE D

Rebellion Smuggler, Henley Gold, Sunchaser, Tiger, Greyhound Cambridge Bitter

Set right in the heart of the pretty village of Bray, this charming pub boasts dark wood panelling and log fires, giving it a characterful, almost medieval feel. Although not far from its alma mater, The Fat Duck, it's light years away in terms of its menu. Heston Blumenthal might be famous for molecular gastronomy, but at The Hinds Head, the food is down-to-earth, with classic, comforting dishes like pea and ham soup or heartwarming oxtail and kidney pudding, and traditional desserts such as Eton mess or strawberry trifle. Dishes are fiercely British and big on flavour; rich, simple and satisfying. This is a proper pub and, as such, is busy with drinkers; the bar is the most atmospheric place to sit, although they don't take bookings here.

CLOSING TIMES
Closed 25-26 December and Sunday dinner
booking essential

PRICES
Meals: £ 28 and a la carte £ 32/48

Typical Dishes

Tea-smoked salmon with soda bread
Shepherd's pie wtih lamb breast & sweetbreads
Quaking pudding

1 mi south of Maidenhead by A 308. Parking in 2 village car parks and opposite the pub.

Bray

3 Royal Oak

Paley Street,
Bray, SL6 3JN
Tel.: (01628)620541
Website: www.theroyaloakpaleystreet.com

Inspectors' favourites

VISA

Fuller's London Pride, Chiswick Bitter and Red Fox

Nick Parkinson is your host and his ability to put guests at ease is clearly one family trait he's inherited from his father, Sir Michael, whose famous encounters are captured in the photos that decorate the place. Boris the dog is usually found snoozing at the front bar, while the rest of the beamed room is given over to dining. The chef is Dominic Chapman, son of West Country hotelier Kit, and, like his father, he champions British food. His cooking displays confidence and a commitment to quality, seasonal ingredients but also suits the place. Fish is handled with particular aplomb, whether it's roast halibut with spicy aubergine or smoked eel with beetroot. He also likes his game. Service is very pleasant and gets the tone just right.

CLOSING TIMES
Closed Sunday dinner

PRICES
Meals: £ 23 (weekday lunch) and a la carte £ 41/61

Typical Dishes

Rabbit lasagne & chervil sauce
Roast turbot, samphire, cockles & mussels
Rhubarb trifle

3.5 mi southwest of Bray by A 308, A 330 and B 3024. Parking.

4

White Oak

Pound Ln,
Cookham, SL6 9QE
Tel.: (01628)523043
Website: www.thewhiteoak.co.uk

VISA MC AE

Greene King - Abbot Ale and Old Speckled Hen Smooth

Having cut his teeth in some of London's original gastropubs, Henry Cripps decided to expand his repertoire by looking further afield. His latest rural venture, The White Oak, is set in a picturesque village and boasts a smart terrace with neat planters and a light, bright, neutrally hued interior; the result of a large-scale contemporary makeover. The cooking here is straightforward and generously proportioned, featuring simple pub-style dishes which consist of quality meats and unfussy accompaniments. There are several options for two, including assiettes of starters and seafood, a charcuterie board and, on Sundays, various roasts to share. Service is cheery and there's a good drinks selection, which includes plenty of wines by the glass.

CLOSING TIMES
Closed dinner Sunday and bank holidays

PRICES
Meals: £ 19 (weekdays) and a la carte £ 25/29

Typical Dishes
Pea soup, black truffle croque monsieur
Salmon fillet with fennel beurre blanc & herbs
Caramelised apple tart

Across the common. Parking.

East Garston

5

Queen's Arms

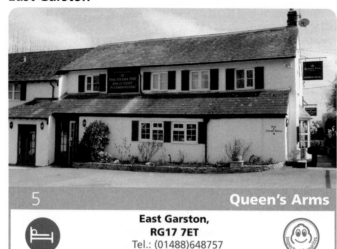

East Garston,
RG17 7ET
Tel.: (01488)648757
Website: www.queensarmshotel.co.uk

VISA AE

Wadworth's 6X, Henry's original IPA, Ramsbury, Loddon, West Berkshire and Butts ales

Situated in the heart of the Valley of the Racehorse, The Queen's Arms is a true thoroughbred among pubs. With its country pursuits theme, it celebrates all things English; catch up with the day's racing results in the atmospheric, antique-furnished bar; its walls lined with fantastic photos of riders and shooters. Rustic British dishes might include shepherd's pie or rib-eye steak with fat cut chips, with the lunch menu providing particularly good value. Superb bedrooms are sponsored by purveyors of country equipment and clothing; for the ultimate extravagance, book 'Miller's Club,' which comes with its own honesty bar and poker table. Don't forget to order your copy of The Racing Post to accompany your generous breakfast the next morning.

CLOSING TIMES
Closed 25 December

PRICES
Meals: a la carte £ 22/32
8 rooms: £ 90/130

Typical Dishes
Pan-roasted pigeon breast with bacon, black pudding & lentils
Stuffed pork shoulder with pease pudding
Jam roly poly & custard

3 mi southeast of Lambourn via Eastbury on Newbury Rd. Parking.

6 Pot Kiln

Frilsham,
RG18 0XX
Tel.: (01635)201366
Website: www.potkiln.org

VISA

Brick Kiln, Mr Chubbs and two guest ales

Part of the old brickworks, The Pot Kiln originally provided refreshment for the workers digging clay from the surrounding fields. Head for the cosy bar and order a pint of specially commissioned Magg's Mild, Mr Chubbs or Brick Kiln beer, then follow the deliciously tempting aromas through to the dining area, where flavoursome British dishes arrive in unashamedly gutsy portions. Chef-owner Mike Robinson takes advantage of the pub's situation in the middle of prime hunting territory and shoots much of the game himself; so you might find pigeon salad followed by pavé of Lockinge fallow deer on the menu. If meat's not your thing, there's plenty of fish too, including local pike, trout and River Kennet crayfish. Service is particularly clued-up.

CLOSING TIMES
Closed 25 December and Tuesday

PRICES
Meals: £ 16 (weekday lunch) and a la carte £ 28/33

Typical Dishes

Warm salad of wood pigeon
Pavé of Linkenholt fallow deer with pomme purée
Sticky toffee pudding

6 mi northeast of Newbury by B 4009 to Hermitage and minor road. Parking.

7

Greene Oak

Oakley Grn,
Windsor, SL4 5UW
Tel.: (01753)864294
Website: www.thegreeneoak.co.uk

VISA · MC · AE

Greene King IPA, Abbott Ale and Old Speckled Hen

It's set on a busy lorry route to Twyford and may not look like much from the outside, but step inside The Greene Oak and it's a different story. There are contemporary soft furnishings and appealing décor in soothing shades of botanical green, a relaxed feel prevails and a warm welcome at the bar is assured. Older sibling to the White Oak in Cookham, it boasts an experienced owner with a background in London pubs, while the chef previously cooked at The Hind's Head in nearby Bray. Dishes might include comforting coq au vin, smoked fish pie or steak with the works, while both the braised Jacob's Ladder and the breaded scallops with pea purée and pancetta come highly recommended. Alfresco dining on the terrace is a delight come summer.

CLOSING TIMES
Closed Sunday dinner
booking advisable

PRICES
Meals: £ 15 (lunch except Friday and Sunday)
and a la carte £ 25/36

Typical Dishes

Steamed asparagus tips, Parma ham crisp & breaded egg yolk

Braised & glazed sticky beef

Crème brûlée & raspberry sorbet

3 mi west of Windsor by A 308 on B 3024 Dedworth Rd. Parking.

8 **Royal Oak**

The Square,
Yattendon, RG18 0UF
Tel.: (01635)201325
Website: www.royaloakyattendon.com

VISA MC

West Berkshire Brewery - Good Old Boy, Mr Chubbs

An eye-catching former coaching inn bursting with country charm, The Royal Oak manages to pull off the tricky feat of being both a true locals pub and a popular destination for foodies. While the picture perfect village and its proximity to the M4 could account in part for the pub's attraction to visitors, it's the cooking which really gets them travelling here from a distance. Honest British dishes might include devilled kidneys, potted shrimps or fish pie, while traditional puddings might be of the bread and butter or sticky toffee varieties. The beamed bar with its blazing log fires is at the pub's hub. There's also a lesser-used restaurant and a pleasant vine-covered terrace at the rear. Comfortable bedrooms boast a country house style.

CLOSING TIMES
Open daily
booking advisable

PRICES
Meals: £ 15 (lunch)
and a la carte £ 27/34
5 rooms: £ 85

Typical Dishes

Devilled kidneys on toast
Roast Barnsley lamb chop
Apricot crumble

6 mi northeast of Newbury by B 4009 and minor road; in the village centre. Parking opposite and in village car park.

Cuddington

9 **Crown**

Aylesbury Rd,
Cuddington, HP18 0BB
Tel.: (01844)292222
Website: www.thecrowncuddington.co.uk

VISA MC

Fuller's London Pride, Adnams and one seasonal guest ale from Red Fox Brewery

Set in the charming village of Cuddington, this Grade II listed 16C building is the very essence of a proper English pub. Whitewashed walls and an attractive thatched roof hide a traditionally styled interior with welcoming open fires, dancing candlelight and a multitude of bygone artefacts; while a loyal band of locals keep up the drinking trade and a friendly serving team help set the tone. There's a blackboard of daily specials and an à la carte that changes with the seasons: so you'll find hearty comfort food in winter – maybe lamb shank or glazed duck breast – and lighter sandwiches and salads in the summer; arrive early if you fancy one of these in a spot in the sun. Tuesday to Friday 'food nights' include steak, curry, pies and fish 'n' chips.

CLOSING TIMES
Closed Sunday dinner

PRICES
Meals: a la carte £ 20/30

Typical Dishes
Grilled field mushroom with spinach & cheddar
Chicken with mozzarella & sweet potato mash
Chocolate & walnut brownie

West of Aylesbury by A 418. Parking.

10 Swan Inn

Village Rd,
Denham, UB9 5BH
Tel.: (01895)832085
Website: www.swaninndenham.co.uk

VISA MC AE

Marlow Rebellion IPA and Wadworth 6X

If you want to escape the hustle of London, this pub may well be the tranquil haven you're after. Close to the A40, M40 and M25 but in a secluded little world of its own, The Swan takes up prime position in this delightful village. Number three in the owner's collection, the Georgian red-brick building is fronted by beautiful cascades of wisteria and framed by manicured trees, with a secluded terrace and gardens to the rear. Menus change with the seasons but their signature bubble & squeak and rib-eye steak are mainstays. This is more than just typical pub food, so you might find confit duck with nutmeg boxty potato and sides such as such as leek, pancetta and parsley crumble. Satisfyingly, they open early for pre-Ascot or Wimbledon champagne.

CLOSING TIMES
Closed 25-26 December
booking essential

PRICES
Meals: a la carte £ 23/28

Typical Dishes

Sautéed duck livers & hearts

Roast saddle of rabbit, pancetta & sage rösti

Rich chocolate torte with violet ice cream

6 mi northeast of Slough by A 412; in the centre of the village. Small car park.

11

Black Horse

Windmill Rd,
Fulmer, SL3 6HD
Tel.: (01753)663183
Website: www.blackhorsefulmer.co.uk

VISA AE

Old Speckled Hen, Greene King IPA and London Glory

Set in the heart of a chocolate box village yet not far from the M40 and M25, this attractive 17C whitewashed inn is the latest addition to the Salisbury group, who own four other pubs nearby. Originally built as cottages for the craftsmen constructing the local church, it boasts a characterful beamed bar complete with nooks, crannies and roaring log fires, as well as a bright dining room overlooking the terrace and gardens. The menu offers a selection of gutsy, modern British dishes such as Scotch duck egg with watercress purée, followed by local Coleshill pork or lamb, or game from nearby Marlow; finished off with maybe a light, crisp apple and sultana strudel. Cooking follows the seasons closely and provenance is of paramount importance.

CLOSING TIMES
Closed 25-26 December

PRICES
Meals: a la carte £ 23/28

Typical Dishes

Wild garlic, sorrel & nettle tart
Spring lamb mixed grill
Glazed rice pudding

2 mi south of Gerrards Cross in centre of village beside St James church.

12 **Three Oaks**

Austenwood Rd,
Gerrards Cross, SL9 8NL
Tel.: (01753)899016
Website: www.thethreeoaksgx.co.uk

VISA AE

Greene King IPA and Rebellion

Turning into the car park and seeing all those smart cars makes you immediately aware that this isn't going to be your typical village local. Sharing the same owner as The White Oak in Cookham Dean and The Greene Oak just outside Windsor, this revamped pub now attracts the local 'smart set'. There's a choice of dining room – go for the brighter one at the back as it looks out over the garden. Bright, enthusiastic service comes courtesy of local boys and girls, all dressed in black. The menu changes often but keeps things British and relatively safe as the customers clearly don't take to anything too unfamiliar. Expect the likes of home-cured salmon, roast lamb with mint jelly or chocolate brownie. There's also a good value lunch menu.

CLOSING TIMES
Closed dinner Sunday and bank holidays

PRICES
Meals: £ 19 (lunch) and a la carte £ 24/38

Typical Dishes

Chicken liver parfait
Braised Orkney beef with honey-roast root vegetables
Strawberry Eton mess

0.75 mi northwest of the town by A 413 following signs for Gold Hill. Parking.

Great Missenden

13 Nags Head

London Rd,
Great Missenden, HP16 0DG
Tel.: (01494)862200
Website: www.nagsheadbucks.com

VISA MC AE

Rebellion IPA, Sharp's Doom Bar, Fuller's London Pride and Tring Brewery Company Ltd ales

This traditional 15C inn is run by the same team behind the Bricklayers Arms in Flaunden and is proving just as popular, so be sure to book ahead, especially at weekends. It has been made over, yet retains a wealth of original features: the two main dining areas have thick brick walls and exposed oak beams, while an extra helping of rusticity comes courtesy of the inglenook fireplace. Original menus mix Gallic charm with British classics, so you'll find things like foie gras or mushroom feuillette alongside eggs Benedict or sausage and mash; food is flavourful and service cheerful and keen. Stylish, modern bedrooms provide a comfortable night's sleep – number one is the best – and the tasty breakfast ensures you leave satiated in the morning.

CLOSING TIMES
Open daily

PRICES
Meals: a la carte £ 25/35
5 rooms: £ 70/140

Typical Dishes

Eggs Benedict with halloumi cheese & paprika
Roasted wood pigeon breast with confit leg & port jus
Chocolate fondant

1 mi southeast by A 413 turning at Chiltern Hospital. Parking.

14 Queens Head

Pound Ln,
Little Marlow, SL7 3SR
Tel.: (01628)482927
Website: www.marlowslittlesecret.co.uk

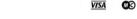

VISA MC

Fuller's London Pride, Brakspear and guest ales

Head towards Little Marlow's 12C church and, tucked away down a lane opposite the village's restored cattle pound, you'll find The Queens Head; a popular pub, with keen young partners at its helm and staff who provide poised, friendly service. Once a spit and sawdust sort of a place, its snug bar used to be a salting room and its priest hole makes it a popular place for filming. The garden gets into full swing during the summer months when hungry walkers gather to refuel; lunch offers either a quick fix with sandwiches, ploughman's and pub classics or more refined dishes on the main à la carte, maybe scallops with black pudding, followed by Baileys brûlée. Menus change every 6-8 weeks and produce is from local farms, forages and shoots.

CLOSING TIMES
Closed 25-26 December

PRICES
Meals: a la carte £ 20/25

Typical Dishes
Potted rabbit & pheasant pâté
Cornish scallops with pea purée and cripsy bacon
Warm poached spiced pear with vanilla panna cotta

3 mi east of Marlow on A 4155 by Church Rd. Parking.

15 **Hand and Flowers**

126 West St,
Marlow, SL7 2BP
Tel.: (01628)482277
Website: www.thehandandflowers.co.uk

Inspectors' favourites

VISA

Greene King IPA, Abbot Ale and Moorland Original

With its softly lit interior, The Hand and Flowers glows enticingly but it's not often you can drop in on the off-chance, as this is Marlow's not-so-well-kept secret. Low beamed ceilings, flagstone floors and a proper bar counter hint at its history, while the professional serving team are a clue as to the quality of the food. Cooking is of the highest order and the chef puts as much care and passion into a lasagne on the set lunch menu as a fillet of beef on the evening à la carte. The selection may be concise but dishes are refined and flavoursome, ingredients marry perfectly and the simple really is turned into the sublime. Characterful cottage bedrooms are equally meticulous, boasting feature baths or showers. Some even have outdoor jacuzzis.

CLOSING TIMES
Closed 24-26 December and Sunday dinner
booking essential

PRICES
Meals: £ 17 (weekday lunch) and a la carte £ 37/48
4 rooms: £ 140/190

Typical Dishes

Parsley soup & parmesan tortellini
Fillet of plaice with asparagus
Vanilla crème brûlée

From town centre follow Henley signs west on A 4155; pub on right after 350 metres. Parking.

16 **Royal Oak**

Frieth Rd,
Bovingdon Green, Marlow, SL7 2JF
Tel.: (01628)488611
Website: www.royaloakmarlow.co.uk

VISA MC AE

Marlow Rebellion IPA and Smuggler

Set less than 15mins from the M40 and M4, this part-17C pub is the ideal escape from the busy streets of London. As you approach, pleasant scents drift up from the herb garden, gentle 'chinks' emanate from the petanque pitch and the world feels at once more peaceful. While away the warmer days on the pleasant terrace or snuggle into pretty cushions beside the wood burning stove in winter, where rich fabrics and heritage colours provide a country-chic feel and freshly cut flowers decorate the room. Not surprisingly, it's extremely popular and the eager team are often stretched to their limit. Cooking is mainly British-led, with the odd Asian influence; you might find pan-roast pork chop with salt and pepper squid or slow-cooked ox cheek pasty.

CLOSING TIMES
Closed 25-26 December

PRICES
Meals: a la carte £ 22/29

Typical Dishes

Home-cured Barbary duck ham

Pan-fried coley fillet, ham hock & pea risotto

Baked dark chocolate soup

1.25 mi west of Marlow by A 4155 and Bovington Green rd. Parking.

17 **Crooked Billet**

2 Westbrook End,
Newton Longville, MK17 0DF
Tel.: (01908)373936
Website: www.thebillet.co.uk

VISA MC AE

Greene King Abbot Ale and Speckled Hen, Wychwood Hobglobin, Everards Tiger and Cottage Brewing's Phoenix

This charming 17C thatched pub is the last place you expect to find on the outskirts of Milton Keynes. Starting life as a farmhouse and later providing refreshments for passing farmers, it eventually evolved into the village pub. The interior is smart yet informal; the owner's artwork adorns the walls and a cheery bunch of locals prop up the bar. Over the last decade it's built up quite a reputation – so much so that you'll need to book. Emma heads the dedicated kitchen team, who create modern, seasonal dishes; lunch offers sandwiches or a three course à la carte and dinner introduces a 7 course tasting menu. Provenance is noted on the menu, as are wine recommendations, and ex-sommelier John happily guides you through the 200-strong wine list.

CLOSING TIMES
Closed 27-28 December, Sunday dinner and Monday lunch
booking advisable

PRICES
Meals: £ 20/24
and a la carte £ 24/41

Typical Dishes

Asparagus with black pudding Scotch egg

Roast pork belly with ham hock rissoles

Pimm's & lemonade jelly with spearmint ice cream

6 mi southwest of Milton Keynes by A 421. Parking.

18 Old Queens Head

Hammersley Ln,
Penn, HP10 8EY
Tel.: (01494)813371
Website: www.oldqueensheadpenn.co.uk

VISA MC AE

Greene King IPA and Old Speckled Hen

This pub may not be quite as old as the ancient beech woodlands that surround it but it does have a part to play in the area's history. Legend has it that Lord Penn inherited the pub when he won a game of cards against Charles II. Whether this is true or not, no one knows but it can be proved from the 1666 deeds that it was purchased by one of the King's physicians. Boasting weathered beams and good views the dining room – formerly a barn – is the oldest part; while the surrounding rooms, although slightly newer, continue the rustic theme with their characterful open fires and cosy nooks. Big, hearty dishes are the order of the day, so you might find pigeon breast on red onion tarte Tatin, followed by beef Bourguignon with oxtail dumplings.

CLOSING TIMES
Closed 25-26 December

PRICES
Meals: a la carte £ 22/29

Typical Dishes

Seared Marlow pigeon breast with thyme rösti

Grilled black bream with clams & leeks

Gooseberry and pear gingerbread crumble

4 mi north of A 40, Junction 2, via Beaconsfield by B 474. Parking.

19 **Three Horseshoes Inn**

Bennett End,
Radnage, HP14 4EB
Tel.: (01494)483273
Website: www.thethreehorseshoes.net

VISA

Brakspear Oxford Gold and Rebellion IPA

This 18C red-brick pub is set in a fantastic hillside location, deep in the countryside. The cosy bar with its attractive flag floor and inglenook fireplace is the place to be – although with space being limited, you might want to head to the restaurant, with its stunning beams and smart, minimalist feel; or in warmer weather, the terrace, which boasts pleasant views over the duck pond to the hills beyond. Menus reflect the chef's background, so you'll find classically prepared dishes with the odd French touch. Lunch consists mainly of soups, salads and pâtés, while dinner offers a more formal à la carte and some lighter tapas dishes; the latter served in the bar and garden. Bedrooms are contemporary and lavish; the Molières suite is the best.

CLOSING TIMES
Closed Sunday dinner and Monday lunch

PRICES
Meals: £ 17/20 and a la carte £ 26/37
6 rooms: £ 85/125

Typical Dishes

Fillet of poached & smoked salmon

Supreme of halibut with champagne sorrel sauce

Hot chocolate fondant with Nuttela ice cream

5 mi west of High Wycombe by A 40 and minor road north. Parking.

20 **Jolly Cricketers**

24 Chalfont Rd,
Seer Green, HP9 2YG
Tel.: (01494)676308

Inspectors' favourites

VISA MC AE

Chilton Vale Brewery, Windsor & Eton Brewery, Fullers London Pride & Marlow Rebellion

Somehow it's hard to imagine a pub called The Jolly Footballers. Indeed, no sport does nostalgia or evokes a spirit of bonhomie quite like cricket and this charming Victorian pub certainly does its bit for the gentleman's game: there's memorabilia aplenty, including signed cricket bats and Test Match programs, and even the menu comes divided into 'Openers, Main Play and Lower Order'. But this is also a pub where people come to eat. The kitchen nicely balances classic dishes with more modern choices, so seasonal asparagus could be followed by monkfish with Moroccan spices and, for dessert, a generously sized and satisfyingly filling fruit crumble. In winter, sit by the fireplace and count down the months until summer comes around again.

CLOSING TIMES
Closed 2 weeks January, Sunday dinner and Monday
booking advisable

PRICES
Meals: a la carte £ 23/39

Typical Dishes

Seared scallops, pork croquette, cauliflower & apple

Ale & cider braised ham & triple cooked chips

Passion fruit soufflé

2.5 mi northeast of Beaconsfield off A355. Parking

21 **George Inn**

High St,
Alfriston, BN26 5SY
Tel.: (01323)870319
Website: www.thegeorge-alfriston.com

VISA MC

Greene King IPA, Olde Trip, Abbot Ale and Brains Rev. James

If it's character you're after, you're in the right place. The picturesque village of Alfriston is on the Southdown Way and boasts its own cricket club, a group of bell ringers and this delightful 14C stone and timber pub. As characterful inside as out, it has vast inglenook fireplaces and more beams than you've ever seen before; there's even one on the floor. For dining, there's the choice between the rustic bar and another spacious, slightly more formal room. The menu offers sharing boards and restaurant-style dishes such as knuckle of lamb or mushrooms with bacon and goat's cheese, and pub classics appear as the specials. Comfy, simply furnished bedrooms are named after scholars; Bob Hall with its 13C wattle and daub murals is the best.

CLOSING TIMES
Closed 25-26 December

PRICES
Meals: a la carte £ 24/32
6 rooms: £ 75/145

Typical Dishes

Pigeon breast with bacon & caramelised pears

Confit of pork belly with bean cassoulet

Dark chocolate & orange mousse

Two public car parks (1min walk) and street parking.

22 **The Ginger Dog**

12 College Pl,
Brighton and Hove, BN2 1HN
Tel.: (01273)620990
Website: www.gingermanrestaurants.com

VISA MC AE

Harvey's Sussex Best Bitter, Sharp's Doom Bar, Hepworth Brewery

The latest addition to the locally based 'Ginger' empire is this shabby-chic, canine-themed pub, with a welcoming atmosphere and relaxed feel. Many of the original architectural features – such as the ornate wood – are juxtaposed with contemporary design touches; note the bowler hats used as lampshades. Tables are smartly laid up behind the bar but you can eat anywhere. Fresh produce is to the fore on the menu, which is mostly British but with the odd nod to Italy, and could include local Rye Bay plaice with shrimps, Scotch quail egg and black pudding salad or a proper trifle. Water and excellent bread are not only brought to the table without hesitation but are not charged for either; and a ginger 'dog' biscuit is served with coffee.

CLOSING TIMES
Closed 25 December

PRICES
Meals: a la carte £ 18/30

Typical Dishes

Salad of shaved Bath chaps

Lamb & ale pie

Chocolate & hazelnut tartlet with honey ice cream

In heart of Kemp Town, just off Marine Parade (A259) towards Lewes. Metered parking nearby.

23 Jolly Sportsman

Chapel Ln,
East Chiltington, BN7 3BA
Tel.: (01273)890400
Website: www.thejollysportsman.com

VISA

Dark Star Hophead, Harvey's Best

Down a myriad of country lanes, in a small hamlet, this grey clapperboard pub attracts locals in their droves, so even midweek you'll have to book. You're greeted by smoky aromas from an open fire and a bubbly team; often even by the owner himself. Choose a spot in the cosy bar, warmly decorated red room, rear extension or large garden and terrace – and prepare for just as much choice when it comes to the food. There are good value set menus, a rustic, European-based à la carte and interesting bar bites such as Cabezada and Guindillas. Blackboard specials quickly come and go but there's always plenty of local meats, offal and fish to be found on the main menu. A very good wine list and plenty of cask ales, cider and perry are offered too.

CLOSING TIMES
Closed 25-26 December
booking essential

PRICES
Meals: £ 16 (lunch)
and a la carte £ 27/35

Typical Dishes

Lobster & mango salad
Rump of Ditchling lamb
Raspberry champagne jelly & panna cotta

5.5 mi northwest of Lewes by A 275 and B 2116 off Novington Lane. Parking.

24 **Griffin Inn**

Fletching,
TN22 3SS
Tel.: (01825)722890
Website: www.thegriffininn.co.uk

VISA AE

Harvey's Best, Kings of Horsham Best, Hogs Back Tea

Under the same ownership for over 30 years, this hugely characterful red and white brick coaching inn is the kind of place that every village wishes for. It boasts a linen-laid dining room, traditional wood-panelled bar and comfy 'Club Room' adorned with cricketing memorabilia, as well as a sizeable garden and terrace – with wood burning oven for sophisticated summer Sunday barbeques. A large freestanding blackboard in the bar offers a huge range of British and Italian classics and there's a more structured à la carte available in the dining room. If you live locally, work it off by joining one of the pub's cricket teams; if not, follow narrow, sloping corridors to one of the individually decorated bedrooms which are dotted about the place.

CLOSING TIMES
Closed 25 December

PRICES
Meals: a la carte £ 20/27
13 rooms: £ 60/145

Typical Dishes

Pan-fried scallops with spiced lentils

Wood-roasted rump of lamb with red onions and chorizo

Rhubarb and ginger beer jelly

In centre of village. Parking.

25 Ginger Pig

3 Hove St,
Hove, BN3 2TR
Tel.: (01273)736123
Website: www.gingermanrestaurants.com

VISA AE

Harvey's Sussex Best Bitter and Sharp's Doom Bar

Set just off the seafront, this smart building displays a mortar relief of a ship above the entrance and a beautifully restored revolving door, harking back to its former days as the Ship Hotel. Inside you'll find a long wood-floored bar and large dining room, and although they take bookings it's worth arriving early, especially at weekends. The à la carte offers precisely prepared, flavoursome British dishes – including plenty of vegetarian options – and there are great value set menus at both lunch and dinner, along with some good wine deals; order a coffee and it'll arrive with a quirky pig-shaped shortbread. They're used to being busy and service copes well under pressure, the only drawback being that it can lack a more personal touch.

CLOSING TIMES
Closed 25 December

PRICES
Meals: a la carte £ 24/34

Typical Dishes

Grilled asparagus & crispy duck egg

Lamb, leek & raisin pie with mash

Tonka bean panna cotta

Off north side of shore road, Kingsway, A 259. NCP car park (2min walk) & parking meters (2hr maximum during day).

26 Ship Inn

The Strand,
Rye, TN31 7DB
Tel.: (01797)222233
Website: www.theshipinnrye.co.uk

VISA MC

Harvey's Best Bitter, Gold Top, Oyster Stout, Ginger Knoll

Fittingly located at the bottom of Mermaid Street, The Ship Inn dates back to 1592, when it was used as a warehouse for impounding smuggled goods. This is a place that proves that smart surroundings aren't a prerequisite for good food. Modern pop art and boars' heads are dotted about the rooms, fairy lights are draped everywhere and if you sit on one of the battered sofas, don't be alarmed if you end up at a quirky angle or even falling through. The quality of the food then, comes as a surprise. Ingredients are well-sourced and preparation is careful. The result: flavoursome, rustic dishes that arrive in generous portions – maybe baked cod or soy-braised pork belly. Compact bedrooms display similarly wacky wallpapers and painted floors.

CLOSING TIMES
Open daily

PRICES
Meals: a la carte £ 23/28

10 rooms: £ 80

Typical Dishes

Duck & fig terrine
Rye Bay fish pie
Chocolate mousse

Close to the Quayside. Local car park close by.

Baughurst

27 Wellington Arms

Baughurst Rd,
Baughurst, RG26 5LP
Tel.: (0118)9820110
Website: www.thewellingtonarms.com

VISA

Wadworth 6X, Henrys IPA, Good Old Boy, Old Father Thames and Andwell's King John

If success relies on the effort put into sourcing local produce and making, growing and rearing everything possible, then The Wellington is a sure-fire winner. A smart, cream-washed building with box hedges framing the doorway, it boasts its own herb and vegetable beds, as well as its own pigs, chickens and bees; it comes as no surprise then, to discover homemade honey, preserves and teas for sale in the bar. It's a cosy, welcoming kind of place, with quarry-tiled floors, low beams and just eight tables on offer. Blackboard menus feature 6 dishes per course – which are rubbed off and replaced as produce runs out – and cooking is generous and satisfying, featuring dishes such as goat's cheese soufflé and beef from a farm just over the fields.

CLOSING TIMES
Closed Sunday dinner
booking essential

PRICES
Meals: £ 19 (weekday lunch) and a la carte £ 18/34

Typical Dishes

Crispy fried pumpkin flowers with ricotta & lemon zest

Rack of lamb, wilted salad leaves & rösti

Elderflower jelly, berries & sorbet

8 mi north of Basingstoke by A 339 and minor road through Ramsdell and Pound Green; south of village on the Kingsclere / Newbury rd. Parking.

28 **Bakers Arms**

High St,
Droxford, SO32 3PA
Tel.: (01489)877533
Website: www.thebakersarmsdroxford.com

VISA

Bowman Ales - Swift One & Wallops Wood

The owners of this pub met whilst working abroad on private yachts, eventually returning to their roots to run this roadside inn. Their experience, effort and enthusiasm have stood them in good stead: cooking is unfussy and filling, with an emphasis on locally sourced ingredients. Main dishes might include venison steak or slow cooked Hampshire beef, with puddings like apple crumble or treacle tart. The pub itself is pleasingly traditional with an open-plan bar, Chesterfield sofas and a roaring log fire; interesting decorative oddments include beer adverts, Victorian photographs and stag heads. Staff are friendly and polite, and the prevalence of local produce continues with the beer, which comes from Droxford-based brewery, Bowman Ales.

CLOSING TIMES
Closed Sunday dinner and Monday

PRICES
Meals: a la carte £ 25/31

Typical Dishes

Local rabbit & black pudding salad

Slow cooked pork belly, polenta chips & salsa verde

Strawberry jelly with vanilla panna cotta

6 mi north of Fareham by A 32. Parking.

East End

29 **East End Arms**

Lymington Rd,
East End, SO41 5SY
Tel.: (01590)626223
Website: www.eastendarms.co.uk

VISA

Ringwood Best and Fortyniner

Owned by John Illsley, bass guitarist of Dire Straits, this traditional country pub boasts a great display of black and white photos of legendary singers, musicians and celebrities from his personal collection. When he bought the place in the late '90s, the locals petitioned for him to keep the place the same, so you'll find a slightly shabby bar with cushioned pews, open fire and dart board, and a slightly smarter pine-furnished dining room behind. Menus are fairly concise, featuring local produce in satisfying, British-based dishes, which are listed in order of price. You might find whitebait followed by pigeon breast, maybe even shark loin. Service is polite if a little lack-lustre. Modern, cottage-style bedrooms provide a smart contrast.

CLOSING TIMES
Closed Sunday dinner

PRICES
Meals: a la carte £ 19/27
5 rooms: £ 68/115

Typical Dishes

Wild mushroom risotto
Rib-eye steak & fries
Creamed rice pudding

3 mi east of Lymington by B 3054. Parking.

30 **Bugle**

High St,
Hamble-le-Rice, SO31 4HA
Tel.: (023)80453000
Website: www.buglehamble.co.uk

VISA AE

Flack Manor, Fagins, Altons Pride, Swift One

This attractive whitewashed pub is set down a cobbled street in the coastal village of Hamble-le-Rice. It's popular with the sailing community – and is owned by a keen seafarer – and its terrace has pleasant views over Southampton Water. The pub menu is served in the bar and offers sandwiches, small plates such as salt and pepper squid or devilled white bait – and pub classics like ale-battered fish and chips or home-cooked honey roast ham. The à la carte is available in the dining room and features more ambitious dishes such as seared local wood pigeon breast, slow-roast pork belly or whole roasted local plaice. Sporting events are popular thanks to the flat screen TVs; equally well-liked are the regular quiz nights and themed food evenings.

CLOSING TIMES
Open daily
booking essential

PRICES
Meals: a la carte £ 20/28

Typical Dishes

Ham hock terrine
Hampshire burger with skinny chips
Chocolate fondant

7 mi southeast of Southampton by A 3024 or A 3025 and B 3397. Parking.

31

Hogget

London Rd,
Hook, RG27 9JJ
Tel.: (01256)763009
Website: www.hogget.co.uk

VISA

Marstons IPA, Ringwood Best and Perfect Union

Its unusual name refers to a boar of between one and two years of age – hence the rather cute sign. Were he still with us, former owner Cornelius Byford, whose picture hangs inside, would no doubt be pleased with the bay windows and heated terrace; the customers certainly seem to like the pub and, despite its location at the junction of the A30 and A287 (with no in-built community to serve), it has become mightily popular. Its success is down to wholesome food and sensible prices; all dishes are homemade using local produce, and choices range from fish and chips or rib-eye steak through to pan-fried fillets of bream or pea and ham risotto. There are breakfasts most mornings and roasts on a Sunday. Polite service comes from cheery staff.

CLOSING TIMES
Closed 25-26 December and Sunday dinner

PRICES
Meals: a la carte £ 30/36

Typical Dishes

Crispy squid with mango & chilli

Rump of lamb with sautéed cabbage & bacon

Apple & sultana oat crumble

At the junction of A 30 and A 287. Parking.

32 Old House at Home

Newnham Green,
Newnham, RG27 9AH
Tel.: (01256)762222

VISA MC AE

Gold Muddler and Wadworth 6X

Tucked away in the corner of a picturesque green, you'll find this mid-19C former post office. Having survived two fires, the owners – one the daughter of cricket commentator 'Blowers' – have restored it nicely and it exudes warmth and charm aplenty. You'll find the local shooting party in most Fridays in season and some of the regulars make appearances at both lunch and dinner, while nearby businesspeople frequent the private rooms. The main room is split in half, with roaring fires on both sides – the original bar being cosier. Cooking is refined and measured, with modern, seasonal dishes such as devilled kidneys or oxtail with blood pudding standing alongside tempura of soft shell crab – followed by a small but impressive dessert selection.

CLOSING TIMES
Closed 25 December and dinner Sunday and bank holidays
booking advisable

PRICES
Meals: £ 18 and a la carte £ 26/34

Typical Dishes

Twice-baked goat's cheese soufflé

Rosemary skewered monkfish and buffalo mozzarella

Strawberry gazpacho

Southwest 1.5 mi by A30 and Newnham Rd on edge of the green off Newham Ln.

Longstock

33 Peat Spade Inn

Village St,
Longstock, SO20 6DR
Tel.: (01264)810612
Website: www.peatspadeinn.co.uk

VISA AE

Flack's Double Drop, Ringwood Best and Fortyniner

Just north of Stockbridge, in the heart of the Test Valley, you'll come across the pretty village of Longstock and this charming 19C inn, where period furnishings and flickering candlelight are accompanied by warming winter fires. Country pursuits are the name of the game, so you'll find plenty of shooters and fishermen inside, alongside local farm workers and those leisurely passing through. Menus offer classically based dishes that have been brought up-to-date; there might be black pudding Scotch egg with apple purée and crispy bacon, followed by roast halibut with squid ink risotto. Stylish bedrooms are split between the main building and the annexe, there's an open-fired residents' lounge and shooting and fishing trips can be arranged.

CLOSING TIMES
Open daily
booking essential

PRICES
Meals: a la carte £ 20/30
6 rooms: £ 145

Typical Dishes
Portland crab tian, pâté, avocado purée & chilli dressing
Greenfield's pork loin with braised shoulder & black pudding
Lemon tart with raspberry coulis

1.5 mi north of Stockbridge on A 3507. Parking.

34 **The Anchor Inn**

Lower Froyle,
GU34 4NA
Tel.: (01420)23261
Website: www.anchorinnatlowerfroyle.co.uk

VISA AE

Alton's Pride and Bowland's Quiver

With its origins firmly in the 14C, this part-whitewashed, part-tile hung pub boasts much more in the way of history than sister establishment, The Peat Spade Inn. Pretty countryside and a little pond set the scene and the interior doesn't disappoint, boasting characterful low-beamed olive green rooms and a pleasing mix of cushioned pews, benches and old chairs. Good-sized menus offer classic pub dishes with a refined edge and cooking is hearty and flavoursome; you might find jellied ham hock, followed by sirloin steak and jam roly poly to finish. Service is fittingly keen and friendly, and there's a concise but well-chosen wine list. Bedrooms are characterful but if you retire before closing, you may be able to hear a gentle hum from the bar.

CLOSING TIMES
Closed 25 December

PRICES
Meals: a la carte £ 27/35
5 rooms: £ 90/150

Typical Dishes

Chicken liver parfait
Beer-battered haddock & triple cooked chips
Jam roly poly

5 mi northeast of Alton by A 31. Parking.

35

Purefoy Arms

Preston Candover,
RG25 2EJ
Tel.: (01256)389777
Website: www.thepurefoyarms.co.uk

Inspectors' favourites

VISA MC AE

Andwells, Ichen Valley, Black Sheep

Don't be fooled by the somewhat austere façade; a charming young couple have totally restored this once crumbling pub, which was last rebuilt in the 1860s. It now comes with an attractive contemporary feel, although many of the original features have been retained. The daily changing menu, with its hints of Spain – especially in the bar nibbles – is very appealing. Some luxury ingredients may appear at weekends but the philosophy is tasty food at competitive prices and everything's homemade, including the bread. There are also dishes to share, such as the suckling pig, which requires pre-ordering. And the chocolates in the bar are courtesy of the owner's father, a retired chocolatier who has set up a studio in one of the barns.

CLOSING TIMES
Closed 1 January

PRICES
Meals: a la carte £ 20/35

Typical Dishes

Pig's head terrine, chicory & mustard salad

Catalan fish stew, aioli & almonds

Churros con chocolate

6.5 mi north of New Alresford on B 3046 in centre of village. Parking.

36 Three Tuns

58 Middlebridge St,
Romsey, SO51 8HL
Tel.: (01794)512639
Website: www.the3tunsromsey.co.uk

Inspectors' favourites

VISA AE

Ringwood Best, Sharp's Doom Bar and Bath Ales Gem

Having been through a number of mismanagements over the last few years, this charming pub, which dates from the 1720s, appears to have finally got the tenants it deserves. Tucked down a quiet road, it oozes charm from the moment you walk in. The low beamed bar with crackling fires is usually full of locals enjoying a drink and some small plates from the blackboard. Beyond is a panelled room where you'll be offered well-priced and reassuringly 'proper' pub food, like steak and kidney pie or home-baked honey-glazed ham and eggs; while dishes like belly of pork with black pudding and Hampshire rhubarb crumble show that this is a kitchen with a deft touch. Service is pitched just right and is provided by a young and very hospitable team.

CLOSING TIMES
Closed Sunday dinner in winter

PRICES
Meals: a la carte £ 15/26

Typical Dishes

Wild rabbit & black pudding terrine
Poached smoked haddock
Rhubarb fool

Towards the western end of the town, off the by-pass. Parking.

37 White Star Tavern, Dining and Rooms

28 Oxford St,
Southampton, SO14 3DJ
Tel.: (023)80821990
Website: www.whitestartavern.co.uk

Inspectors' favourites

VISA AE

Ringwood Best, Fagins, Timothy Taylor, Tribute

You can't miss this striking black pub with its oversized windows and smart pavement terrace. Set in the lively maritime district, it's provided nourishment and shelter for seafarers since the 19C, although you'll find a much more diverse mix of visitors nowadays. It's a spacious place, made up of several different areas organised around a central bar, and displays an eclectic combination of furniture. The à la carte offers a good choice of modern British main courses – finished off with proper old-fashioned puddings – but there's also a selection of tapas-style small plates on offer throughout the day; and they even open early for breakfast. Smart, modern bedrooms boast good facilities; bathrooms are named after legendary White Star Liners.

CLOSING TIMES
Closed 25-26 December

PRICES
Meals: a la carte £ 21/34
13 rooms: £ 79/149

Typical Dishes

Beetroot carpaccio with goat's cheese salad

Fillet of bream with chorizo mash

Vanilla panna cotta

Southeast of West Quay shopping centre, off Bernard Street. Parking meters directly outside and College St car park (2min walk).

38 **Greyhound**

31 High St,
Stockbridge, SO20 6EY
Tel.: (01264)810833
Website: www.thegreyhound.info

VISA MC

Ringwood Best and Upham Ale

It may not be as smart on the outside as some of the other properties in the street but its interior is far nicer than its façade suggests. The bar boasts a low-beamed ceiling and large French bistro posters on the walls, while the comfy lounge makes a great place for coffee and homemade cake. If you fancy a picnic, ask for one of the popular hampers and head for the garden, which runs down to the River Test. Served only inside, the lunch menu offers sandwiches and dishes aimed at people wanting just one course; while dinner consists of a concise à la carte selection featuring old pub recipes but with refined presentation and some restaurant-style touches. Service can sometimes be a little functional. Spacious bedrooms come with huge showers.

CLOSING TIMES
Closed 24-26 December and Sunday dinner

PRICES
Meals: a la carte £ 23/35
7 rooms: £ 70/125

Typical Dishes

Twice-baked blue cheese soufflé

Greenfield pork loin on the bone with a fennel sauce

Plum tarte Tatin

15 mi east of Salisbury by A 30. Parking.

Totford

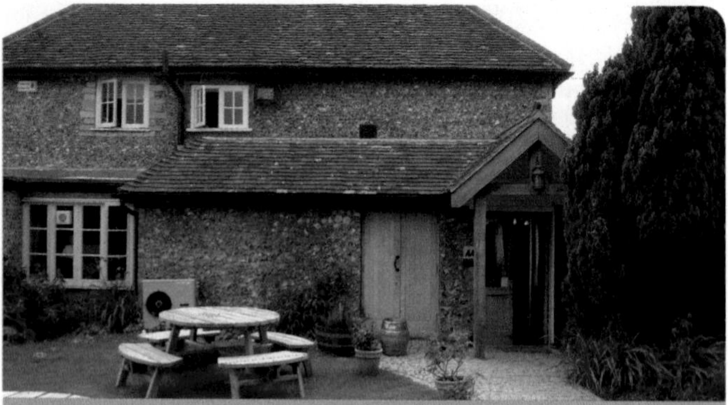

39 **Woolpack Inn**

Totford,
SO24 9TJ
Tel.: (0845)2938066
Website: www.thewoolpackinn.co.uk

VISA AE

Woolpack Ale, King John, Andwell, Copper Ale, Palmers, Bowmans Swift One and Flowerpots Bitter

Flexibility is key at his Grade II listed flint and brick pub: there are two menus available but you can eat what you want, where you want. That could be a roast beef sandwich or Welsh rarebit from the list of Woolpack Classics; or linguine or fishcakes from the dining room menu. The pub's rustic bar and more comfy dining room are popular with walkers and shooting parties – it even has its own drying room. Game features in winter and the pub smokes its own salmon. There are also two wine lists: one of quaffing wines, the other listing some notable French growers and producers. The first Sunday of each month is Quiz Night, when pizzas are cooked in the wood-fired oven. Bedrooms, all named after birds, are housed in a former skittle alley.

CLOSING TIMES
Closed dinner 25 December and bank holiday Mondays

PRICES
Meals: a la carte £ 22/32
7 rooms: £ 85/100

Typical Dishes

Home-smoked warm trout & crispy bacon salad
Confit pork belly, broad beans & peas
Wiltshire lardy cake

3 mi north of New Alresford on B 3046. Parking.

40 **Thomas Lord**

High St,
West Meon, GU32 1LN
Tel.: (01730)829244
Website: www.thethomaslord.co.uk

VISA

Bowman Ales - Wallops Wood, Swift One and Flack Manor Double Drop

This pub is named after the founder of Lord's Cricket Ground, who retired to and is buried in this village – so if you know your stump from your swing and your grubber from your googly, you should feel at home among the bats, county caps and other memorabilia making its home here. Three rooms display a worn, shabby-chic style, with open fires and soft seating; the snug has shelves of second-hand books for sale, with the proceeds going to community projects. Produce is almost exclusively local, with herbs and vegetables from the pub's kitchen garden. The concise menu of British dishes changes at least once a day, depending on what's freshly available and might include crab cakes, Hampshire rarebit, braised lamb or slow-cooked pork belly.

CLOSING TIMES
Closed 1 January,
25 December and Monday

PRICES
Meals: £ 20 (weekdays)
and a la carte £ 26/36

Typical Dishes

Seared king scallops with pea & thyme purée
Pan-roasted duck breast with cherry & thyme compote
Strawberry soup

9 mi west of Petersfield by A 272 and A 32 south.

41 Wykeham Arms

75 Kingsgate St,
Winchester, SO23 9PE
Tel.: (01962)853834
Website: www.wykehamarmswinchester.co.uk

VISA MC AE

Fuller's London Pride, HSB, Seafarer, Goodens Gold and seasonal guest ales

This 18C red-brick inn might be hidden away but that doesn't stop a diverse collection of people from finding it. Tucked away on a cobbled street between the college and cathedral, it's named after Bishop William of Wykeham, who founded the former of these two establishments in the 14C. Made up of various characterful rooms, it's deceptively spacious, with an appealingly shabby style and interesting display of curios; from old school uniform and ex-college desks to Nelson memorabilia, Bishop Pike's mitre and 1,700 tankards. Menus range from soups, pies and pastas through to more elaborate dishes such as lobster. Individually styled bedrooms boast good facilities; those upstairs are the most characterful, those opposite, the most peaceful.

CLOSING TIMES
Open daily
booking essential

PRICES
Meals: £ 15/21
and a la carte £ 29/44
14 rooms: £ 72/145

Typical Dishes
Rosemary-baked goat's cheese with poached pear
Seared rump fillet of beef with oxtail cannelloni
Hot bitter chocolate fondant

Near (St Mary's) Winchester College. Access to car park via Canon Street only. Parking or street parking with permit.

42 Taverners

High St,
Godshill, PO38 3HZ
Tel.: (01983)840707
Website: www.thetavernersgodshill.co.uk

VISA MC

Taverners, Sharps Doom Bar, guest ale every week

In a pretty – and often busy – little village, stands The Taverners, a pleasant whitewashed pub with a cosy, characterful bar and two deceptively large dining rooms. It's the kind of place that's all about the latest island ingredients and handmade, homemade everything. Out front, a blackboard asks for any surplus home-grown produce (in return for a local Taverners beer or two); to the rear, a large garden is home to chickens, herbs and veg; and inside, various boards display food miles and tables of what's in season and when. Cooking is fresh and tasty, mixing traditional pub classics such as lamb burgers with more ambitious daily specials like sea bass fillets. The hand-raised pork pie is a speciality, as is "my nan's" lemon meringue pie.

CLOSING TIMES
Closed first 3 weeks January

PRICES
Meals: a la carte £ 21/24

Typical Dishes

Baked Bembridge crab with watercress

Slow-roast Moor Farm pork belly with bubble & squeak

Lemon meringue pie

4 mi west of Shanklin by A 3020. Parking.

Biddenden

43 The Three Chimneys

Hareplain Rd,
Biddenden, TN27 8LW
Tel.: (01580)291472
Website: www.thethreechimneys.co.uk

VISA

Adnams Lighthouse and St Austell Tribute

This delightful pub dates back to 1420 and has all the character you would expect of a building its age. The low-beamed, dimly lit rooms have a truly old world feel and for sunnier days there's a conservatory, garden and charming terrace. Menus feature largely British dishes such as smoked haddock, finished off with classics like apple crumble, and there are some tempting Biddenden wines, ciders and cask ales on offer. The story surrounding the pub's name goes that French prisoners held at Sissinghurst Castle during the Seven Years' War were allowed to wander as far as the three lanes but were forbidden to pass the junction where the pub was sited. 'Les trois chemins' (the three roads) was then later mistranslated into 'The Three Chimneys'.

CLOSING TIMES
Closed 25 and dinner 31 December
booking essential

PRICES
Meals: a la carte £ 25/36

Typical Dishes

Cheddar rarebit with Serrano ham

Fillet of salmon with tarragon butter

Amaretto parfait with griottine cherries

1.5 mi west by A 262. Parking.

44 **Dove**

Plum Pudding Ln,
Dargate, ME13 9HB
Tel.: (01227)751360
Website: www.thedoveinndargate.co.uk

VISA MC AE

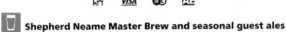

Shepherd Neame Master Brew and seasonal guest ales

Set in the heart of a sleepy hamlet, in the delectable sounding Plum Pudding Lane, this attractive red-brick Victorian pub boasts well-tended gardens and three cosy rooms set with scrubbed pine tables. It's very much a locals pub and villagers pop in and out all day, especially at lunchtime and after work. Phillip, the chef-owner, began his training here at the age of 17 and returned over 10 years later to take the helm. Weekdays he offers a hugely appealing menu of enticing nibbles, pub classics and dishes like smoked cod macaroni: cooking is simple but executed with care and a light touch. Friday and Saturday things step up a gear with a concise, more ambitious menu and prices to match; you might find crab risotto or gurnard with chorizo.

CLOSING TIMES

Closed 1 week February, Sunday dinner and Monday

booking advisable at weekends

PRICES

Meals: a la carte £ 18/34

Typical Dishes

Smoked haddock risotto

Roasted Seasalter marsh lamb, anchovies & asparagus

Warm chocolate brownie

Between Faversham and Whitstable, south of A 299.
Parking.

45 Granville

Street End,
Lower Hardres, CT4 7AL
Tel.: (01227)700402
Website: www.thegranvillecanterbury.com

VISA MC AE

Masterbrew and one seasonal ale

This pub may not look as impressive as the Tudor warship it's named after but it definitely has the size. Set on a small village crossroads, it's a real family affair, with the owner's sister out front and her partner in the kitchen – and, like their other pub, The Sportsman, you can guarantee it'll be busy. With a high ceiling, exposed rafters and an open-plan layout, the interior is a touch Scandinavian; the sofas making a great spot for a quick snack, the hotchpotch of tables beyond being better for a proper meal. A constantly evolving blackboard menu offers unfussy dishes which arrive in generous, flavoursome portions; mostly on chunky wooden platters. Warm oiled pumpkin seeds come with the bread and veg originates from their allotment.

CLOSING TIMES
Closed Sunday dinner and Monday

PRICES
Meals: a la carte £ 21/34

Typical Dishes

Smoked salmon tart with beetroot relish
Roast leg of lamb & potato gratin
Tiramisu

3 mi south of Canterbury on B 2068. Parking.

46 **Red Lion**

Rawling St,
Milstead, ME9 0RT
Tel.: (01795)830279
Website: www.theredlionmilstead.co.uk

VISA MC

Adnams, Harvey's Best, Whistable Native, Copper Top (Old Dairy Brewery)

A 'Red Lion' pub has stood on this spot since Victorian times; the current one belonging to a very capable and experienced couple, who have run numerous pubs in the area over the years. They like to get involved, so you'll find him hard at work in the kitchen and her leading the friendly, engaging service. It's a simple place, featuring a cosy, open-fired bar where the locals tend to gather and a dining room with rich red walls, benches and Lloyd Loom chairs. The ever-changing blackboard menu offers plenty of choice and the Gallic roots of the chef are clear to see; you might find French onion soup, homemade bouillabaisse, cassoulet of lamb shank and Provençale sauces. In true country style, dishes are honest, wholesome and richly flavoured.

CLOSING TIMES
Closed Sunday and Monday
booking advisable
at weekends

PRICES
Meals: a la carte £ 24/32

Typical Dishes

Seared scallop, black pudding & pea purée
Bouillabaisse
Pistachio crème brûlée

South of Sittingbourne signposted off the A2. Parking.

47 Three Mariners

2 Church Rd,
Oare, ME13 0QA
Tel.: (01795)533633
Website: www.thethreemarinersoare.co.uk

Inspectors' favourites

VISA

Shepherd Neame Masterbrew, Early Bird and Late Red

If you've been negotiating the Saxon Shore Way, this 500 year old pub is the perfect place to refresh yourself, as there's a certain warmth and quirkiness about it, from the roaring fires to the smiley team. A constantly evolving à la carte offers an appealing mix of carefully prepared, flavoursome dishes like smoked pigeon salad or skate cheeks; while the two-choice set menus represent great value – the Walkers' Lunch might include potted duck, chicken pie and homemade ice cream, and the Business Lunch, Parma ham, sea bass and artisan cheeses. From starters to desserts, there's always plenty of local produce. Set in a sleepy hamlet, next to a small marina in the Swale channel, it offers pleasant views over the marshes to the estuary beyond.

CLOSING TIMES
Closed Sunday dinner

PRICES
Meals: £ 17 (weekdays) and a la carte £ 25/32

Typical Dishes

Fish soup with tomato, saffron & garlic
Calves liver with sage, crispy pancetta & veal jus
Chocolate tart

1 mi northwest of Faversham by minor road or A 2 and B 2045. Parking.

48 The Sportsman

Faversham Rd,
Seasalter, CT5 4BP
Tel.: (01227)273370
Website: www.thesportsmanseasalter.co.uk

VISA MC

Shepherd Neame - Masterbrew Bitter, Early Bird, Whitstable Bay and Late Red

Set on the edge of town, close to the sea wall, the unassuming-looking Sportsman proves that you should never judge a book by its cover; for while both it's façade and its interior appear rather modest, it's top-class food really steals the show. The daily blackboard menu might read simply but dishes are rarely as straightforward as they seem; true, they may only feature two or three ingredients but they are top quality, locally sourced and prepared with precision. Flavours are extremely well-judged and presentation is original; the homemade bread, butter and salt remain a highlight and the crispy duck and roasted pork belly are favourites. Arrive early if you want the full choice, as dishes disappear off the menu as produce is used up.

CLOSING TIMES
Closed 25-26 December, Sunday dinner and Monday
booking advisable

PRICES
Meals: a la carte £ 32/41

Typical Dishes

Grilled slip sole
Roast pork belly, crackling & apple sauce
Warm chocolate mousse, salted caramel & milk sorbet

2 mi southwest of Whitstable by B 2205 following the coast road. Parking.

49 George & Dragon

Speldhurst Hill,
Speldhurst, TN3 0NN
Tel.: (01892)863125
Website: www.speldhurst.com

VISA MC

Harveys Best, Larkins Traditional and Westerham Georges Marvellous Medicine

Dating back to 1212, this timbered Wealden Hall house boasts an impressive beamed ceiling and displays an unusual Queen's post in the upstairs dining room (unfortunately only used at busier times). It's thought to be the second oldest pub in the country and has even provided refreshment for the soldiers returning from Agincourt. It's a hugely appealing place, with several rooms, characterful flag floors, vast inglenook fireplaces and a contrastingly modern, landscaped terrace. Cooking is generous and strives to keep things local and organic. Lunch offers largely pub classics, while dinner sees more elaborate offerings such as Kentish ham hock and Turners Hill pheasant. The Groombridge belly pork and Ashdown Forest venison are best sellers.

CLOSING TIMES
Closed 1 January, Sunday dinner and bank holiday Monday dinner

PRICES
Meals: a la carte £ 23/31

Typical Dishes
Pigeon breasts with braised baby gems & home-cured bacon
Gloucester Old Spot pork belly with apple compote
Chocolate brownie with honeycomb ice cream

3.5 mi north of Royal Tunbridge Wells by A 26. Parking.

50 Pearson's Arms

The Horsebridge,
Sea Wall, Whitstable, CT5 1BT
Tel.: (01227)773133

Inspectors' favourites

Website: www.pearsonsarmsbyrichardphillips.co.uk

VISA MC

Gadds No.5, Whitstable Brewery IPA, Otter, Timothy Taylor's Landlord, Harveys Best

With the Thames Estuary stretching out in front of it, this characterful pub is in a great spot. Exposed beams and wood floors provide a pleasant rustic style and contemporary furnishings add a touch of modernity. Enter into the bar for a pint from the next door brewery and snacks such as whitebait, jellied eels and crispy pigs' ears or head up to the dining room for superb water views and a more extensive selection of comforting dishes. You might find ham hock and parsley ballotine or lobster and prawn cocktail, followed by wild boar and apple sausages or an assiette of fruits der mer; with flavoursome Kentish produce to the fore. Service is friendly and copes well, and there's a great atmosphere, enhanced by live music every Tuesday.

CLOSING TIMES
Closed Sunday-Tuesday dinner

PRICES
Meals: £ 13 (lunch) and a la carte £ 23/37

Typical Dishes

Scallops baked in shell

Slow-roast belly pork, sage cabbage & grain mustard sauce

Marinated cherry trifle

In centre of town on seafront. Street parking nearby.

51 Sweet Olive at The Chequers Inn

Baker St,
Aston Tirrold, OX11 9DD
Tel.: (01235)851272
Website: www.sweet-olive.com

VISA MC AE

Brakspear, Fuller's London Pride

A red-brick Victorian pub at the heart of an English village; cosy, welcoming and frequented by locals. What sets it apart is its decidedly Gallic feel, attributable in no small part to its French owners. One of the owners also happens to be the chef, so expect to see dishes like Mediterranean fish soup and onglet of beef on the menu; other staples include the more globally influenced tiger prawns in tempura or crispy duck salad, and the thoroughly British ox cheeks and mash or treacle sponge and custard. The old French wine boxes which bedeck the bar offer a clue as to wine list: most are from France, with many from the Alsace region. Oenophiles, or those celebrating, will find plenty to get excited about on the separate fine wine list.

CLOSING TIMES
Closed 3 weeks February, 2 weeks July, Sunday dinner and Wednesday
booking essential

PRICES
Meals: a la carte £ 25/35

Typical Dishes

Tempura tiger prawns & rocket salad with spicy soy dressing

Escalope of venison with port wine sauce

Treacle sponge & custard

4 mi southwest of Wallingford by minor road through South Moreton. Parking.

52 **Kings Head Inn**

The Green,
Bledington, OX7 6XQ
Tel.: (01608)658365
Website: www.kingsheadinn.net

VISA

Various guest ales from Hook Norton, Wadworth's, Cottage and Purity Breweries

This warmly welcoming 15C inn is set on the pretty village green with a stream running alongside. Seats by the fire in its low ceilinged, beamed bar are popular; the dining room is just as comfortable, if perhaps not quite as atmospheric, while the paved terrace is great for alfresco dining in the sun. The same menu is served in all areas and you'll find traditional dishes such as pan-fried lamb cutlets or homemade steak, ale and root vegetable pie, with the odd international influence thrown in. Cooking is robust and rustic in style, with local ingredients well used. Bedrooms are smart, with good facilities and some antique furniture; those in the pub itself are older and more characterful, while the others have a more stylish feel.

CLOSING TIMES
Closed 25-26 December

PRICES
Meals: a la carte £ 21/35
12 rooms: £ 50/125

Typical Dishes

Crayfish, crab & leek terrine

Aberdeen Angus sirloin steak

Peach & almond tart

4 mi southeast of Stow-on-the-Wold by A 436 and B 4450. Parking.

Buckland Marsh

53 Trout at Tadpole Bridge

Buckland Marsh,
SN7 8RF
Tel.: (01367)870382
Website: www.troutinn.co.uk

VISA

Youngs, Ramsbury, White Horse Wayland Smithy, Loose Cannon Abingdon Bridge and Butts Barbus Barbus

If you fancy trying your hand at boating, then The Trout could be the pub for you. Set just off the Thames Path, it boasts a pleasant garden running down to the river, where, upon request, you'll find an electric punt, complete with picnic hamper; and six private moorings. It's a smart place but manages to retain a loyal band of drinkers, who congregate in the characterful flagstone bar; the diners sat beside them or in the airy back room. The concise main menu consists of classical Gallic dishes with the odd contemporary touch, supplemented by a blackboard of daily specials that often include seafood or game. It's a popular place, so you'll need to book but the cheery staff cope well under pressure. Comfortable bedrooms exceed expectations.

CLOSING TIMES
Closed 25-26 December and Sunday dinner November-March

PRICES
Meals: a la carte £ 22/34
6 rooms: £ 70/150

Typical Dishes
Tempura of red mullet
Pan-fried calves liver with spring onion mash
Dark chocolate tart

4.5 mi northeast of Faringdon by A 417, A 420 on Brampton road. Parking.

54 **Carpenter's Arms**

Fulbrook Hill,
Burford, OX18 4BH
Tel.: (01993)823275
Website: www.thecarpentersarmsfulbrook.com

VISA AE

Greene King IPA, Abbot Ale and one regularly changing guest ale

2011 saw another change in the ownership of this pub but the good news is that the new couple seem to know what they're doing. For a start, they've brightened it up a little – the bar has an attractive rustic-designery look that's so typical of the Cotswolds, while the room overlooking the garden is very popular when the sun's out. One thing they sensibly decided not to tinker with too much was the menu which remains an appealing mix of recognisable pub classics alongside other dishes of a Mediterranean bent, as well as some thoughtfully compiled seasonal salads. Most visitors to Burford are in such a rush to get into the town that they'll drive straight past The Carpenter's Arms – this is a shame as this is a pub with much going for it.

CLOSING TIMES
Open daily

PRICES
Meals: £ 17 (lunch)
and a la carte £ 21/27

Typical Dishes
Beetroot-cured salmon & new potato salad
Slow-roasted Gloucester Old Spot pork belly, glazed peas & black pudding
Honey panna cotta

0.5 mi northeast of Burford on A361. Parking.

55 **Highway Inn**

117 High St,
Burford, OX18 4RG
Tel.: (01993)823661
Website: www.thehighwayinn.co.uk

VISA

Hook Norton, Cotswold lager and Cotswold cider

You might say that the Highway Inn's owners were meant to be: a local boy, he met his wife when she came over from Australia to visit her grandmother. They married in Burford, and even spent their wedding night at this 15C inn. Fast forward a few years, and it belongs to them. Twinkly lights in the trees draw you in; grab a table in a bay window or close to the roaring fire and take a look at the menu. Pub dishes like fish and chips and sausage and mash are the staples here, with maybe a lamb or pork burger and specials such as risotto, calves liver or lamb shank. Desserts are delicious and far from dainty, with choices like bread and butter pudding. Cooking is as it should be: simple, honest and fresh. Bedrooms are classical and cosy.

CLOSING TIMES
Closed first 2 weeks January and 25-26 December

PRICES
Meals: a la carte £ 24/34
9 rooms: £ 79/140

Typical Dishes

Pressed pig cheek terrine
Chicken breast with wild mushroom & thyme stuffing
Lemon mousse, lime jelly & shortbread

In town centre. Parking unrestricted on the eastern side of the High St.

56 **Lamb Inn**

Sheep St,
Burford, OX18 4LR
Tel.: (01993)823155
Website: www.cotswold-inns-hotels.co.uk

Inspectors' favourites

VISA MC AE

Hook Norton Hooky Bitter and Old Hooky

Set in picture perfect Burford, once famous for its wool and sheep fairs, it's no coincidence that this 1420s weavers' cottage is set on Sheep Street. You can't fail to be impressed by the cosiness of the place, with its characterful flag-floored bar, elegant columned restaurant, courtyard terrace and cottage garden. As well as main dishes and a fresh fish board, the bar offers nibbles, light bites and afternoon tea; while the restaurant offers more substantial daily market menus and a set selection. Cooking is robust and classical but isn't afraid of pushing boundaries; you might find trio of beef, or scallops and langoustines with vanilla sauce. It's rightly popular and, at times, staff can struggle to keep up. Bedrooms are warm and cosy.

CLOSING TIMES
Open daily

PRICES
Meals: £ 25/39
and a la carte £ 25/38
17 rooms: £ 155/270

Typical Dishes

Crab tortellini with avocado
Pig's trotter & apple
Rhubarb panna cotta

Parking at Bay Tree Hotel.

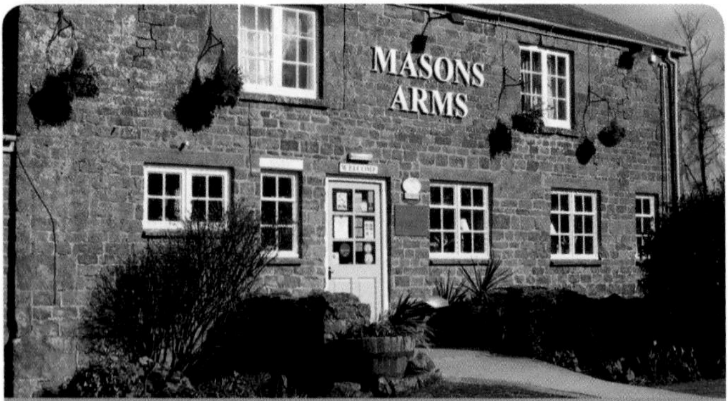

57 Masons Arms

Banbury Rd,
Swerford, Chipping Norton, OX7 4AP
Tel.: (01608)683212
Website: www.masons-arms.com

VISA

Hook Norton Bitter, Brakspear Bitter and Wychwood Hobgoblin

This stone-built inn is the perfect place to be on a lazy summer's day, when you can kick back in the garden, survey the surrounding countryside and linger over a real ale. Don't be out off if the car park looks busy, as although it's a popular destination, there's plenty of room for one and all. They also have the service well and truly sussed, so you'll never have to wait too long. Good value menus present an eclectic mix of unfussy dishes, ranging from the traditional to the more exotic; so you could find anything from a ploughman's to squid tempura or maybe a chicken Jalfrezi. Ingredients are traceable, meats are rare breed, poultry is free range and fish is delivered daily; while terrines, breads and desserts are all homemade.

CLOSING TIMES
Closed Sunday dinner

PRICES
Meals: £ 15 (lunch)
and a la carte £ 20/30

Typical Dishes

Crab & leek fish cakes
Pot-roasted half shoulder of lamb
Buttermilk panna cotta

5 mi northeast of Chipping Norton on A 361. Parking.

58 Crown Inn

Mill Ln,
Church Enstone, OX7 4NN
Tel.: (01608)677262

VISA

Hooky Best, Timothy Taylor, Bombardier

Found in a picturesque village on the edge of the Cotswolds, among pretty stone houses, this 17C inn boasts a welcoming slate-floored conservatory, a beamed dining room and a rustic stone-walled bar; as well as a front terrace and a secluded garden for sunnier days. The chef-owner has built up quite a reputation for his seafood in these parts, so you'll find fishcakes and king scallop and bacon salad as permanent fixtures, alongside beer-battered cod and some more unusual varieties of fish such as Red Gurnard. The daily lunchtime blackboard reads like a top ten of old pub favourites, with the likes of sausage and mash or steak and Hooky ale pie. Meats, fruit and vegetables are sourced from local farms and tasty puddings are made on-site.

CLOSING TIMES
Closed 25-26 December, 1 January and Sunday dinner

PRICES
Meals: a la carte £ 19/29

Typical Dishes

Avocado, bacon & blue cheese salad

Crisp roast belly pork with apple compote

Lemon panna cotta

3.5 mi southeast of Chipping Norton by A 44. Parking.

59 **Eyston Arms**

High St,
East Hendred, OX12 8JY
Tel.: (01235)833320
Website: www.eystonarms.co.uk

VISA AE

Fuller's London Pride and Wadworth 6X

This characterful village is still largely owned by the local estate and although a pub has stood on this site for many years it was once much smaller and – before being knocked through – was adjoined by the estate workers' cottages. Original tiled floors and exposed brickwork remain but it's been given a typical modern dining pub makeover with scrubbed tables, plenty of candles and caricatures of the locals adorning the walls. Staff are equally as warm and welcoming and, as such, they have gained a loyal local following. Menus are kept reasonably simple with the likes of pâtés, fishcakes, char-grilled steaks and Sunday roasts. The sharing antipasti boards are popular choice and desserts often turn out to offer something a little different.

CLOSING TIMES
Closed 25 December and Sunday dinner

PRICES
Meals: a la carte £ 21/32

Typical Dishes

Jumbo king prawns with chilli, lemon & parsley

Trio of local hog

Baked white chocolate & raspberry cheesecake

4.5 mi east of Wantage by A 417. Parking.

60 White Hart

Main Rd,
Fyfield, OX13 5LW
Tel.: (01865)390585
Website: www.whitehart-fyfield.com

VISA

Hooky Bitter, Sharp's Doom Bar

A 15C former chantry house, this intriguing building displays many original features including a two-storey, flag-floored hall with vaulted ceiling (now the dining room), a minstrels' gallery and a secret tunnel; as well as a pleasant terrace and cosy beamed bar with inglenook fireplace. They make good use of the wealth of produce on their doorstep: so you'll find meat from nearby farms or estates; flour – for the homemade bread – from the local mill; and fruit and veg from either the pub's own plot or locals' gardens. Menus offer gutsy, honest British dishes – of they type the owners themselves like to eat – and excellent desserts. Service is slick and friendly, and the annual beer festival and hog roast always makes for a great day out.

CLOSING TIMES
Open daily

PRICES
Meals: £ 19 (lunch)
and a la carte £ 25/35

Typical Dishes

Kelmscott pork, herb & smoked pancetta terrine

Grilled sea trout with herb gnocchi

Summer pudding

10 mi southwest of Oxford by A 420. Parking.

Hampton Poyle

61 Bell at Hampton Poyle

11 Oxford Rd,
Hampton Poyle, OX5 2QD
Tel.: (01865)376242
Website: www.thebellathamptonpoyle.co.uk

VISA AE

Fuller's London Pride and Hook Norton

Tiled flooring and a bright, fresh look make The Bell seem almost Mediterranean in its looks, which is not a style one usually associates with a pub in rural Oxfordshire, but it seems to work. The owners have made the kitchen a very visual element of the operation, with its wood-burning oven and large, open-plan 'pass' and they've created a very accessible menu, which covers all tastes. There's meze, homemade pizza, seafood and charcuterie boards, as well as pub staples such as calves liver and a couple of decent steaks. They tweak it a little with the seasons but also strive to keep prices in check. Some of the bedrooms are above the bar; others are in a small adjoining cottage and are quieter, if a little smaller.

CLOSING TIMES
Open daily

PRICES
Meals: £ 18 and a la carte £ 23/31

9 rooms: £ 140

Typical Dishes

Crispy duck salad
Rump of lamb with elderberry jus
Lemon & raspberry posset

9 mi north of Oxford by A34. Parking.

62

Black Boy

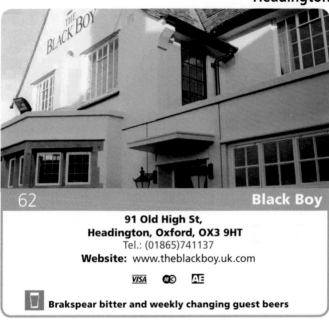

91 Old High St,
Headington, Oxford, OX3 9HT
Tel.: (01865)741137
Website: www.theblackboy.uk.com

VISA MC AE

Brakspear bitter and weekly changing guest beers

It's big and it's bold; it's The Black Boy and it's back to its beautiful best. The chef did a long stint with Raymond Blanc, so it comes as no surprise that there's a French edge to the essentially classic menu, but don't get the wrong idea; this is proper pub food, no messing, with unadorned mains like braised pork belly or sausage and mash for under a tenner. Bring some bling to your Black Boy burger by eating it in the small side restaurant; the low-lit bar is the less popular, but by no means less pleasant, alternative. There are homemade breads and pizzas, a roast goes down a storm for Sunday lunch and Tuesday night is quiz night. Thursday night's for jazz-lovers, and Sunday mornings are when the kids can get creative in the kitchen.

CLOSING TIMES
Open daily

PRICES
Meals: a la carte £ 19/28

Typical Dishes

Crayfish & broad bean risotto

Pork belly with garlic scented mashed potato

Iced white chocolate mousse

East of Oxford off London Rd. Some parking at the front of pub and in nearby streets.

Kingham

63 **Kingham Plough**

The Green,
Kingham, OX7 6YD
Tel.: (01608)658327
Website: www.thekinghamplough.co.uk

VISA

Hook Norton, Purity, Hereford Pale Ale, Donnington

Set on the green of a beautifully unspoilt village in the Evenlode Valley, this pub boasts a rustic bar, laid-back restaurant and easy-going team. It's owned by Emily Watkins, former sous-chef at The Fat Duck, so you'll find the odd dish such as snails on toast that harks back to her Heston days. The majority of dishes are rooted in the gutsy pub vein, however; albeit a very modern one. The bar menu offers a selection of tasty snacks such as scotched quails' eggs or hand-raised pork pie, while the concise restaurant menu features the latest seasonal produce from foraging expeditions and nearby farms or estates – evolving throughout the evening as ingredients arrive. Preparation is careful and slow cooking reigns. Nearby, comfy bedrooms await.

CLOSING TIMES
Closed 25 December

PRICES
Meals: a la carte £ 27/40
7 rooms: £ 75/130

Typical Dishes

Pressed duck terrine
Wild rabbit, with potato dumplings, morels & asparagus
Elderflower & strawberry 'split'

In village centre. Parking.

64 **Tollgate Inn**

Church St,
Kingham, OX7 6YA
Tel.: (01608)658389
Website: www.thetollgate.com

VISA AE

Hook Norton Bitter and regularly changing guest ales

The owners of the Tollgate Inn used to live next door to it – and loved the pub so much, they bought it. It sits proudly at the centre of this unspoiled village, its front terrace bathed in the midday sun, and attracts passing trade as well as loyal locals. The building is a Grade II listed former Georgian farmhouse which dates back to 1720 but the interior is modern and light, with comfy seating and inglenook fireplaces helping to create a relaxed feel. Food-wise, the choice is more than adequate: while the easy-going lunch menu might offer a Cajun chicken salad or lasagne, the more ambitious dinner menu focuses on dishes like roasted duck breast or pan-fried venison. Modern bedrooms are immaculately kept and have a warm, bright feel.

CLOSING TIMES
Closed Sunday dinner and Monday

PRICES
Meals: a la carte £ 20/35
9 rooms: £ 70/100

Typical Dishes

Country pâté
Halibut with crab risotto & crab bisque sauce
White chocolate & raspberry crème brûlée

3 mi southwest of Chipping Norton by B 4450 to Churchill and minor road west. Parking.

65 Five Horseshoes

Maidensgrove,
RG9 6EX
Tel.: (01491)641282
Website: www.thefivehorseshoes.co.uk

VISA

Brakspear Bitter and Oxford Gold

Many a walker can be found sat by the crackling log fire in the bar of this charming, part-17C inn, resting their weary feet and refuelling on one of the pub's renowned doorstop sandwiches. Others take a seat in the splendidly sun-soaked restaurant and wine room, or in the garden, with its stunning views out over the countryside. The chef has dipped into many a famous kitchen and his dishes range from comforting classics like Berkshire pork bangers or rib-eye steak with fat chips to more ambitious offerings such as truffle tagliatelle or smoked rainbow trout with chopped goose egg. In summer, the wood-fired oven is used to cook breads, pizzas and various meats. Homely desserts might include apple and rhubarb crumble or sticky toffee pudding.

CLOSING TIMES
Open daily

PRICES
Meals: a la carte £ 20/30

Typical Dishes
Smoked salmon with celeriac remoulade
Roast haunch of venison with potato purée & baby spinach
Dark chocolate mousse cake

6.25 mi northwest of Henley by A 4130, B 480, and Maidensgrove rd. Parking.

66 **Old Swan**

Minster Lovell,
OX29 0RN
Tel.: (01993)774441
Website: www.oldswanandminstermill.com

VISA MC AE D

Wychwood brewery - Hobgoblin, King Goblin, Wychcraft

They may be a few hundred miles apart but the Old Swan and its sister, the Cary Arms, share a few things in common, including stylish accommodation and a passion for fresh, simply cooked food. The Old Swan is just the sort of place you expect to come across in Oxfordshire, with its smart parquet floor, roaring open fires and collection of horse brasses and Toby jugs. For summer there's boules and a giant chess set in the garden – set next to large herb plots which supply the pub all year-round and contribute to unfussy pub classics and tasty daily specials from the Brixham day boats. Chic bedrooms are accessed via a winding staircase and display period furnishings, quality linens and the latest mod cons – some even boast feature bathrooms.

CLOSING TIMES
Open daily
booking essential

PRICES
Meals: a la carte £ 29/41
16 rooms: £ 125/325

Typical Dishes

Crab & crayfish cocktail
Steak & Hobgoblin ale pie
Rice pudding with winter berry & whisky compote

3.5 mi west of Witney by B 4047. Parking.

67 Nut Tree

Main St,
Murcott, OX5 2RE
Tel.: (01865)331253
Website: www.nuttreeinn.co.uk

VISA AE

Vale Best Bitter, Fuller's London Pride, Hooky Gold, Shepherd Neame Spitfire

You want a good old-fashioned thatched pub with a cosy beamed bar, and a tasty, good quality meal: enter The Nut Tree. It's owned by a local and his wife, and apart from the addition of a smart new restaurant, the building itself has altered little since they bought it. Appealing menus change constantly as the latest seasonal ingredients arrive and produce is organic, free range or wild wherever possible. Breads and ice creams are homemade, salmon is smoked on-site and sausages and pork pies are for sale. In the ultimate bid to ensure only the freshest of meats are used, they even rear their own rare breed pigs and Dexter cattle out back. There's always plenty of choice too, with offerings ranging from baguettes to ambitious tasting menus.

CLOSING TIMES
Closed Sunday dinner and Monday

PRICES
Meals: £ 22 (weekday lunch) and a la carte £ 32/49

Typical Dishes
Pan-fried terrine of pig's head & black pudding
Olive oil poached fillet of halibut, green herb risotto
Sticky toffee pudding & praline ice cream

7 mi from Bicester by A 41 east and a minor road south via Lower and Upper Arncott; at T-junction beyond the motorway turn right. Parking.

68 **Fishes**

North Hinksey,
OX2 0NA
Tel.: (01865)249796
Website: www.fishesoxford.co.uk

VISA

Greene King IPA, Old Speckled Hen and one regularly changing guest ale

This pub's pretty riverside garden, with its fairytale white benches, is a large part of its charm – kick back with a drink on a lazy afternoon or order a picnic, which comes complete with crockery, cutlery and even a blanket on which to sit. Inside, the décor moves seamlessly between the traditional – think stuffed fish in display cases – and the modern – try colourful abstract artwork and low leather seating. The atmosphere is lively, and, the garden apart, the decked terrace and the conservatory are the best places to sit. Food is fresh, free range and available all day: dishes might include sticky pork ribs, rack of lamb or sausage and mash; some choices come in small or large portions and there are a selection of deli boards for two.

CLOSING TIMES
Closed 25 December

PRICES
Meals: a la carte £ 20/40

Typical Dishes

Chicken & summer vegetable terrine

Asparagus & pecorino ravioli

Warm flourless chocolate cake

3 mi west of Oxford city centre by A 420 and minor road south on east side of A 34. Parking.

69 Anchor

2 Hayfield Rd,
Walton Manor, Oxford, OX2 6TT
Tel.: (01865)510282
Website: www.theanchoroxford.com

Inspectors' favourites

VISA

Wadworth 6X and Bishops Tipple, IPA, Everards Tiger, Courage Directors

Located in a smart residential area by the city, this striking art deco pub is one of a handful of town-based establishments left that understand the true meaning of 'community'. Set beside a lovely old convenience store, just a stone's throw from the canal, it hosts a breakfast club on Fridays, a quiz night on Sundays and is home to the local book club. A careful renovation has retained a lovely atmosphere, with coal fires burning brightly among dark wood panelling and characterful furnishings befitting its age. The chef is keen to promote local, seasonal ingredients and produces tasty, gutsy, carefully presented dishes ranging from snack-sized Worcester sauce glazed cocktail sausages to substantial daily specials like whole roast wood pigeon.

CLOSING TIMES
Closed 25-26 December

PRICES
Meals: a la carte £ 24/29

Typical Dishes

Devilled lamb's kidneys

Wood pigeon with pea, broad bean & asparagus risotto

Treacle tart with ginger cream

Just north of city centre off Woodstock Rd. Parking.

70 **Magdalen Arms**

243 Iffley Rd,
Oxford, OX4 1SJ
Tel.: (01865)243159

Inspectors' favourites

VISA MC

Theakston's Best Bitter, Caledonian Double Twist and IPA ,Ringwood Fortyniner

This battleship-grey pub is a relative newcomer to the established Oxford scene but it's already a hit with the locals. The place buzzes – even on a weeknight – and there's always something to keep you entertained, be it a board game or a turn on the bar billiards table. The spacious, open-plan interior boasts deep red walls, quirky old standard lamps and an eclectic collection of 1920s posters, while huge blackboards display nibbles and the twice daily changing menu. Order at the bar for a casual lunch or head through to the curtained-off dining room for table service. The experienced chef uses local ingredients to create tasty, good value dishes; perhaps pork and rabbit rillettes, braised ox cheek or seven hour lamb for five to share.

CLOSING TIMES
Closed 2 weeks August, 24-26 December, 1 January, Sunday dinner, Tuesday lunch, Monday and bank holidays

PRICES
Meals: a la carte £ 26/38

Typical Dishes

Crab soup with Gruyère
Slow-roasted Tuscan style pork
Rhubarb & custard

Southeast of city centre on A 4158. On-street parking.

71 **Orwells**

Shiplake Row,
Henley-on-Thames, RG9 4DP
Tel.: (01189)403673
Website: www.orwellsatshiplake.co.uk

VISA

Brakspear and Oxford Gold

Dating from the 18C – and formerly called The White Hart but renamed in honour of George Orwell who spent his childhood in Shiplake Row – this pub has been leased by the brewery to a local boy with experience in some stellar kitchens. The contemporary interior is neatly divided into three distinct sections: the bar, the cosy conservatory and the imaginatively titled fine dining room, 'The Room'. Food is very much the focus of the operation and the commendable 'use local' ethos is evident throughout: rabbit rissoles or wild garlic risotto could appear on the appealing bar menu, while dishes for the restaurant's dinner menu reveal themselves to be altogether more ambitious and elaborate in design, using modern techniques and styles of presentation.

CLOSING TIMES
Closed first 2 weeks January, first 2 weeks September, 1 week April, Sunday dinner and Monday except bank holidays

PRICES
Meals: £ 16 (lunch) and a la carte £ 25/53

Typical Dishes
Rabbit Scotch egg
Pan-seared fillet of Brixham plaice with crayfish & nettle risotto
Baked Alaska with raspberry yoghurt ice cream

3.5 mi south of Henley-on-Thames off A 4155 on Peppard road towards Binfield Heath. Parking.

72 **Wykham Arms**

Temple Mill Rd,
Sibford Gower, OX15 5RX
Tel.: (01295)788808
Website: www.wykhamarms.co.uk

VISA MC

St Austell Tribute, Sharps Atlantic IPA, Wye Valley Best Bitter, Wadworth 6X

If you're after a true village pub, the 17C Wykham Arms may well be it. Set down narrow lanes in the middle of the countryside, this thatched pub certainly plays its role in the community. It boasts attractive sand-coloured stone walls adorned with pretty climbing plants and a pleasant terrace with cast iron furniture. So as not to price out the locals, menus offer a range of dishes right through from light bites and bar snacks to the full three courses; so you might find Salcombe crab and mango salad, Brixham sea bream or baby deer. Suppliers are proudly noted on the blackboard and the chef is only too happy to answer any questions. There's a good choice of wines and what better way to celebrate than with lobster and champagne on the terrace?

CLOSING TIMES
Closed Monday except bank holidays

PRICES
Meals: a la carte £ 23/31

Typical Dishes

Pan-fried squid with chorizo salad

Rump of Lighthorne lamb with bubble & squeak

Panna cotta with poached rhubarb

8 mi west of Banbury by B 4035. Parking.

73 **Sir Charles Napier**

Sprigg's Alley,
OX39 4BX
Tel.: (01494)483011
Website: www.sircharlesnapier.co.uk

VISA AE

Wadworth 6X

Set in a small hamlet on the hillside, this attractive 18C flint pub might just have it all. The delightful terrace and gardens buzz with conversation in the warmer months, while sculptures of beasts and figures peer out from behind bushes or lie on the lawn. Inside yet more creatures hide about the place – and all are for sale. It's worth heading to the cosy bar with its open fires and comfy sofas, although the beamed dining room adorned with flowers and art is equally as charming. Cooking is refined and has a strong French accent, offering the likes of eel and foie gras terrine followed by noisette of venison or boeuf Bourguignon. Dishes are skilfully prepared and capture flavours to their full. A well-chosen wine list completes the picture.

CLOSING TIMES
Closed 24-26 December, Sunday dinner and Monday except bank holidays
booking advisable

PRICES
Meals: £ 25 (weekdays) and a la carte £ 35/51

Typical Dishes
Scallops with salt cod
Duck breast, pithivier & carrot purée
Vanilla yoghurt with citrus jelly

2.5 mi southeast of Chinnor by Bledlow Ridge rd. Parking.

74 **Fish**

4 Appleford Rd,
Sutton Courtenay, OX14 4NQ
Tel.: (01235)848242
Website: www.thefishatsuttoncourtenay.co.uk

VISA AE

Greene King Abbot Ale

Its owners have brought a taste of La France profonde to The Fish, so expect French pictures, French music and a largely French wine list as well as a profusion of French food and charming Gallic service. Feast on meaty terrines, escargots or moules marinière; such dishes mingle merrily on the menu with British pub classics such as steak and kidney pie, as well as dishes like Gressingham duck breast or fillet of lamb. L'entente cordiale continues on the dessert menu, with crème brûlée clamouring for your attention alongside treacle sponge and profiteroles. This is robust country cooking in its most classic form, with pretty much everything homemade using seasonal ingredients. Head to the rear of the pub for the lovely garden and conservatory.

CLOSING TIMES
Closed Monday except bank holidays and Sunday dinner

PRICES
Meals: £ 17 (lunch) and a la carte £ 24/34

Typical Dishes

Home-smoked chicken & avocado salad

Fillet of halibut with tomato salsa & lemon rice

Lemon cheesecake

Between Abingdon and Didcot on B 4016. Parking.

75 **Swan Inn**

Swinbrook,
OX18 4DY
Tel.: (01993)823339
Website: www.theswannswinbrook.co.uk

VISA MC AE

Hook Norton, Wadworth's, Purity, Adnams

Set on the banks of a meandering river, The Swan Inn is a delightful place – so booking is a must. Outside, you'll find honey-coloured walls covered in wisteria and a lovely garden filled with fruit trees; while the interior boasts an open oak frame and exposed stone walls covered with old lithographs. A well-versed team serve tasty dishes from the daily menu, which features the latest seasonal produce from nearby farms and estates. Cooking is fairly modern in style, with some dishes a contemporary take on older recipes; you might find loin of roe deer carpaccio with truffled mayonnaise, followed by fillet of bream with tandoori crushed potatoes, then baked ginger pudding with hot spiced treacle. Well-appointed bedrooms have a luxurious feel.

CLOSING TIMES
Closed 25-26 December

PRICES
Meals: a la carte £ 20/35
6 rooms: £ 80/120

Typical Dishes

Ham hock terrine
Cornish hake with brown shrimps, lemon & parsley
Summer Bakewell tart

3 mi northeast of Burford by A 40 and minor road north. Parking.

76 **Mole Inn**

Toot Baldon,
OX44 9NG
Tel.: (01865)340001
Website: www.themoleinn.com

VISA MC AE

Hook Norton Old Hooky & Bombardier

The Mole has made quite a name for itself in the area and deservedly so. Beautiful landscaped gardens and a pleasant terrace front the building, while inside attractive beamed ceilings and exposed brick walls create a warm and welcoming atmosphere. The menu is equally appealing, catering for all tastes and appetites; you might find sautéed squid with linguine and chorizo, followed by twice-cooked belly of pork with gratin dauphinoise. Sourcing is a serious business and it's a case of 'first come, first served' if you want the full choice. The Tuesday grill and Wednesday fish night menus are decided the day before, so if there's something you've set your heart on, it's worth calling to reserve your dish. Service remains smooth under pressure.

CLOSING TIMES
Closed 25 December
booking advisable

PRICES
Meals: a la carte £ 27/29

Typical Dishes

Wood pigeon with truffle mash
Venison steak & cottage pie
Apple tarte Tatin

6 mi southeast of Oxford; between B 480 and A 4074. Parking.

Wolvercote

77 **Trout Inn**

195 Godstow Rd,
Wolvercote, OX2 8PN
Tel.: (01865)510930
Website: www.thetroutoxford.co.uk

VISA MC AE

Brakspear's, Oxford Gold, Tribute, Sharp's Doombar, Black Sheep and Adnams

The hustle of Oxford feels a million miles away as you sit on the delightful waterside terrace of this idyllically set Cotswold stone inn, watching the greedy chub. The only problem is, so many people know about it, that if you haven't booked, you could have a lengthy wait. The inn dates back to the 17C but it started life as a hospice for the nearby nunnery. It boasts cosy nooks, crannies and roaring fires, as well as an interesting literary history that includes a visit from the fictional Inspector Morse. Menus focus on Italy, featuring sharing antipasti plates, pizza, pasta, Peroni beer-battered fish and tiramisu; but there are plenty of international influences too, with the likes of Greek meze, Moroccan chicken and teriyaki swordfish.

CLOSING TIMES
Open daily
booking advisable

PRICES
Meals: a la carte £ 22/30

Typical Dishes

Lamb koftas
Classic burger & chips
Chocolate brownie

3 mi northeast of Oxford off A 4114. Parking.

78 **Abinger Hatch**

Abinger Ln,
Abinger Common, RH5 6HZ
Tel.: (01306)730737
Website: www.theabingerhatch.com

VISA MC AE

Sharp's Doom Bar, Ringwood Best, Adnams Bitter, Adnams Regatta, Ringwood Fortyniner, Hogsback Tea, Sharps Cornish Coaster

Deep in the Surrey hills and in prime walking country sits this attractive and lovingly restored 18C inn. With its low beams, leather sofas and roaring log fires it oozes country gentility and the newspapers, magazines and board games show that someone here has an eye for detail. A short à la carte alongside a good value set menu make way for greater choice by the end of the week. The country cooking is fresh, satisfying and a perfect match for the surroundings, be it the charcuterie on a board, lamb pie or gooseberry fool. Lunchtime salads prove popular, as do the Sunday roasts; while hampers are available for those thinking of exploring the countryside in a leisurely fashion. There are plans for four bedrooms in a barn at the back of the pub.

CLOSING TIMES
Open daily

PRICES
Meals: £ 15 (weekdays) and a la carte £ 22/31

Typical Dishes

Smoked salmon pâté
Grilled pork chop & apple compote
Lavender & honey crème brûlée

4.75 mi west of Dorking off A25 in village centre opposite St James' church

Chiddingfold

79 **Swan Inn**

Petworth Rd,
Chiddingfold, GU8 4TY
Tel.: (01428)684688
Website: www.theswaninnchiddingfold.com

VISA AE

Adnams Gunhill, Surrey Hills Shere Drop, Langhams Flor-ale

The elegant tile-hung façade of the Swan Inn hints at its 200 year old heritage, although following a fire in 2003, it's interior is now of a more contemporary vintage. The pub's latest owners moved here from Knightsbridge, swapping the bustling city streets for a more sedate pace of life. Lunchtime sees the Surrey set popping in for maybe Maryland crab cakes or the 'terrine of the day', while the à la carte changes daily depending on the latest local produce available. The experienced owners keep a keen eye over proceedings and cool, contemporary bedrooms complete the picture. Wandering round the green it's hard to believe that eleven glass works once stood here, supplying many of the country's finest buildings, including St Stephen's Chapel.

CLOSING TIMES
Open daily

PRICES
Meals: a la carte £ 22/29
10 rooms: £ 100/125

Typical Dishes

Pan-seared foie gras
Chargrilled rib-eye steak
Date sponge pudding.

On east side of A 283. Parking opposite.

80 Parrot Inn

Forest Green,
RH5 5RZ
Tel.: (01306)621339
Website: www.theparrot.co.uk

VISA

Youngs Ordinary, Ringwood Best, Dorking DBI, Hog's Back TEA, Hobgoblin, Summer Lightning

When a pub sells its own home-grown and homemade produce – bread, cheese, cakes and preserves, as well as eggs and meat from its own farm – you can be pretty much guaranteed that their cooking is going to be fresh and full of flavour. With well-priced, generously proportioned dishes such as vegetable and stilton pie or pork belly with chorizo and baked butter bean, the Parrot certainly doesn't disappoint. This is a pub where they home-cure their own black pudding and aren't afraid to serve less well-known offerings such as oyster sausages or mutton. The 300 year old pub's interior is traditional, with plenty of character in the form of exposed brick, flag floors and low wooden beams. Sup real ale as you watch a cricket match on the green.

CLOSING TIMES
Closed 25 December and Sunday dinner

PRICES
Meals: a la carte £ 20/31

Typical Dishes

Home farm pork & pistachio terrine
Home farm mutton chop curry
Hot chocolate brownie

8 mi south of Dorking by A 24, A 29 and B 2126 west. Parking.

Ockley

81 Bryce's

Old School House,
Stane St, Ockley, RH5 5TH
Tel.: (01306)627430
Website: www.bryces.co.uk

VISA

London Pride and Horsham Best

Although it may look like a traditional pub, this is much more of a dining operation, with just a small copper-topped counter and a couple of tables to make up the lounge. There are two similarly styled dining areas boasting high-backed leather chairs – each has its own menu and one of them is linen-laid. You'll always find a couple of meat dishes but it's the fresh seafood from the South Coast day boats that people come for. The cheaper bar menu offers simple dishes such as herring roes or smoked salmon tart, with several options available in two sizes; while the more adventurous restaurant menu might offer red snapper en papillote or herb-crumbed supreme of cod. There's also a 3 course 'menu of the day' and blackboard specials to consider.

CLOSING TIMES
Closed 25-26 December, 1 January and Sunday dinner January, February and November

PRICES
Meals: £ 16 (weekdays) and a la carte £ 29/34

Typical Dishes

Trio of Arbroath smokie

Assiette of fish with cardamom sauce

Panna cotta with berry compote

8 mi south of Dorking by A 24 and A 29. Parking.

82 Three Horseshoes

25 Shepperton Rd,
Staines, TW18 1SE
Tel.: (01784)455014
Website: www.3horseshoeslaleham.co.uk

VISA MC AE

Sharp's Doom Bar and Ringwood Best

The sister pub to the Red Lion in Woking is this sturdy 17C inn, which has had a full and sympathetic makeover. It's a pretty thing, with a pleasant enclosed garden and an interior divided into three large dining areas, all of which have their own charm and character. Just order at the bar and hand over your credit card – which they keep in the safe, so there's no need to panic. Staff are a cheery bunch who patently care about their customers. The menu is unashamedly traditional but the cooking is done with due care and attention. Calves liver is popular, as are the lighter, tapas-style dishes. There are shared plates, a style of eating which always seems so appropriate in a pub, and the crab sandwiches are also good.

CLOSING TIMES
Open daily

PRICES
Meals: a la carte £ 21/35

Typical Dishes

Smoked haddock & spinach tart

Pan-fried calves liver with black pudding

White chocolate & raspberry crème brûlée

Junction 13 on M 25 southeast 2.5 mi by A 30, A 308 and on B 376. Parking.

83

The Inn @ West End

42 Guildford Rd,
West End, GU24 9PW
Tel.: (01276)858652
Website: www.the-inn.co.uk

VISA MC AE

Fuller's London Pride, Hook Norton Best Bitter and Sharp's Cornish Coaster

A snug and friendly village pub, with a roaring fire in winter and a pleasant garden for alfresco dining come summer. Blackboards tell you all you need to know: there's a small one listing lunchtime sandwiches, which come in brown, white, dainty or doorstop; on Wednesdays there's a board which offers fresh fish and, Mondays, in season, a board which lists a large selection of game. Event nights are also announced in this manner – with the pub's loyal local following ensuring an impressive turnout. The array of menus means there's something for everyone – perhaps chicken liver and black pudding salad, roast rump of lamb or loin of pork and twice-cooked belly. The owner also has a wine business, so expect a large selection by the glass.

CLOSING TIMES
Open daily

PRICES
Meals: a la carte £ 28/40

Typical Dishes

Lightly home-smoked pigeon paté

Calves liver with smoked onion purée

Warm chocolate & macadamia brownie

2.5 mi southeast of Junction 3 on M3 by A 322. Parking (40 spaces).

84 Queen's Head

1 Bridge Rd,
Weybridge, KT13 8XS
Tel.: (01932)839820
Website: www.whitebrasserie.com

VISA

Fuller's London Pride, Sharp's Doom Bar and seasonal Twickenham Ale

It was built in the mid-1700s as a coach house but the Queen's Head has also spent time as a courthouse, complete with gallows. An appealing whitewashed building with small terrace and patio, it's been lovingly restored, and with its series of snug little rooms, warming open fires and a pewter bar, can't fail to impress. Raymond Blanc's name is above the door, so it's no surprise to find French brasserie classics alongside the British pub staples. Start with potted pork, gnocchi with braised chestnuts or a charcuterie or smoked fish board, followed by guinea fowl confit, steamed Loch Fyne mussels or venison sausages. There's also a good value set menu and a well-chosen wine list; sit in the spacious restaurant for a more formal experience.

CLOSING TIMES
Closed 25 December

PRICES
Meals: £ 14/16
and a la carte £ 22/30

Typical Dishes

Grilled Cornish sardine fillets on toast

Free range Cornish rump steak with béarnaise sauce & fries

Steamed lemon sponge

In town centre, just off B 374 (Heath Rd). Limited parking (12 spaces).

Windlesham

85 The Bee

School Rd,
Windlesham, GU20 6PD
Tel.: (01276)479244
Website: www.thebeepub.co.uk

VISA

Sharpe's Doom Bar, Courage Best, Summer Lightning

The espresso machine on the bar is the first clue. Wood floors, eggshell-coloured walls, a mishmash of wooden furniture and a leather Chesterfield make it abundantly clear: this is a pub which has had the gastro treatment – and judging by the number of punters making a beeline for it, it seems to have done the trick. The daily changing menus showcase local, seasonal produce, with precisely cooked dishes such as roast rump of lamb or braised breast of veal; the two course lunch menu is good value, but with starters like pigeon and wild mushroom salad and desserts like sticky toffee pudding, the trouble will be knowing which courses to go for. With a children's play area and regular barbecues, the garden becomes a hive of activity in summer.

CLOSING TIMES
Closed Sunday dinner

PRICES
Meals: £ 16 (lunch)
and a la carte £ 26/38

Typical Dishes

Scallops with curried cauliflower

Brixham monkfish with chorizo spiced lentils

Chocolate & griottine cherry clafoutis

Just off A 30 on B 386. Parking.

86 Brickmakers

Chertsey Rd,
Windlesham, GU20 6HT
Tel.: (01276)472267
Website: www.thebrickmakerswindlesham.co.uk

VISA MC AE

London Pride, Courage Best and Sharpe's Doom Bar

Thus named because workers from the nearby former brickmaking works used to pop in for a pint on their way home, this red-brick pub may appear quite small from the outside – not hard when it's surrounded by houses as grand as some of those nearby – but it actually goes back a long way. It's set in a pretty location and its narrow, immaculately kept garden is quite a feature in summer. If you're dining inside, choose a seat in the linen-laid restaurant which extends out into the conservatory. The other option is the bar, with its comfy sofas and open fire. Food-wise, the choice is between a simple bar menu and a more interesting à la carte. Dishes, which range from sausage and mash to roasted duck breast, are good value and full of flavour.

CLOSING TIMES
Open daily

PRICES
Meals: £ 24 and a la carte £ 23/30

Typical Dishes

Smooth duck liver pâté
Beef fillet stroganoff with steamed rice
Pan-fried calves liver with colcannon, bacon & veal jus

1 mi east on B 386. Parking.

87 Red Lion

High St,
Horsell, Woking, GU21 4SS
Tel.: (01483)768497
Website: www.redlionhorsell.co.uk

VISA AE

Courage Best, Fullers London Pride and Sharp's Doom Bar

This modern take on the pub is concealed within a residential area but is just five minutes from the centre of Woking. It's made up of a large, contemporary main bar, with sofas and wi-fi for those who've brought along their technological gadgetry, and a plethora of boards advertising the cocktail of the day and menu offers. The two large rooms at the back constitute the dining room but the same menu is served throughout. That means lots of pub classics, the highlights being the supremely fresh fish and the shared dishes. Whole gammons are sometimes roasted at weekends, along with spit-roasted chickens and there are all-day dining options too. Add large outside seating, occasional live music and wine tasting and you have a successful operation.

CLOSING TIMES
Open daily
booking advisable

PRICES
Meals: a la carte £ 23/36

Typical Dishes

Mushrooms & spinach on toast
Gressingham duck & parsnip mash
Baked cheesecake & cherry compote

1.5 mi northwest of Woking by Brewery Rd and Church Hill. Parking.

88 George and Dragon

Main St,
Burpham, BN18 9RR
Tel.: (01903)883131
Website: www.gdinn.co.uk

VISA MC

Arundel Sussex Gold, Old Speckled Hen, Green King IPA

Standing close to the green in a peaceful hamlet, the George and Dragon boasts delightful views out over the rolling countryside. Such a good old English name is perfectly fitting for a pub that's been trading since 1736 and the associations don't end there. Cooking features British classics – with pub favourites and daily specials on the blackboard, and a concise à la carte featuring the likes of rib-eye steak, rump of lamb and game from the local estate. The laid-back, classically styled interior is divided in two: there's a formal linen-laid dining room and a rustic bar with scrubbed tables and a large brick fireplace. Exposed beams, twinkling church candles and local artwork feature throughout, and theme nights take place all year-round.

CLOSING TIMES
Open daily

PRICES
Meals: a la carte £ 25/46

Typical Dishes

Seared scallops with crab cream

Aged fillet of beef, foie gras, asparagus & Madeira jus

Sticky toffee pudding

3 mi northeast of Arundel by A 27. Parking.

Charlton

89 **Fox Goes Free**

Charlton,
PO18 0HU
Tel.: (01243)811461
Website: www.thefoxgoesfree.com

VISA MC AE

Fox Goes Free, Ballards Best, Otter Ale

Set in beautiful South Downs countryside, close to Goodwood, this charming 17C flint pub was once the haunt of William III and his Royal Hunting Party. It boasts a pleasant garden with lovely outlook and retains most of its original features, including exposed stone walls, low beamed ceilings, brick floors, inglenook fires and even an old bread oven. There are three dining areas, two with waiter service and one where you order at the bar; behind which you'll find a good selection of hand-pulled ales. Dishes range from simple pub classics on the bar menu to an à la carte of local pork chop, braised venison shank or steak and kidney pie for two. It's deservedly popular, so definitely worth booking ahead. Bedrooms are too modest to recommend.

CLOSING TIMES
Open daily

PRICES
Meals: a la carte £ 21/32

Typical Dishes

Whole roasted camembert

Pork belly with apple chutney

Raspberry cheesecake

6.45 mi north of Chichester by A 286. Parking.

90 **Fish House**

Chilgrove,
PO18 9HX
Tel.: (01243)519444
Website: www.thefishhouse.co.uk

VISA

Harvey's Sussex Best and Arundel Sussex Gold

The Fish House is a stylish, rurally set inn, popular with foodies. With limestone flooring, low beams and a 300 year old fireplace, it retains a characterful sense of history, while contemporary touches like the oyster bar and fish tanks bring it firmly into the 21C. The bar's the most atmospheric place to sit, but if you want a touch more formality, then head for the high-ceilinged dining room. The kitchen focuses on seafood dishes and these range from classics such as potted shrimps or fish and chips to those with a more international flavour such as wok-fried whole bream, with chilli, garlic, spring onions, soy and ginger. Individually styled bedrooms come with every conceivable facility, including espresso machines and iPod docks.

CLOSING TIMES
Open daily

PRICES
Meals: £ 22 (lunch) and a la carte £ 28/60

15 rooms: £ 85/240

Typical Dishes

Selsey crab with wafers & ice cream

John Dory with celeriac, peas & bacon

Peach Melba & lavender parfait

6.5 mi north of Chichester by A 286 on B 2141. Parking.

East Lavant

91 The Royal Oak Inn

Pook Ln,
East Lavant, PO18 0AX
Tel.: (01243)527434
Website: www.royaloakeastlavant.co.uk

Inspectors' favourites

VISA MC AE

Arundle Gold, Sharp's Doom Bar, Skinner's Betty Stogs,

Set in the heart of the village, among some stunning properties, this 18C inn boasts a small outside seating area with immaculately kept planters and a welcoming interior filled with exposed stone, brick and wood. There's a really relaxing feel to the place but you'll have to make like the locals and arrive early if you want to bag a sofa or spot by the fire. Although combinations may be classical, cooking is fairly refined. There are always some interesting vegetarian options, steaks play an important role and there's a good selection of cheese. Produce is delivered from Smithfield, Billingsgate and Covent Garden, and you'll find a fine selection of wines by the glass. Spacious bedrooms are very comfy and well-equipped; breakfast is a treat.

CLOSING TIMES
Open daily

PRICES
Meals: £ 21 (lunch)
and a la carte £ 25/47

8 rooms: £ 110/275

Typical Dishes

Shallot tarte Tatin with melted goat's cheese

Free range local pork loin

Crème brûlée.

Off A 286 after the hump-back bridge. Parking.

92 Duke of Cumberland

Fernhurst,
GU27 3HQ
Tel.: (01428)652280
Website: www.dukeofcumberland.com

VISA MC AE

Harvey's Sussex, Langhams' Best and Hip-Hop

A hidden gem affectionately known as The Duke, this 15C hillside pub nestles in pretty tiered gardens with trickling streams, trout ponds and a splendid view over the South Downs. The pub's interior is as enchanting as the garden, with low beams, flag floors, a huge fireplace, simple wood tables and bench seating; the young serving staff are engaging and the landlord, charming. An appealing menu offers carefully prepared, seasonal dishes; lunch is a two course affair, with choices like pan-seared scallops with rocket or Selsey Crab salad, a selection of organic baguettes and homely puddings like hot chocolate fondant. Dinner offers the full three courses, with dishes that might include potted shrimps, steak and chips or braised lamb shanks.

CLOSING TIMES
Closed Sunday and Monday dinner

PRICES
Meals: a la carte £ 31/41

Typical Dishes

Pan-fried samphire, prawns, lemon & garlic butter

Confit free range pork belly with apple & Calvados glaze

Apple & pear nut crumble

4.5 mi north of Midhurst off A286 at Fernhurst. Parking.

Halfway Bridge

93 Halfway Bridge Inn

Halfway Bridge,
GU28 9BP
Tel.: (01798)861281
Website: www.halfwaybridge.co.uk

VISA MC AE

Betty Stogs, Sharp's Doom Bar, Moondance

Set right on the edge of Cowdray Park – famous for its polo – this charming pub has been here so long that the road in front of it has been re-routed, giving the inn a rather back-to-front appearance. Once inside, you'll find several cosy, fire-lit rooms, their walls filled with local maps and country prints. Dishes tend towards the traditional and might include pan-seared calves liver or slow-cooked belly of pork. There's a fine selection of lunchtime baguettes as well as tasty nursery puddings like apple and rhubarb crumble or sticky toffee pudding. Bedrooms are in converted stables a two minute walk away. Like the pub itself, they blend rustic charm with modern facilities – and in the morning, a deliciously fresh cooked breakfast awaits.

CLOSING TIMES
Closed 25 December

PRICES
Meals: a la carte £ 25/31
6 rooms: £ 75/130

Typical Dishes

Spiced crab with a crayfish gateau

Seared calves liver with caramelised shallot jus

Chocolate fondant

Halfway between Midhurst and Petworth on A 272. Parking.

94 **Ginger Fox**

Albourne,
Henfield, BN6 9EA
Tel.: (01273)857888
Website: www.gingermanrestaurants.com

VISA MC AE

Harvey's Best and Sharp's Doom Bar

The fox in hungry pursuit of a pheasant on the thatched roof of this 17C inn gives a clue as to its charm and character. Inside you'll find beams, open fires and parquet flooring; there's a spacious dining room, a rustic open bar and – the best place to sit – 'The Den.' Cooking is skilful, with a real country flavour; the distinct menu offering unfussy dishes such as duck egg and mushrooms on toast, jellied knuckle of pork, stuffed saddle of rabbit or a whole grilled lemon sole. There's a vegetarian tasting plate, a special children's menu with smaller portions, and puddings with names you will recognise, but which come with a twist. Packed at weekends, the pub is particularly popular with families, who enjoy its spacious garden and slides.

CLOSING TIMES
Closed 25 December

PRICES
Meals: a la carte £ 18/30

Typical Dishes

Pork, smoked bacon & black pudding terrine

Free range chicken & wild mushroom pie

Baked orange blossom & yoghurt pudding

8 mi north of Shoreham by A283 and A2037. Parking.

95 **Earl of March**

Mid Lavant,
PO18 0BQ
Tel.: (01243)533993
Website: www.theearlofmarch.com

VISA MC AE

Fuller's London Pride, Hopback Summer Lightning, Harveys and Ballards Golden Bine

This 18C inn offers the perfect blend of country character and contemporary styling, boasting a wood burning stove and cosy sofas in the bar, a smart restaurant, and a relaxed feel throughout. Its terrace affords amazing views of the South Downs, with the main stand at Goodwood racecourse in the distance, and its private dining room changes use seasonally; home to shooting parties in winter and serving champagne and seafood in summer. The owner spent time as executive head chef at The Ritz, so expect good quality, seasonal produce; dishes are British and mainly classical in style, and might include vegetables soup, lamb chops, pan-fried fillet of Sussex beef or Gressingham duck breast. Desserts are old favourites like sticky toffee pudding.

CLOSING TIMES
Closed Sunday dinner

PRICES
Meals: £ 23 (early dinner) and a la carte £ 30/39

Typical Dishes

Diver-caught scallops with cauliflower purée

Pan-fried venison with roast roots

Lemon posset & mulled berries

3 mi north of Chichester by A 286.

96 **Badgers**

Coultershaw Bridge,
Petworth, GU28 0JF
Tel.: (01798)342651
Website: www.badgerspetworth.co.uk

VISA

Youngs and Sharp's Doom Bar

This white-painted pub close to the River Rother has a satisfyingly homely feel. Log fires blaze in the grate, fresh flowers are dotted about the place and in the evening, candles flicker. A beautiful oak-panelled bar boasts carvings from its former 'Badger and Honeypot' days, while black and white photos depict its original railway inn-carnation. You'll also find an attentive, cheery team and a truly intimate single table alcove. Menus are rather eclectic; offering robust, flavoursome cooking with international influences. You could find anything from lamb's liver or bubble and squeak to prawns with Cajun spices or Spanish fish casserole – while in summer, lobsters picked from the tank are a favourite. Bedrooms aren't currently recommendable.

CLOSING TIMES
Closed Sunday dinner in winter

PRICES
Meals: a la carte £ 25/36

Typical Dishes

Tiger tail prawns in garlic butter
Lamb half shoulder, roasted with garlic & rosemary
Crème brûlée

2 mi south of Petworth by A 285 at Coultershaw Bridge. Parking.

97 Chequers Inn

Rowhook,
RH12 3PY
Tel.: (01403)790480

VISA MC D

Harvey's Best, Sharp's Doom Bar, Arundel Gold and Andwells King John

As you step inside you're instantly surrounded by the oaky aroma of an open fire and the murmur of the day's tales being recounted by groups of cheery locals. The origins of this inn can be traced back to the 15C, which comes as no surprise when you look around the charming stone-floored bar, but there's also a slightly unusual corrugated dining room extension (formerly the village hall), a large paved terrace and spacious garden. The experienced chef-owner loves the hands-on approach, so he's often out in the woods foraging for wild mushrooms and tracking down game, or out in the garden gathering the latest yield; maybe artichoke, pears or greengages. Classically based menus display a good understanding of how best to prepare ingredients.

CLOSING TIMES
Closed 25 December and Sunday dinner

PRICES
Meals: a la carte £ 21/35

Typical Dishes

Confit duck hash
Pork loin with caramelised apple & black pudding
Rosé wine jelly

3 mi west of Horsham by A 281. Parking.

98 Crab and Lobster

Mill Ln,
Sidlesham, PO20 7NB
Tel.: (01243)641233
Website: www.crab-lobster.co.uk

VISA MC AE

Hepworth's Sussex and Sharp's Doom Bar

This historic inn, with its pretty gardens, is superbly located within the striking landscape of Pangham Harbour Nature Reserve; a marshy haven for wildlife, particularly birds. The pub has a light, relaxed feel, with an open main dining room, a snug seating area and a log fire. Cooking places its emphasis on seafood, with starters like sautéed calamari or clam and red mullet chowder and main courses such as fresh cod and chips with homemade tartare sauce or kedgeree with poached egg. Local crab sandwiches go down a storm at lunch and desserts might include deep-fried ice cream with butterscotch or a fine selection of English cheeses. Very comfortable bedrooms have a modern, minimalist style; one has its own garden and an open fired stove.

CLOSING TIMES
Open daily
booking advisable

PRICES
Meals: £ 22 (weekday lunch) and a la carte £ 28/51

4 rooms: £ 80/180

Typical Dishes

Crab, crayfish & smoked salmon parcel
Fillet of halibut with shellfish broth
Dark chocolate tart

5 mi south of Chichester by B 2145, then turn right into Rookery Lane. Parking.

Tillington

99 Horse Guards Inn

Upperton Rd,
Tillington, GU28 9AF
Tel.: (01798)342332
Website: www.thehorseguardsinn.co.uk

VISA

Harleys Sussex Best, Skinners Betty Stogs, Langham's Halfway to Heaven

In an elevated spot in the heart of a quiet village sits this pretty mid-17C inn, with views over Rother valley and the South Downs from its lovely lavender-filled garden. Happily, it's equally charming inside, with its low beams, fireplaces, period features and fresh flowers. Specialities and the names of suppliers are chalked up on the blackboard and there's a good mix of the rustic, like wild mushrooms on toast, and the more elaborate, like stone bass with roast fennel. Local seafood is handled with skill and some of the vegetables and salads come from their own patch. The staff are young, chatty and willing, and contribute considerably to the charm. There are three simple bedrooms available; families can book the cottage opposite.

CLOSING TIMES
Open daily

PRICES
Meals: a la carte £ 22/36
3 rooms: £ 80/105

Typical Dishes
Salad of beetroot & goat's cheese
Fillet of stone bass, asparagus & sautéed potatoes
Chocolate brioche bread & butter pudding

Just off A272 in heart of the village Unrestricted on-street parking.

100 **Keepers Arms**

Trotton,
GU31 5ER
Tel.: (01730)813724
Website: www.keepersarms.co.uk

VISA MC AE

Ballard's Trotton Best and Hophead

The Keeper's Arms is a cheery, welcoming, neighbourhood inn, where the customer is king. Set back from the road and perched halfway up a hill, it affords pleasant countryside views if you're dining alfresco; inside, it's quite compact, with low ceilings, an open fire, a Chesterfield sofa and a host of quirky tables. Cooking is good value and honest, with dishes changing regularly; try a nice bowl of juicy olives to kick you off, then perhaps a warm goat's cheese tart, some char-grilled mackerel or duck cooked two ways. Pudding might mean a simple lemon parfait with fresh raspberries or a good old chocolate brownie – and the wine list changes as often as the food; thus ensuring that you can always find a glass to perfectly complement your meal.

CLOSING TIMES
Closed 25 December, Monday in winter and Sunday dinner

PRICES
Meals: a la carte £ 21/32

Typical Dishes

Sardine fillets with tapenade

Pan-fried halibut with broad beans & chive velouté

Salted peanut parfait

4 mi west of Midhurst by A 272. Parking.

101 **Cat Inn**

Queen's Sq,
West Hoathly, RH19 4PP
Tel.: (01342)810369
Website: www.catinn.co.uk

VISA

Harvey's Best, Larkins Traditional, Dark Star Hophead

This charming inn is located in the centre of a pleasant hamlet, opposite a lovely 11C church and just two minutes walk from The Priest House museum. The pub itself dates back to the 17C and boasts a part-tiled exterior and a myriad of different rooms filled with pewter tankards and hop bines. These include a semi-panelled bar with huge log fire, a room with delightful glass floor panel looking down into an old well, two intimate, rustic areas and two larger, more formally laid dining rooms. There's also a few tables out the front and a large terrace to the rear. The hands-on owners have plenty of experience and are supported by a bubbly team. Menus feature satisfying country-style classics. Bedrooms are modern and extremely comfortable.

CLOSING TIMES
Closed Sunday dinner

PRICES
Meals: a la carte £ 25/32
4 rooms: £ 80/140

Typical Dishes

Vietnamese rare roast beef rolls

South Downs rump of lamb

Rhubarb crumble cake

4 mi southwest of East Grinstead by B2110 and B2028. Parking.

Six hundred miles of relentlessly breathtaking coastline pound the majestic South West, assuring it of a dramatic backdrop whatever the season. Its prestige is bolstered by four UNESCO World Heritage sites: one of them is Dorset's spectacular Jurassic Coast, which includes the 180 billion pebbles of Chesil Beach. Further north, Dartmoor and Exmoor embody the region's untamed beauty. The built environment may be of a more recent time line, but examples are still impressive, ranging from thirteenth century Lacock, home of many a filmed costume drama, to Elizabethan Longleat with its Capability Brown designed parkland, and late Victorian Lanhydrock, "the great house of Cornwall". The same county boasts its very own "theatre under the stars", The Minack, where the drama of nature collides with the drama of the written word. Days out in this unforgettable region come complete with pasties and a pint of local ale, or freshly caught lobster, scallops or mussels enjoyed along the quay.

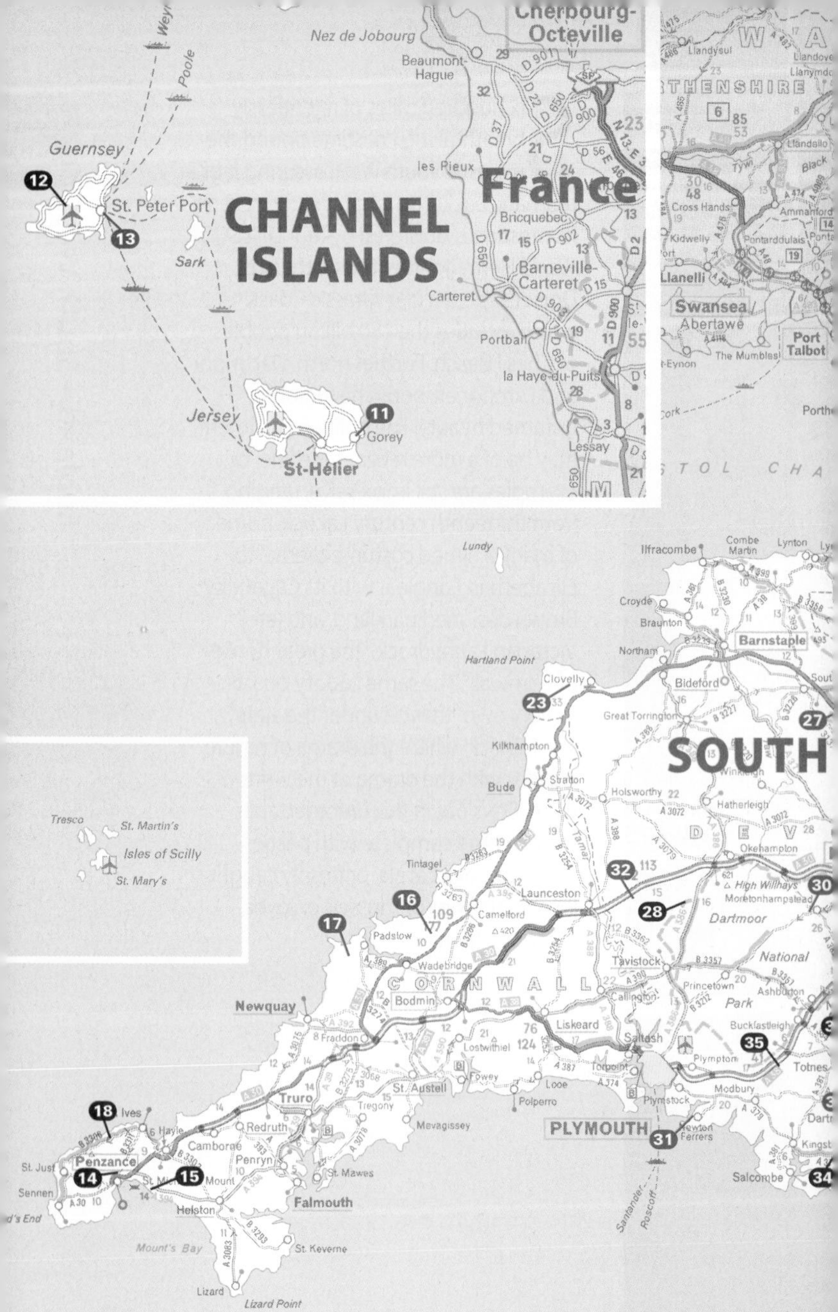

Cherbourg-Octeville
Nez de Jobourg
Beaumont-Hague
les Pieux
France
Bricquebec
Barneville-Carteret
Carteret
Portbail
la Haye-du-Puits
Lessay
CHANNEL ISLANDS
Guernsey
St. Peter Port
Sark
Jersey
Gorey
St-Helier
Poole
Llandysul
Llandovery
Llanymddyfri
Llandeilo
Black
Cross Hands
Ammanford
Kidwelly
Pontarddulais
Llanelli
Swansea / Abertawe
Port Talbot
The Mumbles
Cork
Lundy
Ilfracombe
Combe Martin
Lynton
Croyde
Braunton
Barnstaple
Northam
Hartland Point
Clovelly
Bideford
Great Torrington
SOUTH
Kilkhampton
Stratton
Bude
Holsworthy
Hatherleigh
Winkleigh
Okehampton
Tintagel
Launceston
Camelford
Padstow
Wadebridge
High Willhays
Moretonhampstead
Dartmoor
National
Park
CORNWALL
Tavistock
Princetown
Ashburton
Buckfastleigh
Callington
Bodmin
Liskeard
Saltash
Newquay
Fraddon
Lostwithiel
Plympton
Totnes
Torpoint
Fowey
Looe
Polperro
Truro
St. Austell
Tregony
Mevagissey
Plymstock
Modbury
PLYMOUTH
Newton Ferrers
Kingsbridge
Salcombe
Santander
Roscoff
St. Ives
Hayle
Redruth
Camborne
Penryn
St. Mawes
Falmouth
St. Just
Penzance
Sennen
St. Michael's Mount
Helston
Land's End
Mount's Bay
St. Keverne
Lizard
Lizard Point
Tresco
St. Martin's
Isles of Scilly
St. Mary's

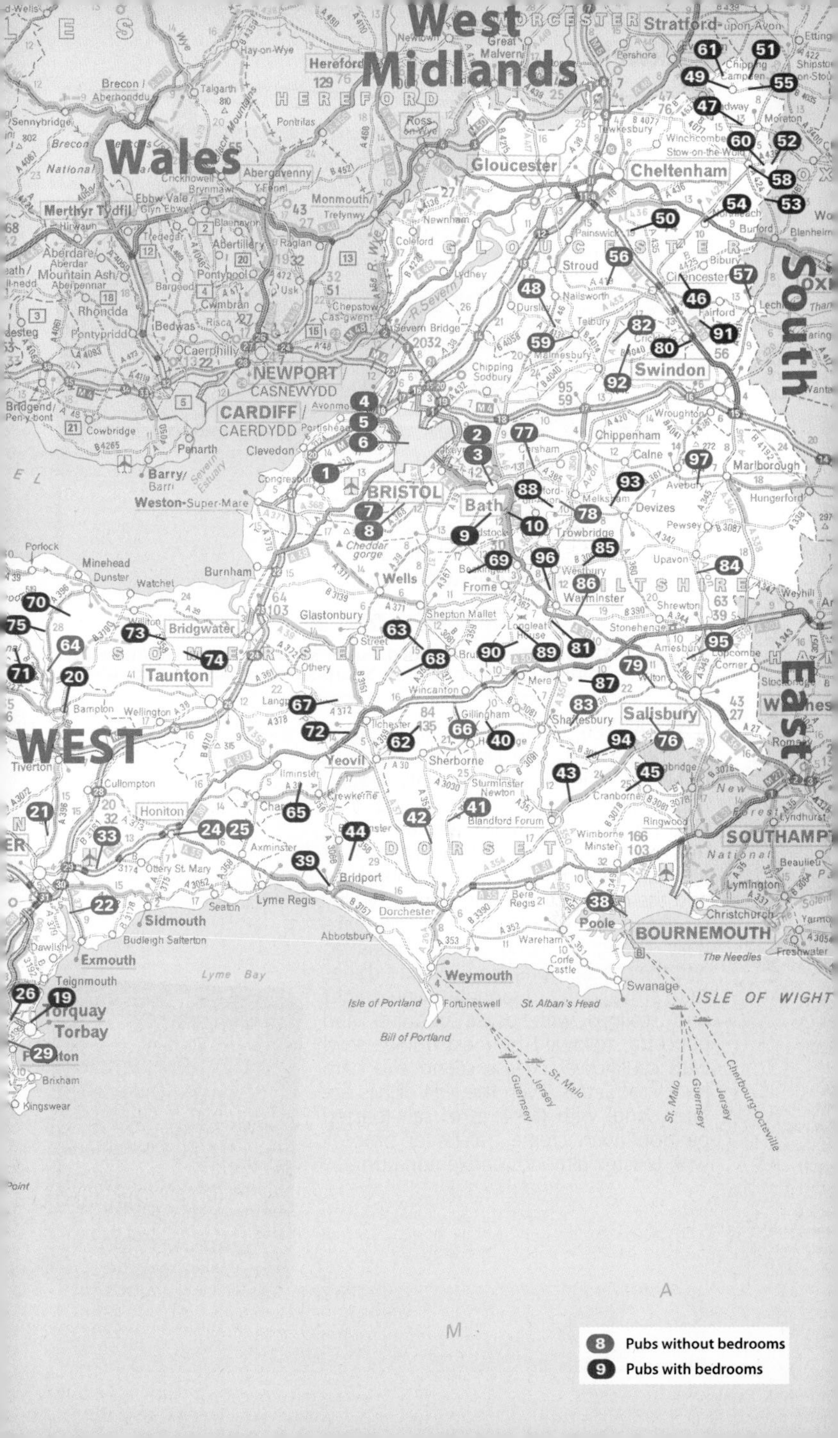

West Midlands
Wales
South East
WEST
Hereford
Gloucester
Cheltenham
Stratford-upon-Avon
Swindon
NEWPORT
CASNEWYDD
CARDIFF / CAERDYDD
BRISTOL
Bath
Chippenham
Marlborough
Devizes
Trowbridge
Warminster
Frome
Wells
Glastonbury
Bridgwater
Taunton
Yeovil
Sherborne
Shaftesbury
Salisbury
Blandford Forum
Dorchester
Weymouth
Poole
BOURNEMOUTH
SOUTHAMPTON
Exmouth
Sidmouth
Torquay
Torbay
Lyme Bay
ISLE OF WIGHT
Pubs without bedrooms
Pubs with bedrooms

Backwell

1 New Inn

86 West Town Rd,
Backwell, BS48 3BE
Tel.: (01275)462199
Website: www.newinn-backwell.co.uk

Timothy Taylor Landlord, Fuller's London Pride, St Austell's Tribute, Butcombe Bitter, Sharp's Doom Bar and Bath Ales

A pretty 18C stone pub with a warm farmhouse feel, The New Inn boasts a lovely open-fired bar with comfy seating and a slightly more formal dining area with polished pine tables and an almost 'tea room' atmosphere. The pleasant staff are as welcoming as the surroundings and the confident cooking is in a stylishly modern vein. Descriptions on the twice daily changing menu sound appealing and the precisely prepared, elegant dishes that arrive don't disappoint: you might find scallops with pease pudding and pancetta, followed by roast guinea fowl with cauliflower cheese cream and ham hock croquettes. Even the side dishes are interesting, with the likes of salt roasted beetroot with crème fraîche or broccoli with toasted almonds and lemon butter.

CLOSING TIMES
Closed 2 weeks January, 25-26 December, Sunday dinner and Monday

PRICES
Meals: £ 16/24
and a la carte £ 27/40

Typical Dishes

Cornish crab, rhubarb, apple & shallots

Roast loin & braised shoulder of lamb with anchovy and lemon

Bitter chocolate & beetroot cheesecake

6 mi southwest of Bristol by A 370. Parking.

2 Marlborough Tavern

35 Marlborough Buildings,
Bath, BA1 2LY
Tel.: (01225)423731
Website: www.marlborough-tavern.com

VISA

Butcombe ales, Timothy Taylor Landlord and Brakspear bitter

If you're a Londoner looking for a home away from home, then this is probably the place for you. Set next to the Royal Victoria Park, this spacious, modern pub boasts funky flock wallpaper, scrubbed wooden floors and displays local artwork on its walls. The chef is very passionate about his craft and carefully sources his ingredients from nearby farms and small independent producers. He favours organic growing methods and traditional rearing techniques, and strives to find produce that originates from sustainable stocks. Menus have a classical base and dishes are unfussy, straightforward and hearty – the pork belly in particular is a firm favourite. Daily specials are chalked on the blackboard and change as new produce arrives at the door.

CLOSING TIMES
Closed 25 December
booking advisable

PRICES
Meals: £ 15 (lunch)
and a la carte £ 26/34

Typical Dishes

Diver caught scallops
Loin of Neston Park venison
Dark chocolate pot

Northwest of city centre on east side of Royal Victoria Park. Parking bays opposite; parking also in the park (50m).

3 **White Hart**

Widcombe Hill,
Bath, BA2 6AA
Tel.: (01225)338053
Website: www.whitehartbath.co.uk

VISA MC

Butcombe Bitter and Sharp's Doom Bar

Situated close to the railway, just over the river, The White Hart has a real neighbourhood feel. It has attracted a loyal local following, so get here early or book ahead as it fills up quickly. Food-wise, the mantra here is 'keep it simple', with the sourcing of ingredients afforded paramount importance. Portions are large and cooking, hearty, with dishes like baked fillet of pork wrapped in bacon, breast of chicken with lentils or whole baked sea bass with lime, ginger and chilli butter. Most people have a main dish and share a side and a dessert, but the smaller tapas plates are also very popular. The pub has a rustic feel, with scrubbed wooden floors and worn wooden tables and the rear terrace is a great spot in warmer weather.

CLOSING TIMES
Closed 25-26 December, Sunday dinner and bank holidays

booking essential at dinner

PRICES
Meals: a la carte £ 13/29

Typical Dishes

Home-smoked duck, green bean & mango salad

Fillets of sea bream with saffron mash

Gooseberry & meringue fool

Southeast of city centre off A 3062. On-street parking.

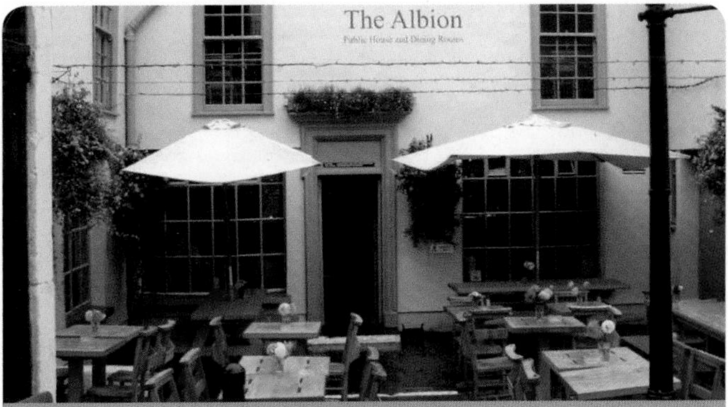

4 Albion Public House and Dining Rooms

Boyces Ave,
Clifton Village, Bristol, BS8 4AA
Tel.: (0117)9733522
Website: www.thealbionclifton.co.uk

VISA AE

Otter Ale, Bath Gem, Sharp's Doom Bar and Cornish Coaster

Tucked away down a cobbled street in a fashionable neighbourhood quarter, the trendy 17C Albion is exactly as a pub should be – fun, friendly and casual – with an equal split of drinkers and those out for a relaxed meal. The benches outside on the terrace make a pleasant spot to take in the comings and goings of the area, as well as providing the setting for the regular Sunday night BBQ. Cooking is highly seasonal and the unfussy British menu changes twice a day as new produce arrives. Everything is homemade, including the rustic bread and nibbles such as goose ham and pickled damsons, but these days the kitchen displays a lighter touch and fish is handled particularly well. Booking is imperative, as drinkers multiply throughout the evening.

CLOSING TIMES
Closed 25 December and Monday lunch
booking essential

PRICES
Meals: £ 31 (dinner) and a la carte £ 31/40

Typical Dishes

Gravadlax with dill & mustard dressing

Smoked trout & crab fishcake with hollandaise

Tarte Tatin

In Clifton Village. Parking in Victoria Square or surrounding roads.

5 Kensington Arms

35-37 Stanley Rd,
Bristol, BS6 6NP
Tel.: (0117)9446444
Website: www.thekensingtonarms.co.uk

VISA AE

Greene King IPA, Moorlands Original, Abbot Ale, Ruddles County

The crest of the Royal Borough of Kensington and Chelsea swings on the board outside, proclaiming the motto 'quam bonum in unum habitare': what a good thing it is to dwell together in unity – and with this pub at the heart of the neighbourhood, what a good thing indeed. With its charming Victorian style, large wood-floored bar and impressive high-ceilinged dining room, you could be mistaken for thinking someone had simply picked up a London pub and dropped it down here. Menus change bi-monthly and have a strong British base, featuring maybe lamb kidneys on toast or venison suet pudding. Seasons play an important role, so you'll find hearty, nourishing dishes and proper homemade puddings in the colder months. Service is particularly warm.

CLOSING TIMES
Closed 25-26 December and Sunday dinner

PRICES
Meals: a la carte £ 29/37

Typical Dishes

Ham hock with apple jelly

Roast belly of pork with black pudding fritters

Chocolate & honeycomb truffle

In city centre. Unrestricted parking outside pub and in nearby streets.

6 **Robin Hood's Retreat**

197 Gloucester Rd,
Bristol, BS7 8BG
Tel.: (0117)9248639
Website: www.robinhoodsretreat.co.uk

VISA MC AE

Skinners Betty Stogs and Wickwar Bab

It's a fair trek from Sherwood Forest, so despite this pub's name, you're unlikely to catch a glimpse of the famous outlaw; although, with eight cask ales on constant rotation, if you stick around until last orders, the chances are you might spot some merry men. Drinkers are certainly welcome, but it's the food that's the focus here; British classics are reinterpreted with a nod to French techniques, the result being hearty, flavourful dishes. The large blackboard menus change daily, but might include dishes like ox cheeks with mash or fried halibut with homemade tartare sauce. This red-brick Victorian pub is situated in a busy part of the city, but a relaxed atmosphere reigns in its characterful bar and its spacious, rustic dining room.

CLOSING TIMES
Closed 25 December
booking advisable at dinner

PRICES
Meals: £ 14 (lunch) and a la carte £ 25/33

Typical Dishes

English Heritage tomato salad
Roast rump of lamb with sweetbreads
Chilled vanilla & lemon rice pudding

In city centre. On-street parking or car park opposite.

7 **Bear & Swan**

13 South Par,
Chew Magna, BS40 8SL
Tel.: (01275)331100
Website: www.bearandswan.co.uk

VISA AE

Fuller's London Pride, Butcombe Bitter, plus guest ales

When Fuller's took over this village pub one of the first things that they did was to make it all a little less formal, so that the bar, with its inglenook fireplace, now merges effortlessly into the adjoining dining room. It has something of a farmhouse feel to it, thanks to its dresser and assortment of old wooden tables. There is now just one menu, for wherever you're sitting, and its influences come from all parts of the world, from Thailand to Italy. Cooking is undertaken with a degree of care and wisely they never forget that this is a pub, so expect to also find classics like homemade burgers and some good quality steaks. This is a welcoming, friendly spot and the 'local' element is enhanced by the bi-monthly quiz night.

CLOSING TIMES
Closed Sunday dinner

PRICES
Meals: a la carte £ 22/35

Typical Dishes

Fresh mussels Thai bloody mary style

Smoked haddock kedgeree

Strawberry custard slice

8.25 mi south of Bristol via A 37 on B 3130. Parking.

8

Pony & Trap

Knowle Hill,
Newtown, Chew Magna, BS40 8TQ
Tel.: (01275)332627
Website: www.theponyandtrap.co.uk

VISA

Butcombe Ale, Sharp's Doom Bar, Spring Ale

With this whitewashed pub on their doorstep, the inhabitants of this tiny hamlet have plenty to smile about. The rear garden with its rolling countryside views is the place to be but the cosy stone-walled bar and oversized dining room windows make it just as welcoming whatever the weather. To say the food is local and seasonal is an understatement: the menu is written twice a day; meats are locally sourced and hung; fish comes from the nearby Chew Valley smokehouse; and eggs are collected from their own chickens out the back. The passionate chef keeps his cooking rooted firmly in the classical British vein, flavours are clean and clear, and the lamb 2 ways is establishing itself as a firm favourite.

CLOSING TIMES
Closed Sunday dinner in winter and Monday except bank holidays
booking essential

PRICES
Meals: a la carte £ 19/36

Typical Dishes

Scallops with hodge podge
Pressed breast of lamb
Cardamom panna cotta

1.5 mi south of the village; follow signs for Bishop Stuttard. Parking.

9 Wheatsheaf

Combe Hay,
BA2 7EG
Tel.: (01225)833504
Website: www.wheatsheafcombehay.com

Inspectors' favourites

VISA

Butcombe Bitter and guest ale

The Wheatsheaf began life as a farmhouse in 1576. Centuries and several seamless additions later, it boasts chic, über-modern styling typified by delightful pink flocked wallpaper and vivid artwork, and a relaxed atmosphere helped on its way by open fires, comfy low sofas and an abundance of books and magazines – not forgetting Milo and Brie, the pub's friendly resident spaniels. The flavourful, seasonal food is presented in a contemporary style – often on slate plates – and dishes might include homemade fish pie, game broth or slow-roasted belly pork with black pudding; with desserts such as chocolate fondant or almond and prune cake. Bedrooms follow the pub's lead, with a spacious, contemporary feel and an emphasis firmly on quality.

CLOSING TIMES
Closed 1 week January, 24-25 December, Sunday dinner and Monday except bank holidays

PRICES
Meals: a la carte £ 23/37
3 rooms: £ 120/150

Typical Dishes

Lulworth Bay scallops with confit pork belly
Herb-crusted lamb with Niçoise garnish
Warm treacle tart

4 mi south of Bath by A 367 and minor road south. Parking.

10 Wheelwrights Arms

Church Ln,
Monkton Combe, BA2 7HB
Tel.: (01225)722287
Website: www.wheelwrightsarms.co.uk

VISA MC

Butcombe Bitter and Sharp's Doom Bar

If you're after a spot of peace and quiet, make a beeline for the sleepy village of Monkton Combe, where you can relax to the sound of birdsong in this charming 18C stone inn. A former carpenter's workshop, it's made up of two main buildings, both displaying attractive parquet floors, exposed stone walls and warming open fires. Menus offer a wide range of classical dishes from sandwiches and sharing plates to good value set lunches and tasty three course dinners. You might find blue cheese, almond and spinach tart, followed by sea bass with ratatouille or rabbit and pork braised in cider. Specials consist mainly of fish and, to finish, the treacle tart is always a good bet. Individually designed bedrooms are modern with rustic overtones.

CLOSING TIMES
Open daily

PRICES
Meals: a la carte £ 22/30
7 rooms: £ 85/150

Typical Dishes

Thai-style mussels
Pan-roasted chicken breast & Puy lentils
Vanilla, rhubarb and strawberry fool

2 mi southeast of Bath city centre by A 3062. Parking.

Gorey (Jersey)

11 Bass and Lobster

Gorey Coast Rd,
Gorey, JE3 6EU
Tel.: (01534)859590
Website: www.bassandlobster.com

VISA MC AE

No real ales offered

A bright, modern pub set close to the sandy beach, with smartly laid wooden tables, a mock wooden floor, some banquette seating and a small decked terrace. Having lived and worked on the island for many years, the experienced owner has built up a network of local suppliers and uses these whenever possible. Fresh seafood and shellfish dominate the seasonal menu and dishes are simply cooked and immensely flavourful: try the roast fillet of local sea bass, the local Chancre crab linguini with prawns or some fantastic steely oysters. Wonderfully earthy Jersey Royals make a great side dish and the prices also bring a smile to one's face, with the lunch menu representing particularly good value. Smooth service comes from a friendly European team.

CLOSING TIMES
Closed Monday lunch and Sunday

PRICES
Meals: £ 13/16
and a la carte £ 27/43

Typical Dishes

Grilled flat cap mushroom

Roast fillet of sea bass with grilled lobster & herb butter

Hazelnut meringue with vanilla cream

On the coast road. Parking.

12 Fleur du Jardin

Grand Moulins,
Kings Mills, GY5 7JT
Tel.: (01481)257996
Website: www.fleurdujardin.com

VISA AE

Fuller's London Pride, Timothy Taylor Landlord, Sharp's Doom Bar and regularly changing guest ales

Set in a small hamlet, not far from the sea, this attractive inn started life as a several stone cottages. The first thing you'll notice is the stylish terrace and lovely landscaped garden, and it will come as no surprise that it hosts regular summer BBQs. Pleasingly, the interior lives up to every expectation too, with its series of charming, adjoining rooms, rustic beams, exposed stone walls and open fires. When it comes to dining, the regularly changing menu ranges from homemade burgers to sea bass with pesto potatoes. Specials feature tasty island seafood and every dish is prepared with care and a lightness of touch. Completing the picture are stylish New England themed bedrooms with luxury bathrooms; there's even a heated outdoor pool.

CLOSING TIMES
Open daily

PRICES
Meals: a la carte £ 21/27
17 rooms: £ 65/138

Typical Dishes

Smoked salmon & haddock fishcakes

Pan-fried pork fillet, apple & red onion jus

Apple & amaretti pudding with toffee sauce

In the centre of the village. Parking.

St Peter Port (Guernsey)

13 **Swan Inn**

St Julian's Ave,
St Peter Port, GY1 1WA
Tel.: (01481)728969

VISA

Patois, Guernsey Ale

From façade to food, this really is a 'proper' pub. The smart bottle-green Victorian exterior makes it easy to spot and its traditional styling is warm and welcoming; especially in winter when the cosy log burners are ablaze. It's owned by a gregarious French fellow – a former manager – and his enthusiasm can be felt right at the heart of the place. If you're after a generous serving of something satisfying try the homemade burgers, legendary club sandwich or popular fish pie. For a more sedate dining experience climb the stairs up to the formal dining room. Here you'll find more ambitious dishes such as pork belly, lamb cutlets or seared fillet of sea bass – alongside some good value set menus that are offered early in the week.

CLOSING TIMES
Closed 25 December and Sunday

PRICES
Meals: a la carte £ 12/18

Typical Dishes

Ham hock terrine
Belly pork
Sticky toffee pudding

St Julian's Ave is opposite South Quay. Parking on South Quay (50yds).

14 Coldstreamer

Gulval,
TR18 3BB
Tel.: (01736)362072
Website: www.coldstreamer-penzance.co.uk

VISA

Otter Bitter, Skinners Betty Stogs, Dartmoor Brewery Legend

This handsome pub is set in the heart of Gulval and, like much of the village, was built by the Bolitho family. Following the death in service of Harry Bolitho it was given to the Coldstream Association, before being taken over by two local brothers. It's a spacious place, boasting a bright dining room and a large bar adorned with Coldstream Guards memorabilia. The concise, seasonal menu features fish from Newlyn, meat from Penzance and products from the village's now retired Smoker, and cooking is clean, generous and modern; lunch might offer salt cod fritters and dinner, more elaborate dishes like lamb rump with caramelised shallots. May sees an asparagus menu and the regular wine dinners prove popular. Bedrooms are fresh and well-appointed.

CLOSING TIMES
Closed 25 December

PRICES
Meals: £ 17 (weekday lunch) and a la carte £ 20/28

3 rooms: £ 60/85

Typical Dishes

Salt pollock with garlic & lemon dressing

Confit pork belly with rhubarb purée

Dark chocolate tart

1.25 mi northeast of Penzance off A 30 in centre of village. Plenty of parking in the square.

Perranuthnoe

15 **Victoria Inn**

Perranuthnoe,
TR20 9NP
Tel.: (01736)710309
Website: www.victoriainn-penzance.co.uk

VISA MC

Sharp's Doom Bar, St Austell Tribute and Bays Gold

Simple but characterful, with a cosy, homely feel, this pink-washed inn sits in the heart of the village and appeals to drinkers and diners alike. Its owners are keen for it to remain a proper pub, so you'll see locals here for a beer alongside families who've hot-footed it in from the beach for lunch; sand between their toes. The short menu offers choices ranging from sandwiches and soups to wholesome pub classics like ham, free range eggs and real chips, as well as dishes like honey-roasted Cornish duck breast. A regularly changing blackboard menu offers seafood specials, and the chef-owner – a local boy returned home – is proud to showcase local produce. The rear terrace provides a pleasant suntrap. Simple bedrooms are nautically themed.

CLOSING TIMES
Closed 25-26 December, 1 January, Monday in winter and Sunday dinner

PRICES
Meals: a la carte £ 27/34
2 rooms: £ 50/75

Typical Dishes

Cornish crab with aioli
Slow-roasted belly pork with hog's pudding
Valrhona chocolate and espresso marquise

3 mi east of Marazion, south of A 394. Parking.

16 St Kew Inn

St Kew,
PL30 3HB
Tel.: (01208)841259
Website: www.stkewinn.co.uk

VISA MC

St Austell's Tinners, HSD, Tribute, Proper Job

St Kew Inn was built in the 15C to serve the masons who constructed the magnificent next door church and boasts flag floors, stone walls and wooden beams. It sits in a quintessentially English location and its attractive front garden is as much of a draw as the pub itself, come the warmer weather. A massive electric umbrella means that sudden summer showers are not a problem, and there are heaters too, should it turn nippy. Cooking is fresh and tasty, with a wide range of appealing, good value dishes from which to choose; lunch means choices like Fowey mussels, Welsh rarebit, corned beef hash and a range of sandwiches, while dinner offers similar (minus the sandwiches), plus perhaps some grilled lemon sole or pan-fried lamb's liver.

CLOSING TIMES
Open daily

PRICES
Meals: a la carte £ 23/34

Typical Dishes

Welsh rarebit
Free range pork sausage with onion gravy
Steamed lemon sponge pudding

3 mi northeast of Wadebridge by A 39 and minor road north. Parking.

17 **Cornish Arms**

Churchtown,
St Merryn, PL28 8ND
Tel.: (01841)532700
Website: www.rickstein.com

VISA

St Austell's Tinners, Tribute, Proper Job and a guest ale

When St Austell Brewery leased this pub to Rick Stein, the locals panicked at the thought of their beloved haunt being turned into a gastropub. They needn't have worried though as, despite the sympathetic refurbishment of the dining room and the addition of a smart terrace, it remains a proper pub, with a proper bar whose low beams, slate floors and pictures of regulars give it an undeniable dose of old world charm. The menu offers classic pub dishes such as ploughman's, ham, egg and chips, homemade curry or apple pie, with fish specials chalked up on boards. Cooking is sound and sensibly priced, but they don't take bookings, so arrive early on busy summer evenings. Every other Friday is open mic night, with local musicians to warm things up.

CLOSING TIMES
Open daily

PRICES
Meals: a la carte £ 18/27

Typical Dishes

Tomato soup with tapenade
Mussels & chips
Sticky toffee pudding

West of Padstow on B 3276. Parking.

18 **Gurnard's Head**

Treen,
Zennor, TR26 3DE
Tel.: (01736)796928
Website: www.gurnardshead.co.uk

VISA MC

Skinners Betty Stogs and Heligan Honey, St Austell's Tribute, Tomos Watkin's Cwrw Braf

Set in a remote location, surrounded by nothing but fields and livestock, The Gurnard's Head provides a warm welcome that sets you immediately at your ease. It's dog-friendly, with stone floors and shabby-chic décor, while blazing fires and brightly coloured walls help create a relaxed, cosy feel. The simple menu relies on regional produce, including some locally foraged ingredients. Dishes might include ham hock terrine with piccalilli, deep-fried gurnard and chips, Provençal fish soup or a modern take on a classic cassoulet. Desserts are in the traditional vein, while the wine list includes a very interesting selection by the glass. Extremely comfy beds feature good quality linen and colourful throws. Breakfast is taken communally.

CLOSING TIMES
Closed 24 and 25 December

PRICES
Meals: £ 17 (lunch)
and a la carte £ 25/29

7 rooms: £ 70/110

Typical Dishes

Pea risotto
Bass with a shellfish vinaigrette
Treacle tart

6 mi west of St Ives by B 3306. Parking.

Babbacombe

19 **Cary Arms**

Babbacombe Beach,
Babbacombe, TQ1 3LX
Tel.: (01803)327110
Website: www.caryarms.co.uk

VISA

Otter Ale, Bays Topsail, Sharp's Doom Bar and St Austell's Tribute

Set in an idyllic spot on the English Riviera, The Cary Arms is built into the rocks, with terraces down to the shore and far-reaching views. Its boutique-chic, New England style bedrooms come with stunning bathrooms complete with roll-top baths. The stylish, ultra-comfy residents lounge continues the nautical theme, and there's even a spa room for treatments. If the rooms are all about luxury, the food, by contrast, is straightforward in style; we're talking reasonably priced pub dishes of simply cooked fish and meats. At the hub of the operation is its atmospheric stone and slate floored bar where you're served by chatty staff; in summer, there's also a wood burning pizza oven on the terrace, to make the most of that wonderful location.

CLOSING TIMES
Open daily

PRICES
Meals: a la carte £ 24/31
8 rooms: £ 105/260

Typical Dishes

Brixham fishcake with chilli dressing
Loin of Devon lamb
Warm chocolate brownie

Parking at adjacent beach car park.

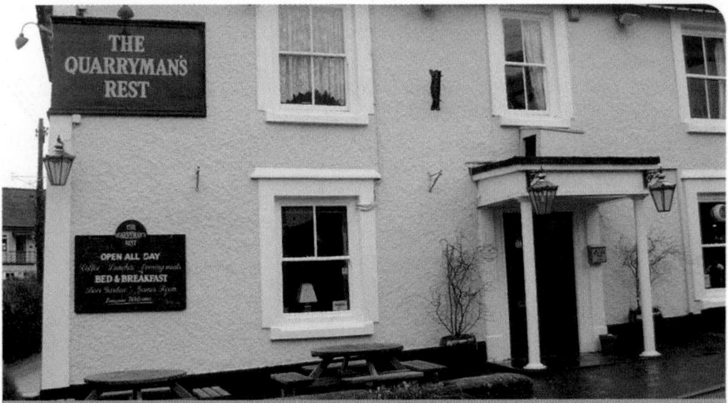

20 Quarrymans Rest

Briton St,
Bampton, EX16 9LN
Tel.: (01398)331480
Website: www.thequarrymansrest.co.uk

VISA MC AE

Sharp's Doom Bar, Otter, Exmoor Gold and Fox, Bays Gold

With its relaxed, traditional open-fired bar, this 17C inn is still very much the village local. Its restaurant, with exposed brick and high-backed leather chairs is, by contrast, a more formal and intimate choice of dining room – but wherever you sit, the menu is the same. Chef-owner Paul prides himself on sourcing the best of local produce and dishes are substantial enough to render side orders redundant. Expect tried-and-tested classics, with the occasional Asian influence; perhaps salmon and crab fishcake, potted wild rabbit with pickles, homemade steak, ale and kidney pudding or braised shank of Devon lamb. The Sunday carvery is popular, staff are cheery and, if you're staying over, you'll find bedrooms clean, fresh and uncluttered.

CLOSING TIMES
Closed 25 December and Sunday dinner

PRICES
Meals: a la carte £ 23/31
3 rooms: £ 55/85

Typical Dishes

Hill Farm smoked pork belly with duo of apple sauce

Fillet of Cornish bass with Jersey Royals

White chocolate cheesecake

6 mi north of Tiverton by A 396 and B 3190.

Brampford Speke

21 **Lazy Toad Inn**

Brampford Speke,
EX5 5DP
Tel.: (01392)841591
Website: www.thelazytoad@btinternet.com

VISA MC

Otter ale, Trelawny and 2 guest ales

Sweet little Grade II listed pub with charming oak-beamed ceilings and slate floors, set in an equally attractive village not far from the River Exe. In summer, head for the beautiful walled garden or lovely cobbled courtyard, once used by the local farrier and wheelwright. If you're only paying a flying visit, opt for a real ale or some of Mo's homemade blackcurrant cordial, along with some tasty homemade pork scratchings; if you've got longer, choose from the interesting Asian-inspired main menu. Much of the produce, including the pak choi, comes from their own polytunnel just across the car park – visit in the spring and you can also sample lamb raised on their smallholding. Prices are kept keen by the chefs' more unusual choice of cuts.

CLOSING TIMES
Closed 3 weeks January, Sunday dinner, Monday and bank holidays

PRICES
Meals: a la carte £ 24/29

Typical Dishes

Home smoked salmon with potato pancake

Pig's head three ways with peas & trotter sauce

Trio of chocolates

4 mi north of Exeter by A 377. Parking.

22 Puffing Billy

Station Rd,
Exton, EX3 0PR
Tel.: (01392)877888
Website: www.thepuffingbilly.co.uk

VISA AE

Otter Bitter and O'Hanlons Yellowhammer

Robert Louis Stevenson once said 'it is better to travel hopefully than to arrive' – but he hadn't been to the Puffing Billy. Set just round the corner from Exton station, this spacious pub is light, modern and boasts a distinct sense of style. The welcome really is first class but it's a popular place, so you might want to reserve your seats. Modern stools and tub chairs fill the bar, while the more formal dining room displays stylish banquettes and high-backed chairs. On your journey through the menu you'll discover something to suit every taste: comforting classics like steak and kidney pie; regionally inspired dishes such as local chicken with Devon cheese; and some more international influences, perhaps crab cakes in chilli and coriander.

CLOSING TIMES
Closed 25 December and Sunday dinner January-15 February

PRICES
Meals: a la carte £ 25/28

Typical Dishes

Smoked salmon Niçoise
Monkfish wrapped in Parma ham
Honey & rosemary crème brûlée

Brown tourist sign off A 376 to Exmouth, 3 mi from junction 30 M 5. Parking.

Hartland

23 Hart Inn

The Square,
Hartland, EX39 6BL
Tel.: (01237)441474
Website: www.thehartinn.com

VISA

Sharp's Doom Bar, Bath Gem and O'Hanlons Yellow Hammer

Boasting stonework dating back to the 14C, this is one of the oldest buildings in Hartland, and the huge beams, open fires and homely furnishings create a warm, friendly atmosphere. Formerly 'The New Inn', it's thought that the name was changed when the draymen kept going to the wrong address; its new title is believed to make reference to it being the 'heart' of the village, where the hunt used to meet. The chef is Norwegian so the regularly changing menu sees some Scandinavian influences, although the produce itself remains local and seasonal: meat and vegetables are supplied by nearby farms and fish is delivered from Appledore. Portions are generous and not for the faint-hearted; dishes could include roast spatchcock or braised Lundy lamb.

CLOSING TIMES
Closed 1 week Spring, Sunday dinner and Monday

PRICES
Meals: a la carte £ 15/24

Typical Dishes

Trio of local sausages
Devon duck breast with pancetta & shallots
Dark chocolate & Earl Grey tart

Between Bideford and Bude off A 39. Parking.

24 **Holt**

178 High St,
Honiton, EX14 1LA
Tel.: (01404)47707
Website: www.theholt-honiton.com

VISA MC

Otter Ale, Otter Head, Otter Bright and Otter Amber

The McCaig family's mission statement is to provide a 'distinctive and sustainable taste of Devon' – and with one brother out front and one behind the scenes in the pub, and mum and dad brewing real ales just down the road, there seems to be no stopping them. Sourcing regional produce is a key part of their ethos, as is sustainability, so you'll find ingredients from small, local suppliers and eco-friendly menus printed on recycled hops and paper. Appealing menus change every 6 weeks, with tapas and light dishes on offer at lunchtime and a more substantial à la carte in the evening. Much of what you'll find on your plate is homemade – including the tasty sausages – and the curing and smoking of meats and fish takes place entirely on site.

CLOSING TIMES
Closed 2 January, 25-26 December, Sunday and Monday

PRICES
Meals: a la carte £ 25/29

Typical Dishes

Smoked salmon, poached egg & asparagus
Roasted rump of lamb
Rhubarb & almond cake

At lower end of High Street. Dowell Street car park (2 min walk).

25 Railway

Queen St,
Honiton, EX14 1HE
Tel.: (01404)47976
Website: www.therailwayhoniton.co.uk

VISA

Regularly changing guest ales including Branscombe Branoc, Black Isle Yellowhammer, Palmers Copper and St Austell's Tribute

A two minute walk from the High Street, this smart, modern pub offers authentic Italian cooking at affordable prices; a combination patently pleasing the people in this East Devon market town. It's managed by a French-born owner who previously ran a deli, and touches like the Bibendum statues and various cookery books dotted around suggest a serious approach, underlined by the pub's strap-line, 'Passionate about Food'. Nibble on olive-oil dipped bread while you peruse the menu: classics like fritto misto sit alongside homemade pasta, steaks and pizzas; warm Sicilian tart is a house favourite and specials might include seared scallops or wild boar terrine. An eclectic wine list, a weekly film club and an olive oil top-up service add to the fun.

CLOSING TIMES
Closed 25-26 December, Sunday and Monday

PRICES
Meals: a la carte £ 25/34

Typical Dishes

Lyme Bay potted brown crab

Devonshire 'nose to tail' pot-au-feu

Vanilla panna cotta

Just off the High Street, via New Street. Parking.

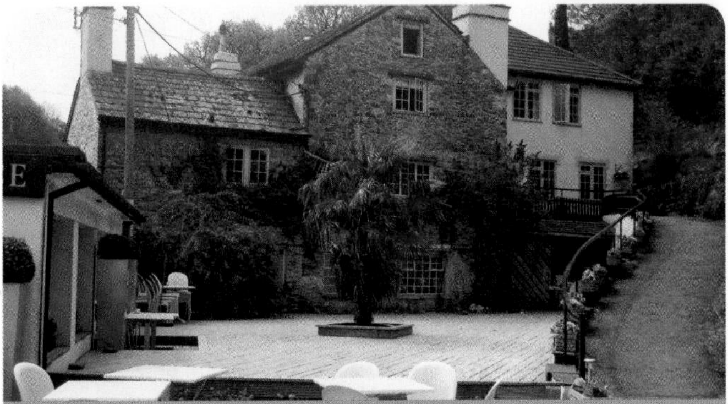

26 **Bickley Mill Inn**

Stoneycombe,
Kingskerswell, TQ12 5LN
Tel.: (01803)873201
Website: www.bickleymill.co.uk

VISA MC AE

Otter Ale, Bays & Teignworthy, Branscombe Brewery, Hunters

This modern-looking former flour mill is the last place you expect to find as you drive down winding country lanes and past a large quarry. You're greeted by a huge decked terrace, gardens built into rocky banks and a contemporary entranceway, and, despite the rustic furnishings, large open fireplaces and cosy bar, it feels decidedly modern inside, too. Menus take on a simple, traditional style and are keenly priced; you might find king prawn cocktail or devilled kidneys on toast, followed by shepherd's pie with cheddar and leek mash, or home-baked ham, free range eggs and chips – while the blackboard displays the latest fish, fresh from Brixham market. Individually designed bedrooms are bold and stylish; Owls and Eaves are two of the best.

CLOSING TIMES
Closed 23-30 December

PRICES
Meals: a la carte £ 18/25
12 rooms: £ 65/130

Typical Dishes

Game terrine
Calves liver & bacon with red wine jus
Lemon posset

3 mi south of Newton Abbot by A 380 and minor road east. Parking.

27 **Masons Arms**

Knowstone,
EX36 4RY
Tel.: (01398)341231
Website: www.masonsarmsdevon.co.uk

VISA AE

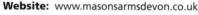

Cotleigh Tawny Ale

This pretty thatched inn is set in a secluded village in the beautiful foothills of Exmoor. It was built in the 13C by the masons who also constructed the village church, and exudes rural charm; its cosy beamed bar with inglenook fireplace often playing host to locals, their guns and their dogs. You'll find French and British classics on the menu, created using the finest of locally sourced produce. Dishes like Devon beef fillet and monkfish loin are sophisticated but never over-wrought; deliciously fresh and attractively presented, with pronounced, assured flavours. Dine beneath a celestial ceiling mural in the bright rear dining room, with delightful views out over the rolling hills towards Exmoor. Charming service complements the food.

CLOSING TIMES
Closed first
2 weeks January,
1 week spring and August,
Sunday dinner and Monday
booking essential

PRICES
Meals: a la carte £ 34/46

Typical Dishes

Salted cod with crushed potatoes & chorizo

Beef fillet & oxtail, red wine jus

Mango parfait & coconut sorbet

7 mi southeast of South Molton by A 361; opposite the village church. Parking.

28 **Dartmoor Inn**

Moorside,
Lydford, EX20 4AY
Tel.: (01822)820221
Website: www.dartmoorinn.com

VISA MC AE

Otter Ale, St Austell's Tribute

Set on the fringes of the Dartmoor National Park, close to Lydford Gorge and the White Lady waterfall, the setting couldn't be more appealing; and this pub's shabby-chic, French farmhouse styling fits it perfectly. There's a cosy bar, a series of individually styled dining rooms, a lovely courtyard and a boutique selling homewares and accessories – as well as a selection of tasty, modern dishes that are a step above your usual pub fare. Choose from the set, easy dining or main à la carte menus, all displayed on a single page; the mixed grill of sea fish for two is a popular choice. Spacious bedrooms are named after the fabrics they feature. Breakfast includes unusual offerings such as herb-crusted goat's cheese with black pudding and bacon.

CLOSING TIMES
Closed Sunday dinner and Monday lunch

PRICES
Meals: £ 24 (lunch) and a la carte £ 26/39

3 rooms: £ 80/130

Typical Dishes

Oxtail soup with parsnip dumplings
Mixed grill of sea fish with chips
Strawberry fritters

1 mi east on A 386. Parking.

Marldon

29 Church House Inn

Village Rd,
Marldon, TQ3 1SL
Tel.: (01803)558279
Website: www.churchhousemarldon.com

VISA

Otter, Tribute, Dartmoor Best and Bays Gold

A charming inn of huge character, originally built in the 14C to provide accommodation for artisans constructing the nearby church, The Church House Inn was rebuilt in the 18C and still displays some of its original Georgian windows. Inside, it's fresh and simple; there are plenty of nooks and crannies in which to settle, and local art hangs on the walls. The menu leans towards the Mediterranean, but with some North African and Asian influences, so expect dishes like slow-cooked shoulder of lamb with Moroccan spiced sultanas or pan-fried king prawns in coriander, lime and ginger butter. Two special Italian main courses are available every Tuesday night and tasting evenings on every fourth Thursday feature cuisine from different countries.

CLOSING TIMES
Closed 25 December and dinner 26 December

PRICES
Meals: a la carte £ 22/35

Typical Dishes

Crab & fennel soup
Grilled fillet of sea bass with braised fennel
Chocolate & Grand Marnier pot

Between Torquay and Paignton off A 380. Parking.

30 White Horse Inn

7 George St,
Moretonhampstead, TQ13 8PG
Tel.: (01647)440267
Website: www.whitehorsedevon.co.uk

VISA MC AE

Dartmoor Legend, Jail Ale, Otter and Butcombe SP

It's hard to believe that this pub, set in the heart of rural Dartmoor, was semi-derelict when its owners took it on. While the locals gather in the bar to watch the sport, diners head for rustic, flag-floored rooms created from the converted stable and barn; or the sunny, Mediterranean-style courtyard. With an actor-turned-chef at the helm you might expect some melodrama in the kitchen; you won't get this, but you will get tasty, unfussy dishes with more than a hint of Italy; think homemade sliced focaccia or crab linguine, set alongside more traditional dishes like duck terrine or roast rare breed pork belly. Thin crust pizzas come straight from a custom-built oven, while desserts such as Eton mess finish your meal off with a flourish.

CLOSING TIMES
Closed Sunday except bank holidays and restricted opening in winter

PRICES
Meals: a la carte £ 18/30

Typical Dishes

Home-cured meat antipasti

West Country shellfish linguine

Grappa panna cotta

In heart of village. Two car parks within 1 min walk.

31 **Ship Inn**

Noss Mayo,
PL8 1EW
Tel.: (01752)872387
Website: www.nossmayo.com

VISA MC AE

Jail Ale, Tribute, Proper Job, Otter and Palmer 200

Wonderful waterside views are one of the main attractions of this fine pub, set in a peaceful spot on the south side of the Yealm Estuary. It's well run, large and very busy, with friendly staff who cope admirably under pressure. Its oldest part dates from the 18C and its characterful interior features wooden floors and open fires, while its collection of maritime memorabilia, including numerous old photographs, gives a tangible sense of seafaring history. The menu offers pub classics such as rib-eye steak, sausage and mash, and ham or free range egg and chips. Desserts come from the tried-and-tested stable and might include lemon panna cotta or bread and butter pudding, while the wine list is well-presented, with a good selection by the glass.

CLOSING TIMES
Open daily

PRICES
Meals: a la carte £ 26/31

Typical Dishes

Seared scallops with saffron risotto

Fillets of sea bass with salsa verde

Trio of favourite puddings

10.5 mi southeast of Plymouth; signed off A 379; turn right onto B 3186. Restricted parking, particularly at high tide.

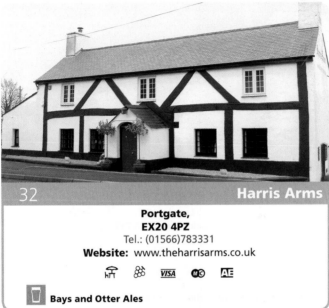

32 **Harris Arms**

Portgate,
EX20 4PZ
Tel.: (01566)783331
Website: www.theharrisarms.co.uk

VISA MC AE

Bays and Otter Ales

With its simple black and white exterior, this is a place that you could easily drive past, but plenty of people already seem to know its secret. Pass through the classical bar-lounge and down the steep steps, and you'll find lovely views across the fields, along with a large decked terrace. The owners constantly flit to and fro but the atmosphere remains cheery and laid-back. Menus offer a concise selection of tried-and-tested dishes, supplemented by daily specials on the blackboard. Presentation is fresh and simple, and there's always plenty of flavour packed in. A well laid out, seasonally changing wine list really reflects the owners' experience in, and passion for, New Zealand and France; keep an eye out for the fundraising wine dinners.

CLOSING TIMES
Closed Sunday dinner and Monday

PRICES
Meals: a la carte £ 20/33

Typical Dishes

Twice-baked goat's cheese soufflé

Confit duck, haricot bean & chorizo ragout

Rich dark chocolate truffle

3 mi east of Launceston by A 388 and side road. Parking.

33 **Jack in the Green Inn**

London Rd,
Rockbeare, EX5 2EE
Tel.: (01404)822240
Website: www.jackinthegreen.uk.com

VISA

Otter Ale, Butcombe Bitter and Sharp's Doom Bar

With its unassuming whitewashed exterior, this is a place that you could easily drive by – but if you did, you'd be missing out. Inside it's warm and welcoming, both in its décor and in the friendliness of the team. Weekend jazz sessions take place on the terrace during summer and the larger than life owner ensures the locals are kept in-the-know by sending out newsletters and recipe cards. They take a very serious approach towards the cooking here and have been supporting local producers for a long time. You'll find everything from pies and steaks to terrines and risottos, supplemented by daily specials – mostly fresh fish from the day boats. Refreshingly, bread, veg and water are all free of charge. Watch out for hot air balloons passing by.

CLOSING TIMES
Closed 25 December-6 January

PRICES
Meals: £ 25 and a la carte £ 33/42

Typical Dishes

Baked parmesan custard
Creedy Carver duck breast with cherry and almonds
Sticky toffee pudding

6.25 mi east of Exeter by A 30. Parking at the back.

34 Tower Inn

Church Rd,
Slapton, TQ7 2PN
Tel.: (01548)580216
Website: www.thetowerinn.com

VISA

Butcombe Bitter, Otter Bitter, St Austell's Proper Job and Sharp's Doom Bar

Leave your car in the car park as you enter the village and make the 10 minute walk up the hill: not only is it the easiest place to park but it's also a pleasant stroll. Built in 1347 as cottages for the workers building the next door chantry, the pub is now overlooked by the ruins of the former tower. It's a charming place, boasting dark red walls, polished tables and roaring fires, not forgetting fresh flowers and flickering candles. Menus differ from lunch to dinner and change every 3 months. It's pub food with an extra little twist; nothing gimmicky, just good cooking that adds something a little different, so your venison sausages might be served with sauerkraut and your fish and chips might come in vodka batter. Simple bedrooms await.

CLOSING TIMES
Closed first 2 weeks January and Sunday in winter

PRICES
Meals: a la carte £ 24/33
3 rooms: £ 65/85

Typical Dishes

Diver-caught scallops
Pan-fried sea bass with fennel purée & chorizo
Chocolate parfait with raspberry crush

6 mi southwest of Dartmouth by A 379. Parking with exceptionally narrow access.

35 **Oak Inn**

Station Rd,
South Brent, TQ10 9BE
Tel.: (01364)72133
Website: www.oakonline.net

VISA MC

Teignworthy Beachcomber, Dartmoor IPA, Otter Ale

South Brent is not the prettiest of villages and most people pass it by when heading on to the coast, so The Royal Oak has its work cut out when it comes to pulling in more than the locals. The décor is clean and fresh yet somewhat traditional: a large bar leads through to a modern, roomy restaurant with an attractive courtyard, while the upstairs function room is used for everything from business meetings to judo session. At lunchtime there's a simple bar menu supplemented by a fish and a dish 'of the day'; while in the evening they offer more complex dishes such as seared pigeon breast or rump of lamb Niçoise. The cheesecakes have become something of a speciality and the various events are always a hit. Bedrooms are modern and spacious.

CLOSING TIMES
Open daily

PRICES
Meals: a la carte £ 15/29
5 rooms: £ 65/130

Typical Dishes

Crayfish with marie rose sauce

Belly of pork with celeriac & potato rösti

Apple & pear frangipane

Off A 38. Free parking in old railway station car park.

36 **Kings Arms**

Dartmouth Rd,
Strete, TQ6 0RW
Tel.: (01803)770377
Website: www.kingsarms-dartmouth.co.uk

VISA MC

Otter Bitter, St Austell's Tribute

Behind its rather dour exterior hides a pub of consequence, serving the best, the wettest and the freshest seafood from Devon's sandy shores. The menu offers classical, honest-to-goodness dishes like herring roes on toast or fillet of turbot. There are oysters, mussels, lobster, crab, scallops and fish in abundance; all locally caught, simply cooked and very tasty. Non-seafood dishes might include confit of duck or steak and chips, with traditional desserts such as sticky toffee pudding. Like the food, the atmosphere is pleasingly down-to-earth. There is a snug bar and a raised dining room with pictures of seascapes on the walls; on a summer's day, head instead for the delightful rear garden which boasts fantastic views out over Start Bay.

CLOSING TIMES
Closed Sunday dinner and Monday in winter

PRICES
Meals: a la carte £ 20/34

Typical Dishes

Seared scallops with braised Puy lentils & Pedro Ximénez syrup

Roast fillet of hake with chilli, lime & coriander butter

Chocolate marquise

4 mi southwest of Dartmouth by A 379. Parking.

Totnes

37 **Steam Packet Inn**

St Peter's Quay,
Totnes, TQ9 5EW
Tel.: (01803)863880
Website: www.steampacketinn.co.uk

VISA

Jail Ale, Courage Best, Sharp's Doom Bar and Otter Ale

Named after the postal ships that used to carry the mail, the Steam Packet Inn is situated in a fantastic location on the River Dart, just five minutes walk from the centre of town. With a vast terrace that catches the sun from dawn til dusk and a large conservatory looking out over the water, this is a great spot to relax and watch the comings and goings on the river – but plenty of other people know this too, so the pleasant serving team are often pushed to their limit. The eclectic, wide-ranging menu has something for everyone and ranges from classic lemon sole and West Country steak to kofta kebabs and even Thai dishes. Fresh fish from Looe is a speciality and a blackboard displays the latest catch. Elegant, contemporary bedrooms await.

CLOSING TIMES
Open daily

PRICES
Meals: a la carte £ 21/26
4 rooms: £ 60/80

Typical Dishes

Prawn & crayfish cocktail
Sea bass fillet with beetroot and spring onion salsa
Lemon and lime posset

Turn right at the bottom of the hill by the river. Parking.

38 **Cow**

58 Station Rd,
Ashley Cross, Poole, BH14 8UD
Tel.: (01202)749569
Website: www.thecowpub.co.uk

VISA MC AE

Ringwood Best, Fuller's London Pride and Wayland's Sixpenny

Pubs next to railway stations are not normally celebrated for their cooking but this bovine beauty bucks the trend. What used to be a local dive has been transformed into a very pleasant stop-off point for a drink or a meal before travelling – as well as a destination in its own right. The lunch menu offers a mix of pub favourites and bistro classics; perhaps bubble and squeak or steak and ale pie. The evening menu – available only in the bistro – steps things up a gear with dishes such as pigeon ballotine or sea bass, while the bar area with its sofas, cow canvases and flat screen TV is principally for drinkers. Anyone wanting an evening meal here must make do with the dish chalked on the board; perhaps shepherd's pie or Thai green curry.

CLOSING TIMES
Closed 25 December and Sunday dinner

PRICES
Meals: £ 25 and a la carte £ 27/40

Typical Dishes

Smoked haddock fishcake

Sirloin of beef, peppercorn sauce & fries

White chocolate & honeycomb mousse

At Parkstone Station. Parking.

Bridport

39 **Bull**

34 East St,
Bridport, DT6 3LF
Tel.: (01308)422878
Website: www.thebullhotel.co.uk

VISA AE

Otter Bitter, Otter Ale

From the moment you set foot in this Grade II listed building and are greeted by a vast contemporary portrait, you realise it's no ordinary place. A regency style former coaching inn, it has undergone a massive transformation, which has left an eclectic mix of period features and chic, contemporary décor – a touch of grandeur amongst the bustling streets of this busy market town. The ground floor is surprisingly compact, featuring a small bar overlooking a courtyard and a simple, fairly informal dining room, where you'll find a mix of English and classic brasserie dishes – crafted from local meats and fresh fish from Lyme Bay. The modern designer bedrooms are equally as appealing; residents' areas include a luxurious ballroom.

CLOSING TIMES
Open daily

PRICES
Meals: a la carte £ 25/40
19 rooms: £ 85/195

Typical Dishes

Lyme Bay scallops with pea purée
Chargrilled sirloin steak & chips
Chocolate fondant

In town centre on south side of main street. Parking.

40 Stapleton Arms

Church Hill,
Buckhorn Weston, SP8 5HS
Tel.: (01963)370396
Website: www.thestapletonarms.com

VISA AE

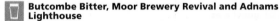

Butcombe Bitter, Moor Brewery Revival and Adnams Lighthouse

Sister to The Queen's Arms in Corton Denham, The Stapleton Arms lies on the fringes of Blackmore Vale and makes an ideal base for exploring the region. Menus are modern British with Mediterranean influences, so you might find rosemary crusted rack of lamb or red and yellow chicory risotto; and if you book ahead, you can even arrange to carve your own Sunday roast at the table. The majority of ingredients are sourced from within 25 miles and local, seasonal produce is delivered daily from the markets and the farm next door. The pub itself has a shabby-chic style, while the individually designed bedrooms with their Egyptian linen and smart bathrooms are more stylish. You can keep your packing light as they provide maps, wellies and picnics.

CLOSING TIMES
Closed 25-26 December

PRICES
Meals: a la carte £ 21/28
4 rooms: £ 72/120

Typical Dishes

Lyme Bay squid with chorizo & salsa verde
Seared hanger steak with braised oxtail cottage pie
Rhubarb & custard cheesecake

7 mi west of Shaftesbury by A 30 and minor road north. Parking.

Buckland Newton

41 **Gaggle of Geese**

Buckland Newton,
DT2 7BS
Tel.: (01300)345249
Website: www.thegaggle.co.uk

VISA

Ringwood Best, Otter Amber, St Austell's Proper Job and guest ales

Instead of Tom and Barbara, it's Mark and Emily pursuing 'The Good Life' here, with acres of room to pursue their dream of self-sufficiency. Out the back there's herb and vegetable beds, an orchard full of fruit trees, and paddocks – where you'll find quail, chickens, goats, sheep and of course, a small gaggle of geese. The pub itself has a relaxed, bohemian feel with shabby-chic styling and even a skittle alley, where the locals take part in a popular winter league. There's always something going on here, be it a theme evening, Morris dancing, the annual charity goose auction or village fête. Drinkers mingle with diners sampling excellent quality produce from constantly evolving, pub-style menus; cooking is hearty but presentation is refined.

CLOSING TIMES
Closed 25 December

PRICES
Meals: a la carte £ 19/27

Typical Dishes

Salt beef hash
Fillet of lamb with slow-cooked kidney
Chocolate fondant

6 mi south of Sherbourne in centre of village. Parking.

42 **New Inn**

14 Long St,
Cerne Abbas, DT2 7JF
Tel.: (01300)341274
Website: www.newinncerneabbas.com

Palmers IPA, Copper and Dorset Gold

The picture postcard village of Cerne Abbas is overlooked by the famous Chalk Giant – and this 16C former coaching inn is another impressively sized and rather ancient village landmark. Its décor is traditional, with exposed beams and dark wood tables, but a little recent revamp has made it slightly less cluttered than it once was. Apart from a few midday sandwiches, the same menu is offered at lunch and dinner. Expect traditional dishes like fishcakes, steak pie or pork belly - good pub grub with no unnecessary fuss; just freshly prepared, ably cooked and using locally sourced ingredients. A pleasant decked area leads out to the pub's vast back garden with its delightful apple trees. Bedrooms are modest but set to improve.

CLOSING TIMES
Restricted opening in winter

PRICES
Meals: a la carte £ 21/29

Typical Dishes

Lyme Bay scallops, spiced pork belly

Loin of venison, dauphinoise & French beans

Eton mess

In the centre of the village. On-street parking.

Farnham

43 **Museum Inn**

Farnham,
DT11 8DE
Tel.: (01725)516261
Website: www.museuminn.co.uk

VISA

Both Bails and Double Drop

Set in the heart of a picture postcard village, this part-thatched 17C country inn was built by the founding father of modern archaeology – General August Lane Fox Pitt Rivers – to provide refreshment and accommodation for visitors to his nearby museum. It retains many original features, including flagstone floors and an inglenook fireplace, and the walls are adorned with hunting artefacts. For dining there's the bar, two adjoining rooms, a conservatory and the 'Shed', a smart, linen-laid room that opens at weekends. The menu offers British classics alongside dishes of a more Mediterranean nature, and cooking is seasonal, unfussy and focused on quality local ingredients. Bedrooms range from small and cottagey to spacious with a four-poster.

CLOSING TIMES
Open daily

PRICES
Meals: a la carte £ 30/34
8 rooms: £ 110/165

Typical Dishes

Twice-baked crab soufflé
Creedy Carver duck with gratin potato
Dark chocolate pavé

7.5 mi northeast of Blandford Forum by A 354. Parking.

44 **Three Horseshoes**

Powerstock,
DT6 3TF
Tel.: (01308)485328

VISA MC

Palmers Copper Ale, Tally Ho!, Palmers 200

It's all about the food here at The 'Shoes. Granted, the pub occupies a lovely spot on the edge of the Dorset Downs but looks-wise, there's really not much here to write home about. But just one glance at the menu will explain the pub's growing reputation – it all sounds so appealing that it's a dilemma deciding what to choose. Great ingredients go into the dishes which come with a proper pubby earthiness, whether that's wild boar Scotch eggs, deep-fried rabbit with coleslaw, Barnsley chop with devilled kidneys or the veal and bone marrow burger. The day's fish specials are chalked up on the blackboard and they make their own breads, ice creams, chutneys and pickles. Prices are sensible and the triple-cooked chips are worth the journey alone.

CLOSING TIMES
Closed dinner
25 December, Monday in winter and Sunday dinner

PRICES
Meals: a la carte £ 21/36
3 rooms: £ 45/70

Typical Dishes

Scallops with cured Bath chaps

Barnsley chop with devilled lamb's kidneys

Custard tart

5.5 mi northeast of Bridport by A 3066. Parking.

Wimborne St Giles

45 **Bull Inn**

Coach Rd,
Wimborne St Giles, BH21 5NF
Tel.: (01725)517300
Website: www.bullwsg.com

VISA

Various guest ales from Hall & Woodhouse Brewery

Down narrow country roads by the Earl of Shaftsbury's estate, you'll come across this smart, modern, olive green pub. Inside neutrally hued walls are covered in countryside prints and there's a mix of older-style furniture. All tables are set for dining, although there is a lounge set aside for drinkers, many of whom are partial to a real ale or two from the local brewery. Dogs are as welcome as their owners and service is helpful and friendly. Menus change daily and sometimes even between services, with produce sourced from their farm and within the county's borders. This is not your usual pub fare: refined dishes use interesting ingredients and unusual cuts, so you might find quince tart or veal tongue. Bedrooms are smart and stylish.

CLOSING TIMES
Open daily

PRICES
Meals: a la carte £ 25/34
5 rooms: £ 65/130

Typical Dishes

Ox tongue with mustard fruits

Lamb chops with mint & feta salad

Custard parfait

From the village, take first right after crossing the River Allen. Parking.

46 **Village Pub**

Barnsley,
GL7 5EF
Tel.: (01285)740421
Website: www.thevillagepub.co.uk

VISA MC AE

Hook Norton, Butcombe, Wye Valley Brewery and two regularly rotating guest ales

One of the trailblazers of the gastro-revolution, The Village Pub ran out of steam somewhat in the late noughties but, now under the expert guidance of Calcot Manor, is once again on the up. With an interior straight out of any country homes magazine, it's got that cosy, open-fired village pub vibe down to a tee. The daily changing menu exudes modern appeal; nibbles like sea trout blinis are an irresistible teaser, there are starters like homemade country terrine, mains like braised lamb hotpot and comforting desserts such as treacle tart or rice pudding. Meat comes from within a 30 mile radius, with charcuterie often from Highgrove and vegetables from partner Barnsley House up the road. Individually styled bedrooms; Six has a four-poster.

CLOSING TIMES
Open daily

PRICES
Meals: a la carte £ 24/31
6 rooms: £ 95/150

Typical Dishes

Ham hock, green bean & lentil salad
Braised lamb hotpot
Sticky toffee pudding

4 mi northeast of Cirencester on B 4425. Parking.

Bourton-on-the-Hill

47 Horse & Groom

Bourton-on-the-Hill,
GL56 9AQ
Tel.: (01386)700413
Website: www.horseandgroom.info

Inspectors' favourites

VISA

Goff's Jouster, Prescott's Track Record, Purity Mad Goose, Donnington's BB and SBA

Situated in a remote Cotswold village on the side of a hill it's not surprising that this Georgian stone pub attracts mainly diners, as, unless you live here, it's a long way to go for a drink. The relaxed atmosphere makes it popular with all ages and the friendly, well-paced service stands the test of even the busiest hour. Original beams, pine flooring and exposed stone feature throughout, while an attractive marble-topped counter steals focus in the bar. Here, two blackboards compete for attention: the first, a growing list of names of those waiting for a table and the second, an appealing list of heartening British classics. Cooking is unfussy and generous, and local produce features highly. Stylish, modern bedrooms await.

CLOSING TIMES
Closed 1 week early January, 25 December and Sunday dinner
booking essential

PRICES
Meals: a la carte £ 21/33
5 rooms: £ 80/175

Typical Dishes

Cornish mackerel, smoked haddock & leek fishcakes
Pork & chorizo meatballs
Yorkshire rhubarb & custard Eton mess

2 mi west of Moreton-in-Marsh by A 44. Parking.

48 **Gumstool Inn**

Calcot,
GL8 8YJ
Tel.: (01666)890391
Website: www.calcotmanor.co.uk

Inspectors' favourites

VISA AE

Butcombe Gold and Butcombe Traditional

Set in the grounds of Calcot Manor Hotel, on a 700 year old Estate, this converted farm out-building is now a highly attractive country pub. With wood-panelled walls, flag flooring and modern furnishings, it successfully combines classic country style with contemporary chic. It's warm and cosy in winter, bright and airy in the spring and the paved terrace is ideal in summer. The wide-ranging monthly menu is seasonal, rustic and hearty, but also accommodates for lighter appetites by offering some scaled-down main courses; while the extensive daily specials provide some interesting choices. Service is polite and friendly but make sure you give back what you get, as in the past miscreants were placed on the local gumstool and ducked in the pond.

CLOSING TIMES
Open daily
booking essential

PRICES
Meals: a la carte £ 24/32

Typical Dishes

Crisp goat's cheese parcel
Chunky beer-battered cod & chips
Bread & butter pudding

3.5 mi west of Tetbury on A 4135, in grounds of Calcot Manor Hotel. Parking.

Chipping Campden

49 **Eight Bells Inn**

Church St,
Chipping Campden, GL55 6JG
Tel.: (01386)840371
Website: www.eightbellsinn.co.uk

VISA

Hook Norton Best, Goff's Jouster, Purity Mad Goose, Wye Valley HPA

If you're following the Cotswold Way Walk, this 14C pub, close to the historic high street of this old wool merchant's town, is well worth a visit. It originally accommodated the stonemasons working on St James's church, and later stored the eight bells from the church tower. Rebuilt in the 17C using the original stone and timbers, it has retained a good old community feel, welcoming drinkers and diners alike. The four neighbouring counties are represented behind the bar in their ale selection and they even offer scrumpy and perry on tap. Cooking is traditionally British – pies are the real thing, puddings are gloriously homemade and specials are just that, so arrive early if you want the full choice. Bedrooms combine character with mod cons.

CLOSING TIMES
Closed 25 December

PRICES
Meals: a la carte £ 23/34
7 rooms: £ 60/125

Typical Dishes
Smoked trout pâté
Mr Lashford's sausages & mash
Lemon posset

In centre of town. Unlimited parking on road.

50 The Green Dragon Inn

Cockleford,
GL53 9NW
Tel.: (01242)870271
Website: www.green-dragon-inn.co.uk

VISA MC AE

Butcombe, Battledown Premium and Directors

This characterful stone pub can be found nestled in a peaceful country lane that borders the grounds of the Cowley Manor hotel. The surrounding area is serious walking territory, so at lunchtime you'll find plenty of ramblers tucking into hearty burgers or sausages – alongside others sampling some of the more unusual dishes, such as deep fried pheasant and chestnut samosas or baked sea bass in a banana leaf. Huge open fireplaces are a focal point in two of the rooms and what better way to start the day than breakfast by a roaring fire? Keep an eye out for the carved mice that hide among the woodwork – the hallmark of Robert 'Mouseman' Thompson. Bedrooms are simple and modern; the St George suite is the best and boasts a super-king-sized bed.

CLOSING TIMES
Closed dinner 25-26 December and 1 January
booking essential

PRICES
Meals: a la carte £ 26/32
9 rooms: £ 70/95

Typical Dishes

Pork meatballs & sweet chilli
Grilled Cajun-marinated salmon
Sticky toffee pudding

5 mi south of Cheltenham by A 435. Parking.

Ebrington

51 Ebrington Arms

Ebrington,
GL55 6NH
Tel.: (01386)593223
Website: www.theebringtonarms.co.uk

VISA

Vale Ale, Uley Bitter, Stroud Organic, Stanny Bitter and one guest ale

This 17C inn snuggles into a charming chocolate box village in the glorious Cotswold countryside; its beamed, flag-floored bar with blazing log fire providing the hub from which locals and visitors come and go, while owners Claire and Jim oversee proceedings with humour and grace. The smart, stylish dining room, with its gilt-framed mirrors, provides an intimate atmosphere for a meal; there are monthly food nights – and fish and chips to take away. Tasty, robust, traditional dishes are cooked using local ingredients and up-to-date techniques; perhaps lamb leg steak or beef, Guinness and horseradish pie – with homemade desserts like passion fruit and orange tart to follow. Comfortable bedrooms with countryside views; Room 3 has a four-poster.

CLOSING TIMES
Open daily

PRICES
Meals: a la carte £ 21/31
3 rooms: £ 95/120

Typical Dishes

Salmon, mackerel & parsley fishcakes
Grilled Cornish plaice with crab linguine
Drambuie scented panna cotta

2 mi east of Chipping Campden by B 4035. Parking.

52 **Fox Inn**

Lower Oddington,
GL56 0UR
Tel.: (01451)870555
Website: www.foxinn.net

VISA MC

Hook Norton, Cotswold Way, Sharp's Doom Bar, Purity Pure UBU

Set in a peaceful Cotswold village, this charming 16C creeper-clad inn boasts exposed beams, flagged floors and open fires. When the sun's out, the pretty garden is the place to be and, as the night draws in, the covered terrace makes the perfect retreat. It's just as appealing in the winter too, with plenty of cosy corners to snuggle into in the candlelit bar or characterful Red Room. Cooking hits just the right note – hearty, with a satisfyingly unpretentious style – and the produce is reassuringly local, with many ingredients sourced from local markets, and game from nearby Adlestrop. Steak and kidney pie is a favourite at lunch and the homemade puddings are a hit whatever the time of day. Uniquely designed bedrooms display lovely antiques.

CLOSING TIMES
Open daily
booking essential

PRICES
Meals: a la carte £ 24/32
3 rooms: £ 75/95

Typical Dishes

Seared scallops with pancetta
Fillet of Cornish turbot with hollandaise
Cherry & almond tart

3 mi east of Stow-on-the-Wold by A 436. Parking.

53 **Feathered Nest**

Nether Westcote,
OX7 6SD
Tel.: (01993)833030
Website: www.thefeatherednestinn.co.uk

VISA AE

Hook Norton, Hobgoblin, Oxford Gold

Set in a small hamlet, this once down-at-heel pub has really come into its own under its latest owners, who spent several years in Portugal gaining experience in the hospitality industry. It's the type of place that offers something for everyone, with a laid-back bar, rustic snug, casual conservatory and formal dining room. Sit on quirky bar stools made from horse saddles and sample dishes such as sardines, pig's cheeks and Cornish pollock, or head through to elegant antique tables for more complex offerings such as confit wood pigeon or scallops with chicory and clementine purée – not forgetting a list of over 200 wines. Once fully sated, make for a comfy bedroom complete with antique furnishings, quality linens and a smart, roll-top bath.

CLOSING TIMES
Closed 25 December
booking advisable

PRICES
Meals: a la carte £ 25/34
4 rooms: £ 110/185

Typical Dishes

Hand-dived scallops, chicory salad

Slow-roasted suckling pig with black pudding

Chocolate & hazelnut brittle

4.75 mi southeast of Stow-on-the-Wold by A 429 and A 424. Parking.

54 **Wheatsheaf Inn**

West End,
Northleach, GL50 3EZ
Tel.: (01451)860244
Website: www.cotswoldswheatsheaf.com

VISA MC AE

Gem Bath Ales, Purity Ales and HPA Wye Valley

The pretty Cotswold town in which this characterful and recently refurbished 17C former coaching inn sits was once famous for its thriving wool trade, and there are many reminders of the town's interesting history including its 12C church and busy market square. There's still plenty going on today: the owners will book guests a day's local fishing or shooting, or organise tickets to events such as the Cheltenham festivals; they also host their own events such as a monthly book club and occasional jazz evenings. Dine in either the stone-floored, open-fired bar or one of two dining areas. The daily changing menus feature flavourful pub classics like steak frites or ham hock terrine and local staff provide friendly service. Individually decorated bedrooms.

CLOSING TIMES
Open daily

PRICES
Meals: £ 15 (lunch)
and a la carte £ 26/33
14 rooms: £ 120/180

Typical Dishes

Devilled kidneys on toast

Warm salad of Bibury lamb

Vanilla panna cotta

In centre of town. Parking.

Paxford

55 **Churchill Arms**

Paxford,
GL55 6XH
Tel.: (01386)594000
Website: www.thechurchillarms.com

VISA

Greene King Abbot Ale, Wye Valley HPA and Hooky Bitter

Despite a troubled past few years, this traditional Cotswold stone inn is on the up. Set in a picture postcard location, it boasts views over pretty stone houses, the nearby church and rolling open fields; as well as a charming interior with exposed beams, stone floors and a large wood burning stove. The enclosed rear garden is popular in summer, especially on a Thursday night, when you'll find the locals playing the old Oxfordshire game 'Aunt Sally'. Cooking displays a real mix of influences, ranging from unfussy pub classics on the blackboard to more restaurant-style dishes on the à la carte; finished off with tasty nursery puddings. Bedrooms are cosy with good country views but be aware that silence doesn't reign until the pub doors close.

CLOSING TIMES
Closed 25 December

PRICES
Meals: a la carte £ 20/36
4 rooms: £ 60/95

Typical Dishes
Stuffed baby squid
Pan-fried sea bass with samphire
Lemon posset

3 mi east of Chipping Campden by B 4035. On-street parking.

56 **Bell**

Sapperton,
GL7 6LE
Tel.: (01285)760298
Website: www.foodatthebell.co.uk

VISA

Uley Old Spot, Otter Bitter, Bath Ales Gem and one guest ale

On a warm summer's day head for this pretty village, where, set above the road, you can relax amongst the neatly-lawned gardens and paved terraces of this charming pub. Exposed stone and wooden beams feature throughout and colourful modern art adorns the walls. The wide-ranging daily menu displays an array of comforting British dishes, with the odd international influence here and there. Lunch offers several dishes in two sizes, dinner boasts some more substantial offerings and the blackboard specials consist mainly of seafood. Cooking is refined yet rustic and a glance at the back of the menu assures you of the local or regional origins of the produce used. Completing the package is an interesting wine list and friendly, well-paced service.

CLOSING TIMES
Closed 25 December and Sunday dinner November-March

PRICES
Meals: a la carte £ 24/35

Typical Dishes

Pan-fried Cornish chilli squid

Loin of Badminton Estate venison

Pear frangipane

5 mi west of Cirencester by A 419. Parking.

Southrop

57 **Swan**

Southrop,
GL7 3NU
Tel.: (01367)850205
Website: www.theswanatsouthrop.co.uk

VISA MC AE

Swan Bitter, Hooky Bitter, Severn Vale's Dursley Steam and Sharp's Doom Bar

Run by an experienced London couple, this swan is a very smart and well-heeled bird; a splendid creeper-clad inn, in a picture perfect village. There are some restaurant-style dishes on the menu, but these are combined with classic pub staples; so expect choices such as chicken liver and foie gras parfait or roast haunch of venison to be found alongside steak, kidney and mushroom pie and Lancashire hotpot. The other influence on the chef's cooking is his mother's Italian roots, hence the bruschetta, ribollita and other Mediterranean delights, including fresh foccacia delivered to the table as you arrive. Modern art graces the walls, flowers brighten the tables and there's a happy mix of visitors and regulars proud to call this their local.

CLOSING TIMES
Closed 25 December and Sunday dinner

PRICES
Meals: £ 19 (weekdays) and a la carte £ 30/37

Typical Dishes

Roast foie gras & toasted brioche
Crisp confit of Kelmscott pork belly
Chocolate fondant

3 mi northwest of Lechlade on Eastleach rd. Parking around the village.

58 White Hart Inn

The Square,
Stow-on-the-Wold, GL54 1AF
Tel.: (01451)830674
Website: www.whitehartstow.com

VISA AE

Arkells Brewery's 3B, 2B and Gold

The second foodie venture for locals Peter and Louise, the 13C White Hart Inn takes up a prominent position on the main town square. A former coaching inn, it now has a contemporary, very individual feel. The small open-fired bar and red leather furnished lounge are popular with drinkers, who can be found nibbling on tasty home-cooked crisps, and there's a characterful, slightly kitsch dining room with a bold feature wall. Menus are fairly concise: lunch offers light dishes and combinations such as half a sandwich and soup; while dinner has classic British dishes to the fore with the likes of shepherd's pie and fruit crumble. Cooking is refined yet hearty and flavoursome. Bedrooms boast antique furnishings; one even has a bath in the room.

CLOSING TIMES
Closed 1 week October and 1 week May

PRICES
Meals: a la carte £ 21/28
5 rooms: £ 70/100

Typical Dishes

Devilled kidneys on toast
Braised lamb shank & celeriac purée
Baked Alaska

In the town centre. Parking at the rear of the inn and in The Square.

59 Trouble House

Cirencester Rd,
Tetbury, GL8 8SG
Tel.: (01666)502206
Website: www.troublehousetetbury.co.uk

VISA MC

Wadworth 6X and Henrys IPA

The 'trouble' in the pub's name refers to rumours of old hauntings but no ghosts have been seen here for a while; well apart from Liam, the chef, who turned up in the kitchen again four years after leaving. The busy roadside setting isn't ideal and the exterior may not seem all that appealing but it's worth stopping off here for the warm welcome and tasty food. The interior has a shabby, homely style and there's a characterful, ultra-low beam in the bar; a place where the owners hope to encourage more of the locals to come and drink. Dishes range from sardines on toast to more ambitious offerings like rib of beef roasted in hay for two; and the Salcombe crab gratin and duck fat chips are favourites. The daily specials usually feature fish.

CLOSING TIMES
Closed 2 weeks January, 25 December, Sunday dinner and Monday except bank holidays

PRICES
Meals: £ 15 (weekday lunch) and a la carte £ 23/36

Typical Dishes
Salcombe crab gratin
Rib of aged beef roasted in hay
Warm lardy cake

2 mi northeast on A 433. Parking.

60 Horse & Groom Village Inn

Upper Oddington,
GL56 0XH
Tel.: (01451)830584
Website: www.horseandgroom.uk.com

VISA

Hereford Pale Ale, Goff's Tournament, Chuffin Ale

Not far from the delightful market town of Stow-on-the-Wold, you'll come across Upper Oddington; designated as an Area of Outstanding Natural Beauty. At its heart stands this part-16C mellow-stone inn, where sunshine floods in through the windows of the lovely central bar and on colder days, a log fire crackles. Flip over the menu and you'll discover that everything here is seasonal, local and ethically sourced, with consideration given to sustainability and organic farming methods. Meat and game are farm and estate sourced, cheese is locally produced and you might even see villagers popping in to swap their home-grown veg for a pint or two. Cosy bedrooms come with a serious breakfast that includes local eggs and Gloucester Old Spot sausages.

CLOSING TIMES
Open daily

PRICES
Meals: a la carte £ 21/33
7 rooms: £ 65/110

Typical Dishes

Bruschetta of char-grilled vegetables
Baked haddock with Welsh rarebit topping
Iced honeycomb & almond parfait

2 mi east of Stow-on-the-Wold by A 436. Parking.

61 **Seagrave Arms**

Friday St,
Weston-sub-Edge, GL55 6QH
Tel.: (01386)840192
Website: www.seagravearms.co.uk

VISA MC AE

Hook Norton Bitter, Purity Bitter, Goff's Cheltenham Gold

This part-Georgian coach house is located just a couple of miles out of Chipping Campden and has been attractively refurbished by its 'ex-London-restaurant' owners. It's pleasingly compact and cosy; be sure to grab a seat by the fire in the bar before moving on to one of the wood-furnished dining rooms. Service is polite and fairly formal – even in the bar drinks are brought to your table – and the food follows suit, with a concise menu of restaurant rather than pub-style dishes. Cooking is ambitious and complex, offering the likes of baked foie gras beignets, neck of lamb with sweetbreads or veal noisettes with salted fennel, and white chocolate parfait. Split between the pub and an outbuilding, bedrooms are stylish, modern and well-equipped.

CLOSING TIMES
Closed first week January and Monday

PRICES
Meals: a la carte £ 26/32
6 rooms: £ 95/115

Typical Dishes

Steamed asparagus with a poached free range egg
Duo of Cotswold lamb
Sticky toffee pudding with vanilla ice cream

3 mi northwest of Chipping Campden. Parking

62 **Queens Arms**

Corton Denham,
DT9 4LR
Tel.: (01963)220317
Website: www.thequeensarms.com

VISA MC AE

Exmoor Ale, Summer Lightning, Moor Beer, Northern Star and two guest Ales

This charming 18C stone pub is set in an attractive area but it's the enthusiastic owner's uncompromising ethos that really drives this place forwards. The regulars, both drinkers and diners, are his top priority, so he does his best to offer top quality produce at realistic prices – from fresh fruit juices and local whiskies to seasonal meats and veg. The menus, which are printed on brown paper, change daily. Lunch focuses mainly one or two courses, maybe slow-cooked autumn fruits with black pudding or a Somerset ploughman's of ham, cheddar and a pork pie; while the evening menu presents a more formal three course selection, with the likes of braised lamb shank or a plate of game for two. Bedrooms are charming, well-appointed and good value.

CLOSING TIMES
Open daily
booking advisable

PRICES
Meals: a la carte £ 22/28
5 rooms: £ 75/120

Typical Dishes

Lyme Bay scallops with aubergine purée
Confit duck leg with shallot & ginger jus
Strawberry shooter with summer pudding ice cream

3 mi north of Sherborne by B 3145 and minor road west. Parking.

Ditcheat

63 Manor House Inn

Ditcheat,
BA4 6RB
Tel.: (01749)860276
Website: www.manorhouseinn.co.uk

VISA MC AE

Butcombe, Otter Ales and Teignworthy Ales

Originally owned by Lord of the Manor Edmund Dawe, this 17C coaching inn on the Somerset Levels boasts exposed stone walls, polished flag floors and roaring log fires. Champion racehorse trainer Paul Nicholls comes from the village and the Bath & West showground is just down the road, so it's no surprise that racing is at the heart of this pub – and you'll often find the locals in the old skittle alley watching the meets. There are no light bites on offer here, just good meaty (and veggie) dishes to get your teeth into. Using locally grown or reared produce, cooking is traditional and honest with international touches; Sunday lunch in particular provides good value and variety. Cosy, well-equipped bedrooms are housed in the former stables.

CLOSING TIMES
Closed 25 December, Sunday dinner and restricted opening Christmas-New Year

PRICES
Meals: a la carte £ 21/31
3 rooms: £ 55/85

Typical Dishes
Pan-fried pigeon breast with a port reduction
Provençal-crusted rack of lamb with red wine jus
Tropical fruit yoghurt parfait

4 mi south of Shepton Mallet by A 37 and minor road left. Parking.

64 **Woods**

4 Banks Sq,
Dulverton, TA22 9BU
Tel.: (01398)324007

VISA

St Austell's Dartmoor and Proper Job

Owned by a highly regarded local publican, this former bakery can't quite decide whether it wants to be a pub or a restaurant. It doesn't really matter though because as soon as you walk through the door you know you're in for a treat: the décor is charming, a great deal of the furniture has been made by the owner himself and the walls are lined with culinary-themed paintings. Local, traceable produce is important and as such, most meat comes from the owner's farm. Cooking offers classical dishes with a French slant – light bites and a few more substantial plates at lunch, with dishes stepping it up a gear at dinner. Once a year the town turns into a mini Marseille, as the chef brings French ingredients together in a culinary celebration.

CLOSING TIMES
Closed dinner 1 January and 26 December

PRICES
Meals: a la carte £ 16/25

Typical Dishes

Bresaola
Roast belly pork with black pudding
Lemon posset

13 mi north of Tiverton by A 396 and B 3222. 3 car parks and on-street parking.

65 **Lord Poulett Arms**

High St,
Hinton St George, TA17 8SE
Tel.: (01460)73149
Website: www.lordpoulettarms.com

VISA

Moor Beers, Branscombe, Otter

The Lord Poulett offers everything you could possibly want from a pub. A picture perfect, lavender-framed terrace overlooks a boules pitch to a wild, untamed secret garden, while inside lovely old tables and squashy armchairs are set in a detailed country interior filled with hops and glowing candles. The kitchen creates an interesting seasonal menu with its roots planted firmly in the Med. Lunchtime sees a selection of gourmet sandwiches and lighter dishes, while in the evening the menu expands: there's always a 'West Bay catch of the day' and an extra mature local steak with tasty triple-cooked chips. These are followed by locally made ice creams, tempting desserts and West Country cheeses. Smart, stylish bedrooms boast feature baths.

CLOSING TIMES
Closed 25-26 December and 1 January

PRICES
Meals: a la carte £ 20/38
4 rooms: £ 60/95

Typical Dishes

West Bay crab tartine
Line-caught cod & triple-cooked chips
Lemon tart

1 mi northwest of Crewkerne by minor road. Parking.

66 **Old Inn**

Holton,
BA9 8AR
Tel.: (01963)32002
Website: www.theoldinnrestaurant.co.uk

VISA

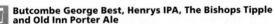

Butcombe George Best, Henrys IPA, The Bishops Tipple and Old Inn Porter Ale

The owner of nearby Clinger Farm always fancied being a chef but never realised his dream. Instead, he bought this 400 year old village pub, added a large, modern restaurant and now delights in seeing the kitchen make good use of his own farm produce, be it Gloucester Old Spot, lamb, corn-fed chicken, or apples and pears; you can even buy his eggs as you leave. The menu is kept short and to the point and the star of the show is the Josper grill, used to chargrill the assorted cuts of meat, as well as the fish from the Brixham day boats. Portions are not for the fainthearted and dishes deliver big, gutsy flavours. The wine list is decidedly Old World, focuses on a limited number of growers and offers a decent selection by the glass.

CLOSING TIMES
Open daily

PRICES
Meals: a la carte £ 26/40

Typical Dishes

Devilled lamb's kidneys on toast

Sirloin steak with hand-cut chips

Mixed iced berries with warm white chocolate sauce

2.5 mi. west of Wincanton by B 3081, A 371, A 357 and minor roads. Parking.

Long Sutton

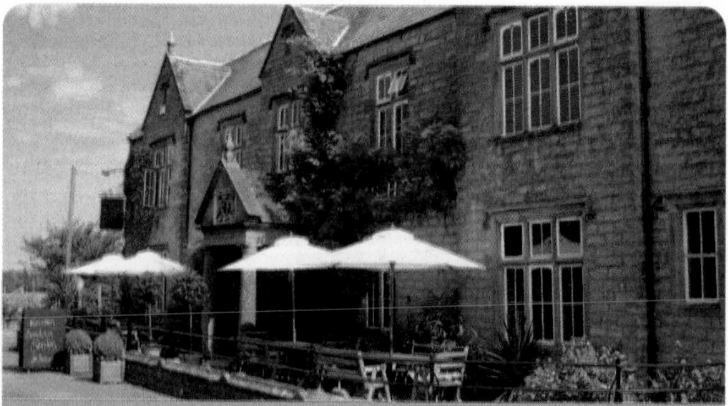

67 **Devonshire Arms**

Long Sutton,
TA10 9LP
Tel.: (01458)241271
Website: www.thedevonshirearms.com

VISA

Moor Revival, Moor Northern Star, Otter Bitter, Otter Amber, Cheddar Ales Potholer

This spacious Grade II listed hunting lodge is set right on the village green and boasts a contemporary interior, with a relaxing, open-plan bar and more formal dining room. The chef is Russian and his menu appealingly eclectic, with plenty of fish and locally sourced meats. It has a French bias but includes influences from all over Europe, so expect to see words like bresaola, brûlée, clafoutis and chorizo as you whet your appetite with nibbles like fresh olives or pistachios. Main dishes could include local chicken livers, pollock with pan-fried squid or veal burger with hand-cut chips, while dessert might mean homemade ice cream or dark chocolate fondant. The extremely comfortable bedrooms boast excellent quality bed linen and toiletries.

CLOSING TIMES
Closed 25-26 December and 1 January

PRICES
Meals: a la carte £ 25/39
9 rooms: £ 78/130

Typical Dishes

Lyme Bay mackerel with horseradish mousse

Slow-cooked shoulder of hogget

Dark chocolate fondant

4 mi east of Langport by A372. Parking.

68 The Pilgrims at Lovington

Lovington,
BA7 7PT
Tel.: (01963)240597
Website: www.thepilgrimsatlovington.co.uk

VISA

Cottage Brewing Co. Champflower

It's set at a main junction, and at first sight is hardly inspiring, but step inside The Pilgrims and it's a different matter entirely. It's pristine and personally run, and whether you sit in amongst the owners' cookbook collection in the bar side of the pub or in the bright, fresh restaurant, the décor is delightful and a relaxed atmosphere reigns. Their motto is 'the pub that thinks it's a restaurant,' and the homemade bread, the Spanish bar nibbles, the interesting wine list and the cider which comes from down the road all prove their point, as does the appealing menu of British and Mediterranean dishes created using quality produce from local suppliers. Contemporary, comfortable bedrooms, luxurious bathrooms and substantial breakfasts.

CLOSING TIMES
Closed first 2 weeks of October, Sunday dinner, Monday and lunch Tuesday

PRICES
Meals: a la carte £ 24/39
5 rooms: £ 90/130

Typical Dishes

Smoked eel & bacon
Monkfish & scallops with wild mushrooms
Selection of local Somerset cheeses

4 mi southwest of Castle Cary by B 3153. Parking.

Lower Vobster

69 Vobster Inn

Lower Vobster,
BA3 5RJ
Tel.: (01373)812920
Website: www.vobsterinn.co.uk

VISA

Butcombe Bitter, Butcombe Blonde

Its owners' propensity to produce good food, coupled with their enthusiastic, hands-on approach has made the Vobster Inn a real destination pub, and though they may have put themselves on the map, they haven't forgotten the locals, so you are as welcome to snuggle up on a sofa for a drink, a bowl of chips and a chat as you are to enjoy a three course meal in the spacious restaurant. Mr and Mrs Davila hail from Galicia in North West Spain, so you might find paella or Spanish omelette alongside cottage pie or Ploughman's on the menu; Mediterranean ingredients and techniques are married with local produce – fish specials come courtesy of the catch at St Mawes - and the cooking has an honest, rustic edge to it. Three cosy, modern bedrooms.

CLOSING TIMES
Closed Sunday dinner and Monday

PRICES
Meals: a la carte £ 19/31
3 rooms: £ 55/95

Typical Dishes

Seared scallops with bubble & squeak
Stuffed breast of lamb & sweet potato purée
Vanilla crème brûlée

6 mi northwest of Frome by A 362 towards Radstock; Vobster is signed after approx 5.5 mi. Parking.

70 **Royal Oak Inn of Luxborough**

Exmoor National Park,
Luxborough, TA23 0SH
Tel.: (01984)640319
Website: www.theroyaloakinnluxborough.co.uk

VISA MC

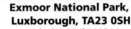

Cotleigh Tawny, St Austell's Tribute, Exmoor Ale and Gold

Set in a secluded wooded valley between the Brendon and Croyden Hills, the beautiful landscapes of Luxborough are a well kept secret. Passing through this peaceful countryside is the Coleridge Way, a walk that follows the routes that the romantic poet took when drawing inspiration for his works. The Exmoor Park authorities are understandably reluctant to put up signs, so it can be tricky finding this red sandstone pub, but it's definitely worth the search. The seasonal menu offers substantial dishes of classically prepared, boldly flavoured foods and despite an international edge to the cooking, focuses on quality, local ingredients, including Exmoor meat and Cornish seafood. Bedrooms are compact but charming; room 14 has its own terrace.

CLOSING TIMES
Closed 25 December

PRICES
Meals: a la carte £ 18/32
11 rooms: £ 55/100

Typical Dishes

Lobster & avocado salad

Roast rump of salt marsh lamb

White chocolate & Grand Marnier cheesecake

South of Minehead by A39 off A396. Parking.

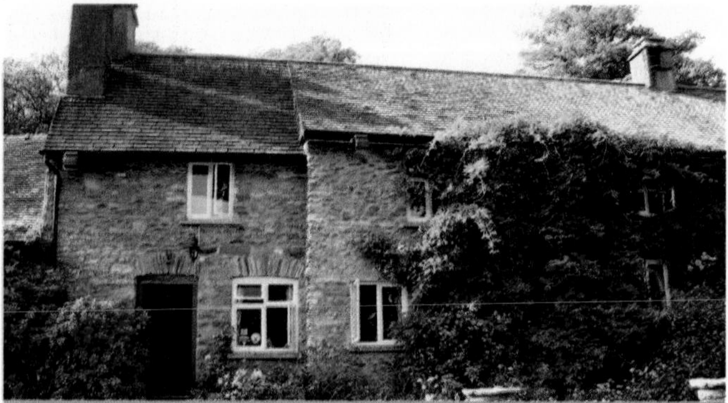

71 **Tarr Farm Inn**

Tarr Steps,
TA22 9PY
Tel.: (01643)851507
Website: www.tarrfarm.co.uk

Exmoor Ale and Exmoor Gold Bitters

At 55m in length and with 17 spans, Tarr Steps is one of Britain's finest clapper bridges. It dates back to around 1000 BC and, according to local legend, was built by the devil in order to win a bet. Here, in the idyllic Exmoor countryside, you'll find Tarr Farm Inn, a true destination pub, run by a highly regarded team who can't do enough for you. There's seating for every occasion, so you can have afternoon tea outside, lunch by the bar and dinner in the restaurant. Lunch ranges from sandwiches to a hearty three courses, while the evening menu displays some more ambitious choices such as Cornish sea bass with cockles and clams. Bedrooms are elegant, luxurious and provide every conceivable extra; and breakfast is definitely not to be missed.

CLOSING TIMES
Closed 1-13 February

PRICES
Meals: a la carte £ 18/36
9 rooms: £ 95/150

Typical Dishes

Wood pigeon breast with pancetta crisps
Loin of Exmoor lamb
Rhubarb & vanilla soufflé

Signed off B 3223 Dulverton to Exford road. Parking.

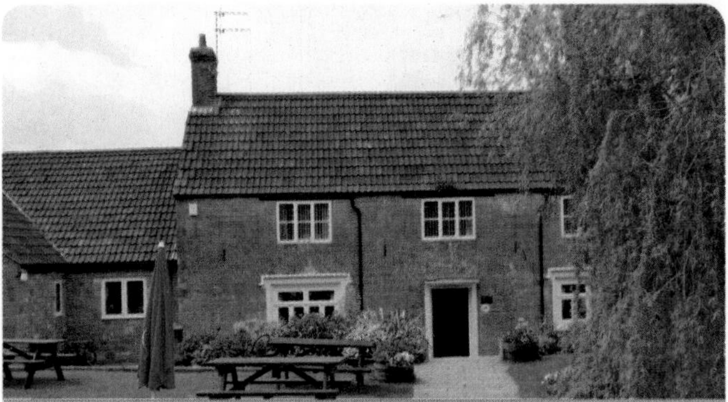

72 **Crown and Victoria Inn**

14 Farm St,
Tintinhull, BA22 8PZ
Tel.: (01935)823341
Website: www.thecrownandvictoria.co.uk

VISA

Butcombe Ales, Cheddar Ales, Yeovil Ales and regularly changing ales from local breweries

This solid stone pub resembles a private house and in a former life, was the local school. It's located next to award winning National Trust gardens but manages to put on a good show itself, with an attractive weeping willow and mature trees on display in its spacious grounds. The owners are very keen and, since they previously ran a training company, only the best team will do – names of staff members and visitor numbers are even listed on the blackboards alongside their suppliers. Mark has a real interest in all things culinary and ensures the ingredients that they source are local, organic and ethically produced. Cooking has an honest, classical base and everything is fresh, tasty and largely homemade. Bedrooms are cosy and welcoming.

CLOSING TIMES
Closed Sunday dinner

PRICES
Meals: a la carte £ 19/32
5 rooms: £ 75/95

Typical Dishes

Dorset crab & avocado
Duck breast with Madeira sauce
Hot chocolate fondant

5 mi northwest of Yeovil by A 37. Parking.

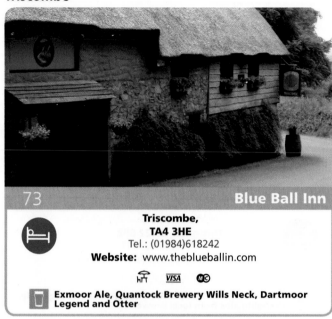

73 Blue Ball Inn

Triscombe,
TA4 3HE
Tel.: (01984)618242
Website: www.theblueballin.com

VISA MC

Exmoor Ale, Quantock Brewery Wills Neck, Dartmoor Legend and Otter

In a rural location in the beautiful Quantock Hills, you'll find this 15C thatched and stone-built former stables. Inside it has a pleasant rustic feel, boasting a narrow, beamed room filled with country pursuit memorabilia, including old photos, mounted stag heads and hunting jackets – while for warmer days, there's a steep garden set over three levels. Menus take on the same format with a fresh soup, warm salad, homemade terrine and some interesting sandwiches at lunch, but the chef has free reign to change the ingredients as and when he pleases. The main à la carte has some hearty offerings; the turbot with crab risotto and mature local beef with a stilton croute are particular favourites. Plush, stylish bedrooms boast quality furnishings.

CLOSING TIMES
Closed 25-26 December, dinner 1 January, Monday and Sunday dinner in autumn and winter

PRICES
Meals: a la carte £ 22/30
3 rooms: £ 65/95

Typical Dishes

Pea & ham risotto with king scallops
Cannon of Exmoor Lamb
Caramelised rhubarb & custard

Northwest : 11 mi by A 358. Parking.

74 **Rising Sun Inn**

West Bagborough,
TA4 3EF
Tel.: (01823)432575
Website: www.risingsuninn.info

VISA MC

Exmoor Ale, Butcombe, St Austell's Proper Job

Having previously survived a fire that raged through the surrounding hillside, the future of this inn was once again in the hands of the gods when it went into receivership. Its prospects were secured, however, when white knights appeared in the form of Jon and Christine Brinkman, an ambitious, experienced couple with no fear of hard work and dedication; who, in just a few months, turned the place around. On the menu you'll find a good balance of traditional and modern dishes, each one crafted from local ingredients and presented with an obvious element of care. A seamless mix of wood and slate creates a warm, intimate atmosphere and you rest assured that with this couple at the helm, the Sun will continue to rise more brightly every day.

CLOSING TIMES
Open daily

PRICES
Meals: a la carte £ 24/34
2 rooms: £ 65/95

Typical Dishes

Baked feta cheese with dates
Belly pork with caramelised apple & cider jus
Sticky toffee pudding

10.5 mi northwest of Taunton off A 358. Parking in the road.

Winsford

75 **Royal Oak Inn**

Exmoor National Park,
Winsford, TA24 7JE
Tel.: (01643)851455
Website: www.royaloakexmoor.co.uk

VISA MC AE

Exmoor Ale, Exmoor Gold, Betty Stogs and Otter

Close to where the Winn Brook ford flows over a winding country lane in Exmoor National Park you'll find the picturesque village of Winsford and the equally delightful Royal Oak. A thatched 12C building full of rustic charm, it was a farmhouse and dairy before finding its calling as a country pub. In tune with its surroundings, the cooking uses local, seasonal produce. Turn right for the bar or left for the restaurant and choose from a selection of tasty, satisfying dishes that range from hearty sausage and mash to chicken liver parfait and roast pork belly with butternut squash purée, sautéed spinach & cider jus. Smart bedrooms offer four-poster, queen or king size beds and come with homemade biscuits and jet powered showers.

CLOSING TIMES
Open daily

PRICES
Meals: a la carte £ 20/27
8 rooms: £ 55/120

Typical Dishes

Local grilled sardines
Exmoor lamb duo with minted jus
Sticky toffee pudding

5 mi north of Dulverston by B 3223; opposite the village green. Parking.

76 **Royal Oak**

Cues Ln,
Bishopstone, SN6 8PP
Tel.: (01793)790481
Website: www.royaloakbishopstone.co.uk

Arkell's Real Ales, Moonlight, Donnington's SBA

At the rurally set Royal Oak, where the décor is rustic and open fires create a relaxing feel, they assert that 'great food starts off with good farming' and they're not wrong. Of course, it helps that the nearby organic farm which supplies it is owned by Helen Browning, who also owns the pub. The menu changes twice daily, according to which ingredients are fresh, local and in season; these might include berries or nettles foraged from the local hedgerows; veal, pork or beef from the farm, and vegetables provided by local growers in exchange for dinner vouchers. Less local are ingredients like cannelloni beans and unfiltered extra virgin olive oil; these come from the Abruzzo region of Italy, courtesy of the chef, who has a house there.

CLOSING TIMES
Open daily

PRICES
Meals: a la carte £ 24/35

Typical Dishes

Asparagus with goat's curd

Grilled pork fillet with garlic mash

Panna cotta

6 mi east by A 4312 off A 420. Parking.

77 **The Northey**

Bath Rd,
Box, SN13 8AE
Tel.: (01225)742333
Website: www.ohhcompany.co.uk

VISA MC AE

Wadworth 6X and Warburtons ales

Having passed from one generation of Warburtons to the next, this traditional-looking coaching inn is a real family affair. It's a sizeable place, with an open-plan interior and fairly modern styling: the bar boasting low level seating and vivid artwork; the large rear dining room, heavy wooden furniture and a more formal feel. The chef has extensive experience cooking in pubs countrywide, so you can rest assured that the appealing monthly menus are as good as they sound, if not better. Dishes are unfussy, seasonal and British, and everything is made on the premises, including the bread. There are always some tasty local steaks to be found and, with seafood arriving fresh from Cornwall, fish dishes – particularly the mussels – are a strength.

CLOSING TIMES
Closed 25-26 December

PRICES
Meals: a la carte £ 22/30

Typical Dishes

Chickpea falafel & spiced chicken salad
Poussin fricassee
White chocolate & raspberry cheesecake

4.75 mi northeast of Bath on A 4. Parking.

78 **Fox**

The Street,
Broughton Gifford, SN12 8PN
Tel.: (01225)782949
Website: www.thefox-broughtongifford.co.uk

VISA

Butcombe Bitter, Otter Bitter, Bath Ales Gem and one changing guest ale

Raising the profile of this pub, both locally and farther afield, has been a labour of love for its young owner, Alex. He's given it one of those clever refurbishments that cost a lot of money but make everything look largely unchanged. It lies at the heart of the community and sponsors the local football team. There's always a great choice of beer on draught but the real surprise is out back: there are raised beds of salad leaves, rhubarb, herbs and fruits, and behind it you'll find his chickens and a pigsty. In a move towards self-sufficiency, the kitchen also makes its own sausages and dries its meat for the excellent charcuterie dishes. And what does Alex do on his day off? He goes foraging for more local produce.

CLOSING TIMES

Closed 25 December, 1 January, Sunday dinner and Monday

booking essential at weekends

PRICES

Meals: £ 18 (lunch) and a la carte £ 24/39

Typical Dishes

Home-reared air-cured ham

Roasted gilthead bream & chips

Vanilla pot

In centre of the village. Parking.

Burcombe

79 **Ship Inn**

Burcombe Ln,
Burcombe, SP2 0EJ
Tel.: (01722)743182
Website: www.theshipburcombe.co.uk

VISA MC AE

Wadworth 6X, Butcombe and Ringwood Best

If you find yourself anywhere near the delightful village of Burcombe on a sunny summer's day, be sure to make your way to this charming 17C pub. Its riverside garden is just the place to linger over a leisurely lunch, with only the wind in the trees and the quack of the local ducks to disturb the silence. If you arrived too late to nab a table, then head inside; with its open fire, low oak beams and chunky wood furniture, the pub itself is an equally enchanting place to dine. The seasonal menu offers honest portions of traditional dishes; perhaps pan-fried pigeon breast, homemade fishcakes, pot-roasted lamb shank or smoked fish kedgeree. Lunch bites offer a lighter alternative and the twice-daily changing specials board adds interest.

CLOSING TIMES
Open daily

PRICES
Meals: a la carte £ 24/35

Typical Dishes

Mushroom risotto croquettes
Crab linguini with sautéed peppers
Chocolate brownie

5.25 mi west of Salisbury by A 36 off A 30. Parking.

80 Red Lion

74 High St,
Cricklade, SN6 6DD
Tel.: (01793)750776

VISA MC

Wadworth 6X, Moles Best, Butcombe Bitter and regularly changing guest ales

Just off the Thames path, you'll find this immensely charming 17C inn. With a cosy, low-beamed interior crammed full of bric-a-brac, it looks like a proper pub; and pleasingly, it adopts a good old English attitude too. The bar serves 4 regular and 5 guest ales, as well as 30 speciality bottled beers, which can be sampled while tucking into a pub classic, dog at feet. Next door is a small but airy stone-walled dining room boasting a beautiful carved slab. Here you'll find classical dishes such as oysters, venison stew and treacle tart, with beer recommendations for every dish. Produce is fresh and extremely local – and if you're down a pound or two, they'll accept some home-grown fruit or veg as payment. Comfy bedrooms are in the old stables.

CLOSING TIMES
Closed Sunday Dinner
booking essential

PRICES
Meals: a la carte £ 21/33
5 rooms: £ 75

Typical Dishes

Red Lion tea-smoked salmon
Roast haunch of venison
Queen of puddings

6 mi northwest by A 419. On street parking.

Crockerton

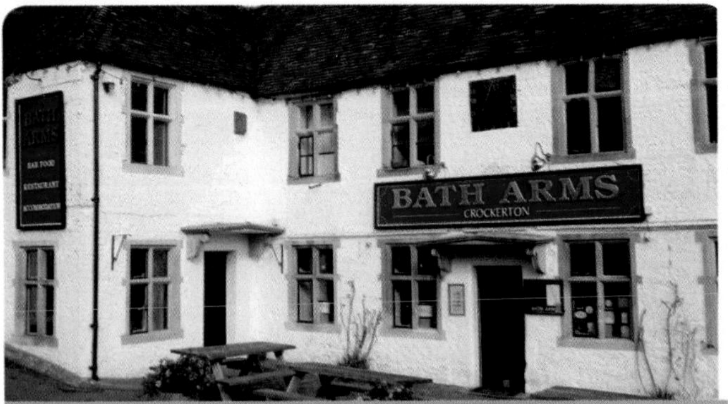

81 **Bath Arms**

Clay St,
Crockerton, BA12 8AJ
Tel.: (01985)212262
Website: www.batharmscrockerton.co.uk

VISA

Porter's Ale, Crockerton Classic and one regularly changing guest ale

The Bath Arms offers a warm welcome, open fires and plenty of country appeal, with a wealth of outdoor space. It is situated on the Longleat Estate and is run by local boy Dean Carr – originally from Warminster – who returned from his culinary experiences in the Big Smoke to put some love back into this community pub. Dishes such as roast scallop with carrot and spicy sultanas or fillet of halibut with asparagus, green beans and pancetta bring a touch of modernity to the menu. The favourites – like the popular fishcakes or the sticky beef – as well as the grills and the snacks keep it practical, while traditional desserts like bread and butter pudding or mixed berry pavlova round things off nicely. Ultra-spacious, contemporary bedrooms.

CLOSING TIMES
Open daily

PRICES
Meals: a la carte £ 21/31
2 rooms: £ 80/110

Typical Dishes

Baked mushroom & Welsh rarebit
Sticky beef with braised red cabbage
Chocolate brownie

2 mi south of Warminster by A 350 on Shearwater rd. Parking.

82 **Potting Shed**

The Street,
Crudwell, SN16 9EW
Tel.: (01666)577833
Website: www.thepottingshedpub.com

VISA MC AE

Timothy Taylor's Landlord, Bath Ales Gem, Butcombe Best and one guest ale

Despite its contemporary name and décor, The Potting Shed is very much a proper pub, where locals gather for a pint and a chat. Situated opposite its sister establishment, the Rectory Hotel, it consists of five spacious, light-filled rooms, with open fires and a relaxing feel. The pub's large gardens provide it with an abundance of fresh, seasonal herbs and vegetables – and the horticultural theme continues inside, with trowel door knobs, wheelbarrow lights and fork and spade bar pump handles. Monthly changing menus offer fresh, satisfying dishes like local trout, wild rabbit fettuccine and apple and blackberry crumble. Lollipops on the bar ensure that the kids are kept happy, while dog biscuits do the same for your four-legged friends.

CLOSING TIMES
Open daily

PRICES
Meals: a la carte £ 23/33

Typical Dishes

Crispy pig's cheeks with sauce gribiche

Duo of new season lamb

Caramelised apricots with white peach & lavender sorbet

4 mi north of Malmesbury by A 429. Parking.

Donhead St Andrew

83 **Forester Inn**

Lower St,
Donhead St Andrew, SP7 9EE
Tel.: (01747)828038
Website: www.theforesterdonheadstandrews.co.uk

VISA AE

Butcombe, Otter and Chuffin ales

Set down narrow lanes in a delightful Wiltshire village, this 13C thatched pub has a gloriously rustic feel. Exposed stone walls feature throughout and vast open fires ensure that it's always cosy. There's a lovely bar crammed with cookery books and two main dining areas – one in a cleverly added extension that's perfectly in keeping. A fine French butcher's block houses the menus, which display a strong seafood base: the constantly changing fish selection originates from the Brixham day boats and there's a daily 3 course menu dedicated to seafood. The owner is passionate about Spain so you'll find plenty of charcuterie and tapas-based dishes in the bar. Puddings are truly warming and the homemade gin and tonic sorbet is well worth a try.

CLOSING TIMES
Closed Sunday dinner

PRICES
Meals: £ 19 (weekdays) and a la carte £ 23/31

Typical Dishes

Potted shrimps
Roast cod with shellfish ragout
Apple tarte Tatin

5 mi east of Shaftesbury by A 30. Parking.

84 **Red Lion Freehouse**

East Chisenbury,
SN9 6AQ
Tel.: (01980)671124
Website: www.redlionfreehouse.com

VISA

Keystone, Three Castles, Stonehenge and Plain Ales

Enthusiastically run, cosy, and proudly impervious to the modern trend for designer pubs, the Red Lion is a charming thatched property with a pretty little garden, set in a tiny hamlet on the edge of Salisbury Plain. Seven simple wooden tables are set around the bar, a wood burner crouches in the inglenook and exposed beams lend a reassuringly solid air. Dishes are pleasingly down-to-earth – yet precisely composed and packed with flavour. There's a great value lunch menu, a roast on Sundays and a daily changing, seasonal à la carte whose dishes might include ox cheek croquettes, wild boar terrine, coq au vin or roast partridge. The resident Springer Spaniel often welcomes you with a wag or six of his tail and service is equally convivial.

CLOSING TIMES
Open daily
booking advisable

PRICES
Meals: £ 18 (lunch)
and a la carte £ 25/33

Typical Dishes

Chicken liver pâté
Roast skate wing with soy braised ox cheek
Red Lion banana bread

The Village is between Pewsey and Amesbury off the A 345. Parking.

Edington

85 Paulet Arms

47 Westbury Rd,
Edington, BA13 4PG
Tel.: (01380)830940
Website: www.pauletarms.co.uk

VISA AE

Wadworth 6X, Henty's IPA, Yeovil Ales Spring Forward

Some wealthy Americans buy football clubs; this one went for a red-brick pub in a small English village and then spent a fortune extending it and doing it up. The wood-furnished garden is a pleasant spot and if the tables are all gone, you can ask for a picnic blanket. Inside it's smart, with a mock-rustic feel courtesy of a low-ceilinged bar, slate flooring and a mix of wood furnishings. On event days, have a guest ale accompanied by an appealing bar snack, maybe a salt cod fritter or pickled egg (the two large mirrors are actually TVs), then head to the dining room for refined pub dishes crafted from quality local produce and served on wooden chopping boards. Smart, boutique-style bedrooms complete the picture and a farm shop is to follow.

CLOSING TIMES
Closed Sunday dinner and Monday

PRICES
Meals: £ 13 (lunch) and a la carte £ 24/35

3 rooms: £ 80/185

Typical Dishes

Smoked duck with red watercress
Lamb shank shepherd's pie
Honey madeleines

On main road through village. Parking.

86 **Angel Inn**

High St,
Heytesbury, BA12 0ED
Tel.: (01985)840330
Website: www.theangelheytesbury.co.uk

VISA AE

Wadworth 6X and Ringwood Best

This pretty looking pub has a typically English feel, its spacious bar home to wood fires and comfy sofas and its beamed dining room packed with locals discussing the shoot and the beer, dogs by their sides. Two further dining areas have a more formal feel; exposed brickwork and open fires adding an air of rusticity. Menus change as and when, depending on what produce is freshly available; maybe a rich homemade cauliflower soup or a salmon and cod fishcake to start, followed by a four-bone rack of lamb or pork tenderloin with cider gravy. Steaks are a speciality, the Camembert for two to share is fast becoming a favourite, and simple pub classics include the ever popular ham, egg and chunky chips. Bedrooms are not currently recommendable.

CLOSING TIMES
Open daily

PRICES
Meals: a la carte £ 20/35

Typical Dishes

Chicken liver & brandy pâté

Plum & ginger spiced duck breast

Sticky toffee pudding

4 mi. southeast of Warminster on A 36. Parking.

Hindon

87 **Lamb Inn**

High St,
Hindon, SP3 6DP
Tel.: (01747)820573
Website: www.lambathindon.co.uk

VISA MC AE

Young's, Tribute and two guest ales

The Lamb is all you'd expect from a 13C inn in the middle of a busy market town; a cosy, characterful collection of bars and dining rooms featuring heavy beams, flag floors, inglenook fireplaces and antique furniture. There's a Scottish theme throughout, so expect a plethora of plaid and tartan to go with the deep red walls and the impressive selection of malt whisky. Extensive menus continue where the décor leaves off, with dishes like pickled Orkney herrings, Macsween haggis and oak-smoked salmon. These sit alongside local dishes like 21-day matured Stourhead farm beef, Wiltshire rarebit and the famous Boisdale burger plus there are a few Mediterranean specials like moules marinière or risotto. Smart bedrooms; some with four-posters.

CLOSING TIMES
Open daily

PRICES
Meals: a la carte £ 20/35
19 rooms: £ 95/180

Typical Dishes

Fishcakes & rocket salad
Chicken stuffed with black pudding
Chocolate & nut brownie

12 mi west of Wilton by A 30 on B 3089. Parking.

88 **Tollgate Inn**

Ham Grn,
Holt, BA14 6PX
Tel.: (01225)782326
Website: www.tollgateholt.co.uk

VISA

Sharp's, Moles, St Austell and Box Steam ales

The Tollgate Inn dates back to the 16C and is very much part of the local community. The comfy seats in its delightfully cosy fire-lit bar are made for curling up in – so don't be surprised to find that one of the pub's cats has beaten you to it. Eat in the more traditional downstairs dining room or upstairs in the former chapel; come summer, the pleasant garden is the only place to be. The daily changing menu focuses on local produce and could include steamed Cornish mussels, confit of duck leg or the ever popular beef Wellington. Puddings might be of the rice or sticky toffee varieties, there's plenty of homemade ice cream; and chutneys and jams are for sale on the bar. Four comfortable bedrooms are named after the aforementioned felines.

CLOSING TIMES
Closed Sunday dinner and Monday
booking essential

PRICES
Meals: £ 20 (weekday lunch) and a la carte £ 23/35
4 rooms: £ 60/110

Typical Dishes
Pan-fried foie gras
Fillet of beef & tomato fondue
Chocolate fondant & liquorice sauce

Midway between Bradford-on-Avon and Melksham on B 3107. Parking.

89

Bath Arms

Longleat,
Horningsham, BA12 7LY
Tel.: (01985)844308
Website: www.batharms.co.uk

VISA MC

Horningsham Pride, Golden Apostle, PIG

This pub is found within the Longleat estate and boasts a rustic, dog-friendly bar with an open fireplace, a grand main dining room and a delightful terrace, witness to some impressive sunsets. Appealing menus offer everything from light dishes, salads and sandwiches through to main courses like stuffed saddle of rabbit or braised shoulder of lamb. The sharing plate is popular and the fishcakes are a veritable institution. Much of the produce comes from the estate – game, specialist cheeses and even flavoured organic vodkas – they rear pigs and even have their own vegetable garden. Staff clearly enjoy their work and are willing to go the extra mile for their customers. Quirky, individually themed bedrooms offer good levels of comfort.

CLOSING TIMES
Open daily

PRICES
Meals: £ 30 (dinner)
and a la carte £ 25/30

15 rooms: £ 95/175

Typical Dishes

Goat's cheese, walnuts, crispy bacon & croutons

Rib-eye of 28-day matured Ashdale beef, béarnaise & chips

Rhubarb fool

3 mi southwest of Warminster by A 362 and minor road. Parking.

90 Somerset Arms

Church St,
Maiden Bradley, BA12 7HW
Tel.: (01985)844207
Website: www.thesomersetarms.org

VISA AE

Wadworth 6X, Henry's Original IPA and Wadworth seasonal ales

Henry the Great Dane provides a larger-than-life greeting and, once ensconced in the open-fired lounge, with its quirky bookshelf wallpaper, mirrors and retro light shades, you'll find the chatty local staff just as hospitable. Dishes on the oft-changing menu might include smoked salmon mousse, confit duck or roasted monkfish. Steaks are a speciality and cooking is hearty, rustic and full of flavour. Wherever possible, produce comes from within a 30 mile radius; eggs come courtesy of their own hens, and some of the vegetables and herbs are grown in the garden. Events like quiz evenings, steak nights and artisan markets pull in the regulars, while visitors will appreciate the contemporary bedrooms, one of which features a free-standing bath.

CLOSING TIMES
Open daily

PRICES
Meals: a la carte £ 18/37

5 rooms: £ 70/110

Typical Dishes

Smoked salmon with rocket & caper salad

Smoked haddock fish cakes

White & dark chocolate brownie

5 mi south of Frome by A 361 and on B 3092. Parking.

Marston Meysey

91 **Old Spotted Cow**

The Street,
Marston Meysey, SN6 6LQ
Tel.: (01285)810264
Website: www.theoldspottedcow.co.uk

VISA MC

Moles Tap, Butcombe, Old Forge, Cottage Brewery, Box Steam, Ramsbury

With its sheep and chickens, and looking for all the world like somebody's private farmhouse, this pub sits firmly in the country dining league. Once neglected but now lovingly restored, it is enthusiastically run by Anna Langley and provides a proper pub for locals with plenty of real ales to accompany the honest, rustic, seasonal cooking. Dishes range from pub classics like devilled whitebait to the more unusual roasted pollock and chorizo or spicy grilled pork belly; a good combination of British sustenance and worldly spices that find their influences in Anna's grandmother's Lancastrian recipes and her own upbringing in Kenya. Popular events include Sunday roasts, barbecues and monthly spice nights. One comfortable, contemporary bedroom.

CLOSING TIMES
Closed Sunday dinner

PRICES
Meals: a la carte £ 19/28
1 room: £ 45/95

Typical Dishes
Devilled kidneys on toast
Crispy Moroccan lamb, spiced broad beans pilaf with harissa
Pancakes with orange curd & dark chocolate sauce

Between Fairford and Cricklade. Parking.

92 Wheatsheaf at Oaksey

Wheatsheaf Ln,
Oaksey, SN16 9TB
Tel.: (01666)577348
Website: www.thewheatsheafatoaksey.co.uk

VISA MC AE

Sharp's Doom Bar and Prescott Hill Climb

The Wheatsheaf is very much a community pub, patronised by locals – the chef-owner and his son even cook lunch for the village school twice a week. With its vast open fireplace, low leather sofas and selection of magazines, the bar is the best place to sit. The rear dining room is the more modern alternative and the fuchsia pink snug is perfect for smaller parties. The blackboard menu changes according to what's fresh in; dishes might include shepherd's pie, or Gloucester Old Spot sausage and mash, with mature local steaks and salmon smoked in-house. The experienced chef spent several years working in Thailand, so expect to see the occasional Asian dish too. There are lighter offerings at lunchtime and appealing nursery puddings.

CLOSING TIMES
Closed Sunday dinner and Monday

PRICES
Meals: a la carte £ 25/36

Typical Dishes

Loch Duart smoked salmon salad

Braised Longhorn beef with horseradish potato purée

Griottine cherry tart

5.5 mi north of Malmesbury; signed from A 429. Parking.

93 **George & Dragon**

High St,
Rowde, SN10 2PN
Tel.: (01380)723053
Website: www.thegeorgeanddragonrowde.co.uk

VISA

Butcombe Bitter, Sharp's Doom Bar

This 16C coaching inn has a rustic feel throughout, its cosy inner boasting solid stone floors, wooden beams and open fires. There's a strong emphasis on seafood, with fish delivered daily from Cornwall to ensure it arrives on your plate in tip-top condition. That the menu is written anew each day also speaks volumes about the pub's take on food; seafood dishes could be a plate of fishy hors d'oeuvres, pan-fried cod with bacon or a whole grilled lemon sole; more meaty choices might include rack of lamb or roast fillet of beef. Some dishes come in two sizes and can be taken as either a starter or a main course. There is also a good value set three course menu. Old-world charm meets modern facilities in the individually designed bedrooms.

CLOSING TIMES
Closed Sunday dinner
booking essential

PRICES
Meals: £ 19 and a la carte £ 21/39

3 rooms: £ 85/125

Typical Dishes

Creamy baked potted crab

Roast monkfish with Parma ham & mustard cream sauce

Chocolate & raspberry roulade

2 mi northwest of Devizes by A 361 on A 342. Parking.

94 **King John Inn**

Tollard Royal,
SP5 5PS
Tel.: (01725)516207
Website: www.kingjohninn.co.uk

VISA AE

Sharp's Doombar, Sixpenny Brewery Gold and Otter Bitter

The owner's interior design background helped take this red-brick Victorian pub from derelict to delicious; now it's all open-plan and open fires, with quarry tiled floors, scrubbed wooden tables and beautiful black and white hunting photos. The daily changing, classically based menu offers unfussy dishes like Welsh rarebit, pigeon breast wrapped in bacon or twice-baked cheese soufflé; local produce is prevalent, with game a speciality in season. Service ranges from friendly to forgetful – although Bumble Bee the Border Terrier evens the balance, attentive to regulars and visitors alike. Stylish, comfortable bedrooms blend antique furniture with modern facilities like flat screens; there's freshly baked bread for sale and a wine shop too.

CLOSING TIMES
Closed 25 December

PRICES
Meals: a la carte £ 29/41
8 rooms: £ 145/195

Typical Dishes

Old Spot pork terrine
Fillet of brill with wild garlic risotto
Chocolate terrine

5 mi southeast of Shaftesbury on B 3081. Parking.

Upper Woodford

95 Bridge Inn

Upper Woodford,
SP4 6NU
Tel.: (01722)782323
Website: www.thebridgewoodford.co.uk

VISA MC AE

Summer Lightning, Wadworth 6X, Ringwood Best

Situated in the Woodford Valley, a few miles south of Stonehenge, the aptly named Bridge Inn stands on the banks of the Avon overlooking the river crossing; its garden, with picnic tables from which to watch the swans and ducks, an alfresco diner's delight. The pub is modern, with a light, airy feel. Its relaxed atmosphere means that locals with dogs rub shoulders with diners and you can peek through the glass windows to see the chefs hard at work in the kitchen. Lunch sees a light bites menu of interesting sandwiches, while the à la carte offers dishes such as fishcakes, pot-roasted lamb shank or the popular pork belly. This is the sister pub to The Ship Inn at Burcombe; get your hands on a loyalty card and you can reap the benefits of both.

CLOSING TIMES
Closed 25 December and Sunday dinner January-February

PRICES
Meals: a la carte £ 24/35

Typical Dishes

Confit of pork belly & black pudding
Chargrilled lamb skewers with yoghurt dip
Lemon curd & raspberry tartlet

North of Salisbury off A 360; follow signs for The Woodfords. Parking.

96 **Angel Inn**

Upton Scudamore,
BA12 0AG
Tel.: (01985)213225
Website: www.theangelinn.co.uk

VISA MC

Wadworth 6X, Butcombe, Crop Circle and Golden Bolt

It may be the dependable village local, but things have moved on at The Angel Inn. True, it looks the same from the outside, but inside it's been flipped back-to-front and the bar's been moved from the upper to the lower level. There's no need to panic though – the large dining room still has a pleasant, cottage-like feel, while the lovely garden and terrace are as appealing as ever, providing a wonderful suntrap. Menus are fairly formal and not your typical pub grub; you might find home-cured gravadlax, roasted venison steak or salt-cured duck breast, with plenty of specials – usually fish – on the board. Lunch offers a good value set menu and puddings are of the good old-fashioned variety. Individually themed bedrooms are cosy and well-kept.

CLOSING TIMES
Open daily

PRICES
Meals: a la carte £ 18/28
10 rooms: £ 80/98

Typical Dishes

Grilled asparagus
Rack of new season lamb & mini shepherd's pie
Cointreau chocolate pot

Village signed off A 350 to the north of Warminster. Parking.

West Overton

97 Bell at West Overton

Bath Rd,
West Overton, SN8 1QD
Tel.: (01672)861099
Website: www.thebellwestoverton.co.uk

VISA

Wadworth 6X, Ramsbury Gold, Stonehenge Pigswill, Moles Best

One way to improve any walk, apart from having proper shoes and fair weather, is to end up at a decent pub. If you've been out on Cherhill Downs then pop in to the Bell of West Overton. The pub was rescued by a local couple, who realised a dream by buying it but who were also sensible enough to hire an experienced pair to run it. The same menu is served in the bar and the restaurant, although the latter is far from stuffy, as they don't want to scare anyone away. What the pub may lack in character, it makes up for in the quality of its cooking. There's an appealing blend of pub classics and dishes of a Mediterranean bent and fish from Cornish day boats is usually a highlight. Presentation is modern but not at the expense of flavour.

CLOSING TIMES
Open daily

PRICES
Meals: £ 21 and a la carte £ 23/43

Typical Dishes

Chicken liver & foie gras parfait

Whole roasted lemon sole with steamed clams

Wiltshire curd tart

4 mi. west of Marlborough on A 4. Parking.

The names Gas Street Basin, Custard Factory and Mailbox may not win any awards for exoticism, but these are the cutting edge quarters fuelling the rise of modern day Birmingham, at the heart of a region evolving from its grimy factory gate image. Even the Ironbridge Gorge, the cradle of the Industrial Revolution, is better known these days as a fascinatingly picturesque tourist attraction. The old urban landscapes dot a region of delightful unspoilt countryside with extensive areas of open moorland and hills, where stands Middle Earth, in the shape of Shropshire's iconic Wrekin hill, true inspiration of Tolkien. Shakespeare Country abounds in pretty villages, such as Henley-in-Arden, Shipston-on-Stour and Alcester, where redbrick, half-timbered and Georgian buildings capture the eye. Taste buds are catered for courtesy of a host of local specialities, not least fruits from the Vale of Evesham and mouth-watering meats from the hills near the renowned gastro town of Ludlow.

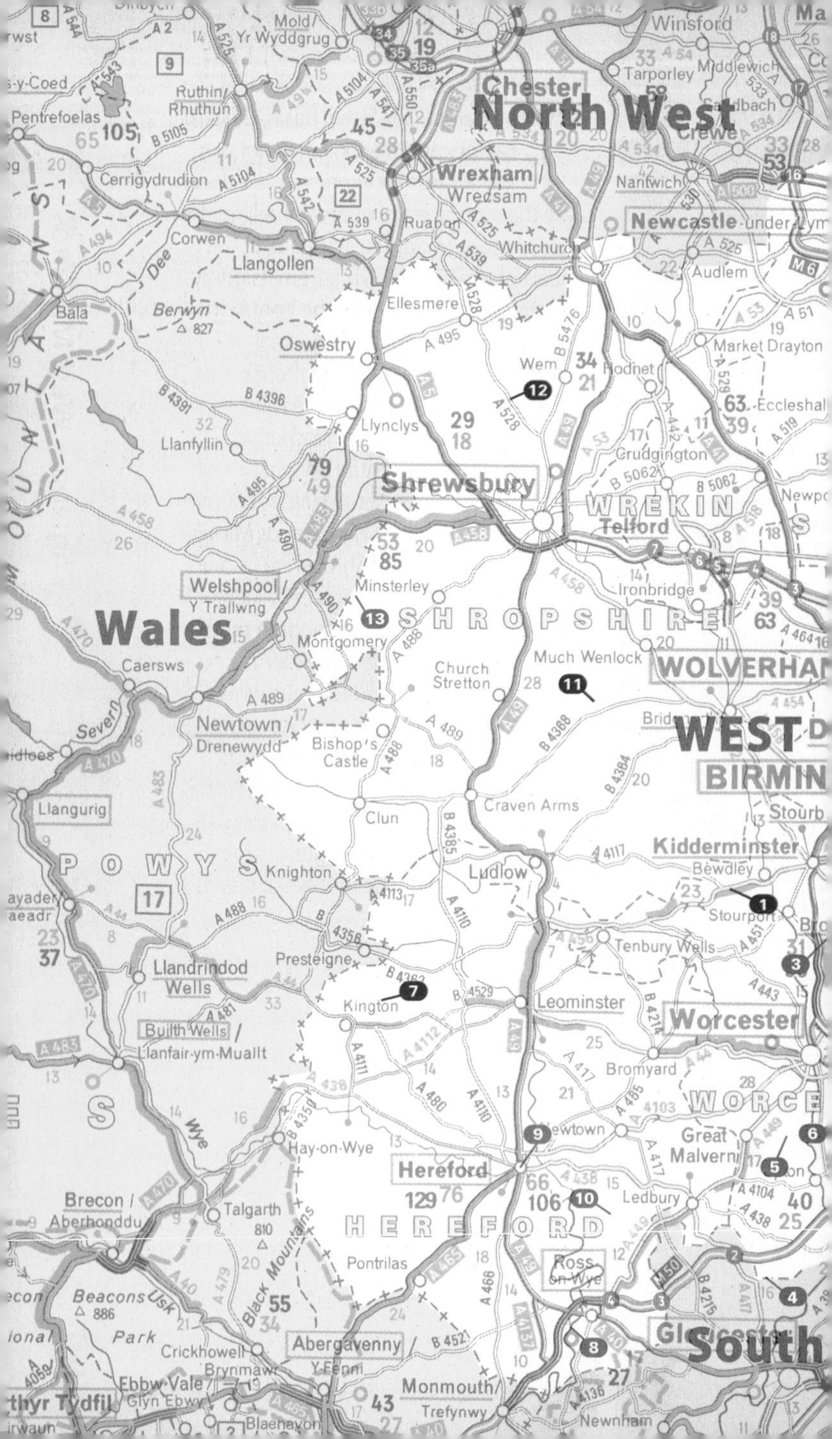
North West
Wales
WEST
South
SHROPSHIRE
POWYS
HEREFORD
WREKIN
Chester
Wrexham / Wrecsam
Mold / Yr Wyddgrug
Ruthin / Rhuthun
Pentrefoelas
Cerrigydrudion
Corwen
Llangollen
Bala
Berwyn
Oswestry
Ellesmere
Whitchurch
Ruabon
Winsford
Tarporley
Middlewich
Sandbach
Crewe
Nantwich
Newcastle-under-Lyme
Audlem
Market Drayton
Eccleshall
Hodnet
Wem
Crudgington
Llynclys
Llanfyllin
Shrewsbury
Telford
Ironbridge
Newport
Welshpool / Y Trallwng
Minsterley
Montgomery
Caersws
Newtown / Drenewydd
Church Stretton
Much Wenlock
WOLVERHAMPTON
Bishop's Castle
Clun
Craven Arms
BIRMINGHAM
Stourbridge
Kidderminster
Bewdley
Stourport
Llangurig
Knighton
Ludlow
Rhayader
Llandrindod Wells
Presteigne
Tenbury Wells
Kington
Leominster
Worcester
Builth Wells / Llanfair-ym-Muallt
Bromyard
Hay-on-Wye
Newtown
Great Malvern
Hereford
Ledbury
Brecon / Aberhonddu
Talgarth
Black Mountains
Pontrilas
Ross-on-Wye
Gloucester
Brecon Beacons National Park
Crickhowell
Brynmawr
Abergavenny / Y Fenni
Ebbw Vale / Glyn Ebwy
Merthyr Tydfil
Blaenavon
Monmouth / Trefynwy
Newnham
Dee
Severn
Wye
Usk

16 Pubs without bedrooms
17 Pubs with bedrooms
East Midlands
MIDLANDS
West
South East
DERBY
NOTTS
LEICESTER
WARWICK
NORTHAMP
OXFORD
BUCKINGHAM
Chesterfield
Mansfield
Newark-on-Trent
Matlock
Bakewell
Chatsworth House
Leek
STOKE-ON-TRENT
Ashbourne
Derby
NOTTINGHAM
Burton-upon-Trent
Stafford
Rugeley
Cannock
Lichfield
Walsall
Tamworth
Loughborough
Coalville
Hinckley
Nuneaton
COVENTRY
Rugby
Solihull
Halesowen
Redditch
Kenilworth
Royal Leamington Spa
Warwick
Henley
Alcester
Stratford-upon-Avon
Evesham
Pershore
Ettington
Shipston-on-Stour
Banbury
Chipping Campden
Broadway
Moreton
Winchcombe
Stow-on-the-Wold
Chipping Norton
Cheltenham
Northleach
Woodstock
Bicester
Buckingham
Brackley
Towcester
Milton Keynes
Daventry
Market Harborough
Lutterworth
Oadby
Melton
Wellingborough
Southam
Sutton Coldfield
Atherstone
Bedworth
Husbands Bosworth
Rothwell
Uppingham
Ilkeston
Long Eaton
Hucknall
Southwell
Bingham
West Bridgford
Swadlincote
Ashby de la Zouch
Uttoxeter
Stone
Sudbury
Abbots Bromley
Brownhills
Ripley
Heanor
Belper
Alfreton
Clay Cross
Sutton-in-Ashfield
Rempstone
Bletchley
Wolverton

1 Royal Forester

Callow Hill,
DY14 9XW
Tel.: (01299)266286
Website: www.royalforesterinn.co.uk

VISA MC AE

Wye Valley Brewery Hereford Pale Ale, Butty Bach, Dorothy Goodbody

Dating back to 1411, The Royal Forester, in the Wyre Forest, is reputedly one of the oldest pubs in Worcestershire and, despite its modern feel, retains a rustic richness of character typified by the dining room's exposed stone walls. Cooking is flavourful, simple in style and reasonably priced, although side dishes can push the bill up. The informative, bi-monthly menu explains what's in season, with produce often supplied by regulars in exchange for dinner credits; perhaps some local venison, or honey from local beekeepers. The atmosphere is easy-going and those of a musical bent will be pleased to hear the tinkle of the grand piano in the bright bar. Food-themed bedrooms are fresh and modern; Aubergine, Pear and Cherry are the largest.

CLOSING TIMES
Open daily

PRICES
Meals: £ 15 (weekdays) and a la carte £ 24/38

7 rooms: £ 55/79

Typical Dishes

Grilled Bewdley asparagus with a poached duck egg
Pavé of beef
Warm chocolate & cranberry brownie.

3 mi southwest of Bewdley. Parking.

2 Bell & Cross

Holy Cross,
Clent, DY9 9QL
Tel.: (01562)730319
Website: www.bellandcrossclent.co.uk

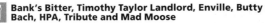

VISA

Bank's Bitter, Timothy Taylor Landlord, Enville, Butty Bach, HPA, Tribute and Mad Moose

Set down a maze of narrow lanes the Bell & Cross stands at what the locals call 'the old crossroads'. Colourful window boxes greet you at the front and round the back there's a spacious, well-kept lawn boasting lovely country views. The inside is made up of a series of rooms: the bar with its red leather banquettes and listed counter is particularly characterful. Football mementoes adorn the hall, harking back to the time when the owner cooked for the England football squad – but it's unlikely that they were given as much choice on their menus: there's sarnies, light bites and pub classics, with more substantial dishes being added at dinner; not forgetting a set menu and some blackboard specials too. Influences range from Asia to the Med.

CLOSING TIMES
Closed 25 December and dinner 26, 31 December, 1 January and Sunday

PRICES
Meals: £ 17 (weekdays) and a la carte £ 21/31

Typical Dishes
Oak-smoked Scottish salmon with sakura & wasabi crème fraîche
Noisette of lamb with chorizo
Cookies and cream chocolate fudge brownie

Between Stourbridge and Bromsgrove off northbound A 491; the pub is on the left hand side in Holy Cross. Parking.

Cutnall Green

3 **Chequers**

Kidderminster Rd,
Cutnall Green, WR9 0PJ
Tel.: (01299)851292
Website: www.chequerscutnallgreen.co.uk

VISA

Wye Valley Brewery, Timothy Taylor Landlord and Purity Mad Goose

If football's your thing, then make for the 'Players Lounge' of this lightly washed roadside pub and sit among photos of the old England team while indulging in a spot of lunch – which may well have been cooked up by the former team chef. Despite the fact that rich burgundy colours and modern furnishings have been introduced, exposed beams and original quarry-tiled floors maintain a cosy, traditional feel throughout the place; while the shelves above the bar counter display a collection of timeless food items such as Colman's mustard and HP and Worcestershire Sauces. Menus are Asian-led but also offer a good selection of light bites and pub classics – while some more adventurous fish and offal-based specials are chalked up on the board.

CLOSING TIMES
Closed 25 December, dinner 26 December and 1 January

PRICES
Meals: £ 17 (weekdays) and a la carte £ 21/30

Typical Dishes

Salad of roasted chorizo & red peppers
Roast chicken breast with mushroom & pepper risotto
Limoncello crème brûlée

3 mi north of Droitwich Spa on A 442. Parking.

4 Butchers Arms

Lime Street,
Eldersfield, GL19 4NX
Tel.: (01452)840381
Website: www.thebutchersarms.net

VISA MC

Wye Valley Butty Bach and Dorothy Goodbody, Shepherd Neame Spitfire and St Austell's Tribute

Apart from the modern sign swinging outside, this pub remains as traditional as ever. Two small rooms display original beams, part-oak flooring and a wood burning stove, while dried hops hang from the bar and memorabilia adorns the walls. A few of the small wooden tables are left for the local drinkers, while the rest are set for around 20 or so diners. With only one person in the kitchen the menu is understandably quite concise but it changes regularly – sometimes even from service to service – and despite the lack of man-power, everything from the bread to the ice cream is homemade, and many of the ingredients are very local. The kitchen makes clever use of less obvious cuts of meat, such as pig's cheek, in thoughtful and tasty dishes.

CLOSING TIMES
Closed 2 weeks early January, 2 weeks late August, Sunday dinner September-May, Tuesday lunch and Monday booking essential

PRICES
Meals: a la carte £ 34/43

Typical Dishes

Pig's cheek with crackling & Bramley apples
Fillet of beef with foie gras & wild mushrooms
Marmalade pudding

8.5 mi north of Gloucester by A417 and signposted off B 4211. Parking.

Guarlford

5 Plough and Harrow

Rhydd Rd,
Guarlford, WR13 6NY
Tel.: (01684)310453
Website: www.theploughandharrow.co.uk

VISA MC

Wadworth IPA and 6X

This white and yellow-washed pub may be off the beaten track but that doesn't stop the owners and their team from putting their hearts and souls into the place. There's a snug feel throughout, from the traditional dark wood bar with its blazing log fire to the more formal dining area in the old timbered skittle alley. Outside, a huge garden and field provide plenty of fruit and veg, which Michael cooks and Juliet brings to the table. Seasonality is key here, with menus often changing daily and local and ethical considerations playing their part. Lunch sees a light menu served throughout, with many dishes available in two sizes, while dinner offers a shorter à la carte (served only in the dining room) and simpler bar snacks during the week.

CLOSING TIMES
Closed 1 week spring,
1 week autumn,
25-26 December, 1 January,
Sunday dinner and Monday

PRICES
Meals: a la carte £ 21/36

Typical Dishes

Grilled smoked salmon & leek tartlet

Rack of lamb with honey-roast parsnips

Banana & toffee pavlova

2 mi east of Great Malvern by B 4211. Parking.

6 **Inn at Stonehall**

Stonehall Common,
WR5 3QG
Tel.: (01905)820462
Website: www.theinnatstonehall.com

Inspectors' favourites

VISA MC AE

Malvern Hills Black Pear Bitter

Just 2 miles from the M5 lies the peaceful little hamlet of Stonehall Common and, at it's heart, this smart, modern dining pub surrounded by a large garden and orchard. Offering lovely views over Evesham Vale towards Bredon Hill, it started life as 'The Fruiterers Arms', providing refreshment for the local fruit pickers, who harvested the now rare Worcestershire black pear – the inn being one of the few places to still have fruiting trees. At the front there's a comfy lounge where they serve light bites and beers from local artisan brewers; to the rear, an airy dining room that looks out over the terrace. Menus are simple and concise, featuring well-prepared, flavoursome dishes that follow the seasons, with desserts something of a speciality.

CLOSING TIMES
Closed first week January, Sunday dinner and Monday

PRICES
Meals: a la carte £ 22/29

Typical Dishes

Wild mushroom & red onion risotto

Homemade faggots with roasted roots & thyme jus

Orange posset

5.75 mi southeast of Worcester by A 38 and Norton rd. Parking.

7 **The Stagg Inn**

Titley,
HR5 3RL
Tel.: (01544)230221
Website: www.thestagg.co.uk

VISA MC AE

Hobson's Best and Ludlow Gold

Situated at the meeting point of two former drovers roads, this characterful part-medieval, part-Victorian pub was once called 'The Balance', as it marked the point where farmers would stop to weigh their wool. Inside, it's delightfully cosy – one room was once a butcher's shop and another still displays an old bread oven. Cooking is fittingly straightforward, relying on classically based recipes, careful preparation and top quality produce; they even raise their own pigs, ducks and geese, so you'll find homemade sausages, duck eggs and preserves for sale too. Menus are short, simple and to the point, while the dishes themselves are truly satisfying. Bedrooms in the pub are snug but can be noisy; opt for one in the nearby former vicarage.

CLOSING TIMES
Closed 2 weeks between January and February, first 2 weeks in November, 25-26 December, Sunday dinner and Monday
booking essential

PRICES
Meals: a la carte £ 29/34
6 rooms: £ 65/150

Typical Dishes

Scallops & parsnip purée
Fillet of Herefordshire beef
3 crème brûlées

3.5 mi northeast of Kington on B 4355. Parking.

8 **Mill Race**

Walford,
HR9 5QS
Tel.: (01989)562891
Website: www.millrace.info

VISA

Wye Valley Ale, Butty Bach

This isn't the kind of place you expect to find in a small country village – but the locals aren't complaining. It looks nothing like a pub, either outside or in; save for the bar counter that is. You enter via a Gothic-style door and pass a board pinpointing their local suppliers. Straight ahead, the chefs are hard at work in the semi open-plan kitchen; follow it round and you'll find a community notice board and leaflets for nearby attractions. It really is the village local, so you'll find regulars standing around the bar and families out for the night in the darker, slate-floored areas. Cooking is fairly simple and lets the ingredients speak for themselves. The small team flit about, coping well when it's busy – which it usually is.

CLOSING TIMES
Open daily

PRICES
Meals: a la carte £ 21/34

Typical Dishes

Wood pigeon with pickled wild mushrooms

Chicken wrapped in ham

Rhubarb crème brûlée

4 mi south of Ross-on-Wye by B 4234. Parking.

9 **Wellington**

Wellington,
HR4 8AT
Tel.: (01432)830367
Website: www.wellingtonpub.co.uk

VISA AE

Hobson's Best, Wye Valley HPA and Butty Bach

Who hasn't idly commented, whilst eating out, that they reckon they could do better? Rare is the person who actually does something about it, however. One exception is the chef-owner of The Wellington, who, before his monumental career change, used to work in PR. He's now at the helm of this bright and airy neighbourhood pub, where locals gather fireside in the spacious bar and all-comers enjoy flavourful dishes in the more formal conservatory dining room. Simple pub classics like fish and chips are chalked on a blackboard in the bar, while the daily changing à la carte offers choices like rabbit ravioli or slow roasted belly of Gloucester Old Spot pork, with desserts such as warm chocolate fondant pudding or rhubarb crème brûlée.

CLOSING TIMES
Closed 25 December, Sunday dinner and Monday

PRICES
Meals: a la carte £ 25/30

Typical Dishes
King scallops with black pudding & pea purée
Salmon fillet with asparagus & broad beans
Warm chocolate fondant

5 mi north by A 49. In village centre. Parking.

10 **Butchers Arms**

Woolhope,
HR1 4RF
Tel.: (01432)860281
Website: www.butchersarmswoolhope.co.uk

Inspectors' favourites

VISA

Wye Valley bitter and Butty Bach, Goldin Valley, Hay Bluff, Hertford Breweries Original Bitter,

Hidden away deep in the countryside, this half-timbered 16C inn boasts a characterful interior with open fires, wattle walls and beams slung so low you're forced to duck. Saws and pitchforks hang from the walls, while the pretty garden, with its babbling brook and weeping willow, offers delightful views over farmland. Chef-owner Stephen Bull was one of the pioneers of modern British cooking; expect the daily changing menu to offer simple sounding, classically based dishes like Goodrich Middle White sausages, mash and onion gravy or his speciality twice-baked soufflé – meticulously executed and full of flavour. A focus on regional produce means that lamb comes from over the road, fruit and veg from nearby farms and herbs from their own garden.

CLOSING TIMES
Closed 25 December, Sunday dinner and Monday except bank holidays

PRICES
Meals: £ 22 (Sunday lunch) and a la carte £ 21/28

Typical Dishes

Hot Ragstone goat's cheese mousse
Braised Goodrich Longhorn brisket
Warm ginger cake

9 mi north of Ross-on-Wye by A 449 and B 4224. Parking.

11 Feathers at Brockton

Brockton,
TF13 6JR
Tel.: (01746)785202
Website: www.feathersatbrockton.co.uk

VISA MC

Hobson's Town Crier and Six Bells Supper

This rustic 16C pub is situated on the edge of the village, in an area popular with walkers. Take your pick from four dining areas: all are snug with warm, homely décor, open fires and lots of stripped wood, exposed beams and thick stone walls. It's a personally run place and the atmosphere is relaxing and unpretentious, with the focus firmly on the food. Having learnt his trade in the Big Smoke, chef-owner Paul returned to Shropshire to open The Feathers back in 2004 – and his tasty cooking has been attracting customers ever since. Mainly traditional in style, with some Mediterranean influences, dishes make use of local produce and might include corn-fed chicken breast, shoulder of lamb or steak and ale pie. Old school puddings follow.

CLOSING TIMES
Closed 26 December, 1 January, Monday and lunch Tuesday

PRICES
Meals: £ 13/15
and a la carte £ 24/30

4 rooms: £ 50/75

Typical Dishes

Garlic king prawns with lemon & parsley

Slow-cooked pork belly, apple chutney & crackling

Warm chocolate fondant

5 mi southwest of Much Wenlock on B 4378. Parking.

12 **Burlton Inn**

Burlton,
SY4 5TB
Tel.: (01939)270284
Website: www.burltoninn.com

VISA MC AE

Robinson's Unicorn, Hartleys Cumbria Way and seasonal ales

Set on a busy road in a small village between Ellesmere and Shrewsbury, this traditional 18C whitewashed inn welcomes you with a colourful flower display. Since the current owners took over it has undergone a transformation – most notably a terrace, fountain and landscaped garden have been added. It's a characterful place with exposed beams, tiled floors, scrubbed pine tables and some soft seating by a wood burning stove. To one side there's a dining area but you can eat throughout; although it can get busy in the bar with local drinkers, especially on a Friday. The straightforward lunch menu offers snacks and pub classics, while in the evening some more adventurous dishes appear too. Neat, wood-furnished bedrooms boast spacious bathrooms.

CLOSING TIMES
Closed 25 December

PRICES
Meals: a la carte £ 21/30
6 rooms: £ 85/105

Typical Dishes

Local asparagus
Slow-cooked pork belly with a crisp Asian salad
Mascarpone & vanilla parfait

8 mi north of Shrewsbury on A 528. Parking.

Marton

13 **Sun Inn**

Marton,
SY21 8JP
Tel.: (01938)561211
Website: www.suninn.org.uk

VISA

Hobsons, Six Bells and Monty's Ales

A welcoming country pub on the English-Welsh border, The Sun Inn is a family affair, with father and son in the kitchen and their respective spouses looking after the customers out front. On one side of the counter is a cosy bar with a wood burning stove; here choices like fish and chips, steak and ale pie and homemade faggots are chalked up on a blackboard. On the other side is a brightly painted restaurant, with chunky pine tables. Here they offer a concise, regularly changing à la carte menu of classic dishes like salmon and prawn mousse, roast loin of local venison or slow-roast belly pork, supplemented by fresh fish boards in the summer. Darts, dominoes and regular events including themed food evenings and quiz nights bring in the locals.

CLOSING TIMES
Closed lunch Monday-Tuesday and dinner Sunday

PRICES
Meals: a la carte £ 22/30

Typical Dishes

Toasted goat's cheese
Slow-roast pork belly with cider sauce
Cappuccino crème brûlée

8.5 mi southeast of Welshpool on B 4386. Parking.

14 George

Alstonefield,
DE6 2FX
Tel.: (01335)310205
Website: www.thegeorgeatalstonefield.com

VISA

Marston's Pedigree, Burton Bitter, Brakspear's Oxford Gold and Jennings Cumberland

The moment you walk in The George, feel the warmth from the roaring fires and start to soak up the cosy, relaxed atmosphere, you just know that it's going to be good. A traditional pub set on the village green, it's simply furnished, with stone floors, scrubbed wooden tables and pictures of locals on the walls. The bubbly manager – the third generation of her family to have owned the pub – brings a woman's touch to the place, with the latest fashion mags for flicking through and candles and fresh flowers on every table. Like the décor, the food is simple but well done. The menus change daily according to the produce available; the team use local suppliers where possible and also grow some of their own vegetables in the garden.

CLOSING TIMES
Closed 25 December

PRICES
Meals: a la carte £ 20/39

Typical Dishes

Ham hock terrine & pea purée
Trio of Tissington sausages
Lemon posset

7.5 mi north of Ashbourne by A 515. Parking.

Aston Cantlow

15 King's Head

21 Bearley Rd,
Aston Cantlow, B95 6HY
Tel.: (01789)488242
Website: www.thekh.co.uk

VISA MC

Greene King Abbot Ale, Purity Gold, Brew XI and Pure Ubu

Set close to the Cotswolds, the picturesque village of Aston Cantlow is home to the 13C Norman church where, in 1557, Shakespeare's parents were married – and this ivy-clad, black and white inn is thought to have provided the setting for their wedding breakfast. Inside, the bar is everything you'd expect, with low beamed ceilings, flagged floors and an open log fire. Seasonal menus feature traditional dishes, with local meats and fish to the fore; choose from pub classics like pie of the week or more comprehensive dishes such as ballotine of chicken or seared fillet of sea bass. Regular duck suppers celebrate the pub's past, when during wartime rationing the landlord was unusually allowed to serve duck – as he reared his own out the back.

CLOSING TIMES
Closed 25 December and Sunday dinner

PRICES
Meals: a la carte £ 22/31

Typical Dishes

Ham hock & glazed parsnip terrine

Duck breast with caramelised red cabbage

Pear & almond tart

6 mi northwest of Stratford signposted off A 46. Parking.

16 **Chequers Inn**

91 Banbury Rd,
Ettington, CV37 7SR
Tel.: (01789)740387
Website: www.the-chequers-ettington.co.uk

VISA

Greene King IPA, St Austell's Tribute, Fullers London Pride

The signs outside scream country gastropub but to assume so would be off the mark; with its chandeliers, brushed velvet furniture and round-backed Regency chairs, this place is anything but formulaic. The open-fired bar is a popular spot with villagers, no doubt pleased with the large selection of beers as well as their local's transformation from run down boozer to smart, contemporary inn. When it comes to the cooking, the menus display a broad international style. There are good old British classics like prawn cocktail, cauliflower cheese and ham hock with bubble and squeak, alongside dishes of a more global persuasion, like rabbit rigatoni, salami platters and other Asian-influenced offerings. Friendly service completes the package.

CLOSING TIMES
Closed Sunday dinner and Monday

PRICES
Meals: a la carte £ 24/34

Typical Dishes
Pork belly roasted in cider
Roasted pollock fillet with chive mash & brown shrimp
White chocolate & raspberry crème brûlée

Southeast of Stratford-upon-Avon where the A 422 crosses the A 429. Parking.

Great Wolford

17 Fox & Hounds Inn

Great Wolford,
CV36 5NQ
Tel.: (01608)674220
Website: www.thefoxandhoundsinn.com

VISA

Purity Pure UBU, Hooky Bitter and 1 guest ale

This unpretentious pub lies at the heart of a small village which, in turn, is nestled in the rolling Cotswold Hills. Built in 1540 from local stone, it's a traditional English country inn – small, cosy and characterful – with flagged floors, a large inglenook fireplace and hops hanging from low beamed ceilings. With the owner out front and her son in the kitchen, it's very much a family affair. Menus are chalked up on the board daily and feature largely rustic pub fare, alongside a few more modern dishes. The chef is passionate about local produce, sourcing Chastleton beef, venison from Todenham and game from nearby shoots; while the bread, bacon and sausages are all made in-house. Simple, pine-furnished bedrooms offer country views.

CLOSING TIMES
Closed first two weeks January, Sunday dinner and Monday

PRICES
Meals: a la carte £ 17/32

3 rooms: £ 60/90

Typical Dishes

Cured mackerel, pickled radish, samphire & cucumber

Pork belly with homemade black pudding

Yoghurt panna cotta

4 mi northeast of Moreton-in-Marsh signposted off A 44. Parking.

18 **Crabmill**

Preston Bagot,
Henley-in-Arden, B95 5EE
Tel.: (01926)843342
Website: www.thecrabmill.co.uk

VISA MC

Greene King IPA, Abbot Ale, Purity UBU,

This characterful timbered pub is the ideal place to kick-back and relax, whether you sit in the lawned garden, on the peaceful terrace or inside the pub itself. It's made up of various beamed snugs and lounges, which display a mix of traditional old wood furniture and contemporary leather chairs set at black wood tables. You can eat anywhere but if you're tucked away in a corner and it's busy – which it usually is – you may need to flag down one of the team to place your order. The good-sized à la carte offers modern Mediterranean-influenced dishes, with some lighter bites available until the early evening. Start with a tasty sharing plate and move onto one of the interesting main courses, maybe ostrich fillet wrapped in Serrano ham.

CLOSING TIMES
Closed Sunday dinner
booking essential

PRICES
Meals: a la carte £ 21/33

Typical Dishes

Sweet potato & corned beef hash

Three rack of lamb, fondant potato & confit garlic

Warm chocolate brownie

1 mi east of Henley-in-Arden on A 4189. Parking.

Hunningham

19 Red Lion

Main St,
Hunningham, CV33 9DY
Tel.: (01926)632715
Website: www.redlionhunningham.co.uk

VISA AE

Greene King IPA, Abbot Ale and Roosters Leghorn

Set close to the River Lemm – and sometimes, in the past, underneath it – this charming, part-17C timbered inn has been lovingly restored. In summer, don't be surprised to find groups of stripy deckchairs down at the end of the garden by the water's edge and maybe a huge inflatable cinema screen or a festival taking place in the adjoining fields. Inside you'll discover a keen, welcoming team, over 300 framed American comics and a ceiling-mounted air pipe that delivers orders to the kitchen. A daily menu offers well-crafted, unfussy pub fare, with the occasional modern touch; you might find haddock and prawn fishcakes, black pudding salad or carpaccio of mid-Shires veal; order at the bar next to the case of tempting, locally made pork pies.

CLOSING TIMES
Open daily

PRICES
Meals: a la carte £ 19/34

Typical Dishes

Weston parsnip soup
8oz Warwickshire steakburger
White chocolate & hazelnut cheesecake

6.25 mi northeast of Royal Leamington Spa by A 425 off B 4455. Parking.

20 Howard Arms

Lower Green,
Ilmington, CV36 4LT
Tel.: (01608)682226
Website: www.howardarms.com

VISA AE

Wye Valley Bitter, Old Hooky, Lady Godiva and Goff's Jouster

This 400 year old Cotswold stone inn, set on a peaceful village green, is the very essence of an English country pub. Bright flower displays welcome you at the front, and round the back there's a small garden and terrace. Inside, you'll find the expected stone-faced walls, exposed beams, flagged floors and a huge inglenook fireplace, and a mix of chairs, pews and benches; there's also a raised-level dining room with a large dresser and fully laid dark wood tables. Blackboards are dotted about the place, displaying hearty dishes that are mainly British-based; you might find braised beef and ale pie or calves liver and bacon. Featuring antique furniture, the original bedrooms are warm and cosy; those in the extension are more contemporary.

CLOSING TIMES
Open daily

PRICES
Meals: a la carte £ 21/29
8 rooms: £ 85/155

Typical Dishes

Warm duck leg & glass noodle salad
Grilled pork loin steak with bubble & squeak
Sticky toffee pudding

Between Stratford-Upon-Avon and Moreton-in-Marsh signposted off A 429. Parking.

Lapworth

21 **Boot Inn**

Old Warwick Rd,
Lapworth, B94 6JU
Tel.: (01564)782464
Website: www.bootinnlapworth.co.uk

VISA MC

London Pride, Tribute, Pure UBU

Whether you're hastening down the M40 or pottering along on a narrow boat, it's worth stopping off at this large, buzzy red-brick pub. Set close to the junction of the Grand Union and Stratford-upon-Avon canals, it draws in a mixed crowd – from the young to the old, businesspeople to pleasure seekers – and you may well wonder where they all come from. With its traditional quarry-floored bar, modern first floor restaurant and large terrace complete with barbeque, it's deservedly popular, so booking is a must. Dishes vary greatly, from bar snacks and burgers through to sharing plates and more sophisticated fish specials. The crispy oriental duck and the bubble and squeak are mainstays, as is the scallop dish, which changes slightly every day.

CLOSING TIMES
Closed dinner 25 December and dinner 1 January
booking essential

PRICES
Meals: £ 16 (weekdays) and a la carte £ 26/38

Typical Dishes

Lamb kofta with kohlrabi salad

Crispy Asian pork belly

Lemon meringue cheesecake

2 mi southeast of Hockley Heath on B 4439; on the left hand side just before the village. Parking.

22 **Red Lion**

Long Compton,
CV36 5JS
Tel.: (01608)684221
Website: www.redlion-longcompton.co.uk

VISA MC AE

Hooky Bitter, Goff's Jouster and Vale IPA

With its flag floors and log fires, this 18C former coaching inn has the character of a country pub, and its stylish interior boasts a warm, modern feel. The seasonal menu offers classic pub dishes like homemade steak and Hook Norton pie, pan-fried calves liver or fish and chips, with old favourites like rhubarb crumble or warm chocolate fudge cake for dessert. These are tasty, home-cooked dishes from the tried-and-tested school of cooking – so if you're after something a little more adventurous, try the daily specials board instead. Staff are pleasant and smartly attired; Cocoa, the chocolate Labrador, also gives a warm welcome. Bedrooms may be slightly on the small side, but are stylish and contemporary, with a good level of facilities.

CLOSING TIMES
Open daily

PRICES
Meals: £ 15 (lunch and early dinner) and a la carte £ 26/36

5 rooms: £ 55/115

Typical Dishes

Smoked salmon with bubble and squeak

Steak & Hook Norton pie

Passion fruit panna cotta

Between Chipping Norton and Shipston-on-Stour on A 3400. Parking.

Offchurch

23 Stag

Welsh Rd,
Offchurch, CV33 9AQ
Tel.: (01926)425801
Website: www.thestagatoffchurch.com

Warwickshire Best, Darling Buds, Purity Mad Goose

Charles and Nigel may have won over the villagers before they even started – by distributing tasty home-baked bread to mark their arrival – but newcomers seem just as taken with this 16C thatched pub. Inside it's surprisingly contemporary, boasting a boldly coloured bar and two modern dining rooms: the first, adorned with deer antlers and animal heads, is cosy, beamed and wood-panelled; the second, overlooking the garden, boasts funky fabrics, large mirrors and dark Venetian blinds. The extensive menu changes with the seasons, offering generous, classical dishes – maybe haddock fishcakes or pan-fried calves liver – and the sharing plates of antipasti, charcuterie and fruits de mer are a hit. Service is efficient and copes well under pressure.

CLOSING TIMES
Open daily

PRICES
Meals: a la carte £ 22/40

Typical Dishes

Chicken liver parfait
Lamb cutlets with rosemary jus
Dark chocolate mousse

3.5 mi east of Royal Lemington Spa signposted off A 425. Parking.

24 **White Horse**

Kenilworth Rd,
Balsall Common, CV7 7DT
Tel.: (01676)533207
Website: www.thewhitehorseatbc.co.uk

VISA MC AE

Wells Bombardier, Purity UBU, Titanic, Timothy Taylor

It may be the village local, but this striking timbered building is far from your typical rustic country pub, having brought with it a touch of glamour from the town. It's a large place, with a decked terrace to the front and a sizeable paved dining area to the rear. Inside, you'll find a spacious modern lounge boasting low-backed leather chairs and an equally stylish L-shaped dining area that provides light relief from the bustle of the bar. Menus are easy-to-read and stick mainly to British pub classics, with dishes such as prawn cocktail or garlic field mushrooms, followed by spit-roast chicken or 21-day aged Hereford steaks. Some more Mediterranean influences can often be found in the way of rustic breads, charcuterie boards and risottos.

CLOSING TIMES
Open daily

PRICES
Meals: a la carte £ 22/30

Typical Dishes

Garlic mushrooms on toasted ciabatta
Roasted cod fillet with pesto cream
Vanilla panna cotta

5 mi northwest of Kenilworth by A 452. Parking.

Chadwick End

25 **Orange Tree**

Warwick Rd,
Chadwick End, B93 0BN
Tel.: (01564)785364
Website: www.lovelypubs.co.uk

Greene King IPA, Fullers London Pride and Purity UBU

Set in a small but affluent village, The Orange Tree is a sizeable place – even without the neat lawned gardens and spacious terrace. Characterful country dining it is not – it's smart, contemporary and can get a tad on the loud side. The large bar is set over various levels, some with characterful wooden beams, all with comfy modern seating; and there's a dining room with chunky wood tables, low-backed chairs and leather banquettes. The same, wide-ranging menu is served throughout and offers something for everyone. You'll find several dishes in a choice of size, as well as salads, sharing plates, pizzas, pastas and grills: the free range spit-roast chicken with a choice of sauces is something of a speciality. Service is polite and friendly.

CLOSING TIMES
Closed 25 December and Sunday dinner
booking essential

PRICES
Meals: £ 16 (lunch and early dinner) and a la carte £ 17/36

Typical Dishes

Lemon & chilli crusted squid

Pork belly with chorizo & watercress

Steamed rum & raisin pudding

On A 4141 midway between Solihull and Warwick. Parking.

England's biggest county has a lot of room for the spectacular; it encapsulates the idea of desolate beauty. The bracing winds of the Dales whistle through glorious meadows and deep, winding valleys, while the vast moors are fringed with picturesque country towns like Thirsk, Helmsley and Pickering. Further south the charming Wolds roll towards the sea, enhanced by such Georgian gems as Beverley and Howden. Popular history sits easily here: York continues to enchant with its ancient walls and Gothic Minster, but, owing to its Brontë links, visitors descend on the cobbled street village of Haworth with as much enthusiasm. Steam railways criss-cross the region's bluff contours, while drivers get a more streamlined thrill on the Humber Bridge. Yorkshire's food and drink emporiums range from quaintly traditional landmarks like the country tearoom and fish and chip shops proudly proclaiming to be the best in England, to warm and characterful pubs serving heart-warming local specialities.

North East
North West
YORKSHIRE
Yorkshire Dales National Park
Peak District National Park
Penrith
Appleby
Ullswater
Patterdale
Shap
Orton
Ambleside
Windermere
Kendal
Tebay
Sedbergh
Whernside
Kirkby Lonsdale
Ingleton
Clapham
Settle
Long Preston
Lancaster
Gisburn
Clitheroe
Skipton
Threshfield
Colne
Keighley
Nelson
Burnley
Padiham
Blackburn
Accrington
Darwen
Chorley
Leyland
Rawtenstall
Rochdale
Bury
Bolton
Wigan
Leigh
St. Helens
Oldham
MANCHESTER
Ashton-under-Lyne
Hyde
Glossop
Stockport
Altrincham
Widnes
Knutsford
Wilmslow
Frodsham
Northwich
Winsford
Middlewich
Macclesfield
Congleton
Tarporley
Whaley Bridge
Chapel-en-le-Frith
Buxton
High Peak
Castleton
Bakewell
Baslow
Chatsworth House
Dronfield
Staveley
Chesterfield
SHEFFIELD
Stocksbridge
Rotherham
Conisbrough
Barnsley
Holmfirth
Huddersfield
Todmorden
Halifax
Brighouse
Dewsbury
Wakefield
BRADFORD
Bingley
LEEDS
Garforth
Castleford
Ilkley
Otley
Harewood
Harrogate
Knaresborough
Fountains Abbey
Pateley Bridge
Ripon
Thirsk
Northallerton
Bedale
Leyburn
Hawes
Reeth
Richmond
Scotch Corner
Darlington
Barnard Castle
Bowes
Brough
Kirkby Stephen
Middleton-in-Teesdale
Bishop Auckland
Newton Aycliffe
Stockton-on-Tees
Eaglescliffe
Spennymoor
Sedgefield
Swale
Wharfe
Ure
Tees
Ribble
Lune
D U R H A M
N O R T H Y O R K
P E N N I N E S
L A N C A S H I R E
C H E S H I R E
M6
M62
M61
M66
M60
M1
A1(M)

16 Pubs without bedrooms
24 Pubs with bedrooms
& THE HUMBER
YORKSHIRE
East Midlands
Hartlepool
Redcar
Marske-by-the-Sea
Saltburn-by-the-Sea
Brotton
Guisborough
Loftus
Middlesbrough
Whitby
Cleveland Hills
North York Moors National Park
Scalby
Scarborough
Helmsley
Pickering
Filey
Easingwold
Malton
Norton
Flamborough Head
E. RIDING
Bridlington
Wetwang
Gt. Driffield
Beeford
Market Weighton
Leven
Hornsea
Beverley
Selby
Barlby
Howden
KINGSTON-UPON-HULL
R. Ouse
Snaith
Goole
Humber Bridge
River Humber
Hedon
Withernsea
Barton-upon-Humber
Patrington
N. LINCS
Immingham Dock
Immingham
Kilnsea
Thorne
Crowle
Scunthorpe
Don
N.E. LINCS
Grimsby
Spurn Head
Doncaster
Brigg
Humberside
Cleethorpes
Epworth
Caistor
Rotterdam
Zeebrugge
Bawtry
R. Trent
Gainsborough
Louth
Market Rasen
East Retford
Mablethorpe
Wragby
Sutton-on
Tuxford
Lincoln
Alford
NOTTS.

South Dalton

1 **Pipe and Glass Inn**

West End,
South Dalton, HU17 7PN
Tel.: (01430)810246
Website: www.pipeandglass.co.uk

VISA

John Smiths, Black Sheep, Wold Top and Old Mill Brewery

Very personally run by its experienced owners – he cooks, while she looks after the front of house – the 17C Pipe and Glass Inn is a deservedly popular place and is also our pub of the year 2012. Grab a drink and a seat beside the log burner or just head straight for a table in the contemporary dining room to enjoy food that's carefully executed, big on flavour and comes in generous portions. Dishes are made with local, seasonal and traceable produce wherever possible, and might include venison and juniper suet pudding or roast loin of red deer; desserts like The Pipe and Glass chocolate plate continue the decadent theme. Luxury bedrooms are equipped with all mod cons and come with their own patios overlooking the estate woodland.

CLOSING TIMES
Closed 2 weeks January, 25 December, Sunday dinner and Monday except bank holidays

PRICES
Meals: a la carte £ 34/45
2 rooms: £ 140/160

Typical Dishes
Wild rabbit, langoustine & Jerusalem artichoke crumble
Rump of lamb with a 'hotch potch' of spring vegetables
Lemon verbena posset

5 mi northwest of Beverley by A 164, B 1248 and side road west. Parking.

2 Crab and Lobster

Dishforth Rd,
Asenby, YO7 3QL
Tel.: (01845)577286
Website: www.crabandlobster.com

VISA MC AE

Golden Pippin Ale, Theakston Best Bitter

From the moment you set eyes on this pub, you'll realise it's no ordinary place. Old advertisements and lobster pots hang from the walls, thatched crabs and lobsters sit on the roof – and even the umbrellas are thatched. Inside it's just as quirky, with charming exposed beams hung with knick-knacks aplenty and all kinds of characterful memorabilia strewn over every surface The menu, unsurprisingly, features plenty of seafood, with the likes of fish soup, fishcakes, fish pie, shellfish and lobster; alongside traditional British favourites such as cheese soufflé, pork cheek confit and crusted loin of lamb. Split between an 18C Georgian Manor and log cabins, stylish bedrooms are themed around world-famous hotels; some boast private hot tubs.

CLOSING TIMES
Open daily

PRICES
Meals: a la carte £ 20/42

Typical Dishes

Yorkshire game terrine
Swordfish loin with curried king prawns
'Crabs' sticky date pudding

4 mi southwest of Thirsk by B 1448 and A 168. Parking.

Aysgarth

3 George and Dragon Inn

Aysgarth,
DL8 3AD
Tel.: (01969)663358
Website: www.georgeanddragonaysgarth.co.uk

VISA

Black Sheep, John Smith Cask, Yorkshire Dales Brewing Company, George & Dragon, Midnight Sun and Grass Wood

Set in the heart of prime walking country, close to the breathtaking waterfalls of the River Ure, this 17C coaching inn makes the perfect base for exploring Wensleydale. This is a proper pub in all senses of the word: there's not a plasma screen in sight and if you've made yourself comfy in the laid-back bar, you're welcome to settle in for the night. The large restaurant winds its way around the front of the building, first taking on a French brasserie style and then ending up in a Victorian themed room; there's also a patio with great views of Pen Hill. Unfussy pub classics include plenty of local meats, game and old-fashioned puddings and there's a good value early evening menu. Bedrooms are comfy and well-priced; some boast whirlpool baths.

CLOSING TIMES
Closed 2 weeks January

PRICES
Meals: £ 13 (lunch)
and a la carte £ 20/30

7 rooms: £ 40/90

Typical Dishes

King prawns with sweet chilli sauce

Chicken wrapped in Parma ham

Lemon meringue cheesecake

7 mi west of Leyburn by A 684. Parking.

4 **Malt Shovel**

Main St,
Brearton, HG3 3BX
Tel.: (01423)862929
Website: www.themaltshovelbrearton.co.uk

VISA

Black Sheep Best Bitter and Timothy Taylor Landlord

The Bleiker family are best known for their successful smokehouse but Jürg, the founder, has left his sons-in-law in charge and moved on to combine his family's two greatest loves – food and music. The Malt Shovel is a rather quirky, shabby-chic pub boasting a panelled, fire-lit bar, an opera-themed 'Red Room', an elegant 'Green Room' and a conservatory. There's a small kiln outside the kitchen and whatever meat, game or fish is in season will be smoking away. Dishes are largely classical with continental flavours, so will feature the likes of moules frites or Wiener schnitzel, with some smaller tapas-style plates available at lunch. On Sundays they host jazz sessions and from time to time son D'arcy and wife Anna give the odd opera recital.

CLOSING TIMES
Closed 25 December, 1 January, Monday, Tuesday and dinner Sunday

PRICES
Meals: a la carte £ 20/40

Typical Dishes

Smoking kiln selection
Slow-cooked pork belly with black pudding mash
Bread & butter pudding

4 mi east of Ripley by B 6165 and Brearton road. Parking.

5 Bull

Broughton,
BD23 3AE
Tel.: (01756)792065
Website: www.thebullatbroughton.co.uk

VISA AE

Copper Dragon Scotts, Dark Horse Hetton Pale Ale, Thwaites Original

The Bull is a member of Ribble Valley Inns – but don't expect some sort of faceless corporate brand – this is the bourgeoning pub company set up by Nigel Haworth and Craig Bancroft, co-proprietors of Lancashire's celebrated Northcote. They have led the way in promoting the specialities of their region and The Bull is no different. Expect real ales, local meats and cheeses, as well as traditional British dishes, rediscovered classics and the sort of puddings that make you feel patriotic. The Bull is an appropriate moniker as this pub is big and solid looking. It's at the side of Broughton Hall and inside is made up of assorted snugs and spaces, with beams, stone floors and log fires. It's cosy in winter and charming on a summer's day.

CLOSING TIMES
Closed 25 December

PRICES
Meals: a la carte £ 19/33

Typical Dishes

Rabbit faggots
Traitor's Pudding with traditional lamb sausages
Yorkshire curd tart

3 mi west of Skipton on A 59. In the grounds of Broughton Hall Country Park Estate. Parking.

6

Red Lion

Burnsall,
BD23 6BU
Tel.: (01756)720204
Website: www.redlion.co.uk

VISA MC

Timothy Taylor, Theakston, Copper Dragon

This appealing stone inn sits at the heart of a small rural community on the banks of the River Wharfe. It has a warm yet worn feel, which isn't all that surprising when you learn that it has cellars dating back to the 12C and a wood-panelled bar from its 16C ferryman's inn days. There's plenty of choice when it comes to where to sit – the cosy bar with its copper-topped counter, the laid-back lounge or the more formally dressed dining room. The choice of food is similarly wide, with a bar menu of pub favourites; an à la carte featuring local lamb in spring, East Coast fish in summer and game in winter; and a blackboard of daily specials. Bedrooms are traditional with modern overtones; those in the nearby manor house are more contemporary.

CLOSING TIMES
Open daily

PRICES
Meals: a la carte £ 20/37
21 rooms: £ 70/158

Typical Dishes

Smoked ham shank
Lancashire hot pot with spring cabbage
Warm pear, chocolate & frangipan tart

7 mi north of Bolton Abbey by B 6160. Parking.

Carlton Husthwaite

7 **Carlton Bore**

Carlton Husthwaite,
YO7 2BW
Tel.: (01845)501265
Website: www.carltonbore.co.uk

VISA MC

Black Sheep Bitter, Hambleton Bitter

Four stuffed boars on the wall named Gordon, Delia, Jamie and Rick show that the owners of this characterful stone inn have a sense of humour. There's nothing funny about the food though: the appealing menu offers plenty of pub favourites, with starters/light bites such as game meatballs or devilled lambs kidneys on toast and main courses like slow-cooked pork belly, braised lamb shank or steak and ale pie. Portions are huge and dishes well-priced; Monday steak nights are particularly good value. Warm and welcoming, this 17C inn has three brightly decorated rooms; the middle room has comfy cushions and tables laid up for dining, while the room next to the bar is more suited to drinkers – and diners who like to be in the thick of the action.

CLOSING TIMES
Closed first 2 weeks January

PRICES
Meals: £ 16 (lunch)
and a la carte £ 23/32

Typical Dishes

Salad Lyonnaise with crispy pig's cheeks
Spring lamb Wellington with ratatouille
Pavlova of local strawberries

5 mi southeast of Thirsk off A 19. Parking.

8 **Fox and Hounds**

Carthorpe,
DL8 2LG
Tel.: (01845)567433
Website: www.foxandhoundscarthorpe.co.uk

VISA MC

Black Sheep Bitter, Worthington's

If you like a bit of history with your lunch, then this ivy-clad stone pub could be the place for you. Photos, curios and old farming equipment cover every surface, and there's an old water pump and anvil on display – the pub having started life several centuries ago as the village smithy. For the last 26 years, the Fitzgerald/Taylor family have been in charge and you'll find present owners Helen and Vincent hard at work in the kitchen, preparing homemade bread and perhaps dressed crab or pies of the steak and kidney or fish variety. Fish is from Hartlepool, meat from Bedale and other products come from the nearby dairy. If you want to take something home, organic flour, honey, and homemade jams and chutneys are for sale.

CLOSING TIMES
Closed 25 December, first week January and Monday

PRICES
Meals: £ 17 (weekdays) and a la carte £ 21/32

Typical Dishes

Salmon & prawn roulade
Rack of lamb with pea purée
Brandy snap basket with bramble ice cream

9 mi north of Ripon by minor road via Wath and Kirklington. Parking.

Colton

9 Ye Old Sun Inn

Main St,
Colton, LS24 8EP
Tel.: (01904)744261
Website: www.yeoldsuninn.co.uk

VISA AE

Timothy Taylors Landlord, Black Sheep and Moorhouse's "Ye Old Sun Inn"

The demise of many a local post office has highlighted their importance in the local community, but Ye Old Sun Inn is a good example of how significant a role the pub plays in local life. This family-run pub does it all: from selling homemade produce from their small deli to holding cookery demonstrations. They are also great ambassadors for local suppliers, several of whom are name-checked on the menu. The open fires and rustic feel make this a very popular place with the local community, although race days at the Knavesmire bring a regular invasion of interlopers. The menus change monthly and are as seasonal as ever. Those not from these parts can take advantage of the three very smart bedrooms in the recently acquired house next door.

CLOSING TIMES
Closed 26 December

PRICES
Meals: a la carte £ 23/30
3 rooms: £ 75/100

Typical Dishes

Confit duck leg
Sea bass with mussels & olives
Trio of strawberries

3 mi northeast of Tadcaster by A 659 and A 64. Parking.

10 **Tiger Inn**

Coneythorpe,
HG5 0RY
Tel.: (01423)863632
Website: www.tiger-inn.co.uk

VISA

Timothy Taylor Landlord, Black Sheep Bitter, Ilkley Brewery Mary Jane

With a name like that you might be expecting something rather exotic, but this is a simple-looking pub, with just the odd picture or cuddly toy giving a nod to the eponymous feline; the inn's moniker apparently comes from local tales about a travelling circus, which purportedly kept its animals here in the late 1800s. These days, The Tiger Inn is a family-owned and popular place, with polite, friendly service and a bustling atmosphere, particularly in the front bar. Cooking is hearty and substantial, with classic pub dishes like fish and chips, Yorkshire hotpot, roast saddle of rabbit or the locally renowned steak and ale pie. The monthly changing menu is supplemented by fish specials – and there are gourmet sandwiches available at lunchtime.

CLOSING TIMES
Closed 25 December
booking advisable

PRICES
Meals: a la carte £ 20/30

Typical Dishes

Warm salad of French black pudding

Roast pork belly with apple sauce & red wine jus

Bramley apple & blackberry crumble

5 mi northeast of Knaresborough by A 59 and minor road north. Parking.

Constable Burton

11 **Wyvill Arms**

Constable Burton,
DL8 5LH
Tel.: (01677)450581
Website: www.thewyvillarms.co.uk

VISA

Theakstons and Hambleton Ales

As you approach this ivy-clad stone pub you might recognise the large Elizabethan stately home immediately in front it; that's if you're a fan of the 2006 film Wind in the Willows. To the rear you'll find pleasant gardens and a small sitting area; while inside classical décor and rustically themed furnishings provide a warm, intimate feel. For dining, there's the choice of a small open-fired bar, a stone-floored area with banquettes and a more formal room with high-backed chairs. There's plenty of choice on the menu too, which features local, traceable produce in carefully prepared, classical dishes. You'll find tasty mature steaks, daily fish specials and Nigel's Yorkshire puddings are a must on Sundays. Bedrooms are simple but well-kept.

CLOSING TIMES
Closed Monday except bank holidays

PRICES
Meals: a la carte £ 20/33
3 rooms: £ 60/80

Typical Dishes
Rolled fillet of sole
Fillet Steak 'black jack'
3 way crème brûlée

3.5 mi east of Leyburn on A 684. Parking.

12 **Durham Ox**

Westway,
Crayke, YO61 4TE
Tel.: (01347)821506
Website: www.thedurhamox.com

VISA MC AE

Black Sheep Best Bitter and Timothy Taylor Landlord

Set in a sleepy little hamlet, next to Crayke Castle, the 300 year old Durham Ox is a bustling, family-run pub which boasts pleasant views over the vale of York and up to the medieval church. You'll receive a warm welcome whether you sit in the carved wood-panelled bar with its vast inglenook fireplace or more formal beamed dining room; but when the weather's right, head straight for the rear courtyard, as this is definitely the place to be. The regularly changing menu features plenty of fresh seafood, steaks and Crayke game; as well as tasty chicken from the rotisserie. Set in converted farm cottages, the cosy bedrooms display original brickwork and quarry tiling; some are suites, some are set over two floors and some have jacuzzis.

CLOSING TIMES
Closed 25 December
booking essential

PRICES
Meals: a la carte £ 24/35
5 rooms: £ 80/100

Typical Dishes

Baked Queen scallops
Rib-eye steak with skinny fries & béarnaise
Vanilla crème brûlée

2 mi east of Easingwold on Helmsley rd. Parking.

England • Yorkshire and The Humber • North Yorkshire

East Witton

13 **Blue Lion**

East Witton,
DL8 4SN
Tel.: (01969)624273
Website: www.thebluelion.co.uk

VISA MC

Black Sheep, Golden Sheep

Set in a delightful village, this former coaching inn boasts a truly rustic interior, pleasingly untouched by the minimalist makeover brigade. Dine in the flag-floored bar or in the high-ceilinged, wood-floored dining room; either way you'll sit at a polished wooden table in the glow of candlelight and enjoy unfussy, hearty cooking made from local produce. The menu is chalked up above the fire in the bar and dishes might include homemade pork pie, cassoulet of duck leg or roast wild venison. The wine list is of particular note and offers bottles at a wide range of prices. Bedrooms in the main house are furnished with antiques, including a four-poster in Room 3, while the rooms in the converted stable are more contemporary in style.

CLOSING TIMES
Open daily
booking essential

PRICES
Meals: a la carte £ 23/44
15 rooms: £ 70/145

Typical Dishes

Parma ham & Yorkshire blue cheese tart

Fillet of line-caught turbot with roast king scallops

Dark chocolate terrine

3 mi southeast of Leyburn on A 6108. Parking.

14 Carpenter's Arms

Felixkirk,
YO7 2DP
Tel.: (01845)537369
Website: www.thecarpentersarmsfelixkirk.com

VISA MC AE

Black Sheep Bitter and Timothy Taylors Landlord

Mentioned in the Domesday Book, Felixkirk's claim to fame is that it was once a local Commandery of the Knights Hospitallers of St John of Jerusalem. Dating back to the 18C, the Carpenter's Arms may not be quite as old but it still boasts its fair sense of history. Consisting of one long, open-fired room, it really is a proper village pub, so you'll often find groups such as the local bell ringers in; and, since being taken over by the owners of the Durham Ox, its popularity has only increased. There's a choice of blackboard specials or dishes from the seasonal main menu, which offers everything from gammon to venison casserole or sea bass with ratatouille; and be sure to save room for pudding before the steep climb back up Sutton Bank.

CLOSING TIMES
Open daily

PRICES
Meals: a la carte £ 21/29

Typical Dishes

Prawn cocktail
Sticky pork ribs with spicy beans & chips
Sticky toffee pudding

Signposted off A 170, 3 mi northeast of Thirsk. Parking.

15 General Tarleton Inn

Boroughbridge Rd,
Ferrensby, HG5 0PZ
Tel.: (01423)340284
Website: www.generaltarleton.co.uk

VISA MC AE

Inspectors' favourites

Black Sheep Bitter, Timothy Taylor Landlord

With four spacious dining rooms, an airy glass-roofed courtyard and alfresco dining in both the garden and on the lovely decked terrace, you're spoilt for choice at this 18C coaching inn. One of the forerunners of today's gastropubs, it still helps to lead the way for others; its menu featuring a strong seasonal base, with traceability and local supplier relationships at its core. Tasty, warming dishes include old favourites such as steak and ale pie, as well as more ambitious offerings like seafood in a pastry bag – their speciality – followed by char-grilled haunch of venison or Goosnargh duckling in gingerbread sauce; finished off with maybe panna cotta and green apple sorbet. Individually styled bedrooms are luxurious and very comfy.

CLOSING TIMES
Open daily

PRICES
Meals: a la carte £ 25/36
13 rooms: £ 75/150

Typical Dishes
Hand-picked North Sea crab with cumin mayonnaise
Taste of rabbit with girolles, broad beans & truffle jus
Passion fruit & vanilla panna cotta

3 mi north of Knaresborough by A 6055. Parking.

16 **Star Inn**

High St,
Harome, YO62 5JE
Tel.: (01439)770397
Website: www.thestaratharome.co.uk

VISA

Black Sheep and regularly changing ales from Leeds Brewery, Wold Brewery and Captain Cook Brewery

It already boasted a cosy bar and a rustic dining area but this charming 14C pub is now also the proud owner of a chic, modern dining room complete with chef's table; not forgetting a smart new garden designed by Jo Campbell, which provides many of the herbs and veg that appear on your plate. Cooking is firmly rooted in tradition but shows evidence of modern techniques, the result being typical pub dishes but with a more sophisticated edge. The ingredients used are the best available: wild mushrooms from just outside, free range poultry, milk-fed piglets and local Whitby fish – if you fancy seeing for yourself, book a place on their 'Chef for the Day' course. Comfy bedrooms can be found nearby in Cross House Lodge, which is also owned by them.

CLOSING TIMES
Closed Monday lunch, Sunday dinner and bank holidays
booking essential

PRICES
Meals: £ 25 and a la carte £ 35/55

Typical Dishes

Corned beef terrine with brown ale jelly
Roast monkfish tail wrapped in York ham
A celebration of Yorkshire rhubarb

2.75 mi southeast of Helmsley by A 170. Parking.

Helperby

17

Oak Tree Inn

Raskelf Rd ,
Helperby, YO61 2PH
Tel.: (01423)789189
Website: www.theoaktreehelperby.com

VISA AE

Black Sheep and Timothy Taylor Landlord

Don't let the Brafferton Helperby sign confuse you – this did, in fact, start life as two even smaller villages; The Oak Tree being in the latter of the two. Younger sister to the Durham Ox and Carpenters Arms, it's a place of two halves: on the one hand there's a large bar, tap room and two snugs; while in the old hay barn there's a smarter dining room with large windows overlooking the terrace. The same menu is available throughout, offering hearty, generous dishes using ingredients from small local suppliers. Everything from bread to petit fours is homemade and combinations are familiar and comforting; service is charming but if you're in a rush, pizzas and wines are also available to take away. Smart, modern bedrooms boast Jacuzzi baths.

CLOSING TIMES
Open daily

PRICES
Meals: a la carte £ 19/29
6 rooms: £ 120/150

Typical Dishes

Prawn cocktail
Baked cod with cured ham
Chocolate tart

5 mi northeast of Boroughbridge on T junction entering village. Parking.

18 Angel Inn

Hetton,
BD23 6LT
Tel.: (01756)730263
Website: www.angelhetton.co.uk

VISA AE

Hetton Pale Ale, Black Sheep, Timothy Taylors Landlord

Don't be fooled by the relatively remote setting – you have to book ahead to get a table in the bar and even then it can be a bit of a scrum. It's jammed with character and charm but the long serving staff all ably anticipate their customers' needs. There is also a more formal dining room available. The flexible menu uses plenty of local bounty; there is something for everyone, at sensible prices and the cooking is eminently satisfying. Wine is a huge draw here – and the cave is well worth a visit. You'll find the luxuriously appointed bedrooms in a converted stone farm building. There is many a chef and restaurateur around the country who owe their success to the formative years they spent at this iconic 18C Yorkshire institution.

CLOSING TIMES
Closed 4 days January
booking essential

PRICES
Meals: £ 15 (lunch and weekday dinner) and a la carte £ 19/34

Typical Dishes

Homemade black pudding
Suckling pig with a red wine sauce
Chocolate brownie cheesecake

5.75 mi north of Skipton by B 6265. Parking.

19 **Black Horse Inn**

Lumley Ln,
Kirkby Fleetham, DL7 0SH
Tel.: (01609)749010
Website: www.blackhorsekirkbyfleetham.com

VISA

Black Sheep, Taylors Landlord, Copper Dragon Pippin, 1816

Originally called The Salutation, this 18C pub was reputedly renamed after a highwayman rode away on his black horse with a local landowner's daughter. Having been taken over by the owners of the Black Bull at Moulton, it's been subtly modernised; still displaying original beams but now with a smart new flagged floor and stylish bedrooms with designer bathrooms. Drinkers and diners sit alongside one another in the candlelit bar, with its Welsh dresser and cushion-filled benches but there's a dedicated dining room too, with painted tables and high-backed chairs. The same menu is served throughout, ranging from sharing boards to flavoursome British classics that are a step above your usual pub fare, maybe Yorkshire game pie or oxtail casserole.

CLOSING TIMES
Open daily

PRICES
Meals: a la carte £ 21/32

7 rooms: £ 75

Typical Dishes

Fishcakes & tartare hollandaise

Crisp confit duck leg with bubble & squeak

Cherry chocolate bar

Midway between Catterick and Northallerton signposted off B 6271. Parking.

20 **Charles Bathurst Inn**

Langthwaite,
DL11 6EN
Tel.: (01748)884567
Website: www.cbinn.co.uk

VISA

Theakstone, Timothy Taylors, Black Sheep Best, Riggwelter

This characterful 18C hostelry is named after a local land and lead mine owner, and former resident. Sitting on the edge of the Pennine Way, high in the hills of Arkengarthdale, it boasts commanding views over the surrounding countryside and is so remotely set, that the only sound you'll hear is the 'clink' of quoits being thrown by the locals. Inside you're greeted by open fires, various timbered snugs and a charming dining room hung with old monochrome photos and sepia lithographs. Unusually inscribed on a mirror, the daily menu offers refined yet hearty classical British dishes, with the likes of asparagus and Wensleydale tart, followed by local meats; maybe fillet of beef on oxtail terrine. Bedrooms are spacious and extremely comfy.

CLOSING TIMES
Open daily

PRICES
Meals: a la carte £ 20/27
19 rooms: £ 77/137

Typical Dishes

Fishcake with hollandaise sauce
Duck breast with a green pepper sauce
Rhubarb panna cotta

3.25 mi northwest of Reeth on Langthwaite rd. Parking.

Leyburn

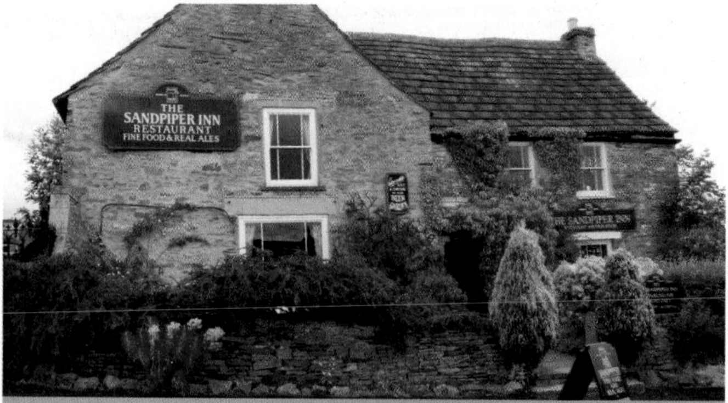

21 Sandpiper Inn

Market Pl,
Leyburn, DL8 5AT
Tel.: (01969)622206
Website: www.sandpiperinn.co.uk

VISA MC AE

Black Sheep, Theakston, Copper Dragon Brewery, Daleside and Yorkshire Dales Brewing Co. Ltd

A friendly Yorkshire welcome is extended to the Dale walkers who come to refuel at this stone built part 16C pub, situated just off the main square.Visitors can rest their blistered feet by the fire in the split-level, beamed bar, or plump for a seat in the more characterful dining room. A small enclosed terrace out the back provides a third alternative for when it's sunny, but you'll have to come inside to read the blackboard menus, found hanging on the walls amidst the general clutter of decorative pictures, books and ornaments. Subtle, refined cooking offers a modern take on the classics, so expect dishes like ham hock terrine and piccalilli, pressed Dales lamb or slow-cooked Wensleydale beef. Two homely bedrooms are on the first floor.

CLOSING TIMES
Closed Monday

PRICES
Meals: a la carte £ 22/35
2 rooms: £ 75/90

Typical Dishes
Wood pigeon with blood orange & walnut salad
Selection of fish, pasta, crayfish & fennel
Terrine of three chocolates

In town centre. Limited parking available in the Market Place.

22 **Punch Bowl Inn**

Low Row,
DL11 6PF
Tel.: (01748)886233
Website: www.pbinn.co.uk

VISA

Timothy Taylor Landlord, Theakston Best Bitter, Black Sheep Bitter and Riggwelter

A traditional 17C stone-built inn whose rustic exterior is a complete contrast to its modernised, shabby-chic style interior, with its open fires and scrubbed wooden tables. It's a popular stop off point for walkers, who refuel on classic dishes like duck liver parfait, braised local lamb shank or beef and red wine casserole; but don't go looking for a paper menu, since dishes are listed on mirrors above the fireplace. There's a selection of filled ciabatta at lunchtime, tasty desserts such as spiced apple tart and custard and bi-monthly steak nights which prove popular with the villagers. Supremely comfortable bedrooms are decorated in a fresh, modern style; all of them have views over Swaledale, while the superior rooms are more spacious.

CLOSING TIMES
Closed 25 December

PRICES
Meals: a la carte £ 22/32
11 rooms: £ 102/129

Typical Dishes
Pan-fried pigeon breast, smoked bacon & black pudding salad
Loin of lamb, garlic mousse, parsnip purée & lamb jus
Yorkshire curd tart

In the middle of hamlet. Parking.

Newton-on-Ouse

23 Dawnay Arms

Newton-on-Ouse,
YO30 2BR
Tel.: (01347)848345
Website: www.thedawnayatnewton.co.uk

VISA

Timothy Taylor Golden Best, Landlord, Black Sheep, Hambleton Ales, Wold Top

This capacious 18C inn boasts a handsome rustic style, thoroughly in tune with its rural surroundings. It's got the low beamed ceilings and the roaring fires. It's got the walls filled with countryside art and the solid stone floors. It's got the locally-crafted chunky wood tables. All that, and a stuffed armadillo too. A native Yorkshireman cooks up tasty, good value dishes in the kitchen, with everything fresh, homemade and seasonal; the lunch menu offers sandwiches and pub classics like shepherd's pie alongside fish stew or slow roast rump of lamb, while the dinner menu might tempt you with confit pork belly or ballotine of chicken. The more formal rear dining room looks out over the terrace and gardens and down to the River Ouse.

CLOSING TIMES
Closed 1 January, Sunday dinner and Monday except bank holidays

PRICES
Meals: £ 15 (lunch)
and a la carte £ 23/34

Typical Dishes

Warm salad of wood pigeon, bacon & egg

Fillet of pork Wellington with celeriac & apple purée

Warm chocolate cake

8 mi northwest of York by A 19 and minor road west. Parking.

24 **Black Swan**

Oldstead,
YO61 4BL
Tel.: (01347)868387
Website: www.blackswanoldstead.co.uk

VISA

Black Sheep Best Bitter and Copper Dragon Best Bitter

The Black Swan is a proper village pub and a real family affair. The Banks have lived and farmed in Oldstead for generations – and still do. The pub is stone-built and has a characterful beamed, flag-floored bar with welcoming open fires, where you'll find top-rate bar meals such as beef casserole. Head to the upstairs dining room for more ambitious but expertly crafted dishes like duck terrine with foie gras, followed by herb-crusted fillet of wild turbot. Cooking is modern and highly skilled but remains satisfyingly unpretentious, and they are particularly proud of the sourcing of their meats. Antique-furnished bedrooms boast modern fabrics, luxurious bathrooms and patios overlooking the surrounding farmland.

CLOSING TIMES
Closed 2 weeks in January and lunch Monday-Wednesday

PRICES
Meals: £ 25 (lunch) and a la carte £ 35/48
4 rooms: £ 165/310

Typical Dishes
Scallops with cauliflower purée
Lamb 4 ways
Set lemon custard

Signposted off A 170 7.5 mi southwest of Helmsley. Parking.

25 Golden Lion

6 West End,
Osmotherley, DL6 3AA
Tel.: (01609)883526
Website: www.goldenlionosmotherley.co.uk

VISA MC

Harvieston Bitter & Twisted, Fools Gold, and Timothy Taylor Landlord

The Golden Lion has probably done more to invigorate walkers than sunshine and a following wind. Found in the historic village of Osmotherley, it represents the starting line for those about to set off on the Lyke Wake walk or at least those contemplating the walk. There's nothing fancy about this place and that's the beauty of it – just a rustic, warm interior with open fires, great beers and staff who make you feel instantly at ease. The food also fits neatly into these surroundings. There's a bit of French, a little Italian with some pasta dishes but, above all, food that satisfies, whether that's a piece of roasted halibut or a local mature steak accompanied by a pint in front of the fire. The bedrooms are quite modern in style.

CLOSING TIMES
Closed 25 December, lunch Monday and Tuesday except bank holidays

PRICES
Meals: a la carte £ 24/33
5 rooms: £ 65/90

Typical Dishes

Nidderdale trout, spinach & mayonnaise
Grilled halibut with samphire & beurre blanc
Vanilla ice cream with poached pear and hot chocolate sauce

6 mi northeast of Northallerton by A 684. Parking in the village.

26

Crown Inn

Roecliffe,
YO51 9LY
Tel.: (01423)322300
Website: www.crowninnroecliffe.com

VISA

Theakston's, Timothy Taylor Landlord, Black Sheep bitter and Ikley Gold

Delightfully set by the village green, this smart 16C inn displays a stylish country interior with stone floors, exposed beams and open fireplaces. Out the front there's a small terrace and inside, the choice of three different rooms – one decorated in red, one in green, and the last, housing the bar counter. The good-sized menus are chalked up the board as well as being printed out and display a nice balance of meat and fish. Dishes like the crab soup, tempura prawns, fish pie and belly pork are mainstays and the dedicated 'meat free' menu ensures that vegetarians are well-catered for. A carefully chosen wine list provides the perfect accompaniment. Smart new bedrooms boast antique-style furnishings, feature beds and free-standing baths.

CLOSING TIMES
Closed Sunday dinner

PRICES
Meals: a la carte £ 25/30
4 rooms: £ 82/120

Typical Dishes

Smokehouse tasting plate
Duck breast with roasted figs & purple endive
Iced tiramisu parfait

1 mi west of Boroughbridge by minor road. Parking.

Sawdon

27 Anvil Inn

Main St,
Sawdon, YO13 9DY
Tel.: (01723)859896
Website: www.theanvilinnsawdon.co.uk

VISA MC

Guest ales from Great Newsome, Leeds, and Northumberland Breweries

As its name suggests, this charming inn was formerly a smithy, and much of the associated paraphernalia remains, including bellows, an open forge and the original anvil. In marked contrast, but blending in seamlessly, is the boldly coloured, contemporary sitting room. Cooking is classical in essence, with the odd international influence, so expect crispy duck and pancakes alongside Shetland mussels or slow-roasted daube of beef. Local chef Mark prides himself on the use of locally sourced produce; eggs come from the pub's own hens and the local Stillington pork is a firm favourite. There are only seven tables in the intimate restaurant, so be sure to book ahead; particularly for Sunday lunch, which has become something of an institution.

CLOSING TIMES
Closed 25-26 December, 1 January, Monday and Tuesday

PRICES
Meals: a la carte £ 21/30

Typical Dishes

Leek & potato cake

Seared king scallops with black pudding dauphinoise

Panna cotta, sorbet & tart of Yorkshire rhubarb

12 mi southwest of Scarborough by A 170 to Brompton and minor road north. Parking.

28 **Hare Inn**

Scawton,
YO7 2HG
Tel.: (01845)597769
Website: www.thehareinn.co.uk

VISA MC AE

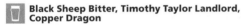

Black Sheep Bitter, Timothy Taylor Landlord, Copper Dragon

The appeal of many a pub lies in its far-flung setting and The Hare's location couldn't be more remote – it nestles in the depths of the North Yorkshire Moors, close to Rievaulx Abbey and Sutton Bank, which, as many gliders know, is where you'll find some of the country's best views. But The Hare is more than just a hideaway – it's also got plenty of character, with parts of the pub dating back to the 13C. For some, it even resembles a smart scout hut and would certainly win a badge for hospitality. The food is equally pleasing and local, whether that's the local asparagus, whole roast sea bass, sweet new season lamb or 'proper' puddings like lemon posset. It gets pretty jam packed at weekends so a little patience is sometimes required.

CLOSING TIMES
Closed 25 December, Sunday dinner and Monday

PRICES
Meals: a la carte £ 23/34

Typical Dishes

Twice-baked cheese soufflé
Breast of chicken with tarragon mousse and a wild mushroom sauce
Soft chocolate cake

Between Thirsk and Helmsley off north side of A 170. Parking.

Sinnington

29 **Fox and Hounds**

Main St,
Sinnington, YO62 6SQ
Tel.: (01751)431577
Website: www.thefoxandhoundsinn.co.uk

VISA MC

Copper Dragon Best Bitter, Wold Top Bitter,

It's easy to see why this handsome stone pub, dating from the 18C, is something of a local institution: it has charm, is run smoothly and offers something for everyone. It's divided into a number of areas; if you want to chat to the good burghers of Sinnington sit in the bar but there's also a dining room at the back. The menu is all about flexibility, with virtually all the starters available in larger sizes for main courses. Local specialities include the Bleikers smoked salmon, the scallops with black pudding or the Swaledale 'Old Peculiar' cheese soufflé. There is something comforting about the main courses, such as slow-cooked shoulder of lamb or fish pie. If staying overnight, then book ahead as the bedrooms get snapped up quickly.

CLOSING TIMES
Closed 25-26 December

PRICES
Meals: a la carte £ 22/37
10 rooms: £ 59/130

Typical Dishes

Twice-baked cheese soufflé

Fish platter: fish pie, tiger prawns, sea trout, fish & chips

Yorkshire rhubarb

Just off A 170 between Pickering and Kirkbymoorside. Parking.

30 **Coachman Inn**

Pickering Rd West,
Snainton, YO13 9PL
Tel.: (01723)859231
Website: www.coachmaninn.co.uk

VISA MC AE

Wold Top and Wold Top Gold

This Grade II listed inn dates back to 1776 and was the last staging post before Scarborough for the coaches taking the York mail. It boasts a well-tended garden to the rear and a charming interior: there's a rustic bar displaying quarry tiles and chunky wood furniture and a spacious linen-clad dining room which runs the length of the building, finishing in a small garden room at the end. The place is run with some formality – menus are presented in smart folders and cooking is very much in the classical vein, although with a modern, refined style of presentation. Produce is seasonal and of good quality but prices remain fair. Lunch offers simpler pub favourites and the concise wine list is well thought out. Bedrooms are smart and spacious.

CLOSING TIMES
Open daily

PRICES
Meals: a la carte £ 19/30
5 rooms: £ 60/85

Typical Dishes

Crispy belly pork with pea purée & black pudding
East coast cod with a watercress sauce
Dark chocolate fondant

West of the village on B 1258. Parking.

31

Blackwell Ox Inn

Huby Rd,
Sutton-on-the-Forest, YO61 1DT
Tel.: (01347)810328
Website: www.blackwelloxinn.co.uk

VISA

Timothy Taylor Landlord, John Smiths Cask, Black Sheep Bitter, Copper Dragon Golden Pipin

A smart, contemporary inn with a homely bar/lounge and a more formal, linen-clad dining room. There are snacks chalked on a board plus a daily changing à la carte menu; starters like foie gras on toasted brioche may feature but these sit alongside more down-to-earth dishes like pan-fried pigeon breast, or creamy garlic wild mushrooms on toast. Main courses could include local rib-eye steak with chips or half a roast chicken and desserts range from bread and butter pudding to cherry and boozy prune clafoutis. Bedrooms are spacious and stylish, with excellent modern bathrooms. Some feature four-poster beds and Room 2 has a roll-top bath in the room; such a high standard finish makes sense when you know that the inn is owned by a local builder.

CLOSING TIMES
Open daily

PRICES
Meals: £ 15 (lunch) and a la carte £ 20/30
7 rooms: £ 65

Typical Dishes

Breast of pigeon wrapped in pancetta
Fillet of beef with blue cheese & red wine
Vanilla panna cotta

8 mi north of York by B 1363. Parking.

32 **Rose & Crown**

Main St,
Sutton-on-the-Forest, YO61 1DP
Tel.: (01347)811333
Website: www.rosecrown.co.uk

VISA MC AE

Black Sheep Best, Hambleton Stallion

The small, cosy front bar creates a welcoming and intimate atmosphere and the dining room and conservatory add to the overall charm. There is a bewildering array of menus available, from 'early bird' to 'light bites', from the à la carte to a list of 'classics' – but don't be frightened off as you'll almost certainly find something that appeals – to your appetite and your pocket – whether that's the sirloin of Yorkshire beef, pork cutlet with black pudding, ham hock terrine or just a Caesar salad. Local cheeses go into the potato cakes; the piccalilli is homemade and the haddock uses a local York beer for its batter. Perhaps the pub's best feature is the enclosed rear garden which comes with a super terrace and an impressively sized gazebo.

CLOSING TIMES
Closed Sunday dinner and Monday
booking essential

PRICES
Meals: £ 18 (lunch)
and a la carte £ 26/30

Typical Dishes

Smoked salmon & crab with crème fraîche
Venison with butternut squash & blackberry jus
Iced mango parfait

On B 1363 north of York. Parking.

Wighill

33 White Swan

Main St,
Wighill, LS24 8BQ
Tel.: (01937)832217
Website: www.whiteswanwighill.co.uk

VISA

Black Sheep, Moorhouses and Rudgate Beers with other local ales

It may have been closed for two years but surprisingly, the model swan outside managed to survive unscathed. Now under the control of the team behind Ye Olde Sun Inn at Colton, this traditional pub has a warm, welcoming feel. There's a cosy little snug that's popular with the locals, a choice of several comfy dining rooms and a small shop selling bottled beers, chutneys and the like. Specials are chalked on the blackboard and supplement the main monthly menu, which features pub classics like fish and chips or gammon steak, alongside maybe cheddar cheese soufflé, confit duck leg or roast hake with parsley sauce. They also serve a range of 'Yorkshire Tapas', which is proving particularly popular, and hold regular theme evenings and quiz nights.

CLOSING TIMES
Open daily

PRICES
Meals: a la carte £ 19/24

Typical Dishes

Terrine of the day
Beer-battered haddock, chips & tartare sauce
Crème brûlée

Signposted off A 659 3 mi north of Tadcaster. Parking.

34 **Milestone**

84 Green Ln,
Sheffield, S3 8SE
Tel.: (0114)2728327
Website: www.the-milestone.co.uk

VISA MC AE

Sheffield micro breweries; Kelham Island and Wentworth

That the owners of The Milestone can boast their own herd of free range pigs speaks volumes about their approach to food: passionate about organic, locally sourced produce, they consider the quality of their ingredients to be the key to their success and don't believe in buying in things like bread, pasta and puddings, since they can make them in-house. Some of the hearty dishes on the 'gastro' menu – like the lamb burger, and the beef Bourguignon – have become classics, but the emphasis here is on evolution and seasonality, so what's on offer changes frequently. While downstairs is spacious, with understated décor, simple wood tables and banquettes, the beamed first floor room provides a more formal dining space, with a menu to match.

CLOSING TIMES
Closed 25-26 December and 1 January

PRICES
Meals: a la carte £ 26/30

Typical Dishes

Fillet of mackerel with sesame cucumber & fennel jam
Corn-fed chicken breast with blue cheese
Apricot & almond tart

Between A 61 and River Don. Parking in Green Lane and Ball Street.

35 **Cricket Inn**

Penny Ln,
Totley, S17 3AZ
Tel.: (0114)2365256
Website: www.relaxeatanddrink.co.uk

VISA

Thornbridge Brewery Jaipur, Kipling and Hopton ales

Hidden away in a delightful spot in the valley, next to the cricket ground, this is a proper pub in every sense of the word. Three rooms boast open fires and rustic wood floors; the walls are filled with cricketing paraphernalia, while the scrubbed tables are home to bottles of Sheffield's spicy Henderson's sauce. Food comes in big, hearty portions, not for the faint-hearted, and there's something for everyone, from sandwiches and snacks like home-roasted pork scratchings, to things like cheese on toast or homemade fishcakes, as well as dishes such as steak and ale pie or slow-braised shoulder shank of lamb. 'Cricket Inn boards' come in ploughman's and fisherman's varieties, there's a little person's menu and some nice nursery style puddings.

CLOSING TIMES
Open daily

PRICES
Meals: £ 25 and a la carte £ 21/39

Typical Dishes

Potted ham hock & chilled pease pudding
Tasting of pork with sweet & sour cabbage
Warm treacle tart

6 mi southwest of Sheffield by A 61, A 621 and Hillfoot Rd. Parking.

36 Shibden Mill Inn

Shibden Mill Fold,
Halifax, HX3 7UL
Tel.: (01422)365840
Website: www.shibdenmillinn.com

VISA AE

Moorhouse's, Little Valley Brewery and Theakstons ales

Set in the valley, overlooking a stream, this whitewashed inn started life as an early 14C corn mill, was later used for spinning and, in 1890, was sold to a brewing company. Today, you'll find a charming open-fired bar full of nooks, crannies and locals, and a rustic upstairs restaurant with recently exposed original oak beams. Menus offer plenty of choice, with dishes ranging from the traditional – maybe home cured corned beef hash, roast rib-eye or treacle tart – to the more modern, such as crab trifle with lemon cocktail, scallops with bacon crème caramel or butternut squash fondant. For something a little different, come to a gourmet dinner evening or experimental guinea pig night. Individually appointed bedrooms are comfy and cosy.

CLOSING TIMES
Closed dinner
25-26 December and
1 January

PRICES
Meals: £ 13 (lunch)
and a la carte £ 28/33
11 rooms: £ 105/123

Typical Dishes

Duo of Calderdale rabbit

Braised English Veal breast with white polenta mash

Glazed lemon tart

Northeast : 2.25 mi by A 58 and Kell Lane (turning left at Stump Cross public house) on Blake Hill Rd. Parking.

37 **Butchers Arms**

38 Towngate,
Hepworth, HD9 1TE
Tel.: (01484)682361
Website: www.thebutchersarms.co.uk

VISA AE

Black Sheep, Timothy Taylor Landlord and Copper Dragon ales

Set on the fringes of a sleepy hamlet this stone-built inn really is hidden away but with its rustic bar, smart dining room and a choice of delightful terraces, it's well worth searching out. A vibrant sign outside proudly announces the owner's philosophy – 'The Butchers Arms, A great place to meat' – and the skilled cooking offers suitably robust, country style dishes. The bewildering array of menus ranges from your usual daily blackboard and à la carte selections to more interesting Yorkshire tapas choices and even a water menu. All produce comes from within a strict 75 mile radius but most originates from closer to home; be it trugs of gooseberries left on the doorstep by the neighbours, game shot just down the road or homemade chutneys.

CLOSING TIMES
Open daily
booking essential

PRICES
Meals: £ 17 (weekday lunch) and a la carte £ 33/45

Typical Dishes

Pressed ham terrine
Pan-seared Cornish sea bass fillet with wood roast peppers
Warm apricot and almond tart

2 mi southeast of Holmfirth by A 635 and B 6106. Parking.

38 **Olive Branch**

Marsden,
HD7 6LU
Tel.: (01484)844487
Website: www.olivebranch.uk.com

VISA

Regularly changing Greenfield Ales

Set on a busy main road, this stone-built drovers' inn houses many small and characterful rooms, each adorned with food-themed pictures, sepia photos, old menus and more. Most tables are set for dining and there's a chatty, bustling atmosphere, while for warmer weather, a decked terrace and secluded garden are hidden round the back. The large menu displays an even split between meat and seafood, ranging from pigeon and venison to sea bass and monkfish; with daily specials displayed on large yellow post-it notes around the bar. Taking on a traditional style, cooking is robust, straightforward and uses local produce wherever possible. Service is friendly, if sometimes lacking a little in direction. Bedrooms are modern, comfy and very unique.

CLOSING TIMES
Closed first 2 weeks January
dinner only and Sunday lunch

PRICES
Meals: a la carte £ 26/41
3 rooms: £ 65/80

Typical Dishes

Scottish mussels in wine, cream & garlic
Smoked haddock with spinach and soft poached egg
Lemon tart

1 mi northeast on A 62. Parking.

Rishworth

39 **Old Bore**

Oldham Rd,
Rishworth, HX6 4QU
Tel.: (01422)822291
Website: www.oldbore.co.uk

Black Sheep and Timothy Taylor Landlord

Hidden away in a charming landscape dotted with reservoirs and traversed by pleasant walks, this 19C stone coaching inn makes the ideal stop off point for anything from a refreshing northern ale to a full 3 course dinner. It's a cosy, characterful place bursting with knick-knacks and memorabilia, from quirky hunting scene wallpaper and stag antler chandeliers to framed food-related articles and pewter tankards. Service is smooth and welcoming, and matched by appealingly robust cooking. Produce is seasonal and local game is usually a feature; you might find braised beef brisket or game suet pudding on offer, along with options such as coquilles St Jacques with wild mushroom sauce on Fish Fridays. Theme nights and jazz evenings are common.

CLOSING TIMES
Closed 2 weeks January, Monday and Tuesday

PRICES
Meals: a la carte £ 30/38

Typical Dishes

Seafood tasting slate
Spring lamb Wellington
Chocolate fondant

6 mi southwest of Halifax by A 58 and A 672. Parking.

40 **Woodman Inn**

Thunder Bridge,
HD8 0PX
Tel.: (01484)605778
Website: www.woodman-inn.co.uk

VISA

Timothy Taylor Best and Landlord, Black Sheep Best Bitter and Copper Dragon Golden Pippin

If you're following one of the many footpaths that pass by the Southern Pennines, be sure to seek out this peaceful wooded valley and the small hamlet of Thunder Bridge. Here you'll find this traditional 19C Yorkshire-stone inn, with its wood-faced bar – complete with convivial locals – leather furnished lounge and more formal linen-laid restaurant which opens in the evening. Service is polite and efficient wherever you sit: the restaurant is great for special occasions but the bar is more atmospheric. Extensive menus change with the seasons and have a distinct British bias. Lunch sees hearty classics served in generous portions, while dinner takes on a more ambitious approach. Simple, well-kept bedrooms are located in old weavers' cottages.

CLOSING TIMES
Closed 25-26 December

PRICES
Meals: a la carte £ 21/34
12 rooms: £ 48/85

Typical Dishes

Vegetable rösti with poached egg
Monkfish wrapped in Parma ham with spinach risotto
Trio of chocolate

5.75 mi southeast of Huddersfield by A 629; after Kirkburton follow signs to Thunder Bridge. Parking.

Scotland may be small, but its variety is immense. The vivacity of Glasgow can seem a thousand miles from the vast peatland wilderness of Caithness and Sutherland's Flow Country; the arty vibe of Georgian Edinburgh a world away from the remote and tranquil Ardnamurchan peninsula. And how many people link Scotland to its beaches? But wide golden sands trim the Atlantic at South Harris, and the coastline of the Highlands boasts empty islands and turquoise waters. Meantime, Fife's coast draws golf fans to St Andrews and the more secretive delights of the East Neuk, an area of fishing villages and stone harbours. Wherever you travel, the scent of a dramatic history prevails in the shape of castles, cathedrals and rugged lochside monuments to the heroes of old. Food and drink embraces the traditional, too, typified by Aberdeen's famous Malt Whisky Trail. And what better than Highland game, fresh fish from the Tweed or haggis, neeps and tatties to complement a grand Scottish hike…

Lewis
Stornoway
St. Kilda
Tarbert
North Uist
Lochmaddy
Uig
Dunvegan
Portree
South Uist
Lochboisdale
Skye
Kyle of Lochalsh
Barra
Castlebay
Sea of the Hebrides
Rhum
Mallaig
Coll
Tiree
Tobermory
Mull
Craignure
Fionnphort
Oban
Firth of Lorn
Colonsay
Lochgilphead
Islay
Port Askaig
Jura
Port Ellen
Kintyre
Campbeltown
Brodick
Arran
Firth of Clyde
The Minch
Lochinver
Tongue
Dunnet
Lairg
Ullapool
Brora
Dornoch
Dingwall
Nairn
Inverness
Loch Ness
Aviemore
Newtonmore
Cairngorm Mountains
Braemar
Fort William
Ben Nevis
HIGHLANDS
SCOTLAND
R. Tay
Crianlarich
Perth
Stirling
Kinross
Dunoon
Dumbarton
Rothesay
Greenock
Falkirk
GLASGOW
EDINBURGH
Ardrossan
Kilmarnock
Lanark
Ayr
Moffat
Hawick
Cairnryan
Stranraer
Dumfries
Kirkcudbright
Solway Firth
Carlisle
Workington
Whitehaven
Keswick
Windermere
Man
Peel
Ramsey
Malin Head
Buncrana
Giant's Causeway
Portrush
Letterkenny
Londonderry / Derry
Coleraine
Ballycastle
Antrim Glens
Donegal
Northern Ireland
Bundoran
Omagh
Ballymena
Larne
Sligo
Enniskillen
Lough Neagh
Lisburn
BELFAST
Bangor
Armagh
Boyle
Monaghan
Newry
Newcastle
Ireland
North West

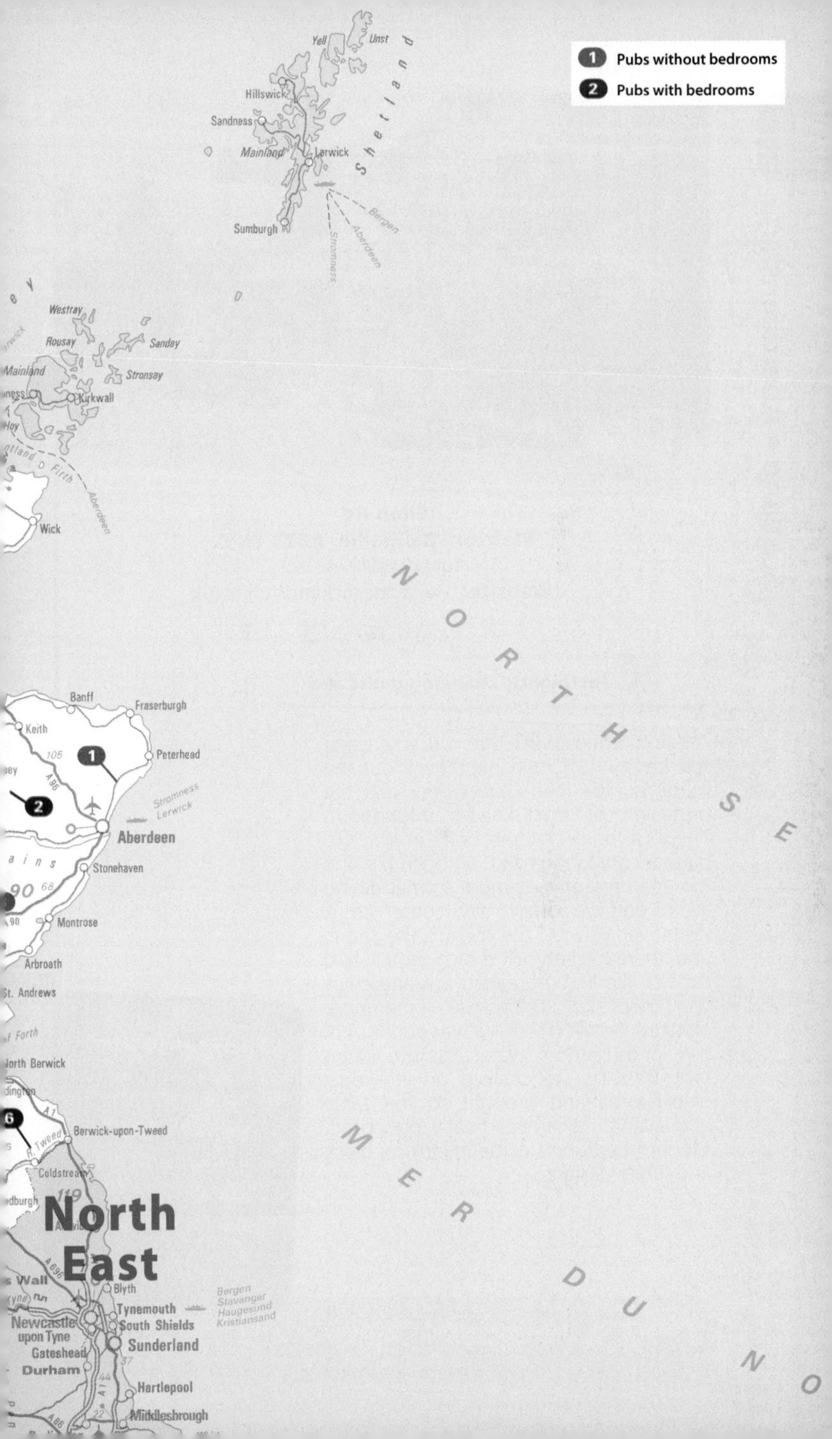

Pubs without bedrooms
Pubs with bedrooms
Shetland
Yell
Unst
Hillswick
Sandness
Mainland
Lerwick
Sumburgh
Bergen
Aberdeen
Stromness
Westray
Rousay
Sanday
Stronsay
Mainland
Kirkwall
Hoy
Firth
Aberdeen
Wick
NORTH SEA
MER DU NORD
Banff
Fraserburgh
Keith
Peterhead
Stromness
Lerwick
Aberdeen
Stonehaven
Montrose
Arbroath
St. Andrews
North Berwick
Berwick-upon-Tweed
R. Tweed
Coldstream
North East
Blyth
Tynemouth
Newcastle upon Tyne
South Shields
Gateshead
Sunderland
Durham
Hartlepool
Middlesbrough
Bergen
Stavanger
Haugesund
Kristiansand

Balmedie

1 **Cock and Bull**

Ellon Rd,
Blairton, Balmedie, AB23 8XY
Tel.: (01358)743249
Website: www.thecockandbull.co.uk

VISA AE

Fortnightly changing guest ales

A quirky, atmospheric pub with a sense of fun befitting of its name; check out the mural on the men's toilet door and the profusion of knick-knacks throughout. There's a choice of three rooms in which to dine: a cosy lounge with an open fire and low leather sofas, a more formal dining room and an open, airy conservatory. Wherever you sit, the menu's the same, and there's plenty of choice. You'll find classics like home-breaded fish and chips or Cullen skink, alongside some more restaurant-style dishes such as confit pork belly or mushroom, watercress and ricotta tart. Desserts are chalked on individual blackboards and brought to the table and everything arrives neatly presented. Modern bedrooms come in striking black and white designs.

CLOSING TIMES
Open daily

PRICES
Meals: a la carte £ 26/48

Typical Dishes

Game & roast vegetable terrine
Halibut with dill pomme purée
Sticky toffee pudding

On A 90 6 mi north of Aberdeen. Parking.

2 Glenkindie Arms

Glenkindie,
AB33 8SX
Tel.: (01975)641288
Website: www.theglenkindiearms.co.uk

Inspectors' favourites

VISA

Trade Winds, Lia Fail, Ossian and Peters Well

The Glenkindie Arms is a rustic Highland inn, set in a remote location in the middle of prime hunting and fishing territory; and at 400 years old, it has plenty of charm. The large bar with its roaring open fire, tartan carpets and huge collection of malt whiskies honours its Scottish roots and provides good views out across the surrounding countryside. The daily changing menu is chalked up the blackboard and offers four choices per course; you might find cullen skink or Peterhead mackerel, followed by lamb's liver, rabbit or mature steak. Dishes make the most of what's in season and available locally (including wild mushrooms that grow just outside the door), and are straightforward, well-cooked and tasty. Simple bedrooms complete the picture.

CLOSING TIMES
Closed 25-26 December, restricted opening in winter
booking essential

PRICES
Meals: £ 28 and a la carte £ 24/44

3 rooms: £ 40/90

Typical Dishes

Highland smoked bacon & broad bean risotto

Roast Hebridean lamb rump with rosemary jus

Dark chocolate & Armagnac fondant

In the heart of Strathdon on the A 97 between Ballater and Huntly. Parking.

3 **Drovers Inn**

Memus,
DD8 3TY
Tel.: (01307)860322
Website: www.the-drovers.com

VISA AE

Orkney Corncrake, Deuchar's IPA, Ossian

Good cooking relies on good ingredients, so if the owner of a pub also has estates nearby that supply much of the produce it's little wonder that the chef seems so contented. This remote Highland inn with its immaculate lawns was once a crofter's cottage and the bar with its open fires is a lovely spot. There's also a more formal dining room, to which the freshly baked breads add their wonderful aroma. Gone is the plethora of confusing menus offered in the past and in their place is now a single, well-priced menu that makes particularly good use of all that local produce, such as game from the shoots. Further value for money is provided by a wine list that eschews the usual 'mark-ups' and instead makes a uniform corkage charge.

CLOSING TIMES
Open daily

PRICES
Meals: a la carte £ 15/26

Typical Dishes

Linguine with creamed Arbroath smokie

Loin of pork, Stornaway black pudding spring roll & grain mustard mash

Chocolate tart

4 mi north of Kirriemuir by B 955 and minor road east.
Parking.

4 Oyster Inn

Connel,
PA37 1PJ
Tel.: (01631)710666
Website: www.oysterinn.co.uk

VISA MC AE

Deuchar's IPA

With views over the Falls of Lora and across to the mountains, this brightly coloured inn is steeped in history. The 18C Ferryman's Bar got its name from serving nearby ferry passengers, although it was better known as the Glue Pot because people used to get 'stuck' waiting for the return boat. It boasts stone walls, log fires and a pleasant rear terrace – as well as a pool table, a dartboard and a menu of pub classics. The smarter pine-furnished restaurant is adorned with lobster pots and nautical memorabilia and offers a regularly changing seafood menu and lovely views of the sun setting over the bay. Bedrooms boast pine furniture, colourful prints and contemporary throws; budget bunk rooms are available. Touch a glue pot to bring you luck.

CLOSING TIMES
Closed 25-26 December

PRICES
Meals: a la carte £ 27/57
11 rooms: £ 55/130

Typical Dishes

Moules marinière
Rack of Argyllshire lamb with a port & rosemary jus
Sticky toffee pudding

5 mi north of Oban by A 85. Parking.

5 **Tayvallich Inn**

Tayvallich,
PA31 8PL
Tel.: (01546)870282
Website: www.tayvallichinn.co.uk

VISA MC

Fyne Ales; Avalanche, Pipers Gold and Hurricane Jack

The Tayvallich Inn's sign shows the silhouette of a lobster, which gives a clue as to what this pub is all about: the chef knows a thing or two about seafood and you can expect to see plenty of locally caught, seasonal fish and shellfish including langoustines, mussels, lobster and lemon sole, as well as scallops by the bucket load. The menu also offers classic pub dishes like steak and chips and a popular curry of the day; the owners worked on local fish farms before taking over the reins here and make the most of their extensive local connections to source the best produce possible. Dine in the bar, in the more formal dining area or out on the decked terrace, with its rustic style bench seating and picturesque views out over the bay.

CLOSING TIMES
Closed Monday November-March

PRICES
Meals: a la carte £ 19/32

Typical Dishes

Scallops with sweet chilli & ginger
Salmon with prawn caper sauce
Drambuie crème brûlée

12 mi west of Lochgilphead by A 816, B 841 and B 8025; on west shore of Loch Sween. Parking.

6 **Wheatsheaf**

Main St,
Swinton, TD11 3JJ
Tel.: (01890)860257
Website: www.wheatsheaf-swinton.co.uk

VISA MC

Belhaven IPA

Set in the heart of the village overlooking the green, this substantial stone inn is far from your typical pub. Inside there are numerous sofa-filled rooms and two small dining areas – one boasting linen-laid tables and leather chairs; the other an attractive pine ceiling and matching furniture. The hands-on owners are extremely passionate about food but drinkers are equally as welcome. The lunchtime menu displays pub classics, while the concise evening à la carte is slightly more adventurous, offering maybe smoked duck with poached pear, followed by loin of venison. Well-presented plates feature flavoursome local produce, with seafood from Eyemouth and meat from the surrounding border farms. Bedrooms are spacious, cosy and well-equipped.

CLOSING TIMES
Closed 24-26 December

PRICES
Meals: a la carte £ 22/40
10 rooms: £ 75/112

Typical Dishes
Wild mushroom & smoked roe buck salad
Sirloin of Scottish Borders beef
Lemon mousse

In the centre of the village. Plenty of parking on the road.

Sorn

7 Sorn Inn

35 Main St,
Sorn, KA5 6HU
Tel.: (01290)551305
Website: www.sorninn.com

Inspectors' favourites

VISA MC

Texas Ale, Braveheart

It's a family affair here, with the father checking you in to one of the bedrooms and his son cooking your meals. The first clues as to the quality of food are the framed menus along with the copy of 'Larousse', the chefs' bible. Wisely, they've made the pub less formal, so the same menu is now served throughout, whether you're in the small bar or the dining room. The chef adopts an international approach, a result of his time spent on the QE2. Along with homemade pasta, steak pie and prime Scottish beef are dishes like wood pigeon with polenta and chicken with banana rice. There's flexibility too, so you can have some dishes as a starter or main course and the lunch menu is a steal. Bedrooms are popular in the shooting season.

CLOSING TIMES
Closed 10 days January and Monday

PRICES
Meals: £ 14 (lunch)
and a la carte £ 19/27
4 rooms: £ 40/70

Typical Dishes

Mackerel with horseradish jelly

Highland venison, fricassee of peas, asparagus & cabbage

Warm almondine sponge

In centre of village. Parking.

8 Ship on the Shore

24-26 The Shore,
Leith, EH6 6QN
Tel.: (0131)5550409
Website: www.theshipontheshore.co.uk

VISA MC AE

No real ales served

With its neat blue façade inset with ship's navigation lights and modelled on the Royal Yacht Britannia, this period building on the quayside looks ready to set sail. Inside, the walls are papered with European maritime charts, scrubbed wooden floors mimic a ship's deck, and it's filled with nautical bric à brac. Regulars prop up the bar and a friendly service team buzz around. The kitchen follows a philosophy of 'sustainable Scottish seafood served simply with style', and 99% of the menu is just this. Popular classics are a mainstay, while fresh daily specials are featured on numerous blackboards; you'll find everything from Cullen Skink to whole roast sea bass, and the odd meat dish on offer too. Try the Arbroath smokies for breakfast.

CLOSING TIMES
Closed 24-26 December

PRICES
Meals: £ 17 and a la carte £ 29/41

Typical Dishes

Smoked salmon, caper & lemon salad

Whole roast sea bass with garlic butter

Croissant & pain au chocolat pudding

On east side of river. On-street parking.

9 Babbity Bowster

16-18 Blackfriars St,
Glasgow, G1 1PE
Tel.: (0141)5525055
Website: www.babbitybowster.com

VISA AE

Deuchar's IPA, Kelburn Misty Law and guest ale

If you're wondering about the name, 'babbity' means to 'bob', a 'bowster' is the wheelshaft of a watermill and the 'babbity bowster' is an old country dance which used to be performed at Scottish balls. Located on the edge of the Merchant City, this double-fronted Georgian building has become part of tradition itself, and one glance at the fiercely Scottish décor and regional memorabilia tells you why. The cheery owner always goes the extra mile; although it's hard not to be satisfied when there's such a fine selection of local ales and whiskies around. Cooking is firmly rooted in tradition, with straightforward, seasonal Scottish favourites including cullen skink, neeps and tatties. For more elaborate dishes, head to the upstairs restaurant.

CLOSING TIMES
Closed 25 December and 1 January

PRICES
Meals: a la carte £ 25/34

Typical Dishes

Scottish smoked salmon with walnut & raisin bread

Duck confit leg with haricot beans

Vanilla pot

In city centre east of the Central railway station.

10 **Summer Isles (Bar)**

Achiltibuie,
IV26 2YG
Tel.: (01854)622282
Website: www.summerisleshotel.com

VISA

An Teallach, Suilven, "Auld Buie"

Set to the side of the Summer Isles Hotel, this was originally an old crofters' bar and dates back to the mid-19C. Still popular with the locals today, it boasts two snug rooms filled with black ash tables, a large lawned area with bench seating and a small two-table terrace affording glorious views over the Summer Isles themselves. Daily changing menus have a strong seafood base but there are plenty of other Scottish-sourced ingredients on offer too, with dishes such as fresh pea soup, chicken breast stuffed with skirlie or local Aberdeen Angus steak. The star of the show, however, has to be the plump, tasty langoustines; which are best enjoyed with a chilled glass of Sauvignon Blanc. Comfy bedrooms are available in the adjoining hotel.

CLOSING TIMES
April-October

PRICES
Meals: a la carte £ 14/30

Typical Dishes

Trio of salmon
Rib-eye steak
Plum & almond flan

15 mi northwest of Ullapool by A 835 and minor road west from Drumrunie. Parking.

Applecross

11 **Applecross Inn**

Shore St,
Applecross, IV54 8LR
Tel.: (01520)744262
Website: www.applecross.uk.com

VISA

Red Cuillin, Hebridean Gold, Blavern

Set between the mountains of the mainland and the Isle of Skye, the Applecross Peninsula provides a tranquil haven from the world outside. It seems miraculous that this charming Highland inn can get so busy, as access to the tiny fishing village is either via a 24 mile coastal track or steep zigzagging mountain pass; albeit accompanied by panoramic views over the Kintail Mountains and Outer Hebrides. Menus offer local, seasonal produce, and with stunning views over the water to the distant hills of Skye, you might even be able to see where many of the ingredients come from. Fresh seafood arrives regularly from Applecross Bay and venison from the nearby estate. Smart, comfy bedrooms are set in old fishermen's cottages and boast sea views.

CLOSING TIMES
Closed 25 December and 1 January
booking essential

PRICES
Meals: a la carte £ 18/27
7 rooms: £ 70/120

Typical Dishes

Haggis flambéed in Drambuie

King scallops with crispy bacon, garlic & lemon butter

Raspberry cranachan

From Kishorn via Belach nam Bo (Alpine Pass) or round by Shieldaig and along the coast. Parking.

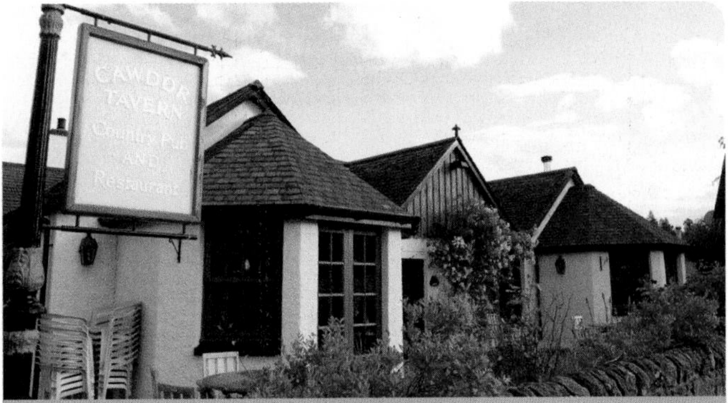

12

Cawdor Tavern

The Lane,
Cawdor, IV12 5XP
Tel.: (01667)404777
Website: www.cawdortavern.co.uk

VISA MC AE

Orkney Dark Island, Red McGregor, Three Sisters

Macbeth may have died several centuries before it was built, but the next door castle is well-known for its role in Shakespeare's tragedy, and this smart whitewashed pub was once its joiners' workshop. It's an immensely charming place and is very passionately run by the owner – who, having purchased both the Orkney and Atlas breweries, isn't short of an award winning ale or two. Exposed beams and wooden-panelling abound and it's hard to choose between the lovely open-fired bar, characterful lounge and traditional restaurant. The wide-ranging, classical menu offers a good selection of frequently changing dishes; you might find trio of Scottish black pudding, haggis and white pudding, followed by Highland venison with bramble and juniper jus.

CLOSING TIMES
Closed 2 weeks January, 25 December and 1 January
booking essential

PRICES
Meals: a la carte £ 18/27

Typical Dishes

Home-smoked duck breast with black pudding croutons
Highland venison with caramelised apple
Belgian chocolate truffle torte

5 mi south of Nairn by B 9090. Parking.

13 **Kylesku (Bar)**

Kylesku,
IV27 4HW
Tel.: (01971)502231
Website: www.kyleskuhotel.co.uk

VISA MC

An Teallach and Suilven

Breathtaking views of Loch Glendhu and the spectacular surrounding scenery make this inn an essential stop-off point if you're ever in the area. Friendly staff welcome guests and there's a cosy, homely atmosphere in the spacious, fire-lit bar. Sup on local ale while you trade tales with walkers and cyclists, before settling down to eat seafood so local it practically swam in the door. Langoustines and fish come from the jetty in front of the bar and mussels are rope grown 200 yards away. Classic dishes might include salmon fishcakes or a fish pie, a satisfying bowl of soup or a platter of mature local cheeses, while if you're after something a little more meaty, try a mature local steak. Eight comfortable bedrooms upstairs in the hotel.

CLOSING TIMES
March-October

PRICES
Meals: a la carte £ 22/38

Typical Dishes

Battered langoustine with pea purée
Local seafood platter
Honey panna cotta

32 mi north of Ullapool by A 835, A 837 and A 894. On street parking.

14 Loch Ness Inn

Lewiston,
IV63 6UW
Tel.: (01456)450991
Website: www.staylochness.co.uk

VISA

Cairngorm Tradewinds and Belhaven's 80 Shilling

Aside from the name, there's nothing inside to suggest a link with the mythical monster, or even Scotland for that matter; making this an honest local pub rather than just a tartan-clad tourist attraction. You'd never guess that it had once stood derelict, especially when you're rubbing shoulders with the locals in the buzzing bar or relaxing on the wood-furnished terrace. The dining area consists of two spacious rooms featuring exposed stone walls, black slate floors and new timbered beams; where at lunchtime you'll find a small blackboard menu of pub classics, and at dinner, more restaurant-style dishes such as risotto or confit of duck. Named after local lochs and glens, the individually styled bedrooms have a pleasant, country feel.

CLOSING TIMES
Open daily

PRICES
Meals: a la carte £ 19/32
12 rooms: £ 69/112

Typical Dishes

Applecross Bay prawns
Rack of lamb with roasted sweet potatoes
Sticky toffee pudding

14 mi southwest of Inverness by A 82. Parking.

Plockton

15 Plockton Hotel

41 Harbour St,
Plockton, IV52 8TN
Tel.: (01599)544274
Website: www.plocktonhotel.co.uk

VISA MC AE

Plockton Bay, Crags Ale, Trade Winds

Set on the waterfront overlooking Loch Carron, this building started life as two small cottages before being transformed into an inn. Boasting an unusual black exterior, it stands out among the other whitewashed buildings in this small National Trust village; and not just on appearance. Owned by the Pearson family for over 20 years, it has a friendly, welcoming feel. The bar is the centre of activity but there's a small terrace and restaurant if you fancy something quieter. Their speciality is seafood but you'll also find Highland meats and plenty of locally grown Scottish produce, in dishes like casserole of venison, seafood bake or Plockton smokies. Bedrooms are split between the pub and an annexe; those to the front boast great bay views.

CLOSING TIMES
Open daily

PRICES
Meals: a la carte £ 16/38
15 rooms: £ 40/130

Typical Dishes

Plockton smokies
Seared hand-dived local scallops
Cranachan & raspberries soaked in whisky

5 mi north of Kyle of Lochalsh. Parking 50 yards away in village car park.

16 **Stein Inn**

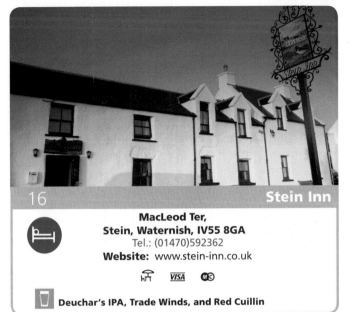

MacLeod Ter,
Stein, Waternish, IV55 8GA
Tel.: (01470)592362
Website: www.stein-inn.co.uk

VISA

Deuchar's IPA, Trade Winds, and Red Cuillin

Set towards the northwest end of the island, on the Waternish Peninsula, this whitewashed building dates back to 1790 and beyond, and is the oldest inn on Skye. Large black lettering on the side wall states its purpose; to the rear there are picnic benches for the warmer months; and inside, a characterful wood-panelled bar and stone-walled lounge with an open fire form the heart of the pub. At lunchtime you'll find the likes of fresh crab sandwiches, ploughman's with Scottish cheeses and maybe even a haggis toastie; while dinner is more substantial and might include Skye scallops, local venison or Scottish salmon. Bedrooms are simple and well-kept, and with no TVs, you're free to watch the comings and goings of picturesque Loch Bay instead.

CLOSING TIMES
Closed 1 January and 25 December

PRICES
Meals: a la carte £ 15/22
5 rooms: £ 46/110

Typical Dishes

Pan-fried scallops with bacon
Local beer battered haddock
Sticky toffee pudding

22 mi west of Portree by A 87, A 850 and B 886; on the shore of Loch Bay. Parking.

17 **Sun Inn**

Lothian Bridge,
Dalkeith, EH22 4TR
Tel.: (0131)6632456
Website: www.thesuninnedinburgh.co.uk

VISA AE

Sun Inn IPA, Foxy Blonde

Set on the main road from Edinburgh to Galashiels, this smartly refurbished pub started life in the 17C as a blacksmith's, only later becoming a coaching inn. It's a large place, consisting of two open-fired rooms with part wood and part stone-faced walls; all hung with contemporary black and white photos of the area. Menus are extensive and feature good quality local produce, with suppliers listed on a blackboard. Lunch keeps things simple – you might find ham hock potato cakes, kipper pâté or liver and bacon – while dinner is more ambitious, with the likes of monkfish wrapped in ham, pigs cheek and black pudding or sea bass with saffron risotto. Completing the picture are smart, modern bedrooms boasting handmade furniture and Egyptian cotton.

CLOSING TIMES
Open daily

PRICES
Meals: £ 14 (lunch and early dinner) and a la carte £ 13/28

5 rooms: £ 70/175

Typical Dishes

Braised local pig's cheek & black pudding
Pan-roast duck breast with confit duckling
Sea buckthorn crème brûlée

2 mi Southwest of Dalkeith on A 7. Parking.

18 Tormaukin Inn

Glendevon,
FK14 7JY
Tel.: (01259)781252
Website: www.tormaukinhotel.co.uk

VISA MC

Harviston Bitter and Twisted and other guest ales

After a breathtaking drive along the A823, stop at the door of this characterful inn, where the owner and manageress will welcome you in as if you're old friends. Across the threshold, a huge granite fireplace greets you; pass by it and you'll come to a dark, beamed bar and spacious, traditionally decorated dining room – with a conservatory breakfast room for residents beyond. Carefully executed dishes are largely traditional – you might find smoked salmon or shank of lamb – but there's also the odd contemporary nod with offerings such as Strathdon blue cheese mousse or seared tuna with ginger and soy; while tasty homemade breads and ice creams come at either end. Tartan-floored bedrooms are spread between the inn, stable block and chalet.

CLOSING TIMES
Open daily

PRICES
Meals: a la carte £ 18/35
13 rooms: £ 55/80

Typical Dishes

Seared scallops with black pudding
Wild duck breast with raspberry jus
Lemon posset

In centre of village on A823. Parking.

19 **Strathardle Inn**

Kirkmichael,
PH10 7NS
Tel.: (01250)881224
Website: www.strathardleinn.co.uk

VISA MC

Thrappledouser, Pentland IPA, Beltane, Tradewinds

As you leave the village of Kirkmichael, heading south towards Blairgowrie on the A924, you pass by this 18C drover's inn, opposite the river. Stop off instead and experience the warm welcome extended by the owners; they hail from Yorkshire originally but are now deeply rooted in this beautiful part of Scotland – a fact that reveals itself in their judicious use of seasonal produce from the surrounding countryside. Cooking is robust and technically sound, with a Scottish twist. The concise lunch menu offers pub favourites like fish and chips, while dinner might feature local venison, smoked salmon or sirloin steak highlander and can be taken in either the bar or the dining room, both of which boast open fires. Bedrooms are simple and modern.

CLOSING TIMES
Closed Tuesday-Friday lunch November-March and Monday lunch

PRICES
Meals: a la carte £ 21/31
8 rooms: £ 45/80

Typical Dishes
Clapshot pancakes with melted goat's cheese
Medallions of local wild venison
Lanark Blue cheese with handmade oatcakes

Between Pitlochry and Blairgowrie on A 924. Parking.

It's nearly six hundred years since Owen Glyndawr escaped the clutches of the English to become a national hero, and in all that time the Welsh passion for unity has bound the country together like a scarlet-shirted scrum. It may be only 170 miles from north to south, but Wales contains great swathes of beauty, such as the dark and craggy heights of Snowdonia's ninety mountain peaks, the rolling sandstone bluffs of the Brecon Beacons, and Pembrokeshire's tantalising golden beaches. Bottle-nosed dolphins love it here too, arriving each summer at New Quay in Cardigan Bay. Highlights abound: formidable Harlech Castle dominates its coast, and Bala Lake has a railway that steams along its gentle shores. Hay-on-Wye's four pubs and eighteen bookshops turn perceptions on their head, and Welsh cuisine is causing a surprise or two as well: the country teems with great raw ingredients now employed to their utmost potential, from the humblest cockle to the slenderest slice of succulent lamb.

6 Pubs without bedrooms
7 Pubs with bedrooms
BAILE ÁTHA CLIATH
Douglas (I. of Man)
Liverpool
Belfast
Dublin
Holyhead / Caergybi
Holy Island
Isle of Anglesey
ANGLESEY
Amlwch
Llanerchymedd
Llangefni
Rhosneigr
Beaumaris
Menai Bridge
Newborough
Great Ormes Head
Llandudno
Colwyn Bay / Bae Colwyn
Rhyl
Conwy
Bangor
Penmaenmawr
Llanfairfechan
Bethesda
Carnedd Llewelyn
Abergele
St Asaph
Denbigh / Dinbych
Llanrwst
Capel Curig
Betws-y-Coed
Caernarfon
Caernarfon Bay
Llanberis
Snowdon
Snowdonia
Beddgelert
Blaenau Ffestiniog
Ffestiniog
Pentrefoelas
Cerrigydrudion
Nefyn
Lleyn Peninsula
Pwllheli
Abersoch
Aberdaron
Criccieth
Porthmadog
Penrhyndeudraeth
Harlech
GWYNEDD
SNOWDONIA
National
Park
Bala
Corwen
Llangollen
Berwyn
Oswestry
Dolgellau
Barmouth
Cader Idris
Tywyn
Aberdovey
Machynlleth
Mallwyd
Caersws
Newtown
Welshpool / Y Trallwng
Llanfyllin
Llynclys
Shrewsbury
Ruthin / Rhuthun
Mold / Yr Wyddgrug
Prestatyn
Mostyn
Holywell
Flint / Fflint
Queensferry
Chester
Wrexham / Wrecsam
Ruabon
Ellesmere
Whitchurch
Wem
Hodnet
Market Drayton
Eccleshall
Newport
Telford
WREKIN
Ironbridge
Bridgnorth
Minsterley
Montgomery
Stretton
SHROPSHIRE
WALES
West Midlands
North West
LIVERPOOL
Liverpool Bay
Southport
Lytham St. Anne's
Preston
Leyland
Chorley
Darwen
Bury
Bolton
Wigan
Ainsdale
Formby
Ormskirk
Skelmersdale
St. Helens
Warrington
Widnes
Runcorn
Frodsham
Leigh
Altrincham
Wallasey
Bootle
Hoylake
Birkenhead
Bebington
Ellesmere Port
Northwich
Winsford
Middlewich
Sandbach
Tarporley
Crewe
Nantwich
Newcastle under Lyme
Audlem
Severn

WALES
POWYS
CEREDIGION
CAMBRIAN MOUNTAINS
CARMARTHENSHIRE
PEMBROKESHIRE
HEREFORD
South West
BRISTOL CHANNEL
Pembrokeshire Coast National Park
Brecon Beacons National Park
Black Mountains
Strumble Head
St. David's Head
St. Bride's Bay
St. Govan's Head
Worms Head
Carmarthen Bay
Severn Estuary
Lundy
Fishguard
Abergwaun
Haverfordwest
Hwlffordd
Milford Haven/
Aberdaugleddau
Pembroke Dock/
Doc Penfro
Pembroke
Tenby/
Dinbych-y-pysgod
Saundersfoot
Carmarthen
Caerfyrddin
St. Clears
Llanelli
Swansea/
Abertawe
Port Talbot
Neath/
Castell-nedd
Bridgend/
Pen-y-bont
Merthyr Tydfil
Brecon/
Aberhonddu
Abergavenny/
Y Fenni
Monmouth
Trefynwy
NEWPORT/
CASNEWYDD
CARDIFF/
CAERDYDD
Barry/
Barri
Cardigan
Aberteifi
Aberaeron
New Quay
Llanrhystud
Devil's Bridge
Tregaron
Lampeter
Llandovery
Llanymddyfri
Llandrindod Wells
Builth Wells/
Llanfair-ym-Muallt
Hay-on-Wye
Rhayader
Rhaeadr
Knighton
Presteigne
Kington
Hereford
Ross-on-Wye
Gloucester
Worcester
Kidderminster
Ludlow
Leominster
Ledbury
Great Malvern
Chepstow
BRISTOL
Bath
Weston-Super-Mare
Clevedon
Wells
Glastonbury
Bridgwater
Burnham
Minehead
Ilfracombe
Barnstaple
Lynton
Lynmouth
Porlock
Exmoor
Frome
Rosslare
Cork

Rhoscolyn

1 **White Eagle**

Rhoscolyn,
LL65 2NJ
Tel.: (01407)860267
Website: www.white-eagle.co.uk

VISA

Marston's Best, Cobblers, Weetwood and various guest ales

Set in a small coastal hamlet on the peninsula, this pub boasts stunning sea views from its spacious decked terrace. From the outside it may look more like a restaurant but swing a right through the door and you'll find locals playing on slot machines in a cosy open-fired bar. It's rightly popular, so you might have to wait for a table; fill your time by glancing over the display of the owners' business history – they also own Timpson Shoe Repairs. The monthly menu offers something for everyone and dishes arrive well-presented, in a contemporary style; whether it's the huge battered haddock and chips or pan-fried salmon with prawn and chorizo butter. Daily fish specials, regular pie or sausage weeks and weekend beer festivals also feature.

CLOSING TIMES
Open daily

PRICES
Meals: a la carte £ 22/33

Typical Dishes

Lamb medaillons
Rump steak
Sticky toffee pudding

5 mi south of Holyhead by B 4545 and minor road south. Parking.

2 New Conway

53 Conway Rd,
Cardiff, CF11 9NW
Tel.: (029)20224373
Website: www.theconway.co.uk

VISA MC

Greene King IPA, Otley, Vale of Glamorgan, Newmans, Wickwar

Set in a residential area just north of the city and very much a place for local drinkers, The New Conway offers everything from a pint and a bowl of chips whilst you watch the rugby, through to a three course meal and a bottle of wine from the well-priced list. A makeover has given the pub a light, modern feel, with comfy sofas by the fire and shelves crammed with books and board games. Although prone to the odd over-elaboration, their approach to food is, in the main, pleasingly simple: using fresh, seasonal and local produce to create tasty pub classics like steak and chips, toad in the hole or apple and raisin crumble. Having chosen from the daily changing blackboard menu, place your order at the bar; service is friendly and efficient.

CLOSING TIMES
Open daily

PRICES
Meals: a la carte £ 25/34

Typical Dishes

Scotch egg with aioli
Barnsley chop with minted broad bean & pea salad
Sherry trifle

Parking in neighbouring roads.

3 **Y Polyn**

Nantgaredig,
SA32 7LH
Tel.: (01267)290000
Website: www.ypolynrestaurant.co.uk

VISA MC AE

Otley 01 and Otley 03 Boss

Collectively, the owners here have a wealth of experience, gleaned from their various backgrounds, so you can be sure that they know what they're doing. Set in a great corner location, next to a stream and with views across the surrounding fields, this pub attracts diners from far and wide. Contemporary colours lead the way in the dining room but it also manages to maintains some of its original rustic style – yet despite the casual attire of the servers, most guests still dress to the nines. Cooking is in the classical vein but has a modern edge and, as you would expect, is hearty, tasty and uses local produce wherever possible. Lunch offers an à la carte and 'express' 3 course menu, while in the evening there's a fixed price selection.

CLOSING TIMES
Closed Sunday dinner and Monday

PRICES
Meals: £ 15/30
and a la carte £ 21/30

Typical Dishes

Scallops, crispy Carmarthen ham & chive dressing

Sewin with beurre blanc

Rhubarb Eton mess

1 mi south on B 4310. Parking.

4

Harbourmaster

Quay Par,
Aberaeron, SA46 0BA
Tel.: (01545)570755
Website: www.harbour-master.com

VISA MC

HM Best Bitter, Cwrw Glasglyn, Dark side of the Moose

With its vibrant blue exterior, you'll spot this place a mile off; not that the owners need worry about being noticed, as their reputation for good food and hospitality goes before them. As the name suggests, it once belonged to the harbourmaster, and, as such, offers lovely views across the water. Inside, there's a modern bar-lounge with an oval pewter-topped counter and open-plan kitchen, as well as a more traditional wood-panelled dining room – make a play for 'cwtch', a table offering excellent harbour views. Choose between the bar menu or a more substantial evening à la carte supplemented by daily specials. Split between the house and nearby cottage, bedrooms are comfy and brightly decorated; some boast oversized windows or terraces.

CLOSING TIMES
Closed 25 December

PRICES
Meals: a la carte £ 32/41
13 rooms: £ 65/195

Typical Dishes

Crab spring rolls
Rib of beef with skinny fries & béarnaise
Hot chocolate fondant with salted caramel

In town centre overlooking the harbour. Parking on the harbour road.

Llanfihangel-y-Creuddyn

5 **Y Ffarmers**

Llanfihangel-y-Creuddyn,
SY23 4LA
Tel.: (01974)261275
Website: www.yffarmers.co.uk

VISA MC

Guest beers from Purple Moose and Felinfoel Breweries

More than just the village pub, the passionately run Y Ffarmers is also the village hub. A characterful whitewashed building in a remote, picturesque valley, it was originally a farm and later a tax collector's office. With no village hall, life here really revolves around the place, which hosts everything from yoga classes and quiz nights to meetings of the local choir and bee keeping group. Turn right for the locals bar or left for the homely, open-fired restaurant, which opens out into the garden. The concise, monthly à la carte offers a good range of satisfying, original dishes that are big on flavour. Most produce is from the valley, including locally grown organic veg, game from nearby shoots, and lobster and crab from Cardigan Bay.

CLOSING TIMES
Closed first week January, Monday except bank holidays, Sunday dinner and lunch Tuesday-Wednesday

PRICES
Meals: a la carte £ 17/29

Typical Dishes

Crab cake with saffron aioli
Sirloin steak with béarnaise sauce
Penlanlas strawberries & meringue

7.75 mi southeast of Aberystwyth by A 487 and A 4120, turning right after Pant-y-crug. Parking in the village square.

6 **Pen-y-Bryn**

Pen-y-Bryn Rd,
Upper Colwyn Bay, Colwyn Bay, LL29 6DD
Tel.: (01492)533360
Website: www.penybryn-colwynbay.co.uk

VISA MC AE

Brunning and Price Original, Timothy Taylor Landlord, Purple Moose Snowdonia

You might need your sat nav, as even when you've located the right residential street, you could easily pass Pen-y-Bryn by. Looking more like a medical centre than a place to dine, it boasts impressive panoramic views over Colwyn Bay, especially from the garden and terrace. The spacious, open-plan interior is crammed full of pictures, bookcases and pottery, yet despite these and the oak floors, old furniture and open fires, it has a modern, laid-back feel. The extensive all-day menu offers plenty of choice, ranging from a classical ploughman's to more adventurous pheasant-based dishes; while during 'Beer and Bangers' weeks 12 varieties of sausage and over 20 beers are also offered. Large tables make it ideal for families or groups of friends.

CLOSING TIMES
Closed 25 December

PRICES
Meals: a la carte £ 17/24

Typical Dishes

Spicy potted shrimps
Chinese crispy beef salad with sweet chilli dressing
Bread & butter pudding

1 mi southwest of Colwyn Bay by B 5113. Parking.

7 **Kinmel Arms**

The Village,
St George, LL22 9BP
Tel.: (01745)832207
Website: www.thekinmelarms.co.uk

VISA

Thwaites Original and beers from Great Orme, Facers and Conwy Breweries

This early 17C stone inn is hidden away in a hamlet by the entrance to Kinmel Hall. It's the type of pub that's not entirely sure if it wants to be a pub or a restaurant. True, there's a delightful open-fired bar with slate-topped counter and low-level seating which hosts regular events for the locals. But, there are also two spacious dining areas – one with chunky wood furniture, the other, with a conservatory feel – where the service and the food are much more formal; you might find confit of duck, rack of lamb or locally shot game. They keep cows, sheep and chickens, and even grow their own fruit and herbs in a small polytunnel. Stylish, contemporary bedrooms boast large kitchenettes, so you can have your continental breakfast in your PJs.

CLOSING TIMES
Closed 1 January, 25 December, Sunday, Monday and bank holidays

PRICES
Meals: a la carte £ 23/41
4 rooms: £ 115/175

Typical Dishes
Seafood assiette
Duo of Welsh spring lamb
Steamed rhubarb pudding

In the centre of village. Parking.

8

Groes Inn

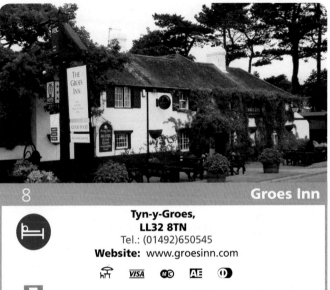

Tyn-y-Groes,
LL32 8TN
Tel.: (01492)650545
Website: www.groesinn.com

VISA MC AE

Great Orme Brewery and Groes Ale

Located in the foothills of Snowdonia, with the estuary in front and the mountains behind, the setting couldn't be more beautiful. Flowers greet you at the door and the characterful beamed interior is filled with pictures, copperware and china; all bathed in flickering firelight. If you're after nooks and crannies, there are several small rooms encircling the comfy bar, as well as an airy conservatory and an intimate dining room. The bar menu features local Welsh and British dishes in neatly presented, generous portions, while at dinner the restaurant steps things up a gear. Specials feature fish from the nearby waters, lamb reared on the salt marshes and game from local estates. Bedrooms have lovely views; some boast balconies or terraces.

CLOSING TIMES
Closed 25 December

PRICES
Meals: a la carte £ 18/42
14 rooms: £ 95/190

Typical Dishes

Welsh rarebit with black pudding
Seafood platter
Banana & hazelnut pancake

3 mi south of Conwy on B 5106. Parking.

9 **Glasfryn**

Raikes Ln,
Sychdyn, Mold, CH7 6LR
Tel.: (01352)750500
Website: www.glasfryn-mold.co.uk

VISA AE

Snowdonia Ale, Flowers Original

An early example of Arts and Crafts architecture, this glazed red-brick building was intended to be a judges' residence for the nearby courts but, never used, was turned into a farmhouse, before later falling into disrepair. It's a sizeable place, able to cater for a few hundred at every sitting, with some tables seating up to 20 at a time. Order at the large central bar and watch your order whizz past in the vacuum tube system on its way to the kitchen. Menus offer plenty of choice, from pub classics such as fish and chips to culinary classics such as plaice Véronique, with some lighter dishes alongside. Portions are generous, prices are sensible and service is surprisingly swift. The garden and terrace boast nice views over the town below.

CLOSING TIMES
Closed 25 December

PRICES
Meals: a la carte £ 22/33

Typical Dishes

Morecambe Bay potted shrimps

Braised chicken in red wine

Hot waffle with honeycomb ice cream

1 mi north by A 5119 on Civic Centre rd. Parking.

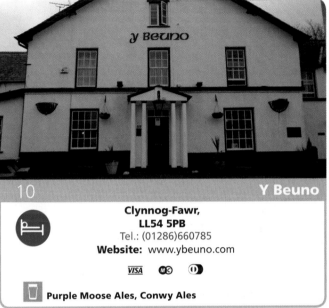

10 **Y Beuno**

Clynnog-Fawr,
LL54 5PB
Tel.: (01286)660785
Website: www.ybeuno.com

VISA

Purple Moose Ales, Conwy Ales

Named after Saint Beuno, whose church is located opposite, this historic coaching inn was originally built by the Lord of Newburgh, who owned a vast estate to the North of Caernarfon. It's a sizeable place, set just 100 yards from the coast, and consists of a delightfully rustic bar and a series of snug, homely rooms. At first glance the menu may not seem anything out of the ordinary but head for the daily specials boards and think again. The key here is to choose a classic Gallic dish from the chef's homeland; maybe a homemade mallard terrine, followed by a perfectly executed Rossini-style steak. In summer, local seafood is a feature, with fresh, unfussy fish dishes filling the boards. Bedrooms are comfy and modern, and some boast bay views.

CLOSING TIMES
Restricted opening in winter

PRICES
Meals: a la carte £ 23/34
7 rooms: £ 75/135

Typical Dishes

Wild mallard pâté
Fillet of beef Rossini
Chocolate fudge cake

Southwest 9 mi from Caernarfon by A 487 and A 499. Parking.

Llandenny

11 **Raglan Arms**

Llandenny,
NP15 1DL
Tel.: (01291)690800
Website: www.raglanarms.com

VISA MC AE

Wye Valley Butty Bach and Breconshire Brewery

With fireside leather sofas, simply laid scrubbed pine tables and vases filled with fresh flowers, The Raglan Arms offers a wholesome cosiness; dining happens mostly in the front of the room, while drinkers tend to congregate in the conservatory at the back. Menus change slightly at each service and are short and to the point. The kitchen is clearly serious about food, using local produce wherever possible and employing a range of cooking styles. Dishes could include home cured bresaola, imam bayildi with mint and crème fraîche or goujons of lemon sole, while dessert might mean a panna cotta or some homemade ice cream and sorbets. There is always a sandwich available at lunch, and main courses offer particularly good value for money.

CLOSING TIMES
Closed 25-26 December

PRICES
Meals: a la carte £ 29/36

Typical Dishes

Local ox tongue with Puy lentils

Bryngwyn lamb loin & breast

Valrhona bitter chocolate & bran torte

In centre of the village. Parking.

12 **White Hart**

Llangybi,
NP15 1NP
Tel.: (01633)450258
Website: www.thewhitehartvillageinn.com

VISA

Tomos Watkin Brewery - Chwarae Teg, Abercwrw

The 16C White Hart became the property of Henry VIII as part of Jane Seymour's dowry and a century later, during the civil war, Oliver Cromwell used it as his Monmouthshire headquarters. The characterful interior proudly shows off 11 fireplaces from the 1600s, ornate Tudor plasterwork and a priest's hole; if that's not enough, it's even referred to by TS Elliot in the poem 'Usk'. Lunchtime sees a blackboard menu, while dinner offers a more ambitious à la carte, with a good value 'Market Menu' Tuesday to Thursday. Restaurant-style dishes are well-prepared and precisely presented – with many arriving on slates – and most ingredients come from within a 10 mile radius. You might find smoked salmon risotto, duck confit or roast loin of veal.

CLOSING TIMES
Closed Monday except bank holidays

PRICES
Meals: a la carte £ 29/38

Typical Dishes

Soy & sesame quail
Duck breast with chorizo & lentils
Pineapple carpaccio

2 mi south of Usk turning left after bridge over river Usk on to road signposted to Llangybi. Parking.

Skenfrith

13 **Bell at Skenfrith**

Skenfrith,
NP7 8UH
Tel.: (01600)750235
Website: www.skenfrith.co.uk

VISA

Wye Valley Bitter, Wye Valley Hereford Pale Ale

The Bell offers uncomplicated warmth: a seat in a comfy sofa by the inglenook, candles and meadow flowers on the tables and friendly, unobtrusive service. The weekly changing menu features dishes with an innovative modern twist; these might include rolled fishcakes, confit of duck leg or sirloin of Brecon Beef with mini steak and kidney pudding. Ingredients are allowed to speak for themselves, with local suppliers credited on the menu and much produce coming from their own organic kitchen garden. Fruits of the vine are also taken seriously, with a large selection of wines by the glass and an impressive choice of champagnes and cognacs. Bedrooms are understated in their elegance, with super-comfy beds, fluffy towels and personalised toiletries.

CLOSING TIMES
Closed last week January and first week February
booking essential

PRICES
Meals: £ 20 (lunch) and a la carte £ 26/36
11 rooms: £ 120/220

Typical Dishes
Stuffed loin of local rabbit with braised leg rillettes
Loin of Welsh bred pork with black pudding
Poached meringues with vanilla & thyme panna cotta

11 mi west of Ross-on-Wye by A 49 on B 4521. Parking.

14 Felin Fach Griffin

Felin Fach,
Brecon, LD3 0UB
Tel.: (01874)620111
Website: www.felinfachgriffin.co.uk

VISA

Wye Valley Brewery, Otley Brewery, Breconshire Brewery and Monty's Brewery

A terracotta-coloured former farmhouse set in picturesque countryside, this pub is rather unique, in that you'll find visitors aged from 1-100 and from all walks of life – which creates an almost bohemian atmosphere. Bright paintwork, colourful art and the scattering of magazines about the place provide a very 'lived in' feel and the atmosphere is extremely laid-back. The young staff interact well but, just as importantly, have a good knowledge of what they're serving. Starters like local goat's curd with black olive purée or brawn with apricot chutney are followed by Welsh Cobb coq au vin or red mullet with salt cod brandade – and are a cut above your usual pub grub. If you've eaten yourself to a stand still, super-comfy bedrooms await.

CLOSING TIMES
Closed 25 December

PRICES
Meals: £ 19/27
and a la carte £ 25/33

7 rooms: £ 75/115

Typical Dishes

Leek & potato soup
Roast rib of Welsh beef
Pink rhubarb trifle

4.75 mi northeast of Brecon by B 4602 off A 470. Parking.

Crickhowell

15 **Bear**

High St,
Crickhowell, NP8 1BW
Tel.: (01873)810408
Website: www.bearhotel.co.uk

VISA MC AE

Rhymney, Reverend James, Henry's and guest ale

The well-maintained Bear stands proudly on the main street of this small town, its hanging baskets creating a riot of colour. Step through the front door into its hugely characterful lounge bar, with its shiny brass and open fireplaces, and you can well believe that it has been here since 1432. Diners can sit here or in the more formal restaurant; the latter may be more romantic but the former is undoubtedly the more appealing. The menu offers tasty, tried-and-tested dishes such as prawn cocktail, Welsh rarebit, fish and chips or lasagne. The 'specials' add interest and a young cheery team provide swift and assured service, even when busy. Bedrooms are available in the hotel: the most characterful feature beams, four-posters and fireplaces.

CLOSING TIMES
Closed 25 December

PRICES
Meals: a la carte £ 22/35

Typical Dishes

Scallop & crayfish salad

Lamb's liver, shallots, bubble & squeak

Bread & butter pudding

In the town centre. Parking.

16 **Old Black Lion**

26 Lion St,
Hay-on-Wye, HR3 5AD
Tel.: (01497)820841
Website: www.oldblacklion.co.uk

VISA MC AE

Old Black Lion, Sharp's Doom Bar

This part-13C pub stands on the site of the old gates in this ancient market town and would once have provided refuge for travellers passing from Ireland to England. Although its visitors have now changed – here for the antique shops and annual literary festival – the pub has not. Inside you'll find low beams, scrubbed wooden tables and plenty of old world charm, albeit among more modern, brightly coloured walls. The food here is tasty, honest and arrives in hearty portions, and menus offer a seemingly endless list of dishes – with even more favourites chalked up on the board – maybe duck on parsnip purée or herb crusted lamb. Bedrooms in the main building display antique furnishings; those opposite boast rich colours and modern bathrooms.

CLOSING TIMES
Closed 24-26 December

PRICES
Meals: a la carte £ 23/34
10 rooms: £ 53/90

Typical Dishes
Goats' cheese salad
Herb-crusted rack of local Welsh lamb
Chocolate cheesecake

In the town centre. Parking.

17

Three Tuns

4 Broad St,
Hay-on-Wye, HR3 5DB
Tel.: (01497)821855
Website: www.three-tuns.com

VISA MC AE

Wye Valley Bitter, Butty Bach

After being devastated by fire in 2005, the future of this Grade II listed pub – thought to be the oldest surviving building in Hay-on-Wye – was left hanging in the balance. Thankfully though, two dedicated locals picked up the pieces, saving many original features including cruck truss beams, a period dog-leg staircase and large inglenook fireplace. Downstairs, the bar leads through to cosy sofas set beneath a big glass roof and then on to the terrace; find a seat, study the wide-ranging, classical menu and make for the bar to order. The deep-fried cod in local Wye Valley Butty Bach beer-batter is a favourite but if you'd rather have it crab-crusted, wait 'til the evening and head for the more formal first floor with its friendly table service.

CLOSING TIMES
Open daily

PRICES
Meals: a la carte £ 22/32

Typical Dishes

Black Mountain smoked salmon

New seasons lamb's liver and crispy cured Talgarth ham

Ginger cake & poached pear

In the town centre. Parking in pay and display car park nearby on Oxford Rd.

18 Harp Inn

Old Radnor,
LD8 2RH
Tel.: (01544)350655
Website: www.harpinnradnor.co.uk

VISA

Timothy Taylor, Spitfire, Tribute and locally brewed ales

Built to house workers constructing the medieval church, this 15C stone inn welcomes its drinkers and diners alike. On a warm summer's day take a seat outside and make the most of the glorious view; in colder weather, head through to find a charming, flag-floored room with warming open fire, its beams hung with hop bines. 'Seasonality' and 'sustainability' are keywords here; breads, ice creams and crackers are homemade and everything else is locally sourced. Menus may be concise but dishes are original; you might find leek and ale rarebit, scrambled egg and home-spiced chorizo or mackerel fillet with fennel spelt risotto – while the Welsh Black beef with triple-cooked chips has become a mainstay. Simple bedrooms come with wonderful views.

CLOSING TIMES
Closed Monday except bank holidays and lunch Tuesday-Friday - restricted opening in winter

PRICES
Meals: a la carte £ 22/28
5 rooms: £ 50/85

Typical Dishes

Vegetable soup with homemade bread

Welsh Black rump steak with triple cooked chips

'Kuku U Kul' chocolate mousse

Signposted south off A 44 east of Llandrindod Wells just before crossing the border into England. Parking.

Pontdolgoch

19 Talkhouse

Newtown,
Pontdolgoch, SY17 5JE
Tel.: (01686)688919
Website: www.talkhouse.co.uk

VISA

Montys Midnight, Montys Mischief

Run by an experienced husband and wife team, The Talkhouse has the look and feel of a small house. There's a comfy lounge with old photos of the village on the wall, and a cosy bar with seats around the fire for the drinkers. The colourful rear garden, with its gazebo and terrace, is the owners' pride and joy and the best tables in the house are those in the back room which overlook it. Cooking has a very masculine feel, with hearty portions and bold flavours; the menu is chalked up on a blackboard and changes daily. Dishes might include Welsh lamb rump or pan-fried fish; desserts are read out at the end and might include cheesecake or sticky toffee pudding. Bedrooms have antique pine furniture and colourful furnishings; Myfanwy is the best.

CLOSING TIMES
Closed 2 weeks January, Monday and Tuesday
booking essential

PRICES
Meals: a la carte £ 25/35
3 rooms: £ 70/125

Typical Dishes

Smoked haddock rarebit
Fillet of beef with rösti potato & pan juices
Crème brûlée

1.5 mi northwest of Caersws on A 470. Parking.

20 Blue Anchor Inn

East Aberthaw,
CF62 3DD
Tel.: (01446)750329
Website: www.blueanchoraberthaw.com

VISA MC

Wadworth 6X, Brains Bitter, Wye Valley IPA, Theakston Old Peculiar and Hereford Pale Ale plus one guest beer changing weekly

The name of this pub dates back to 1380, when East Aberthaw was a bustling trading port and the ships that moored in the bay would leave with their anchors covered in a distinctive blue mud. Inside the stone walls and thatched roof of this medieval pub you'll find low beamed ceilings, exposed brick walls, and nooks and crannies aplenty. You enter into a slate-floored drinkers bar and dimly lit dining area but the real surprise is the vast upstairs restaurant which is open for dinner and Sunday lunch. Cooking is traditional and wholesome with straightforward presentation and flavoursome combinations. At lunch you'll find simple dishes such as grilled gammon or beef stew, and in the evening, more interesting offerings like pan-seared wood pigeon.

CLOSING TIMES
Closed Sunday dinner

PRICES
Meals: a la carte £ 17/28

Typical Dishes

Twice-baked cheese soufflé

Pan-fried hake loin with a shellfish velouté

Strawberry parfait

Turn south off B 4265 past cement factory following the road for 0.75 mi. Parking opposite the pub.

Gresford

21 **Pant-yr-Ochain**

Old Wrexham Rd,
Gresford, LL12 8TY
Tel.: (01978)853525
Website: www.pantyrochain-gresford.co.uk

VISA MC AE

Titanic Stout, Snowdonia Ale, Weetwood Eastace, BSP Ltd and Flowers Origional

This is neither a typical rustic inn nor a 21C dining pub – but a classical country manor house in disguise. With Tudor wattle and daub walls backing a 16C inglenook fireplace, the place is steeped in history. Outside, mature gardens and well-manicured lawns stretch down to a small lake; and on a warm summer's day, lunch on the terrace or lawn is hard to beat. In rainier weather, follow the polished quarry tiled floors to the large central bar and choose from one of the numerous rooms surrounding it; some with ancient beams and exposed brick walls, all with nooks and crannies aplenty. The daily changing menu offers hearty, wholesome, all-day dishes, ranging from pies and casseroles to more interesting offerings like hake with crab butter.

CLOSING TIMES
Closed 25 December

PRICES
Meals: a la carte £ 20/31

Typical Dishes

Crab, crayfish, pink grapefruit & avocado salad
Fish pie
Sticky toffee pudding

4.5 mi northeast of Wrexham by A 483 and B 5445. Parking.

22 Hand at Llanarmon

Llanarmon Dyffryn Ceiriog,
LL20 7LD
Tel.: (01691)600666
Website: www.thehandhotel.co.uk

VISA MC

Weetwoods Eastgate, Wye Valley HPA, Three Tuns 1642

Set at the crossroads of two old drovers' roads, The Hand has been providing hospitality for several centuries and its current owners are continuing the tradition with flair, providing a warm welcome and hearty meals to travellers through this lush valley. Rustic charm abounds in the form of stone walls, open fires and ancient beams; there' s a cosy bar, a spacious dining room, a pool room and quite a collection of taxidermy. The daily changing menu offers loads of choice, with plenty of wholesome pub classics like steak and kidney pie or slow braised lamb shank. Portions are generous and cooking is fresh and flavoursome. Cosy bedrooms have hill views and recently modernised bathrooms – plus a decanter of sherry for a late night tipple.

CLOSING TIMES
Open daily

PRICES
Meals: £ 20 and a la carte £ 21/33
13 rooms: £ 50/128

Typical Dishes

Llyn Peninsula crab plate
4-hour braised Welsh lamb shoulder
Bramley apple crumble

At the head of Ceiriog Valley northwest of Oswestry. Parking.

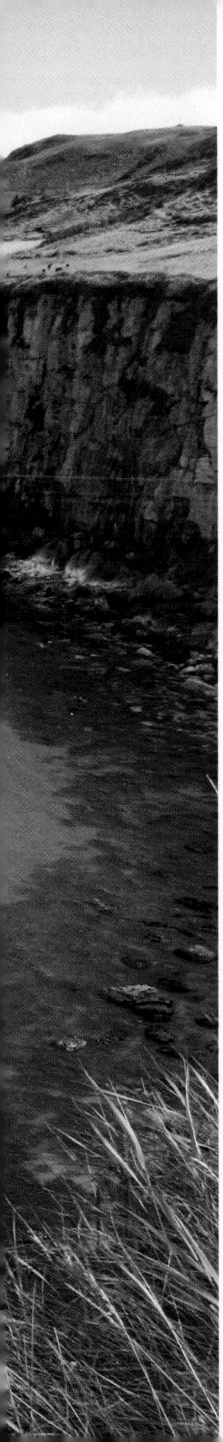

The presiding image of Northern Ireland for outsiders is buzzing Belfast, lying defiantly between mountain and coast. Its City Hall and Queen's University retain the power to impress, and it was within its mighty shipyards that the Titanic first saw the light of day. But the rest of the Six Counties demands attention, too. The forty thousand stone columns of the Giant's Causeway step out into the Irish Sea, part of a grand coastline, though Antrim can also boast nine scenic inland glens. County Down's rolling hills culminate in the alluring slopes of Slieve Donard in the magical Mourne Mountains, while Armagh's Orchard County is a riot of pink in springtime. Fermanagh's glassy, silent lakelands are a tranquil attraction, rivalled for their serenity by the heather-clad Sperrin Mountains, towering over Tyrone and Derry. On top of all this is the cultural lure of boisterous oyster festivals and authentic horse fairs, while farmers' markets are now prominent all across the province.

2 Pubs without bedrooms
3 Pubs with bedrooms
Scotland
NORTHERN IRELAND
Ireland
Wales
Coll
Tiree
Tobermory
Mull
Craignure
Fionnphort
Oban
Colonsay
Lochgilphead
Islay
Port Askaig
Jura
Rothesay
Port Ellen
Kintyre
Brodick
Campbeltown
Arran
Malin Head
Giant's Causeway
Buncrana
Lough Foyle
Portrush
Letterkenny
Londonderry / Derry
Coleraine
Ballycastle
Antrim Glens
Donegal
Bundoran
Omagh
Larne
Lough Neagh
Lisburn
Bangor
BELFAST
Sligo
Enniskillen
Armagh
Monaghan
Boyle
Newry
Newcastle
Cavan
Stranraer
Cairnryan
North Channel
Dundalk
Longford
Roscommon
Ardee
Lough Ree
Drogheda
Navan
Athlone
Mullingar
Kinnegad
R. Boyne
Ballinasloe
IRL
Tullamore
DUBLIN
Naas
Dún Laoghaire
Birr
Portlaoise
Roscrea
Bray
Glendalough
Wicklow
Carlow
Kilkenny
Arklow
Cashel
Clonmel
Caher
New Ross
Enniscorthy
R. Barrow
R. Suir
Peel
Anglesey
Holyhead
Caernarfon
Snowdon
IRISH S
Liverpool
1
2
3
4
5
6
7

1 **Pheasant**

410 Upper Ballynahinch Rd,
Annahilt, BT26 6NR
Tel.: (028)92638056
Website: www.thepheasantrestaurant.co.uk

VISA MC AE D

No real ales offered

Set in the heart of County Down, this sizeable yellow-washed inn has a typically Irish feel; right through from the old Guinness posters to the warm welcome and laid-back atmosphere. It has a Gothic style, featuring stained glass, hunting murals and ornaments aplenty; the traditional open-fired bar being the place to sit when it's cold and the patio providing the ideal spot in warmer months. Cooking uses seasonal produce, with local seafood the speciality in summer and game from the nearby estate in winter – and children are well catered for too, with a dedicated selection of freshly prepared dishes; not forgetting toys and climbing frames. It's a popular place, so if you're in a group it could be worth booking the snug or Gamekeepers Loft.

CLOSING TIMES
Closed 12 July and 25-26 December

PRICES
Meals: £ 10/12 and a la carte £ 15/30

Typical Dishes

Warm Chinese duck salad

Fillet steak with tobacco onions

Cheesecake indulgence

1 mi north of Annahilt on Lisburn rd. Parking.

2 Coyle's

44 High St,
Bangor, BT20 5AZ
Tel.: (028)91270362
Website: www.coylesbistro.co.uk

VISA MC

Strangford Lough Ales

If you're after a quiet drink and a good meal then this black painted, typically Irish pub is the place to come: there are no rowdy groups or noisy sports fans, just families and friends catching up and couples out for dinners à deux. There's the choice of laid-back bistro with small bar area or smarter first floor restaurant – each with a different menu, but both highlighting a selection of low fat dishes. In the bar you'll find the likes of macaroni cheese, fishcakes or steak, as well as more international flavours such as chilli and ginger chicken. While the bistro menu steps things up a gear with offerings such as smoked salmon and blini gâteau, followed by scallops with spinach risotto or red pepper crusted pork with gnocchi Romana.

CLOSING TIMES
Closed 25 December

PRICES
Meals: a la carte £ 19/30

Typical Dishes

Duck samosa
Silver hake with red wine dressing
Italian red fruit ricotta cheesecake

In the town centre. Pay and display parking 2 min walk.

3 **Salty Dog**

Bangor,
BT20 5EY
Tel.: (028)91270696
Website: www.thesaltydogbistro.com

VISA

Belfast Blonde, Headless Dog

Sister to Grace Neill's in Donaghadee, this large Victorian pub is situated at the head of the harbour, overlooking the lifeboat station. It was once a hotel, dating back to the times when Bangor was a busy seaside resort, and affords pleasant views out over the sea; in summer head for the glass-fronted terrace. Inside it has had a makeover, giving it a smart, modern feel – there's an area of low-level leather seating and twinkling tea lights, a snug bar and a dining room with polished wood tables. Cooking is unfussy, offering everything from fish and chips, whitebait and Strangford Lough mussels, to local meats and game specials, and there's a 2-choice set menu that evolves throughout the day. Good-sized bedrooms come with period charm.

CLOSING TIMES
Closed 25-26 December
booking advisable

PRICES
Meals: £ 19 (lunch)
and a la carte £ 19/28
15 rooms: £ 50/95

Typical Dishes

Pigeon breast & carrot salad
Glenarm salmon with Jersey potatoes
Chocolate pot

By the harbour. Pay and display car park 1min walk away.

Donaghadee

4 **Grace Neill's**

33 High St,
Donaghadee, BT21 0AH
Tel.: (02891)884595
Website: www.graceneills.com

Inspectors' favourites

VISA

No real ales offered

Having first opened as The King's Arms in 1611, the oldest pub in Ireland is still going strong. Renamed in the 1900s after a former landlady who would greet every visitor with a kiss, it boasts characterful beamed snugs crammed full of antique bottles and old pictures; and is the place where smugglers once gathered to plot and scheme. The extensive menu is satisfyingly classical; you might find Portavogie prawn cocktail or Strangford Lough mussels, followed by homemade burgers or local beef and Guinness pie – supplemented by a list of daily seafood specials. For those tight on time, lunch also presents the option of an 'express' menu. Live music is a feature at the weekends and a guitar and tin whistle can always be found behind the bar.

CLOSING TIMES
Open daily

PRICES
Meals: £ 18 (lunch)
and a la carte £ 18/38

Typical Dishes

Pan-fried scallops with smoked salmon

Roast loin of Lough Erne lamb

Dark chocolate & lime mousse

In town centre. Parking.

5 **Pier 36**

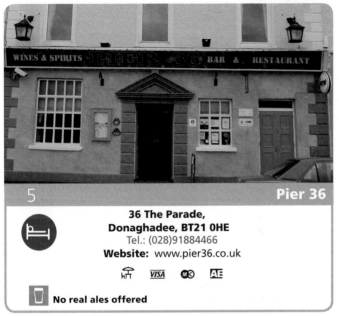

36 The Parade,
Donaghadee, BT21 0HE
Tel.: (028)91884466
Website: www.pier36.co.uk

VISA MC AE

No real ales offered

You couldn't pick a better spot for this family-run pub – it sits on the quayside overlooking the picturesque harbour. But it's not just the location that marks it out – the hospitality here is pretty good too and the owners are continually working hard to give their customers what they want, which explains why so many of them keep coming back. The menus are traditionally based and there's something for everyone. They purchase only the freshest seafood so you can't go wrong with local sole or mussels; they also sell an impressive number of steaks which is due, no doubt, to the fact that they hang and mature the meat themselves to ensure their quality. The bedrooms are bright and in good order; some have great harbour and sea views.

CLOSING TIMES
Closed 25 December

PRICES
Meals: a la carte £ 18/38

7 rooms: £ 50/99

Typical Dishes

Confit of duck

Fillet of cod with smoked salmon & pea risotto

Bread & butter pudding

On the harbour front. Parking in the street and at the rear.

6 **Parson's Nose**

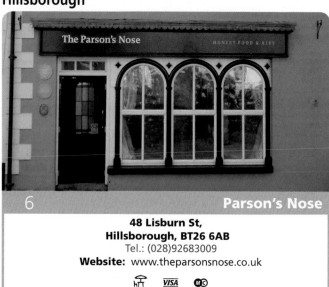

48 Lisburn St,
Hillsborough, BT26 6AB
Tel.: (028)92683009
Website: www.theparsonsnose.co.uk

VISA MC

No real ales offered

The second venture for Danny Millar and Ronan Sweeney is this characterful Georgian inn, which started life as a private house built by the first Marquis of Downshire and dates back to the 18C. The rustic, open-fired bar displays a collection of brewing and distilling paraphernalia, while the dining room above overlooks the Queen's Lake in the grounds of the castle. Food is important here and those in the know will immediately get the culinary reference in the pub's new name. Menus are unashamedly traditional and portions are generous; Dundrum oysters and mussels play a big part and the daily fish specials are always a hit – as is the slow-cooked Dexter shin pie. Puddings are classical and comforting, and the service, quick and efficient.

CLOSING TIMES
Closed 25 December
booking advisable

PRICES
Meals: £ 17/22
and a la carte £ 21/34

Typical Dishes

Mussels in white wine
Dexter beef shin with Belfast stout pie
Vanilla rice pudding

In centre of the town. On-street parking.

7

Plough Inn

3 The Square,
Hillsborough, BT26 6AG
Tel.: (028)92682985
Website: www.bar-retro.com

VISA MC AE D

Hilden Real Ale selection, Old Speckled Hen

From its lush forest and glistening 40 acre lake to its impressive 17C castle and steep streets lined with antique shops, picturesque Hillsborough has plenty to offer, including the locally acclaimed Plough Inn. Having been trading since 1752, it's extremely well-established in the local community – but it's not your usual type of pub. Inside it's almost three establishments in one: the regulars and older folk can be found dining on pub classics in the dark wood bar or on seafood and steak in the similarly styled dining room, while the younger crowds gather upstairs in the stylish bistro, which offers a modern, international menu. Families usually settle next door in the all day café-cum-weekend nightclub and there are plenty of terraces too.

CLOSING TIMES
Closed 25 December

PRICES
Meals: £ 12/20
and a la carte £ 15/25

Typical Dishes

Strangford oyster, crab & sweetcorn broth
Trio of meats
Buttermilk brûlée

At the top of the hill in The Square. Parking.

It's reckoned that Ireland offers forty luminous shades of green, and of course an even more famous shade of black liquid refreshment. But it's not all wondrous hills and down-home pubs. The country does other visitor-friendly phenomena just as idyllically: witness the limestone-layered Burren, cut-through by meandering streams, lakes and labyrinthine caves; or the fabulous Cliffs of Moher, unchanged for millennia, looming for mile after mile over the wild Atlantic waves. The cities burst with life: Dublin is now one of Europe's coolest capitals, and free-spirited Cork enjoys a rich cultural heritage. Kilkenny mixes a renowned medieval flavour with a taste for excellent pubs; Galway, one of Ireland's prettiest cities, is enhanced by an easy, boho vibe. Best of all, perhaps, is to sit along the quayside of a fishing village in the esteemed company of a bowl of steaming fresh mussels or gleaming oysters and the taste of a distinctive micro-brewery beer (well, makes a change from stout…).

3 Pubs without bedrooms
5 Pubs with bedrooms
Northern Ireland
REP. OF IRELAND
IRL
Tiree
Islay
Port Ellen
Malin Head
Buncrana
Lough Foyle
Portrush
Giant's Cause
Letterkenny
Londonderry/Derry
Coleraine
R. Bann
Strabane
Donegal
Omagh
Bundoran
Belmullet
Sligo
Enniskillen
Ballina
Achill
Armagh
Lisburn
Castlebar
Boyle
Monaghan
Newry
Westport
Knock
Cavan
Clifden
Lough Mask
Connemara
Dundalk
Longford
Lough Corrib
Roscommon
Lough Ree
Ardee
Drogheda
Galway
Navan
Athlone
Mullingar
Ballinasloe
Kinnegad
R. Boyne
Aran
Loughrea
Tullamore
DUBLI
Cliffs of Moher
Ennistimon
Lough Derg
Naas
Dun Laoghaire
Bray
Glendalough
Limerick
River Shannon
Listowel
Wicklow
Carlow
Tipperary
Kilkenny
Cashel
Arklow
Dingle
Tralee
R. Suir
R. Barrow
Lakes of Killarney
Killarney
Clonmel
Caher
Enniscorthy
Cahersiveen
Macgillycuddy's Reeks
Mallow
Fermoy
Carrick-on-Suir
New Ross
R. Blackwater
Ring of Kerry
Kenmare
Wexford
Waterford
Rosslare
Dungarvan
Cork
Youghal
Glengarriff
Bantry
Cobh
Carnsore Point
Skibbereen
Swansea
St. George's Channel
St. David's
Milford Haven

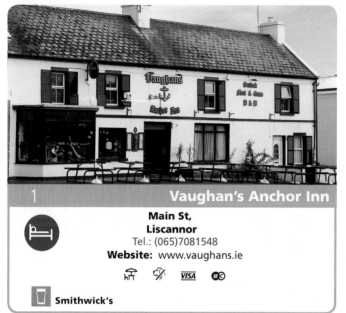

1 Vaughan's Anchor Inn

Main St,
Liscannor
Tel.: (065)7081548
Website: www.vaughans.ie

VISA

Smithwick's

There aren't many pubs where you can sit and sip a pint of the black stuff, have a natter over a seafood platter and then pick up your groceries. One such place is to be found in the picturesque fishing village of Liscannor, along the rugged road to the much-visited Cliffs of Moher. A proper, family-run pub, it has built up a fine reputation over the last three decades, and chef Denis' seafood-based menus are a big part of the reason why. Eat at simple wooden tables in the cosy, old-style bar or in the newer but equally informal restaurant; typical pub favourites are on offer at lunch, with more adventurous, elaborate meals - from oysters and lobster to duck and foie gras - served in the evening. Bright bedrooms with modern bathrooms.

CLOSING TIMES
Closed 25 December

PRICES
Meals: a la carte € 28/48
7 rooms: € 50/70

Typical Dishes

Beef brisket with oyster tempura
Roast monkfish with cauliflower & parmesan cream
Guinness desserts

2 km from Lahinch by coast road, on main route to Cliffs of Moher. Parking.

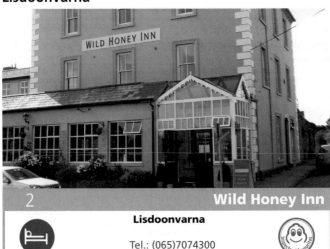

2 **Wild Honey Inn**

Lisdoonvarna

Tel.: (065)7074300
Website: www.wildhoneyinn.com

VISA MC

Smithwick's and Galway Hooker

With the Cliffs of Moher and the limestone landscape of The Burren on the doorstep, this roadside inn makes a great base for exploring County Clare; but it's also a great place to discover some tasty cuisine. The chef-owner has plenty of experience and with his wife and daughter out front, is well supported. There's a sizeable bar complete with turf fire, a linen-laid dining room used mainly for parties and a peaceful residents' lounge for those staying in one of the comfy, simply furnished bedrooms. Lunch consists of soups, salads and sandwiches, while dinner offers a wider selection of classics, but the specials are where the chef's skill really comes into its own – they may sound simple but the results are truly satisfying and great value.

CLOSING TIMES
Closed first week January-12 February, 24-26 December, and restricted opening November-December and February-April

PRICES
Meals: a la carte € 24/40
14 rooms: € 55/90

Typical Dishes

Black pudding & foie gras terrine

Fillet of hake with piperade

Apple tarte fine

On the edge of the town on the Ennistimon rd. On street parking.

3 **Poacher's Inn**

Clonakilty Rd,
Bandon
Tel.: (023)8841159
Website: www.poachersinnbandon.com

VISA MC

Smithwick's

It's not big, brash or colourful, but that doesn't mean the Poacher's Inn is lacking in a good old Irish pub atmosphere; in fact, if you're looking for the locals, this is probably where you'll find them. Inside, it's almost two operations in one. The ground floor is the more 'pubby' of the two: the front room displaying framed maps and local prints on wood-panelled walls, and the cosy snug, simple stool seating and low-level tables. Here you can choose from a light snack menu – the steak sandwich on homemade bread being a particular favourite. The more formal upstairs restaurant opens at the end of the week, offering a hearty, classical menu of locally caught fish and seafood, with Kinsale sole, monkfish and scallops all featuring highly.

CLOSING TIMES
Open daily

PRICES
Meals: € 25 and a la carte € 25/40

Typical Dishes

West Cork seafood plate

Baltimore monkfish with lemon

Meringue with summer berries

1.5 km southwest on N 71. Parking.

Castletownshend

4 Mary Ann's

Main St,
Castletownshend
Tel.: (028)36146
Website: www.westcorkweek.com/maryanns/

VISA

No real ales offered

You've little chance of missing this boldly painted pub or, for that matter, its larger than life owner. It's set in the heart of a sleepy village, up a steep, narrow street and the walk is sure to help you work up an appetite. If not, then while away some time in The Warren, the pub's art gallery, where the owner proudly displays his collection of modern Irish art. After this, head for the rustic bar, linen-laid restaurant, or if the weather's right, the garden, where an enclosed dining area boasting gingham tablecloths and a mature fruiting vine provides the perfect suntrap. Menus are all-encompassing and offer plenty of choice; seafood is usually a feature and there's often several authentic Asian dishes courtesy of the Malaysian chefs.

CLOSING TIMES
Closed 9 January-1 February, Monday-Tuesday October-March and 24-26 December

PRICES
Meals: a la carte € 20/42

Typical Dishes
Goat's cheese salad
Grilled Dover sole
Chocolate pecan tart

Between Rosscarbery and Skibbereen, south of N 71. Parking on the main street.

5 **An Súgan**

41 Wolfe Tone St,
Clonakilty
Tel.: (023)8833719
Website: www.ansugan.com

VISA MC

No real ales offered

Offering charm aplenty and a real sense of history, this salmon-pink pub with its traditional shop front, is everything you could ask for. Run by a capable family team, it has established itself as something of a local institution, but along with the regulars you'll also find plenty of visitors. The logo – depicting a fish, a lobster and several shellfish – provides a good idea of what to expect, with menus based around the daily arrival of fresh, local seafood. The all day selection offers light dishes such as seafood salad or salmon and potato cakes, while more substantial evening offerings might include coquille of seafood or salmon in filo pastry. Specials might involve stuffed crab claws or black sole. Bedrooms boast bold feature walls.

CLOSING TIMES
Open daily

PRICES
Meals: € 25 (dinner)
and a la carte € 22/43

7 rooms: € 30/100

Typical Dishes

West Cork tasting plate
Seafood basket
Crème caramel

On the eastern side of town. Parking in the street.

6 Cronin's

Crosshaven

Tel.: (021)4831829
Website: www.croninspub.com

VISA MC AE

No real ales offered

Having been in the family since 1970, this good old Irish pub is now being run by the third generation of Cronins – although you'll still likely to find Mr Cronin Snr about the place, only this time on the other side of the bar. The keen team welcome one and all and, being just a stone's throw from the harbour, that usually includes a yachtsman or two. The long bar is adorned with interesting artefacts, while the back room is filled with boxing memorabilia. During the week, they serve straightforward seafood dishes, while at weekends and midweek in summer, the restaurant is open for dinner, offering maybe wild scallops with leeks, fresh salmon tartare or their renowned shellfish platter. Produce is from nearby Oysterhaven and Ballycotton.

CLOSING TIMES
Closed 25 December and Good Friday
lunch only and dinner Friday-Saturday

PRICES
Meals: a la carte € 15/35

Typical Dishes
Oysters
Smoked tuna Niçoise
Lemon tart with cream

In the centre of town with free parking adjacent.

7 **Rising Tide**

Glounthaune

Tel.: (021)4353233
Website: www.therisingtide.ie

VISA MC

No real ales offered

Glounthaune is one of those places most people have heard of yet, for some reason, have never actually been to; set beside the water, it's very pleasant – and it's where you'll find this friendly little pub. It's more modern inside than you might expect, with a bright colour scheme, walls filled with photos of Lady Gaga's visit and a contemporary montage of the 'seven deadly sins'; not forgetting nautical knick-knacks, memorabilia about the village and quotes from John Masefield. Local workers pop in for unfussy chowders, homemade fishcakes or freshly roasted meats at lunchtime, while the seafood tank at the entrance plays a key role in the evening, offering oysters and mussels cooked several ways, alongside maybe tian of crab or fillet steak.

CLOSING TIMES
Closed Good Friday and 25 December

PRICES
Meals: a la carte € 34/48

Typical Dishes

Spiced beef & Cashel blue cheese salad
Fillet of pork with apple & cider jus
Baileys cheesecake

East of Cork city, the village is signposted off N 25. Parking.

Kinsale

8 Toddies at The Bulman

Summercove,
Kinsale
Tel.: (021)4772131
Website: www.thebulman.ie

No real ales offered

Named after the Bulman Buoy, this pub is in a great location, affording excellent views over Kinsale and the bay. Its décor is fittingly maritime themed, with an interesting mural of Moby Dick and a carving of the famed buoy on the ceiling. Scrubbed tables and open fires give a rustic feel and pictures from yesteryear fill the walls. Lunch offers simple pub classics served in the cosy bar, which also plays host to regular live music nights, when locals and visitors alike can be found enjoying the craic. The well-travelled owner – formerly of Toddies restaurant – can be seen cooking carefully prepared, globally influenced dishes in the more formal, first floor restaurant. Unsurprisingly, fresh, local seafood remains the star of the show.

CLOSING TIMES
Closed Good Friday, 25 December and Sunday dinner

PRICES
Meals: a la carte € 25/45

Typical Dishes

Local crab gratin
Toddies lobster risotto
Pineapple carpaccio

Head east 2 km towards Summercove. Small free car park opposite; difficult parking in summer.

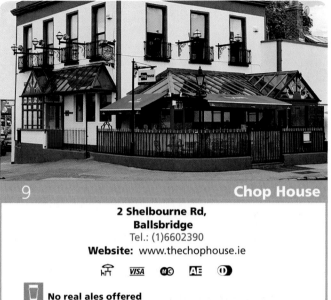

9 Chop House

2 Shelbourne Rd,
Ballsbridge
Tel.: (1)6602390
Website: www.thechophouse.ie

VISA MC AE

No real ales offered

In a prominent position on the main interchange, just a drop goal from the Arval Stadium, you'll find this imposing square-shaped pub. Once a rather spit 'n' sawdust affair, it's been given a new lease of life by a local restaurateur – so much so, that dinner bookings are now advisable. For warmer days there's a small terrace; in colder weather head up the steps, through the bar and into the bright conservatory area. Lunchtimes see a relaxed menu of maybe beer-battered cod, wild mushroom tagliatelli or Landes chicken with vinaigrette but to truly experience the kitchen's full talent come for dinner, where you'll discover the likes of raw tuna with teriyaki glaze, North African spiced lamb breast with orange confit or dry-aged Charolais beef.

CLOSING TIMES
Closed Saturday lunch

PRICES
Meals: a la carte € 26/49

Typical Dishes

Smoked haddock risotto
Braised neck of lamb
Chocolate pots

5min walk from Lansdowne Rd DART station.

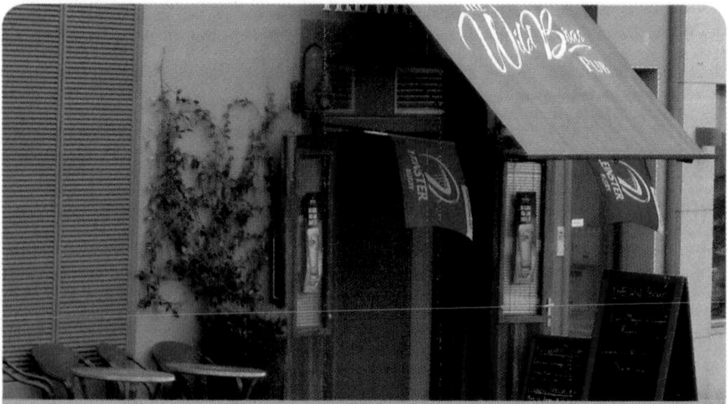

10 Wild Boar

Enniskerry Rd,
Stepaside
Tel.: (01)2052025
Website: www.thewildboar.ie

VISA MC AE

O'Hara's Red Ale and Irish Pale Ale

The Wild Boar is different from most pubs in both setting and style. Firstly, it's situated beneath a small, new-build apartment block and secondly, it looks nothing like a pub. It's very modern inside but there's still the long bar counter and a TV showing the latest rugby or football matches, and sat in front of that, a group of locals. Dining takes place in a former wine merchants shop, amongst shelves filled with wines for sale. There's plenty of choice, from breakfast and afternoon tea right through to filling lunches and dinners, and there are always some blackboard specials and a pie of the day. Quality ingredients are cooked with care and passion and flavours speak for themselves. Homemade chutneys and breads are available to take home.

CLOSING TIMES
Closed Good Friday and 25 December

PRICES
Meals: a la carte € 21/34

Typical Dishes

Shrimp cocktail with Guinness bread

Beef & O'Hara's Red Ale pie

Rhubarb & custard

In the centre of the village. Free parking at rear.

11 Moran's Oyster Cottage

The Weir,
Kilcolgan
Tel.: (091)796113
Website: www.moransoystercottage.com

VISA MC AE

Galway Hooker, Smithwick's

The name says it all: it's been run by seven generations of Morans; it's speciality is oysters; and with whitewashed walls and lovely golden thatch, it's every bit a country cottage. Set in a tiny hamlet down winding country lanes, you'd never find it unless you knew it was there – and on a summer's day it'll soon become apparent that plenty of people do. The latest Moran to take the helm, Michael, continues to follow the family's philosophy of straightforward cooking and good hospitality. The menu barely changes – but then why change something that works so well? Throughout the year you'll find tasty prawns, mussels, crab, smoked salmon and lobster, and daily baked brown bread. September is native oyster season, so is the best time to visit.

CLOSING TIMES
Closed Good Friday and 24-26 December

PRICES
Meals: a la carte € 30/60

Typical Dishes

Native oysters
Selection of Seafood
Chocolate torte

5 min from the village of Clarinbridge. Parking in road.

12 **O'Dowds**

Roundstone

Tel.: (095)35809
Website: www.odowdsbar.com

VISA MC

No real ales offered

The O'Dowd family have been dispensing gastronomic delights at this eye-catching blue-hued pub for over one hundred years. Sit in either the cosy, fire-lit bar or the more spacious, wood-panelled dining room to enjoy fresh, simply cooked seafood. Tender, sweet crab arrives straight from the shore, teamed with a glorious garlic butter to make the perfect meal; while the likes of brill, turbot and plaice are given the respect they deserve – simply lightly dusted with flour and then shallow fried. If you're coming for dinner, be sure to book ahead, and if lunch is your thing, then arrive early, otherwise you may find yourself watching enviously from the quayside as others tuck into home-baked soda rolls and steaming bowls of seafood chowder.

CLOSING TIMES
Closed 25 December
booking advisable

PRICES
Meals: a la carte € 22/31

Typical Dishes

Seafood chowder
Fish & prawns in a curry sauce
Raspberry & apple crumble

On R 341 13 km from Clifden. Parking outside and on the quayside.

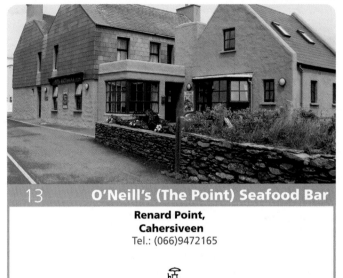

13 O'Neill's (The Point) Seafood Bar

Renard Point,
Cahersiveen
Tel.: (066)9472165

No real ales offered

This striking blue pub has been run by the O'Neill family for over 150 years and, satisfyingly, several different generations are still involved. Standing beside the Valentia Island car ferry terminal, right by the slipway, visitors come and go in waves, as the ferries arrive and depart. The interior has a pleasantly dated feel, with family photographs adorning the walls, alongside various items of seafaring memorabilia. The menu has a strong seafood base, cooking is traditionally Irish and the portions are generous. Salmon comes from the adjacent smokehouse and local fishermen bring their day's catch – which might include squid, monkfish or lobster – to the door. Unusually, they don't take credit cards and don't serve chips or puddings.

CLOSING TIMES
Closed November-February

PRICES
Meals: a la carte € 28/38

Typical Dishes

Hot crab claws with chilli
Pan-fried hake in garlic
Irish Coffee

West of Cahersiveen: follow the signs for the ferry. Parking.

14 **QC's**

3 Main St,
Cahersiveen
Tel.: (066)9472244
Website: www.qcbar.com

VISA

No real ales offered

Named after the owners, Quinlan and Cook, this cosy little pub really delivers when it comes to character. Flagged floors, exposed stone walls and wood burning stoves feature, and there's a strong nautical theme running throughout, with oars, port holes and charts scattered about the place. Diners can eat either in the bar or pre-laid raised area towards the back. The menu is seafood-orientated, which comes as no surprise once you learn that the family also owns a local fish wholesalers. Cooking is fresh, unfussy and relies on classic combinations, with some more unusual choices appearing on the specials board; so you'll find everything from fish and chips to sautéed squid with pesto. Spacious, modern bedrooms are set just around the corner.

CLOSING TIMES
Closed Monday-Wednesday in winter and Sunday lunch

PRICES
Meals: € 20 (dinner) and a la carte € 31/46

5 rooms: € 60/110

Typical Dishes

Valentia crab meat & prawn bisque

Turbot with garlic & chilli sauce

Affogato

In the centre of Town. Parking on the street.

15 Ballymore Inn

Ballymore Eustace

Tel.: (045)864585
Website: www.ballymoreinn.com

VISA MC AE

No real ales offered

Set in a small village close to the Aga Khan's stud, this pub's claim to fame is that Clint Eastwood and Larry Hagman have popped in on their way to the races. To the rear, a large bar screens sporting events and hosts live music, while to the front there's a spacious dining area with red leather banquettes, mosaic flooring and a Parisian brasserie feel. Lunchtime sees salads, homemade pizzas, stir fries and risottos, with some more substantial dishes appearing at dinner. The owner is keen to promote small artisan producers, so you'll find organic veg, meat from quality assured farms and farmhouse cheeses. Portions are generous but you won't want to miss the tasty bread or homemade tarts and pastries. Pleasant staff always go the extra mile.

CLOSING TIMES
Open daily

PRICES
Meals: € 22/35
and a la carte € 28/39

Typical Dishes

Black pudding with apple salad

Hake with braised lentils & red wine sauce

Rhubarb & ginger tart

9 km south of Naas by R 411. Parking.

Carrick-on-Shannon

16 **Oarsman**

Bridge St,
Carrick-on-Shannon
Tel.: (071)9621733
Website: www.theoarsman.com

VISA MC

Galway Hooker Pale Ale

With the River Shannon just 50m away and always a boatman or two inside, this pub's name is perfectly apt. Its double-fronted windows are filled with pottery, county flags and old artefacts, while a plethora of objects adorn the walls and an array of fishing tackle is displayed above the bar. This is a traditional pub through and through, family-owned, with rough wooden floors, old beams and stone-faced walls – and, unsurprisingly, frequented by the locals, especially at lunch. Snacks are available in the afternoon and there's a fairly substantial bar menu in the evening, while later in the week the comfy upstairs area offers dishes such as confit of Thornhill Farm duck or trio of Kettyle lamb. Cooking is simple and produce, laudably local.

CLOSING TIMES
Closed 25-26 December, Easter Friday, Sunday and Monday

PRICES
Meals: € 20/35
and a la carte € 21/43

Typical Dishes

Seared scallops & butternut squash purée

Loin of Roscommon lamb

Pear tart

In the town centre. On-street meters and parking at rear of pub.

17 **Fitzpatricks**

Rockmarshall,
Jenkinstown
Tel.: (042)9376193
Website: www.fitzpatricks-restaurant.com

VISA MC

McArdles Ale

On the coast road to the peninsula, at the foot of the Cooley Mountains, you'll find this classical whitewashed pub overlooking Dundalk Bay. To call it characterful would be an understatement: this is a place where you can take in the whole of the Irish experience. The car park and gardens are filled with colourful flowers set in old bicycles, boots and even a bed; while inside there's a beautiful bar with brass rails and memorabilia aplenty, including a fascinating collection of old chamber pots and Victorian toiletries. The extensive menu features hearty, flavoursome portions of traditional dishes, with local seafood and steaks something of a speciality. More adventurous offerings can be found in the restaurant, which opens later in the week.

CLOSING TIMES
Closed Good Friday, Monday September-May except bank holidays and 25 December

PRICES
Meals: € 25 (dinner) and a la carte € 36/45

Typical Dishes

Chilli & garlic prawns
Stuffed Dover sole
Wexford strawberries & bourbon ice cream

9 km northeast of Dundalk following N 52 on R 173. Parking.

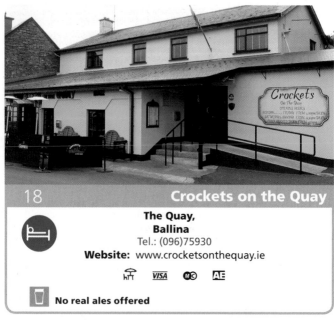

18 **Crockets on the Quay**

The Quay,
Ballina
Tel.: (096)75930
Website: www.crocketsonthequay.ie

VISA MC AE

No real ales offered

This pub's vibrant orange exterior is matched on the inside by a lively atmosphere where there's always something going on, be it a poker night, traditional Irish music session or trivia quiz; and sports fans aren't forgotten either, with TVs in almost every corner, as well as two plasma screens and a pool table in the garden. The place itself is rather dimly lit, but the light fittings that are located above each worn table really put the spotlight where it matters – on the food. They don't serve lunch here but there's a popular early evening menu, which is followed by a larger selection of generously proportioned dishes and local Irish steaks. Bedrooms are modest, affordable and well-kept; those above the restaurant are the most peaceful.

CLOSING TIMES
Closed 25 December and Good Friday
dinner only and lunch Saturday and Sunday

PRICES
Meals: a la carte € 26/36
8 rooms: € 30/50

Typical Dishes

Clew Bay mussels in a white wine sauce
Roast rack of Mayo lamb
Sticky toffee pudding

On the northeast edge of town by N 59 besides the River Moy. Parking.

19 **JJ Gannons**

Main St,
Ballinrobe
Tel.: (094)9541008
Website: www.jjgannons.com

VISA

Courage Directors, Blanchester Bomber, Double Century

The eponymous Gannon family have welcomed guests to this pub for more than 75 years; it's now run by the third generation, who offer as cheery a reception as their predecessors. The building dates from 1838, but its interior is modern in style. There's an atmospheric front bar, a dimly lit chill-out area and a smart, spacious restaurant, which provides extra space when the bar gets too busy. Cooking is satisfying and reassuringly familiar. Traditional dishes might include local beef or slow-roasted shoulder of local lamb; fish features as a special and desserts might include warm apple pie or traditional bread and butter pudding. Weekly themed evenings are popular; stay overnight afterwards in one of the spacious, comfortable bedrooms.

CLOSING TIMES
Closed 25 December

PRICES
Meals: € 25 (dinner)
and a la carte € 21/40

10 rooms: € 65/150

Typical Dishes

Clew Bay sushi
Rib-eye steak with foie gras & merlot
Warm chocolate fondant

In the centre of town on the one-way system. Parking.

20 **Sheebeen**

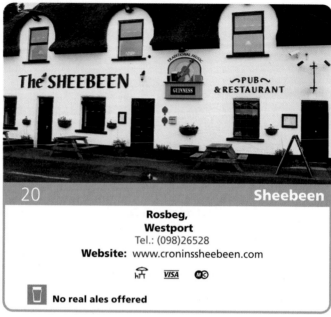

Rosbeg,
Westport
Tel.: (098)26528
Website: www.croninssheebeen.com

VISA

No real ales offered

This attractive whitewashed, thatched pub is situated to the west of town, looking out over Clew Bay and in the shadow of famed mountain, Croagh Patrick. According to legend, this was where St. Patrick fasted for 40 days and 40 nights before banishing all the snakes from Ireland. Fasting not your thing? Cooking here is fresh and simple – everything is homemade, including the bread – with the more interesting dishes to be found among the large selection of daily specials. Try the local fish and seafood, which is accurately prepared and full of flavour – perhaps cod terrine, lobster, sea trout or John Dory. Live music nights take place every Friday and Saturday; but during the week, don't be surprised to hear Peggy Lee blasting out instead.

CLOSING TIMES
Closed Good Friday, 25 December and lunch weekdays November-mid March

PRICES
Meals: a la carte € 23/42

Typical Dishes

Honey-roast ham terrine
Pan-fried king scallops
Buttermilk panna cotta

West of the town beyond Westport Quay. Parking.

21 Hargadons

4/5 O'Connell St,
Sligo
Tel.: (071)9153709
Website: www.hargadons.com

VISA MC AE

No real ales offered

Built in 1864 by a local merchant-cum-MP, this building started life as a grocer's (the original comestible drawers are still on display), before being acquired by the Hargadon brothers in 1909. To say its characterful would be an understatement. There's a narrow passageway with booths, anterooms with oak-topped tables, thick walls hung with Guinness and Jameson's memorabilia and a sloping stone floor designed to prevent flooding; there's also a lovely little "Ladies' Room" complete with serving hatch. Cooking is warming and hearty, offering the likes of bangers and mash, Irish stew and bacon and cabbage, followed by tasty nursery puddings. They also have a good wine list, which makes sense when you see the large wine shop that adjoins it.

CLOSING TIMES
Open daily

PRICES
Meals: € 11 (lunch)
and a la carte € 21/28

Typical Dishes

Seafood chowder
Chicken pesto with Cajun potatoes
Chocolate brownie

In the centre of town. Public parking nearby.

Garrykennedy

22 Larkins

Garrykennedy

Tel.: (067)23232
Website: www.larkinspub.com

VISA

White Gypsy Ruby Ale

Set in a charming location on the shores of Lough Derg, this thatched, whitewashed pub dates back around 300 years and is popular with the sailing set, particularly in the summer. As traditional inside as out, it boasts old flag and timber floors, a long wooden bar and original open fireplaces; and plays host to regular Irish folk music sessions and traditional Irish dancing groups. Throughout the day, the bar menu offers straightforward, unfussy dishes such as seafood chowder, homemade burgers or steak. In the evening, however, things step up a gear, with the likes of honey-roast duckling, herb-crusted fillet of cod or pan-fried lamb cutlets. Having come from farming backgrounds, the owners are passionate about sourcing local Irish produce.

CLOSING TIMES
Closed 25 December, Good Friday and Monday-Tuesday November-April

PRICES
Meals: a la carte € 20/37

Typical Dishes

Atlantic mussels in white wine & garlic
Prime Irish Hereford sirloin steak
Selection of Tipperary cheese

9 km west of Nenagh by R 494 and minor road north. Free public car park opposite.

23 Fatted Calf

Glasson

Tel.: (09064)85208
Website: www.thefattedcalf.ie

VISA MC AE

O'Hara's Cumin Gold Wheat Beer, Schiehallion

With the Farrell family having finally hung up their glass cloths, this pub has been left in the safe hands of Feargal O'Donnell, who formerly worked in the kitchen of nearby Wineport Lodge. Aside from the name, the pub's changed little since he took over, with original Guinness and Gilbeys signs still adorning the attractive wood panels of the bar, and locals gathering around the TV and pool table in the snug. Having spent years working in the area, Feargal knows all of the best local suppliers, and his experience has definitely stepped the cooking up a gear. Dishes range from handmade sausages to local rabbit terrine, while tasty specials and bar snacks, such as duck rillette or black pudding on treacle bread, appear later in the evening.

CLOSING TIMES
Closed Good Friday, 25 December and Monday except bank holidays

PRICES
Meals: a la carte € 22/44

Typical Dishes

Black pudding & Glasson mushrooms

Roast rack of spring lamb with cannelloni beans

Chocolate orange pot

On the N 55 in the centre of the village. Parking

24 **Lobster Pot**

Ballyfane,
Carne
Tel.: (053)9131110

VISA AE

Smithwick's

If you're on your way to the ferry crossing at Rosslare or returning from a stroll along the nearby beach, this bold green pub is definitely worth calling in at. The interior is spotless and as soon as you see the staff in their smart waistcoats, you know they take things seriously here. Make for a cosy, characterful nook amongst the huge array of memorabilia and study the extensive menu of tasty, home-style cooking, which offers a simple selection of light bites at lunch and a dinner menu exclusively for adults – as children must leave by 5pm. There are a few grills, but, as the name suggests, it's mostly seafood, with oysters and lobster cooked to order the specialities. Be sure to arrive early, as this is Carne's not-so-well-kept secret.

CLOSING TIMES
Closed January,
25-26 December,
Good Friday and Monday
except bank holidays

PRICES
Meals: a la carte € 25/45

Typical Dishes

Crab Mornay
Grilled Dover sole with lemon butter
Sticky toffee pudding

South of Rosslare Harbour. Parking.

Index of towns

M

N

O

P

R

Index of pubs & inns

D

E

F

G

H

I – J

K

Q – R

S

eating out in pubs

Michelin Maps & Guides

Michelin Maps & Guides
Hannay House,
39 Clarendon Rd
Watford WD17 1JA
Tel: (01923) 205247
Fax: (01923) 205241
www.ViaMichelin.com
eatingoutinpubs-gbirl@
uk.michelin.com

Manufacture française des pneumatiques Michelin

Société en commandite par actions
au capital de 504 000 004 EUR.
Place des Carmes-Déchaux
63 Clermont-Ferrand (France)
R.C.S. Clermont-Fd B 855 200 507

Dépôt légal Septembre 2011
Printed in France 09-11

Typesetting:

NORD COMPO, Villeneuve-d'Ascq (France)
Printing and binding:
La Tipografica Varese, Varese (Italy)

Photography

Project manager: Alain Leprince
Agence ACSI – A Chacun Son Image
242, bd. Voltaire– 75011 Paris

Location Photographs:

Jérôme Berquez, Frédéric Chales, Ludivine Boizard, Jean-Louis Chauveau/ACSI

Thanks to:
The Pipe and Glass Inn, South Daiton
P12: Ariy/Fotolia.com
P20: Full moon/Fotolia.com
P22: C. Labonne/Michelin
P54: D. Hughes/Fotolia.com
P118: C. Eymenier/Michelin
P187: A. Jon/Hemis.fr
P188: Robert/Fotolia.com
P204: K. Eaves/Fotolia.com
P241: A. Jon/Hemis.fr
P242: D. Hughes/Fotolia.com
P347: A. Jon/Hemis.fr
P348: C. Jones/Fotolia.com
P449: A. Jon/Hemis.fr
P450: D. Hughes/Fotolia.com
P479: Steheap/Fotolia.com
P480: S. Smith/Fotolia.com
P524: O. Forir/Michelin
P547: D. Hughes/Fotolia.com
P548: L. Green/Fotolia.com
P574: O. Forir/Michelin
P584: O. Forir/Michelin
P611: R. Mattes/Hemis.fr